Although the German Empire of 1871–1918 was basically an authoritarian regime, its national elections were held under a democratic franchise and characterized by vigorous election campaigning and high levels of voter turnout. In *The Kaiser's voters*, Jonathan Sperber analyzes the thirteen general elections held in pre-1914 Germany. Using advanced mathematical methods, but presenting their results in understandable, non-technical language, his work offers estimates of the proportion of eligible voters from different confessional groups and social classes choosing the different political parties, and traces the flow of voters among the parties and between voting and abstention from one election to the next. Refuting a number of long-held propositions about the nature of the electorate in Imperial Germany, he presents a new interpretation of voting behavior in the formative years of the modern German political system, considers its consequences for German electoral politics in the twentieth century, and compares electoral trends in Germany with those in other European and North American countries in the age of universal suffrage.

The Kaiser's voters

The Kaiser's voters

Electors and elections in Imperial Germany

Jonathan Sperber

Department of History, University of Missouri

CAMBRIDGE UNIVERSITY PRESS

PUBLISHED BY THE PRESS SYNDICATE OF THE UNIVERSITY OF CAMBRIDGE
The Pitt Building, Trumpington Street, Cambridge CB2 1RP, United Kingdom

CAMBRIDGE UNIVERSITY PRESS
The Edinburgh Building, Cambridge, CB2 2RU, United Kingdom
40 West 20th Street, New York, NY 10011-4211, USA
10 Stamford Road, Oakleigh, Melbourne 3166, Australia

First published 1997

Printed in the United Kingdom at the University Press, Cambridge

Typeset in 10/12 Plantin

A catalogue record for this book is available from the British Library

Library of Congress Cataloguing in Publication data

Sperber, Jonathan, 1952–
    The Kaiser's voters: electors and elections in Imperial Germany /
Jonathan Sperber.
        p.   cm.
    Includes bibliographical references and index.
    ISBN 0 521 59138 4
    1. Elections–Germany–History–19th century.   2. Elections–
Germany–History–20th century.   3. Germany–Politics and
government–1871–1918.   I. Title.
JN3838.S67   1997
324.943′083–dc21   96-45553   CIP

ISBN 0 521 59138 4 hardback

Contents

Figures

Tables

Acknowledgements

Most of the work for this book was done in a period of cutbacks and retrenchment, and it might be seen as an example of scholarship accomplished with modest means. I am all the more grateful to those individuals and institutions who were able to offer assistance in straitened circumstances.

The University of Missouri Research Board provided the funds for the purchase of the hardware and software necessary for the statistical investigations. A one-year research leave, obtained from the University of Missouri Research Council (not the same body as the Research Board), allowed me the time to take the stacks of printouts sitting on my desk and turn them into a book. I need to thank all my colleagues in the history department at the University of Missouri, Columbia, who allowed me a whole academic year in which I was not obligated to attend one single meeting, and, in particular, to thank Steven Watts who offered a number of helpful suggestions on how to express technical matters in non-technical language. I have benefited substantially from my discussions with Thomas Alexander, Emeritus Professor of History at the University of Missouri, and one of the pioneers in the use of quantitative methods. For assistance with the difficult problems posed by ridge regression, I am deeply indebted to Professor Paul Speckman, Department of Statistics, and especially to Dr. Linda Okamura, Campus Computing, University of Missouri, Columbia. The standard disclaimer is particularly true in this case: all the help I received did a lot for any positive features of the book, but its errors and problematic assumptions are my sole responsibility.

Ms. Josephine Johnson of Interlibrary Loan, Ellis Library, University of Missouri, processed an appalling number of forms on my behalf, and did not flinch once. Without her efficient and friendly help this book could not have been written. Richard Fisher and Caro Drake of Cambridge University Press have made the transition from diskette and typescript to published book about as easy as it could be. During the year I was writing the book, Adam Philip Sperber would remind me every morning, "Dad, don't forget to type and click!" I haven't; this book is for him.

Introduction

Posing the problem

When one thinks of democracy, Germany is generally not the first country that comes to mind. Yet as early as 1848 national elections with a broad, if indirect and not quite universal franchise, were held there. Universal and direct manhood suffrage was introduced with national unification in 1867–71, that is to say at the same time as in the United States. German women received the vote in 1919, another early date by international standards. A democratic franchise for national elections has thus characterized German politics for over a century and Germans have made vigorous use of this right to vote from the very beginning. About half the eligible voters cast their ballots in the first nationwide direct elections in 1871 and turnout reached the impressive figure of 85% of eligible voters in the general elections of 1907 and 1912, the last before the First World War. In some ways this is not surprising because, as a number of historical studies have reminded us, widespread and active political organization, vigorous electioneering, and a strong popular wish to participate in the process were typical of national elections in Germany for decades before 1914.[1]

This explanation, however, points to the problem and the reason that Germany and democracy might seem like an odd combination. While the deputies to the national parliament of Imperial Germany, the Reichstag, were elected by a democratic franchise, the elaborate and peculiar constitutional system of the empire reduced to a bare minimum the powers and prerogatives of the democratically elected people's representatives.

---

[1] Two recent general works that have emphasized this point of view are Stanley Suvall, *Electoral Politics in Wilhelmine Germany* (Chapel Hill: University of North Carolina Press, 1985) and Margaret Anderson, "Voter Junker, *Landrat* Priest: The Old Authorities and the New Franchise in Imperial Germany," *American Historical Review* 98 (1993): 1448–74. More generally, on the history of elections in Germany, see the excellent review article of Thomas Kühne, "Wahlrecht–Wahlverhalten–Wahlkultur: Tradition und Innovation in der historischen Wahlforschung," *Archiv für Sozialgeschichte* 33 (1993): 481–547.

Parliamentary government as understood in the usual sense, the election of the head of government and his/her fellow ministers by a majority of the deputies, did not exist. The chancellor, head of the Imperial government, along with his assistants, was chosen by the emperor, without formal or informal consultation of the Reichstag.

Even as a law-making body, the powers of the Reichstag were less than impressive. The parliament could not pass binding legislation of its own accord; all laws required the consent of the Bundesrat, the empire's federal executive organ, itself once again dominated by the representatives of the emperor, this time in his role as king of Prussia. Indeed the Reichstag did not even have the right of initiative; all proposed legislation had to come from the Bundesrat. The only real power the Reichstag possessed was a negative and obstructionist one: a majority of its members could refuse to agree to a law proposed by the executive, particularly legislation relating to Imperial finances, and use this refusal as a weapon to force concessions – a weapon blunted by the executive's right to dissolve an intransigent Reichstag and call for new elections.

Scholars have disagreed about just how much actual power this refusal to consent to legislation gave the people's representatives, with some asserting that the Imperial legislature remained little more than a rubber-stamp body throughout the peacetime years of the empire, while others note a gradual accumulation of political power in the hands of the elected parliamentarians, especially in the first decade of the twentieth century.[2] Yet there can be no doubt that compared to similar parliamentary bodies of the time, to say nothing of today's legislatures, the Reichstag was not a very powerful institution. In other words, the people could express their will but the government had considerable latitude in ignoring it. This conjunction of a broad, democratic franchise with an authoritarian or, in the twentieth century, dictatorial government has been characteristic of much of modern Germany's history.

It is the combination of democratic suffrage, energetic and massive political participation, and an authoritarian regime that marks the starting point for the problems posed in this book. What was all the electoral shouting about? Or, to put it differently, why were Germans so actively involved in choosing the members of a parliament that was, at best, not very powerful? In this book, I will try to provide a very partial answer to this question, by offering a rigorous, quantitative analysis of voting behavior in the formative years of the German electoral system, 1871–1912. Using sophisticated statistical methods, I will identify which Germans

<hr />

[2] A brief but useful discussion of this controversy is in Volker R. Berghahn, *Imperial Germany 1871–1914: Economy, Society, Culture and Politics* (Providence and Oxford: Berghahn Books, 1994), pp. 190–205.

voted, which parties they chose, and how their choices – of one party or another, or of voting and not voting – differed from election to election. To make sense of such quantitative results and indeed to guide the statistical questions one might ask in the first place, one needs an intellectual framework, a model for understanding voting behavior.

Different approaches

Currently one of the most influential general theories of the electoral process is Anthony Downs's economic theory of democracy. Reducing the main idea to its simplest formulation, it is that elections are a sort of bargaining process between candidates and the electorate, directed by individual self-interest. Politicians desire the prerogatives and spoils of office so they promise voters that if they are elected, they will carry out policies profitable for those who vote for them.[3]

This approach seems singularly ill-suited to the study of elections in Imperial Germany. Since there was no parliamentary government and little parliamentary power, there were no spoils of office as goals of politicians' aspirations: office-holding and patronage were out; deputies drew no salaries and did not even receive a per diem expense allowance until 1906.[4] Politicians could promise the voters all manner of things should they be elected, but it is hard to see why rationally minded voters – or even not so rationally minded ones – would have believed these promises in view of the parliamentarians' lack of power to formulate either government policy or new legislation.

Another approach is needed to understand voting behavior in Imperial Germany and the one adopted most often has been proposed by sociologist Rainer Lepsius. Lepsius asserted that the German political parties were an expression of what he called "sociomoral milieus," formed by the intersection of religious, cultural and regional traditions, economic circumstances, social structure, and forms of voluntary associations. Putting aside several smaller groups, such as the national and regional minorities, Lepsius identified four major milieus in Imperial Germany, three of which – the Catholic, the urban Protestant middle class and the rural Protestant – were formed in the first sixty years of the nineteenth century, predating German national unification and the introduction of universal manhood suffrage. Voting for a political party in Lepsius's model was not a means of asserting one's individual or collective self-interest, but an act

---

[3] Anthony Downs, *An Economic Theory of Democracy* (New York: Harpers, 1957).

[4] On the history of the question of compensation for deputies, see Elfi Pracht, *Parlamentarismus und deutsche Sozialdemokratie 1867–1914* (Pfaffenweiler: Centaurus-Verlagsgesellschaft, 1990), pp. 304–9.

of affirming one's membership in such a milieu and the function of the major political parties was to represent their respective milieus. Indeed, Lepsius tends to take the stability of voting results for a party or group of parties as proof of the existence of a milieu, understanding the Center Party as the expression of the Catholic milieu, the liberal parties as the expression of the urban Protestant middle-class one, and the conservative parties as the expression of the rural Protestant milieu.

These three milieus did not just predate the national political system of universal manhood suffrage, they predated large-scale industrialization as well. With its progress in the last third of the nineteenth century, there developed a substantial proportion of the population – urban, at least nominally Protestant, working-class – that was outside the three major milieus. These were the voters of the Social Democratic Party, whose spectacular rise in support was the major long-term change in voter preferences throughout the history of the empire. Lepsius takes his thesis further and asserts that the relationship between the Social Democratic Party and its supporters developed into precisely the same sort of milieu that characterized the other major party groupings. By the early twentieth century the vast majority of the German electorate had been parcelled out among these four mutually impermeable, largely static voting blocs. The electoral system remained that way, Lepsius goes on to argue, surviving the First World War, the economic crises of the post-war era, the territorial changes of 1919, the introduction of a republican and parliamentary form of government, the expansion of the electorate to women and young adults, and the introduction of a system of proportional representation until the rise of the Nazis after 1928. The Nazi regime and the Second World War then destroyed the infrastructure of the sociomoral milieus, allowing for the emergence of an interest-based and so more flexible and more mobile electoral system in the Federal Republic of Germany.[5]

Lepsius's thesis has been enormously influential and a good deal of the scholarship in the last two decades on voting and elections in Imperial Germany, including the work of this author, has made use of his concept of sociomoral milieus.[6] An understanding of the electoral process as centered around social identification rather than bargaining between politicians and voters is particularly well suited to the constitutional and political realities of the German Empire. However, there is a price to be

[5] M. Rainer Lepsius, "Parteisystem und Sozialstruktur: zum Problem der Demokratisierung der deutschen Gesellschaft," in (among other places) Gerhard Albert Ritter (ed.) *Die deutschen Parteien vor 1918* (Cologne: Kiepenheuer & Witsch, 1973), pp. 56–80.
[6] On Lepsius's milieu thesis and its importance for historical studies of elections, see Kühne, "Wahlrecht–Wahlverhalten–Wahlkultur," pp. 508–13.

paid for this understanding, namely a static view of the electoral system. In Lepsius's explanation of past German politics, voters and their parties were tied together in a milieu constituted before the creation of the political system in which these milieus operated; there could be little or no movement between these milieus. Results at elections were basically fixed in advance; the only major changes that occurred were when non-voters not belonging to any milieu – and these two terms are identical in Lepsius's model – identified with a new party and created a new milieu of their own, as Lepsius argues occurred with the growth of the labor movement among urban Protestant workers. This summary is a bit unfair to the nuances of Lepsius's work, since he notes that movement took place between parties of the same milieu (between the left-wing liberal parties and the more moderate National Liberals, for instance) or that over time milieus gradually dissolved under the pressure of social and economic change, a process he notes in the decline in the proportion of Catholic voters supporting the Center Party. Nonetheless, stasis predominates over movement in Lepsius's view of German elections before 1914, and to some extent before 1928: all the sound and fury of election campaigns, all the massive organization and remarkable rates of voter turnout produce little change.

The political scientist Karl Rohe, in a series of recent studies, has developed a variation on Lepsius's work that allows for more change in the model. He introduces the concept of "camp" (*Lager*) that serves as an intermediary between milieu and political party or groups of parties. Camps were made up of one or more milieus, as well as individuals not within any milieu at all, and were characterized less by their internal homogeneity (as in Lepsius's milieu) than by their sharp delineation from other political camps. Rohe identifies three such camps in German politics – a socialist, a Catholic (both reasonably close to Lepsius's comparably named milieu) and a "national" camp, encompassing individuals from Lepsius's liberal and conservative milieus. Like Lepsius's milieus, Rohe's camps were characterized by strong internal cohesion: voters moved back and forth between different parties within their camp but were unlikely to choose a party outside of it.

This theoretical construction allows Rohe to explain the possibilities of movement in a political system structured around relatively static milieus. Milieus may become part of a camp, as Rohe asserts occurred with the Catholic milieu in the 1870s. Under the pressure of the government's persecution in the course of the *Kulturkampf*, voters from the Catholic milieu, who had previously supported several different political parties, became firmly loyal to an explicitly Catholic political party, the Center, thus creating a Catholic political camp. Groups of voters may also change camps, not fluctuating back and forth between them (this would go against the terms of the model), but moving over in one go. If seeing the rise of the Social Democratic Party primarily in terms of the mobilization of previous non-voters, as does Lepsius, Rohe also offers examples of whole groups of workers going over at one election from the national camp to the socialist one and then remaining there. Finally, whole camps may change the political party they support. While Lepsius sees the rise of Nazis as the result of the collapse of the milieus, Rohe sees it primarily as a consequence of voters in the national camp switching their loyalties from various parties of the center and the right to the NSDAP.

Both of these last two possibilities point to an unusual and explicitly delineated feature of Rohe's view on elections, the denial of the existence among voters of a political spectrum going from left to right, even if such a spectrum could be found through comparison of the parties' programs, or characterized the relations of the deputies' caucuses in the Reichstag. Voters in the different camps were identified by their mutual exclusion. There was no exchange of votes between, say, the left-liberal parties and the socialists, although the positions publicly taken by the two groups of parties were closest to each other. Conversely, there was nothing to be suprised about in the movement of voters from the liberal parties to the Nazis, in spite of the considerable ideological distance between them; it was part of a broader switch of loyalties among members of the national camp.

Rohe's model also allows for a continuity of political traditions between the pre- and post-1945 eras. Since party and milieu are not directly aligned in his model, but linked via the political camps, the rise of new political parties in the Federal Republic, particularly the CDU/CSU, does not imply a total revision of the social and political system but can be understood as a realignment of political camps, coupled with more gradual social changes affecting the existence of sociomoral milieus. The upshot is a political model that stresses both the elements of continuity and those of a new beginning in West German politics and also provides a way to understand the changes in voting behavior since the 1950s.[7]

This work is an impressive achievement, with a good deal of analytical power. At times, though, Rohe's incorporation of additional concepts to an existing model – besides milieu and camp, he also discusses "cleavages" or lines of division between social, regional or confessional groups, that may or may not be expressed politically – is remniscent of those

---

[7] Rohe has handily summarized his own work and that of his students in *Wahlen und Wählertraditionen in Deutschland* (Frankfurt: Suhrkamp, 1992). Kühne, in "Wahlrecht–Wahlverhalten–Wahlkultur," pp. 517–22, has some very astute comments on Rohe's approach.

medieval astronomers who added ever more epicycles to reconcile Aristotelian geocentric theories with their observations of the cosmos. A number of English-speaking historians, most prominently Geoff Eley and David Blackbourn, have argued that the whole approach based on milieus is too static to capture the reality of a political process that was more mobile. Starting from the realignments of party organization, the changes in campaigning, participation and political style that they have observed and generally dated to the decade of the 1890s, they have gone on to argue that these both reflected and encouraged changes in voting behavior. Where Lepsius and, to a lesser extent Rohe, see stability and voter loyalty, they see fluctuation and swings in voter support. The main motif in this explanation of political behavior is protest, reaction to changing social and economic circumstances and to government policies. Voters responded to new and often unfavorable conditions by holding politicians responsible, even if they were not, and the latter had to respond to their constituents' anger if they were to be re-elected. The responses they found in turn rechanneled voter loyalties, thus further changing the electoral system.[8]

Ecological inference

Although this brief sketch does not enumerate exhaustively all the possible approaches to studying elections in Imperial Germany, it does suggest some of the main lines of interpretation, in particular the distinction between statically and dynamically oriented modes of explanation.[9] The

[8] In more general terms, see Geoff Eley, *Reshaping the German Right : Radical Nationalism and Political Change after Bismarck* (Yale and New Haven: Yale University Press, 1980) and David Blackbourn, *Class, Religion and Local Politics in Wilhelmine Germany: The Centre Party in Württtemberg before 1914* (New Haven and London: Yale University Press, 1980). Specific formulations include David Blackbourn and Geoff Eley, *The Peculiarities of German History: Bourgeois Society and Politics in Nineteenth-Century Germany* (Oxford and New York: Oxford University Press, 1984), pp.72–73, 93; Geoff Eley, "The German Right, 1860–1945: How It Changed," in Geoff Eley (ed.) *From Unification to Nazism: Reinterpreting the German Past* (Boston, London and Sydney: Allen & Unwin, 1986), pp. 231–53, esp. pp. 239–40; and Geoff Eley, "Notable Politics, the Crisis of German Liberalism, and the Electoral Transition of the 1890s," in Konrad Jarausch and Larry Jones (eds.) *In Search of a Liberal Germany: Studies in the History of German Liberalism from 1789 to the Present* (New York, Oxford and Munich: Berg Publishers, 1990), pp. 187–216. As for other English-language historians, Stanley Suvall's work has more in common with Lepsius's milieu thesis, while Margaret Anderson, although disagreeing with Blackbourn and Eley about almost everything else, does tend to share their notion of protest as a moving factor in German voter behavior.

[9] For a discussion of additional interpretive models, see Peter Steinbach, "Reichstag Elections in the Kaiserreich: The Prospects for Electoral Research in the Interdisciplinary Context, " in Larry Eugene Jones and James Retallack (eds.) *Elections, Mass Politics and Social Change in Modern Germany: New Perspectives* (Cambridge and New York: Cambridge University Press, 1992), pp. 119–46.

question inevitably arises as to which (if any) is right, and it is not an easy one to answer. In part, there are problems of interpretation of evidence. If, over some thirty-five years the share of votes cast for a given group of parties drops from 38% to 25%, is that proof of change or of stability?[10] It is a decline of some 34%, a pretty substantial figure, but at a rate of only 1.1% per year, which could be seen as proof of the long-term stability of the political system. Similarly, studies of individual constituencies or of regions in given periods designed to demonstrate either change or stability suffer from the problem of typicality. They may neither represent what was happening elsewhere in Imperial Germany, a large and diverse country, nor what was happening at other times in the forty-one years between its first general election and its last.

There is a more basic problem confronting these interpretations: the gap between what they explain and the material available to explain it. All the explanations are at least implicitly about the voting of individuals or of social and confessional groups. Lepsius's model, for instance, suggests that all or at least the vast majority of individuals who voted for, say, the conservative parties at one election would be likely to do so at subsequent ones, that the large majority of Catholics supported the Center Party, or that Protestant, blue-collar voters generally cast their ballots for the Social Democrats. A more change-oriented explanation, on the other hand, would suggest that such stability of individual and group choice was not always present; for instance, that at some elections in the 1890s a significant proportion of liberal voters switched over to the anti-Semites and perhaps at a later election came back to the liberal parties or even went on to the Social Democrats, or that a significant number of Catholic industrial workers stopped voting for the Center and began to support the Social Democrats.

Answering these sorts of questions is the very staple of contemporary electoral analysis and political scientists have a simple way of finding out how voters cast their ballot: they ask them, or at least a random sample of them. Unfortunately, we can no longer do this for the voters of the German Empire. Since the voting age was twenty-five and the last prewar elections were in 1912, the very youngest voters in Imperial Germany were born in 1887 and are no longer with us to be surveyed. There were, to be sure, very extensive returns compiled for the general elections to the Imperial parliament, and carried out with the thoroughness and accuracy traditionally associated with German administration. Many of these returns are available in published form. The problem is that the returns,

---

[10] These figures are the share of votes cast for the liberal parties at the general elections of 1874 and 1907.

whether at the level of the precinct, the constituency, the larger administrative unit, or the entire nation, give the votes cast in specific areas, not the votes cast by individuals or social or religious groups. They are, in the jargon of electoral analysis, "ecological" or "aggregate" in nature.

A very simple example of the problems that arise in drawing inferences about individual behavior from information collected on an ecological basis can be seen in the pioneering essay of Rainer Lepsius that has informed so much of the study of elections in Germany before the First World War. Lepsius developed and supported his theory of the existence of sociomoral milieus by noting that the total percentages of votes cast for groups of parties across all of Germany remained reasonably stable for several decades.[11] This could have been the result from the same or similar (in terms of confession, region or social class) individuals casting votes for the same group of parties in these different elections, which is presumably what Lepsius had in mind, and which would support his idea of a basically static electoral system. Yet it is entirely possible for a party to receive a similar percentage of votes at different elections but to have very different individuals cast these votes. If this were the case, then there would have been a good deal of fluctuation among individual voters or groups of them; such a result would suggest a much more dynamic electoral system than could be reconciled with the theory of sociomoral milieus.

The basic issue in studying the national elections of Imperial Germany, or any other elections with a secret ballot and no polling data, is thus how to find out something about individual and group voting preferences from election returns consisting of individual votes aggregated together into geographical areas – the problem generally known as "ecological inference." For a long time, this was thought to be impossible: the very idea of inferring individual or group characteristics from aggregate data was regarded an an example of statistically incorrect thinking, the celebrated "ecological fallacy." Recent scholarship has demonstrated that such a sweeping assertion is incorrect and itself involved faulty statistical reasoning. Proceeding with caution and employing certain at least partially testable assumptions, ecological inference is indeed possible.[12]

There are a number of different approaches to ecological inference.[13]

[11] Lepsius, "Parteiensystem und Sozialstruktur," p. 63.
[12] E. A. Hanushek, J. E. Jackson, and J. F. Kain, "Model Specification, Use of Aggregate Data, and the Ecological Correlation Fallacy," *Political Methodology* 1 (1974): 87–106; Søren Risbjerg Thomsen, *Danish Elections, 1920–1979 A Logit Approach to Ecological Analysis and Inference* (Århus: Politicia, 1987), pp. 37–38, 47–48, 64.
[13] For a general introduction to these and other possible approaches, see Laura Irwin Langbein and Allan Lichtman, *Ecological Inference* (Beverly Hills and London: Sage Publications, 1978).

The simplest and technically least demanding involves the use of correlation coefficients, Pearson's r. If, for instance, one were interested in determining which voters supported a given political party, one would take for each aggregate unit (which could be a precinct, a constituency or a district) the vote for that party and the characteristic one wished to use to explain that party's vote – say the proportion of the voters in that unit belonging to a given religious confession or social class – and systematically compare the vote and the explanatory characteristic for all the units in the election returns. The result, the coefficient of correlation, ranges from −1 (which means that when one of these two characteristics – or variables, to use the technical term – increases, the other decreases in linear fashion) through zero (showing that the two have no linear relationship) to +1 (meaning that when one variable increases, the other also increases linearly). The general interpretation of these results would be that when r is close to 1, the voters designated by the explanatory variable were supporters of the party; when r is close to −1, they likely rejected it.

Unfortunately, there is a large gap between the value of Pearson's r and the explanatory power sometimes attributed to it. First of all, coefficients of correlation are often neither close to +1 nor to −1, but lie somewhere in the middle. Karl Rohe, for instance, cites research showing that the coefficient of correlation between the proportion of voters in a given area casting ballots for the National Liberal party in the 1893 Reichstag elections and the proportion of Catholics in that area was −0.29. Since the figure is negative, it means that an increase in Catholics went along with a decrease in National Liberal votes, but since the figure is not far from zero, it means that this relationship was not linear (not regular or steady in straight-line fashion). Did a lot of Catholics vote for the National Liberals, some, a few, or virtually none? The result does not really tell us. In fact, it tells us very little, since the explanatory power of Pearson's r is found by squaring it: −0.29 squared is 0.084: in other words 8.4% of the change in the National Liberal vote from area to area is explained by the proportion of Catholics living in these areas. What about the other 91.6%?

Even when r is substantial (close to +1 or −1), it does not tell us as much as we might wish to know. For those same Reichstag elections in 1893, the coefficient of correlation between the proportion Catholic and the vote for the Catholic political party, the Center, is the very high figure of 0.85: an increase in the proportion Catholic meant a linear increase in the proportion of Center voters. Linearity is not everything, though. Such a coefficient of correlation is compatible with two very different situations, one in which a large increase in the proportion of Catholic voters led in linear fashion to a small increase in the proportion of Center votes, and one in which a small increase in the proportion of Catholic voters led, once again in linear fashion, to a large increase in the Center vote percentages. Each of these cases would suggest something quite different about Catholic voters and the Center Party.

There is one additional problem with simple correlation coefficients, and that is their simplicity. Turning again to Rohe's figures on the 1893 elections, he notes that the coefficient of correlation between those employed in the service sector and the vote for the Social Democratic party is 0.57, a reasonably high figure, explaining about 32% (0.57^2) of the difference in the Social Democratic vote from area to area. However, the r between the Social Democratic vote and those employed in industry and crafts is 0.65. If areas with a large proportion of the labor force employed in industry and crafts are also ones with a large proportion employed in the service sector, then it might be that the correlation between the Social Democratic vote and those working in the service sector is really measuring the relationship between the Social Democratic vote and those employed in industry and crafts, a classic example (if this were the case) of the ecological fallacy. Using simple coefficients of correlation often means not exercising the necessary cautions to avoid the ecological fallacy.[14]

Much to be preferred to simple correlation coefficients in ecological inference is multiple regression analysis. Its results provide answers to all the questions that coefficients of correlation leave open. In multiple regression analysis one can measure not only the linearity of the relationship between variables, but also the extent to which changes in one affect the other (in technical terms, the slope of the regression line) and, finally, the influence that each variable has, taking into account the influence of the other variables. An example from Stanley Suvall's study of politics in Wilhelmine Germany might help make this clear.

Suvall wanted to determine the influence of occupation, confession and urbanization on the votes for the conservative parties. For 47 larger administrative units he took the conservative vote in 1907, the percentage of the population that was Roman Catholic, the percentage of the male labor force engaged in industry, crafts and mining, and the percentage of the population living in cities with over 10,000 inhabitants. The standardized multiple regression coefficient for the percentage of the male workforce engaged in industry, crafts and mining was -0.623. What this

[14] Figures are from Rohe, *Wahlen und Wählertraditionen*, p. 272. Lest these criticisms be thought to demonstrate a know-it-all attitude, I should note that much of my own previous work in electoral analysis in *Popular Catholicism in Nineteenth Century Germany* (Princeton: Princeton University Press, 1984), displays some of these problems, too.

means is that if we imagine two administrative units with identical percentages of Catholic and urban populations, but one having a percentage of the industrial labor force that was one standard deviation higher than the other, then the conservative vote in that first unit would be 0.623 standard deviations lower. The coefficient of determination, R^2, is 0.636, showing that the combination of confession, occupation and urbanization that Suvall investigated explains 63.6% of the difference in the conservative vote among his 47 administrative units.[15]

While multiple regression analysis is clearly superior to correlation analysis, it still leaves some questions open. The standardized regression coefficients are expressed in units of standard deviations, whose exact interpretation is not always clear. If the standard deviations of the different variables were given (simple to calculate, but almost never done), one could translate statements such as that of Suvall's given above into percentage points; in other words, an increase of so many percentage points in the industrial labor force, all other things being equal, would result in a decrease of so many percentage points in the conservative vote. An implicit assumption usually made (as it is in Suvall's book) in interpreting the results of multiple analysis, although very rarely explicitly stated, is that the higher the standardized regression coefficient for a given variable, the stronger the support of the group indicated by that variable; the lower the coefficient – especially if it is negative – the weaker the support.

This may usually be true, but is not always the case. It is even possible for a majority of members of a given group to support a given political party, yet the multiple regression coefficient for that group can be negative, provided there is another group that supports the party even more strongly. If one is alert to such a possibility, it can be detected, but the basic problem remains: what we really would like to know is not how changes in one group affect the vote for a given party, but what percentage of a given group voted for the party – or, in the example from Suvall's work, just how many voters employed in industry, crafts and mining voted for the conservative parties in 1907. In effect, it would be most helpful if we could obtain information comparable to that obtained today by public opinion polls in an era when such polls were not taken.

There is a way to do so, the procedure known as ecological regression. It involves using multiple regression analysis, with appropriately selected variables. The results can be interpreted as estimates of the percentages of members of individual groups supporting given political parties. In other words, they are in a form requiring no special statistical training to under-

---

[15] Figures from Suvall, *Electoral Politics*, p. 99.

stand, and they are comparable to results obtained by modern survey research.[16]

For all these advantages, ecological regression has a number of limitations. It does not give reliable estimates of the voting behavior of very small groups (say those under 5% of the electorate), or of groups present in about the same percentage in each area of observation. The validity of its results are based on a number of assumptions, not all of which can be directly tested.[17] The frequent and annoying problem of impossible results, of estimates that greater than 100% or less than 0% of a given group supported a particular party, shows that on many occasions all these assumptions do not entirely correspond to actual circumstances. Finally, ecological regression shares a problem with all other forms of ecological inference: missing or incompatible information. Ecological inference is based on the availability of aggregate data. If one does not know how many members of a given group were present in each area under observation, one cannot develop estimates of how members of that group voted. If election returns and information on group membership are aggregated differently and incompatibly – if, for instance, the boundaries of constituencies and of census districts are sufficiently different – then once again the development of estimates is impossible.

This enumeration of limitations and difficulties suggests some caution about the use of ecological regression. It is not a magic wand that can be waved over past election returns to produce information as exact or as detailed as that obtained by contemporary public opinion polls. But the problems with ecological regression do not make it an impossible procedure. There is enough aggregate data available for the German Empire to calculate the voting behavior of important social, confessional and political groups. Some of the calculations do give impossible results, but there exist procedures – admittedly, fairly complicated ones – to adjust these results to produce possible and plausible estimates. Field tests on recent elections have shown that estimates obtained through ecological regression are very close to the figures from survey research. There is even one study of nineteenth-century American elections with an open ballot, which compared results from ecological analysis with the recorded

[16] Two useful introductions to ecological regression are J. Morgan Kousser, "Ecological Regression and the Analysis of Past Politics," *Journal of Interdisciplinary History* 4 (1973): 237–62, and Lichtman and Langbein, *Ecological Inference* .
[17] A succinct discussion of the assumptions implicit in ecological regression can be found in Jan-Bernd Lohmoeller, Jürgen Falter, Andreas Link and Johann de Rijke, "Unemployment and the Rise of National Socialism: Contradicting Results from Different Regional Aggregations," in Peter Nijkamp, Helga Leitner and Neil Wrigley (eds.) *Measuring the Unmeasurable* (Dodrecht Boston and Lancaster: Martinus Nijhoff Publishers, 1985), pp. 357–70, esp. p. 365.

individual votes, which once again obtained quite similar results.[18] All these suggest (and this is not unusual for statistical procedures) that even if all the assumptions behind ecological regression are not met in stringent fashion, the procedure can still produce reasonably reliable estimates.

Ecological regression has been used to study past elections in a wide variety of venues in Europe and North America, from Sweden to Alabama.[19] The most elaborate project involving its use, and certainly the best-known example of its application to the study of German history, has been the work of the political scientist Jürgen Falter and his team on the rise of the Nazi party in the German general elections of the years 1928–33. Starting from the basic question of who voted for the Nazis – more specifically, what proportions of different social and confessional groups supported the Nazis and which parties had Nazi voters supported before they voted for the Nazis – Falter and his co-workers have developed a wealth of information about voting behavior during the Weimar Republic. If, as will be seen in the final chapter, not all their results are above reproach, they have convincingly demonstrated the intellectual potential of ecological regression and have also made important methodological contributions, further improving and refining its practice.[20]

---

[18] Paul F. Bourke and Donald A. DeBats, "Individuals and Aggregates: A Note on Historical Data and Assumptions," *Social Science History* 4 (1980): 229–49; J. Morgan Kousser, "Speculation or Specification: A note on Flannigan and Zinagle," *Social Science History* 10 (1986): 72–84; and Søren Risbjerg Thomsen, Sten Berglund, and Ingemar Wörlund, "Assessing the Validity of the Logit Method for Ecological Inference," in Sten Berglund and Søren Risbjerg Thomsen (eds.) *Modern Political Ecological Analysis* (Åbo: Åbo Akademis Förlag, 1990), pp. 12–62.

[19] A few examples would include J. Morgan Kousser, *The Shaping of Southern Politics: Suffrage Restriction and the Establishment of the One Party South, 1880–1910* (New Haven and London: Yale University Press, 1974); William Gienapp, *The Origins of the Republican Party 1852–1856* (Oxford and New York: Oxford University Press, 1987); Leif Lewin, Bo Jansson, and Dag Sörbom, *The Swedish Electorate 1887–1968* (Stockholm: Almqvist & Wiksell, 1972); Thomsen, *Danish Elections*; and a number of the essays in Berglund and Thomsen (eds.) *Modern Political Ecological Analysis*.

[20] Falter and his team have published their results widely, if not always consistently. Some of the major publications of his empirical findings include Jürgen Falter, *Hitlers Wähler* (Munich: Beck, 1990); Jürgen Falter, "Die Wählerpotentiale politischer Teilkulturen, 1920–1933," in Detlef Lehnert and Klaus Mengerle (eds.) *Politische Indentität und nationale Gedenktage: Zur politischen Kultur in der Weimarer Republik* (Opladen: Westdeutscher Verlag, 1989), pp. 281–305; Jürgen Falter, "War die NSDAP die erste deutsche Volkspartei?" in Michael Prinz and Rainer Zitelmann (eds.) *Nationalsozialismus und Modernisierung* (Darmstadt: Wissenschaftliche Buchgesellschaft, 1991), pp. 21–47; Jürgen Falter and Dirk Hänisch, "Die Anfälligkeit von Arbeitern gegenüber der NSDAP bei den Reichstagswahlen," *Archiv für Sozialgeschichte* 26 (1986): 179–216; Jürgen Falter and Reinhard Zintl, "The Economic Crisis of the 1930s and the Nazi Vote," *Journal of Interdisciplinary History* 19 (1988/89): 55–85; and Jürgen Falter, "The Two Hindenburg Elections of 1925 and 1932: A Total Reversal of Voter Coalitions," *Central European History* 23 (1990): 225–41. Two important methodological articles are Jan-Bernd

The results of Falter's work on the late 1920s and early 1930s are relevant to the various theories developed to explain the way Germans voted in national elections before the First World War. In some ways, Falter's conclusions confirm elements of all the different and mutually contradictory approaches. His analysis of the Nazi electorate led him to describe the NSDAP as the first German people's party, as a catch-all party of protest that garnered support from all social and confessional groups. Implicitly, this is a confirmation of Lepsius's analysis of the politics of sociomoral milieus and their collapse. Unlike the political parties of the German Empire and the early years of the Weimar Republic, whose support, according to Lepsius, was limited to internally homogeneous groups, support for the Nazis cut across previous lines of affiliation, thus showing the collapse of the closed and static world of the milieus. Yet one could also see this conclusion as a confirmation of the ideas of Lepsius's English-speaking critics. They have pointed to the 1890s as a period of the transformation of conservative politics in Germany, from an affirmative, weakly organized and pro-governmental stance, to an independent, tightly organized anti-governmental protest movement, one whose support cut across previous party lines and involved voter realignments. The Nazis would thus appear as the further development and radicalization (a result of the First World War and the subsequent economic and political crises) of this realignment of right-wing politics.

If Falter has shown that the Nazi vote was spread out over different social classes, his results also demonstrate that a disproportionately large share of Nazi voters had previously supported the liberal and conservative parties, precisely those groups that make up Karl Rohe's "national" camp of German politics. This would make the Nazi electorate socially heterogeneous but possessing a common political past, characterized by the rejection of labor and clerical parties, a rejection preserved in the support for a new party, one that opposed the labor and clerical parties even more vehemently than conservatives or liberals had done. These circumstances – varied social structure, common political past, persisting opposition to other political groups, in spite of changes in party loyalties – fit very well Rohe's definition of a political camp and his distinction between it and a sociomoral milieu.

All these differing conclusions involve, implicitly or explicitly, a comparison between voters' choices in the late years of the Weimar Republic and the period before the First World War. The contention that the Nazis were

Lohmoller and Jürgen Falter, "Some Further Aspects of Ecological Regression Analysis," *Quality & Quantity* 20 (1986): 109–25 and Lohmoeller, Falter, Link, and de Rijke, "Unemployment and the Rise of National Socialism."

the first people's party in Germany means that other political parties previously obtaining similar levels of support, such as the Social Democrats in the last elections prior to the First World War, did not receive votes across a broad social and confessional spectrum, but instead obtained the vast majority of the votes of more narrowly delineated groups, along the lines of Lepsius's milieus. Understanding the Nazi vote as the latest manifestation of a national camp in the German electorate would mean demonstrating the long-term existence of such a camp. Similarly, the perception of the 1890s as a period of the reorientation of German right-wing politics, showing similarities with the Nazis, would, at one level anyway, require a study of shifts in the electorate during that decade.

Studying the voters in Imperial Germany

It is precisely such studies of voting behavior in Imperial Germany that are lacking. There have been a few works discussing pre-1914 German elections using various forms of ecological inference, but these have not been comprehensive, instead just discussing selected elections or the voting in particular regions. With one important exception, such studies have been technically less advanced, sometimes rather crude, at best not up to the high standards set by Falter and comparable works on elections in other countries.[21] By far the best of these works is the recent study of Falter's student, Jürgen Winkler, on the development of the German electorate between 1871 and 1933. Methodologically at a very high level and offering a number of important insights, Winkler's work is an impressive contribution to the study of the nineteenth-century German electorate. As the reader will see, I have often drawn on Winkler's study in this book, and have tried to note explicitly the points where the results of our analy-

---

[21] Besides Suvall's *Electoral Politics*, other studies of pre-1914 voting using ecological inference include Horst Nocker, *Der preußische Reichstagswähler in Kaiserreich und Republik 1912 und 1924: Analyse, Interpretation, Dokumentation* (Berlin: Colloquium Verlag, 1987) and William Claggett, Jeffrey Loesch, W. Phillips Shively and Ronald Snell, "Political Leadership and the Development of Political Cleavages: Imperial Germany, 1871–1912," *American Journal of Political Science* 26 (1982): 644–63. A particular disappointment is the recent, massive study by Jürgen Schmädeke, *Wählerbewegung in Wilhelmischen Deutschland* 2 vols. (Berlin: Akademie Verlag, 1995), which is technically backward, uses a number of questionable assumptions and, in spite of its bulk, offers few new or convincing insights. Mention should also be made of the 1928 work of Johannes Schauff, reprinted as *Das Wahlverhalten der deutschen Katholiken im Kaiserreich und in der Weimarer Republik* ed. Rudolf Morsey (Mainz: Matthias-Grünewald-Verlag, 1975). Methodologically quite primitive – since it was written before modern statistical methods, to say nothing of calculation hardware, had been developed – it is unusually comprehensive in its scope and demonstrates great care (not always shared by more recent authors with more possibilities at their disposal) in handling the available election returns.

ses agree and where they suggest different conclusions, as well as the reasons for these convergences and divergences (generally involving technical issues of the choice of data and the methods used to analyze it). Overall, however, our works are more complementary than overlapping, since in discussing the *Kaiserreich*, Winkler limits himself primarily to the elections of the 1870s, with a brief glance at those of the early twentieth century, and thus offers only a partial account of developments in the empire.[22]

This book will attempt to provide a methodologically rigorous and temporally and spatially comprehensive analysis of national elections in Imperial Germany. The analysis is based on three groups of ecological regressions that I have carried out. The first group concerns movements of voters from one election to another. For every pair of elections in the *Kaiserreich*, from the first (1871–74) to the last (1907–12), I have calculated estimates of how the voters (or non-voters) in the first of each pair of elections voted in the second. These estimates make it possible to trace the movement or lack of it from one party or group of parties – including the important "party" of the non-voters – to another. The second group of estimates gives the voting choices of confessional groups for every single national election from 1871 to 1912. The third involves estimates of choices of the voters, differentiated by both social class and religious confession, for the elections of the Wilhelmine era, from 1890 to 1912. These two last groups offer evidence on which groups of voters actually came out to vote and, for those who did, which parties they supported.

One might understand this book as a running commentary on the results of this statistical analysis, a commentary directed at interpretations of voting behavior under the distinct political and constitutional circumstances of Imperial Germany. One focus of the commentary will be the three broad interpretations of the nature of the electoral system discussed earlier in this introduction. I rather dislike the social science language of "testing theories," but there will be a consideration of the extent to which the results of the ecological regressions are compatible with the different interpretations, as well as an attempt to note their strong and weak points, and to develop a new understanding of the movements of the electorate and the bases of support for the different political parties during the empire, one that builds on the strong points of existing efforts, but avoids their empirically questionable elements.

---

[22] Jürgen R. Winkler, *Sozialstruktur, politische Traditionen und Liberalismus: Eine Empirische Längsschnittstudie zur Wahlentwicklung in Deutschland 1871–1933* (Opladen: Westdeutscher Verlag, 1995); and Winkler, "Die soziale Basis der sozialistischen Parteien in Deutschland vom Ende des Kaiserreichs bis zur Mitte der Weimarer Republik 1912–1924," *Archiv für Sozialgeschichte* 19 (1989): 137–72.

The second focus of the commentary will be a broader consideration of popular political life under the Kaiser. For this book, I have not done any of my own research into primary sources – the periodical press, the reports of the state bureaucracy, or the investigations of the Reichstag committees that received complaints of fraud and irregularities and passed on the validity of contested elections. I have, however, drawn extensively on the very large literature on political parties, election campaigns and political or quasi-political organizations in Germany before the First World War. Most of these studies are not analytical or statistical but descriptive in nature, using what historians with a bent for quantification sometimes call, not very flatteringly, "literary" sources. I would like to see how the electoral process observed in this way compares with the view from election returns. In part, this comparison will help ascertain whether such works, drawing their evidence largely from official expressions of the political parties or of articulate political activists, provide a good account of the anonymous mass of voters in a system of universal and secret suffrage. The comparison also works the other way: as a reminder that ecological inference produces estimates of voting behavior, ones that depend on certain, often untestable mathematical assumptions. If, for instance, the estimates show a large swing in voting support of a particular social group between two elections, but contemporary politicians or commentators took no notice of it, one might wonder whether contemporaries were paying attention, but one might also suspect that the assumptions necessary to develop the estimates were not valid, so that the estimates are far off the mark.

Studies of politics in Imperial Germany can be divided into four categories, each of which tends to center around certain themes or debates. Some of these themes are similar to the issues posed by Lepsius and other students of the entire political system while others point in quite different directions. In any event, each of these themes offers the possibility for comparison with the estimates of the election returns. Studies in one category are concerned above all with the rhetoric of political campaigning, in particular with the tendency of the state authorities and certain, usually right-of-center, political parties to use a language of polarization and absolute condemnation of their rivals.[23] Here, one would like to know the effects of such rhetoric on the voters, whether it encouraged them to turn

---

[23] Two examples of this sort of work are Peter Steinbach, *Die Zähmung des politischen Massenmarktes: Wahlen und Wahlkämpfe im Bismarckreich im Spiegel der Hauptstadt- und Gesinnungspresse* 2 vols. (Passau: Wissenschaftsverlag Richard Rothe, 1990), and Elfi Bendikat, *Wahlkämpfe in Europa 1884 bis 1889: Parteiensysteme und Politikstile in Deutschland, Frankreich und Großbritannien* (Wiesbaden: Deutscher Universitäts-Verlag, 1988).

out, or kept them from the ballot box. One might also be curious about whether the voters themselves were as polarized as the rhetoric of politics was.

A second category of works deals with political organization and participation. The driving theme here has been the distinction between notables' politics (*Honoriatorenpolitik*) and mass politics (*Massenpolitik*). In the former, politics at the local level was run by self-selected groups of the local elite, who employed informally constituted and temporary political organization and who believed that election campaigns should consist primarily of statements of principle published in newspapers. A distinguishing feature of mass politics, in contrast, was the mass membership political party, with a large dues-paying membership, supporting a paid permanent staff. Mass political parties were thus permanently present and continuously active, unlike the notables' committees, formed at election time and disbanded once the votes were counted, not to be revived until the next election. Another related distinguishing feature of mass politics was, of course, mass agitation, vigorous election campaigns with rallies, speeches, get-out-the-vote drives, and poll-watchers on election day.

Historians have tended to view the 1890s as the dividing line, when a political system characterized primarily by notables' politics gave way to one dominated by mass politics. They have often seen this process as a sort of cascade, begun by the labor party, the SPD, once the laws prohibiting it were allowed to lapse in 1890. Indeed, the SPD of Wilhelmine Germany generally serves as the very model of a mass political party. The style of mass politics was then taken up by the other parties, starting with the Catholic party, the Center, then the conservatives and, finally and most reluctantly, by the liberal parties. It was not so much that these parties turned themselves into mass membership parties, although they did take a few steps in that direction, as that they retained the structure of notables' parties while developing or cultivating auxiliary mass membership organizations – the People's Association for Catholic Germany, the Agrarian League, the Navy League, the veterans' groups, or the economic special interest groups – that engaged in the campaigning of mass politics and were linked to the parties' notable leadership by a system of interlocking directorates.[24]

There is something of a counter-argument that has developed, one that

[24] The classic account of this development is in Thomas Nipperdey, *Die Organisation der deutschen Parteien vor 1918* (Düsseldorf: Droste, 1961). Both Eley, in *The Reshaping of the German Right*, and Blackbourn, in *Class, Religion and Local Politics*, have strongly endorsed and further developed this notion of the 1890s as a period of transition for political styles.

accepts the categories of notables' politics and mass politics, but suggests
a different and much earlier date for the transition from one form to the
other. Studies along these lines have identified the transition to universal
and direct manhood suffrage as the distinguishing factor and argued that,
at least in certain regions, a vigorous mass politics, complete with permanent organizations and very active campaigning could be found in the
1870s.[25] An analysis of election returns cannot decide this issue, but it
can provide some notion of when and where voters were mobilized, which
voters were mobilized at what time, and whether voters who had previously been mobilized were subsequently demobilized. At the very least,
this might provide some idea of just how effective different political styles
were. Although it seems very counter-intuitive, transitions to mass politics may have been accompanied by declining turnouts and in some cases
notables' politics may have gotten more voters to the polls than a more
active and participatory style of campaigning.

The third major category of works on politics in the *Kaiserreich* involves
the study of individual general elections, either one or many, and on a
local, regional, or national level.[26] These works are generally not centered
around common themes or avenues of inquiry, which is not entirely surprising in view of the great diversity of circumstances found in a large
European country over the course of four decades. Still more unfortunately, such works do not adequately represent the diversity of circumstances in Germany, a state of affairs that is a consequence of the Cold
War. Most local and regional election studies were composed after 1945
and the Marxist-Leninist historiography of the former German

---

[25] See, for instance, Norbert Schloßmacher, *Düsseldorf im Bismarckreich: Politik und Wahlen Parteien und Vereine* (Düsseldorf: Schwann, 1985); or Anderson, "Voter, Junker, *Landrat*, Priest," pp. 1470–71. A nice reflection on the debate, simultaneously a case study arguing for the 1890s as the transition period, is found in Donald G. Schilling's "Politics in a New Key: The Late Nineteenth Century Transformation of Politics in Northern Bavaria," *German Studies Review* 17 (1994): 33–57.

[26] Three studies at the national level are George Dunlop Crothers, *The German Elections of 1907* (New York: Columbia University Press, 1941); Jürgen Bertram, *Die Wahlen zum Deutschen Reichstage vom Jahre 1912* (Düsseldorf: Droste, 1964) and Brett Fairbairn, "Interpreting Wilhelmine Elections: National Issues, Fairness Issues and Electoral Mobilization," in Jones and Retallack (eds.) *Elections, Mass Politics, and Social Change* pp. 17–48. (Fairbairn's full-scale, book-length study of the 1898 and 1903 elections was not yet available when this manuscript was completed.) There are an enormous number of local and regional studies of elections. A few particularly good ones, whose results point towards broader issues, include Hermann Hiery, *Reichstagswahlen im Reichsland: Ein Beitrag zur Landesgeschichte von Elsaß-Lothringen und zur Wahlgeschichte des Deutschen Reiches 1871–1918* (Düsseldorf: Droste, 1986); Fred Ludwig Sepainter, *Die Reichstagwahlen im Großherzogtum Baden: Ein Beitrag zur Wahlgeschichte im Kaiserreich* (Frankfurt and Bern: Peter Lang, 1983) or the older but still useful work, Robert Frank, *Die Brandenburger als Reichstagswähler: Erster Band 1867/71 bis 1912/14* (Berlin: Carl Heymanns Verlag, 1934).

Democratic Republic tended to discourage preoccupation with such distinctly non-revolutionary activities. Consequently, these works usually deal with the areas that would be in the territory of the West Germany of the years 1949–90.

Nonetheless, one important issue emerges from a large number of individual election studies, the periodization of election outcomes. I have found three ways of doing so particularly helpful and will apply these schemes throughout the book. One is a very simple contrast between the general elections of Bismarckian Germany, from 1871 to 1887, and those of the Wilhelmine era, from 1890 to the last prewar balloting in 1912. Although such a distinction is taken from the realms of diplomatic history and the narrative of high politics, it proves to fit changes in voting behavior strikingly well. There was certainly a remarkable difference between the years when the Iron Chancellor determined his country's political destiny – and the analysis of election outcomes shows that such a statement is not just a figure of speech – and those overshadowed by the moody, eccentric Wilhelm II, when state policy, political parties, and the German voters all went their separate ways. A second, equally simple form of periodization is by decade, and in fact the elections of the 1870s, 1880s, 1890s, and the initial years of the twentieth century all had their own distinct patterns of voting choices. The third, and somewhat different way to understand election returns is to contrast those general elections that brought a victory to the parties of the right – 1878, 1887, 1893, and 1907 – with those where the left-wing parties were victorious – 1881, 1890, 1903, and 1912 – and those where the remaining elections that saw no unambiguous winner, or, as in 1874, were characterized by the victory of the Catholic Center, a party not easily placed on a left–right political spectrum.

These sorts of questions are tailor-made for quantitative electoral analysis. To take just one example, one can compare the voter movements that brought victories to the parties of the right, with those bringing success to the left, seeing the extent to which the mobilization of previous non-voters or the attraction of previous supporters of opposing parties provided the margin of victory in the two different cases. A comparison of these sorts of results with the dominant issues in given elections is an important clue to the broader nature of voting behavior in Imperial Germany.

The fourth and most extensive group of studies are accounts of individual political parties. Like the previous group, these are also an extraordinarily varied and diverse category. However, there is rather more in the nature of a common thematic core, or, rather, cores, since different questions tend to be asked about different political parties. For the Social

Democrats, one of the main questions was first posed in the Wilhelmine era itself and has been debated down to the present day. Was the SPD a "workers' party," drawing its support predominantly or exclusively from a blue-collar clientele, or was it a "people's party," with a broader range of supporters? In view of the steadily increasing success of the SPD at the polls before 1914, the answer to this question is crucial to understanding the entire electorate of Imperial Germany, not just the SPD supporters.[27]

The Center Party is handled differently in the literature. There is little debate about who its supporters were; everyone agrees that the party drew its votes from the Roman Catholics in the German electorate. Rather, the question, also first raised in the Wilhelmine era, and more insistently in the Weimar Republic, was whether the party could retain the loyalties of its supporters. In other words, as the issue is usually explained, could a common confessional identity suffice to keep together an electorate when social and economic issues tended to split it apart? The smaller parties of the national and regional minorities have been studied in a similar vein, highlighting the contrast between the common identity of their voters as French, Poles, or Hanoverians, and other factors that over time might have moved them in different political directions.[28]

The liberal and conservative parties tend to be considered still differently. If the SPD was a labor party and the Center a Catholic party, the liberals claimed to be a universal party, representing general interests. A main theme in the study of liberal politics in Imperial Germany has been the failure of such a universal aspiration, the way that internal divisions among liberals, confessional differences, and diverging socioeconomic interests limited and increasingly constricted the potential universe of liberal voters. If growth in support is the central issue in studies of the SPD, and stability of support the main item for consideration of the Center, explanations for decline in support – usually centering around the hetereogeneity of the electorate – have tended to structure investigations of the history of the liberal parties in the *Kaiserreich*.[29]

---

[27] A recent book, summarizing the extensive literature on the topic and presenting some of the latest scholarship is Gerhard A. Ritter (ed.) *Der Aufstieg der deutschen Arbeiterbewegung: Sozialdemokratie und Freie Gewerkschaften im Parteiensystem und Sozialmilieu des Kasierreichs* (Munich: R. Oldenburg, 1990).

[28] See, for instance, Margaret Anderson, *Windhorst: A Political Biography* (Oxford: Clarendon Press, 1981); Wilfried Loth, *Katholiken im Kaiserreich: Der politische Katholizismus in der Krise des wilhelmischen Deutschlands* (Düsseldorf: Droste, 1984); Hiery, *Reichstagswahlen im Reichsland*; Hans-Georg Aschoff, *Welfische Bewegung und politischer Katholizismus 1886–1918: Die deutsch-hannoversche Partei und das Zentrum in der Provinz Hannover während des Kaiserreiches* (Düsseldorf: Droste, 1987).

[29] On this point, I will cite only two main works of synthesis out of many possible studies: James J. Sheehan, *German Liberalism in the Nineteenth Century* (Chicago and London: University of Chicago Press, 1978) and Dieter Langewiesche, *Liberalismus in Deutschland*

In contrast to the liberals, the particularity of the conservative parties is generally taken for granted. There is general agreement that their strongholds were in the rural populations of the areas of large landed estates in East Elbian Germany. The question sometimes posed of the conservatives is the extent to which they were able to move beyond this, to attract support from other regions, urban areas, or social groups other than the farming population. This question is generally investigated in terms of the development of new forms of right-wing politics in the 1890s, and the growth of anti-Semitic and agrarian political movements on the fringes of the previously existing conservative parties. The assumption connecting these two points is that encompassing new constituencies required new kinds of politics.[30]

It should be clear that use of ecological inference to develop estimates of class and confessional preferences in voting and of movements of voters between elections can help provide answers to all these questions about the individual parties. Such estimates give us information about the representation of different social and confessional groups among SPD voters; about the proportion of Catholics who supported the Center, voted for other parties or did not vote; about the composition of the liberal electorate or about what happened to former liberal voters when they stopped voting for the liberal parties; about who supported the conservatives and when they did so. More than just answering previously posed questions, this procedure also offers the opportunity to consider new ones. One could take themes typical for one party and apply them to others: asking, for instance, about the class composition of the Center electorate or the confessional composition of the SPD's; trying to ascertain what happened to former SPD voters when they stopped voting for the labor party, or which parties new liberal or conservative voters had previously supported. More generally, one can disaggregate net swings between elections, that is, see how a particular party's net loss or gain of voters was made up of a mosaic of interchanges, both gains and losses, between that party and the other parties as well as the non-voters.

These are the sorts of questions that I will attempt to answer in this book, which is divided into two parts. The first deals with the individual parties and considers the nature of and trends in their electoral support. It has chapters on the Social Democrats; the parties of the religious,

(Frankfurt: Suhrkamp Verlag, 1988), for whom this question is central to the discussion of liberalism in the Kaiserreich.

[30] Hans-Jürgen Puhle, *Agrarische Interessenpolitik und preußischer Konservativsmus im wilhelmischen Reich 1893–1914* (Hanover: Verlag für Literatur und Zeitgeschehen, 1966); James Retallack, *Notables of the Right: The Conservative Party and Political Mobilization in Germany, 1876–1918* (London: Unwin Hyman, 1988).

national and regional minorities; and, to use Karl Rohe's phrase, the "national" parties (i.e. the liberals and the conservatives). In the second part, the focus of the analysis moves from parties to elections, considered both individually and in various groupings, with chapters on the balloting in Bismarckian and in Wilhelmine Germany. A final chapter will offer a general discussion of the nature of the electorate in Imperial Germany and some suggestions about ways to go about studying it. It will also provide some comparisons, contrasting my findings on pre-1914 elections, with those of Jürgen Falter's work on voting during the Weimar Republic and with the results of survey research in the Federal Republic after the Second World War.

As a student of a student of a student of Friedrich Meinecke, I share the historicist emphasis on the particularities of time and place, and am skeptical of political scientists' efforts to develop universal theories of voting behavior. However, the long-term perspective developed in this final chapter might enable us to see what was unique about voters in Germany, and what they had in common with their counterparts elsewhere in Europe or in North America. That chapter and the book will end with a return to the question posed at the beginning: how did the peculiar combination of democratic franchise and authoritarian regime shape patterns of voting in Germany? Did it, in the very long run, make much difference?

Some necessary caveats, limitations, and explanations

There are two points I need to make about the limitations of this study. First, it is an account of nationwide, general elections. State and local elections, which were generally held during the *Kaiserreich* under a different, less democratic franchise than the national elections, are an interesting topic of study in their own right, one in which historians have shown a growing interest in recent years.[31] The study of such elections, and their interaction with those for the Reichstag is a line of investigation that I will not pursue in this book. Similarly, individual by-elections for the Reichstag, or supplementary elections (*Nachwahlen*), held when a candidate was elected in more than one constituency, are not a topic for this work. Instead, this study focuses exclusively on the thirteen times that all German voters were summoned to the polls between the founding of the empire in 1871 and the last prewar balloting under the Kaiser in 1912.

Second, I fear that such a work, oriented toward statistical analysis, will be less than exciting to read. I have done my best to prevent this book

---

[31] See, for example, Thomas Kühne, *Dreiklassenwahlrecht und Wahlkultur in Preußen 1867–1914: Landtagswahlen zwischen korporativer Tradition und politischem Massenmarkt* (Düsseldorf: Droste, 1993).

from being just one table of figures after another, but a study that is primarily an analysis of election returns and a commentary on theories explaining them, is simply not going to be a thriller. I can only hope that it will make somewhat lighter fare than many others of the same genre.

To that end, I have kept technical considerations in the six expository chapters to a minimum, with a detailed discussion of them reserved for the appendix. There, the reader will find an account of the data used in the study, the methodology of ecological inference, and how I applied the methodology to the data. The appendix also contains tables giving the main results of the analysis for each general election or pair of elections between 1871 and 1912. I hope that the appendix will provide a clear view of the statistical foundations of this work, that it will explain the dilemmas posed by the sources and my responses to them, the different methodological alternatives and my reasons for choosing among them, and the assumptions and approximations necessary for these choices. Although both mathematical formulae and technical expressions will be unavoidable, I have tried to explain my work in the simplest terms possible, in part in the hope that it may help clarify issues for historians and provide some guidance to those who wish to do their own ecological analysis. Until quite recently, this sort of work was restricted to those who had mastered the arcane commands used on mainframe computers or who had at their disposal a small army of research assistants, but in an age of easy-to-use graphical interface statistics packages and inexpensive but powerful desktops, everyone has the potential to be a "computer historian."

Readers interested in the technical details can turn straight to the appendix. Those who are not, but who wish to see the results of the analysis, should read the following non-technical description of the three kinds of ecological regressions whose results form the basis for this work. Reading this account will help make the presentation of the results in the following chapters easily understandable.

First, there ought to be a word of reminder about the electoral system. Those eligible to vote in German national elections between 1871 and 1912 were adult men over the age of twenty-five, who were not active-duty soldiers, had not lost their civic rights because of conviction on felony charges or commitment to an asylum for the insane or the retarded, had not received poor-relief or changed address in the previous three months. Elections to the Reichstag took place in 397 single-member constituencies.[32] They were never reapportioned over the entire

---

[32] Except for the first elections in 1871, which were not held in the fifteen constituencies of Alsace-Lorraine.

history of the *Kaiserreich* in view of the changes in population among them – not an entirely democratic procedure, but one that makes life much easier for the historian.

Election of a deputy required the absolute majority of votes cast. If no candidate received such a majority in the first round of balloting (as happened in a minority of cases, albeit different constituencies at each election) a run-off was held between the two top candidates of the first round. All the results in this book are calculated from the first round of elections only! The question of how voters in the first round of elections voted in the second is interesting, but needs to be calculated on a constituency by constituency basis, using precinct-level election returns from the archives or contemporary newspapers.

The first group of regressions I have calculated are the "voter transition probabilities," estimates of how voters at one election voted in the next one. This is, in principle, quite straightforward. As there was no redistricting, one has the same 397 units of observation, each of the constituencies, to serve as the basis for the regressions.[33] However, two difficulties emerge at this point.

One has to do with the nature of the German party system. Of the individual political parties, only one, the Social Democrats, put up candidates in all, or almost all, constituencies, and that only after 1890. Most parties were present in half or less of the constituencies and to reduce both the number of observations with zeros (which can distort the regressions) and the number of variables (to the number which the statistics package I used can handle) I had to group the different political parties together. Thus, the results are not based on the individual parties, but on five party groups. Group 1 is the conservative parties, including the Conservatives, the Free Conservatives, and the extreme right-wing parties appearing after 1887, the anti-Semites and the Agrarian League. (Note the difference between small c "conservatives" – all the parties of the right and the extreme right – and capital C "Conservatives," the largest of these parties.) Group 2 constitutes the liberal parties, made up of the National Liberals and the various left-liberal and bourgeois-democratic parties. (I will often refer to the latter, generically, as small p "progressives," once again to be distinguished from capital P "Progressives," the name of several of these parties.) Group 3 consists of the parties of the religious, national and regional minorities. The Center, the Catholic political party, accounted for

---

[33] Since elections were not held in Alsace-Lorraine in 1871, calculations for the first pair of elections 1871–74, are based on the 382 constituencies in which elections were held in both years.

about 75% of the votes in this group; the rest were scattered among the Polish, French, Danish and Lithuanian nationalists, the Hanoverian and Hessian particularists, and, after 1890, the Bavarian Peasant League. Group 4 is the Social Democrats, before their 1875 unification both the Lassalleans and the Eisenachers; between 1875 and 1890, officially entitled the Social Democratic Labor Party; from 1891 onwards, going under the same designation they preserve today, the Social Democratic Party of Germany, or SPD. The final group, Group 5, comprises the non-voters, and also includes those who cast invalid or scattered ballots.

These groupings are not arbitrary, but represent parties with ideological affinities and frequent electoral alliances.[34] Parties in each group usually did not run candidates against each other. To be sure, this was not always the case and points to a limitation in these results, namely that voter movements within the party groups – for instance, from the National Liberals to the progressives and vice-versa, from the Center to the Polish nationalists, or from the French nationalists to the Center – which certainly took place, cannot be directly ascertained. The one thing that I can do about this, is to recalculate the regressions using different party groupings. I performed these recalculations for the elections of the 1880s, when there was a somewhat different political alignment, most notably at the elections of 1887, but characteristic of the entire decade. Instead of conservative and liberal groups, I calculated results for the Kartell, the pro-governmental alliance of Conservatives, Free Conservatives and National Liberals (named after an electoral arrangement of 1887), and the left-liberal opposition parties. Results from these regressions are compatible with those calculated using the other party groups and throw some light on the politics of the 1880s, a decade whose electoral history is rather less well-studied than other periods of the empire.[35]

The second problem is basic to all attempts at estimating, via ecological inference, voter choices over two or more elections: the electorate did not stay the same. Between two general elections some eligible voters died, while others reached voting age; voters moved from one constituency to another, or left the country altogether. Unfortunately, it is impossible to take these changes into account, since there are no figures on voter fluctuations. Encouragingly, studies of population movement show that most people who moved were either under age for voting, or just temporarily

---

[34] For a discussion of grouping schemes, and the application of one fairly close to that used in this book, see Winkler, *Sozialstruktur*, pp. 56–63.

[35] Kühne even describes the 1880s as "the 'dark ages' of research into the *Kaiserreich*." "Wahlrecht–Wahlverhalten–Wahlkultur," p. 521.

resident in a given area, and permanently domiciled in their home town or village.[36]

What one can do easily from the available data is calculate the change in the number of voters between two elections in each constituency. This figure, which I call net new voters, is a composite, made up of voters reaching voting age between the two elections, minus eligible voters who died, plus voters who moved into the constituency, less those who left. If one were to take net new voters as a percentage of eligible voters in each constituency and graph this percentage on a line, one would see a cluster of points around the average percentage increase, a few off to the right, signifying a large increase in the electorate – typically in large cities – and rather fewer off to the left, showing a slower population growth or even an absolute decline in the number of voters, characteristic of some rural areas in eastern Germany. The net new voters are therefore not an actual group of individuals, but a measure of the renewal of the electorate, brought about primarily by natural causes, to a lesser extent by internal migration from rural to urban areas.

Particularly during the Wilhelmine era, when elections were held every five years instead of every three as they had been until 1893, and when there was quite rapid population growth, the overall increase in the electorate was considerable. About 8% of the electorate in 1912 consisted of net new voters, quite a lot when one notes, for instance, that the conservative parties received the votes of 13% of the electorate that year. Conversely, in the election pairs 1877–78, and 1878–81, there was almost no net increase in the electorate, making the effect of the renewal of the electorate sufficiently small to allow it to be ignored.

What this discussion of changes in the body of voters from election to election means for the presentation of results can be seen from this example. Considering the votes for the conservative parties in 1907, the results would include the percentage of conservative voters in the previous election of 1903 who voted for the conservatives in 1907, the percentage of 1903 liberal voters supporting the conservatives in 1907, the percentage of 1903 voters of the minority parties voting conservative in 1907, the percentage of SPD voters in 1903 supporting the conservatives four years later, the percentage of 1903 non-voters mobilized to support the conservatives in 1907, and the percentage of net new voters in 1907 who voted for the conservatives. This pattern is maintained for all the pairs of elections, from 1871–74 to 1907–12, with the exception of the

---

[36] On this point, see the model study of Stephan Bleek, *Quartierbildung in der Urbanisierung: Das Münchener Westend 1890–1933* (Munich: R. Oldenbourg Verlag, 1991). Pages 32–36, 42–54, 133–34, 155, 186, 189–90 include not only his own results, but also an excellent critical survey of the literature in the field.

two pairs 1877–78, and 1878–81 when the electorate did not increase in size, so there is no figure for net new voters.

There is one final point about these results. I have calculated the regressions for all of Germany, and also used a very crude regional breakdown, calculating results for Prussia and for non-Prussian Germany.[37] At least at certain points, these results – not too surprisingly – are somewhat different and point to political differences between the Prussian monarchy and the rest of the German Empire. It is also possible to calculate figures for all of Germany by averaging the results of Prussia and non-Prussian Germany. These are usually extremely close (differing by no more than a percentage point or two) for the results obtained for the whole country directly. At some elections, and for some smaller groups, rather greater divergences emerge. For technical reasons, discussed in the appendix, the estimates developed directly for the whole country are rather more reliable than those developed by averaging two regions. I mention this since I will sometimes present both regional and national estimates, and someone calculating the national estimates from the regional ones might notice that the two do not coincide perfectly.

Fortunately, the second group of regressions, estimating the percentages of different confessional groups supporting the different parties, is much simpler both to calculate and to explain. The operative confessions are Roman Catholic and Protestant, because the other religious groups – Mennonites, Jews, those of no religion or Eastern Orthodox, Muslims and the like – were such a small percentage of the electorate that their votes cannot be estimated using ecological inference. All these small groups were lumped together with the Protestants, so when I talk of Protestant voting the reader may always mentally include the others.[38]

An additional attraction of this group of regressions is that it is possible to disaggregate the party groups somewhat. The results will show the percentage of Catholics and of Protestants (plus the others) who supported the conservative parties, the National Liberals, the progressives (not just the liberal parties as a group), the Center, the national and regional minority parties (distinguishing between the Center and the smaller

---

[37] Ideally, one would like to divide the country into many more regions, corresponding with the development of political traditions. The problem is that the more regions, the fewer observations (=constituencies) available for the regressions and the more problematic the results. There are some interesting and successful regional analyses in Winkler, *Sozialstruktur*, ch. 3, while a number of instances in Schmädeke, *Wählerbewegung* (1: 167, or 340, n. 91) demonstrate how this work ought not to be done.

[38] To study the electoral preferences of such smaller groups would require looking at precinct-level data from individual constituencies or groups of constituencies where these groups were present in larger proportions than they were in material drawn from constituency-level data.

minority parties), the SPD, or who did not vote. The annoying problem of change in the electorate coming in with voter transition probabilities does not appear here, since the regressions are done one election at a time. I have also calculated the confessional vote on the same regional breakdown: Prussia vs. non-Prussia. Happily, in this case the results for all of Germany obtained by averaging the Prussian and the non-Prussian results are very close to those obtained by calculations based on the entire country.

The third group of regressions, giving estimates of voting by class and confession, is the most problematic, as a consequence of difficulties arising from the nature of the evidence. The previous two groups of regressions are based on figures from the published election returns for each of the 397 Reichstag constituencies. Material on the social composition of the electorate is not available in this way; it must be developed from the returns of the commercial and industrial censuses. The earlier censuses of 1875 and 1882 are inadequate for this purpose; only the 1895 and 1907 censuses can be used. Since the rapid progress of industrialization in Imperial Germany meant an equally rapid change in social and economic structure, the census results can only be used to study elections close in time to them. Basically, this means the elections of the Wilhelmine era, 1890–1912. I have also calculated estimates for the 1887 elections, but as these are based on a census taken eight years later, they are a good deal more speculative.

However, this is just the beginning of the difficulties created by the sources. The largest problem is that the areas for which the census and election returns are reported are not compatible; in order to obtain comparable areas for analysis, it is necessary to combine administrative units together. At the end of this combination process is a much lower number of observations: from the 397 constituencies that form the basis for the two other groups of regressions, one is left with 77 observations for the 1895 census and, because of minor adminstrative changes, 78 for its counterpart of 1907. The more observations, and the smaller the units they represent, the more exact and secure the results of the ecological inference drawn from them. One can expect good results from 397 observations; 78, one-fifth as many, is rather pushing the lower limit.[39]

The upshot is some limitations on the results. The analysis is based on the five party groups, considered in the first series of regressions; with

[39] Two good discussions of the problem of unit size in ecological inference are Svante Ersson, "Model Specification and Ecological Inference," and Svante Ersson and Ingemar Wörlund, "Level of Aggregation and Ecological Inference: A Study of the Swedish Elections in 1944 and 1979," both in Berlund and Thomsen (eds.) *Modern Political Ecological Analysis*, pp. 111–30 and 131–47, respectively.

only 78 observations, the finer analysis in the estimates of confessional voting is not possible. The social and confessional groups themselves have to be few in number and hence rather crude. The results have been calculated for six groups: (1) Catholic farmers, including owners, tenants, administrators, and laborers involved in agriculture; (2) Catholic blue-collar workers; (3) the Catholic middle class, consisting of independent businessmen, salaried employees, civil servants, professionals and rentiers; (4) Protestant farmers (here, once again, Protestant includes all non-Catholics); (5) Protestant blue-collar workers; (6) the Protestant urban middle class.[40] Readers familiar with similar work by Jürgen Falter and other scholars on the Weimar Republic, with their very fine social detail, distinguishing industrial workers from workers in craft enterprises, independent businessmen from salaried employees, rentiers from those actively exercising an occupation, and the like, may be disappointed, but need to be reminded that Falter's regressions are based on 800 observations, over ten times as many as are available for the *Kaiserreich*.[41]

Additionally, I should note that technical problems in performing regressions with these variables and observations require some fancy statistical footwork (for details, please consult the appendix). Under these circumstances, the reader may wonder about the accuracy of the results. There are three points I can make and a general conclusion arising from them. First, there is a virtue in using these 78 cases, namely the fact that the 1895 and 1907 censuses give figures on social distribution, broken down by confession: the number of Catholic farmers in each area, for instance, and the number of Protestant ones. Such a cross-tabluation is unique to these censuses; one does not find it in the otherwise much more detailed returns of the 1920s and 1930s. Second, the results of these regressions based on such 78 observations are very close to the second set, based on the more reliable 397 cases. If one adds up the estimates of, say, the percentage of Catholic farmers supporting the minority parties in 1903, the percentage of Catholic workers and of the Catholic urban middle class doing so, the result is within one or two percentage points of the estimates of all Catholics supporting these parties derived from the second group of regressions. Finally, the results obtained do not seem

---

[40] Results for the 1903 elections, for instance, would give: (1) the percentage of Catholic farmers voting for the conservative parties, the liberal parties, the minority parties, the SPD, and not voting that year; (2) the percentage of Catholic workers supporting each of these party groups; (3) the percentage of the Catholic urban middle class doing so; and (4) the same figures for these groups' Protestant counterparts.

[41] The 1895 and 1907 census returns do include material from smaller administrative units, more comparable with the election constituencies. Schmädeke and Winkler have used these data in their work. However, there are a number of problems with this material that led me to reject its use, as explained in the appendix.

impossible, or worse, implausible; rather, they are within the same universe as figures derived from ecological inference in the 1920s, or from survey research after 1945.

Since greater detail ought to produce more precision, it is regrettable that the nature of the available sources means that the results on class and confession – perhaps the most interesting of all the estimates – are less comprehensive and more uncertain than those on confession alone. Still, for all the difficulties involved in developing and interpreting these estimates, they are based on data with certain unique advantages, and whose analysis provides plausible figures on developments in German politics after 1890, ones which stand up to cross-checking against results produced in different ways. Although I will be a bit more cautious about citing my results on voting by class and confession than with the figures obtained from the other regressions, pointing out possible alternative interpretations and limits on the data, I nonetheless think they offer a generally valid picture.

Let me mention two final, small points before proceeding to the results. First, the reader will note that percentages often sum to 99 or 101 instead of 100. This is always a consequence of rounding-off error. Second, unless otherwise specifically noted, all results presented in tables or graphs are from the three groups of regressions I have described above, or from the electronic database used to calculate them and described in the appendix. It seems simplest to mention these points now, at the beginning of the book, rather than to repeat them each time.

Part 1

The parties

1   The Social Democrats

In this first part of the book, the focus will be on the individual parties, or groups of parties, and the long-term trends in voting patterns relating to them. Each chapter will contain an overview of electoral support for the party throughout the history of the empire; a consideration of the fluctuation of voters between that party and the others – always including among them the "parties" of the non-voters and the net new voters; a discussion of the confessional bases of support; and a presentation of the figures from the Wilhelmine era on class and confession. Although the overall structure of each chapter will stay the same, the specific results presented, the order of their presentation, and the discussion of their implications will differ slightly, taking into account the differing questions posed by the scholarly literature on each of the parties.

An ascendant party

Of all the political parties in Imperial Germany, the Social Democrats had the most dramatic electoral history. An insignificant splinter group – actually, two insignificant splinter parties – at the first elections in 1871, the Social Democrats received more votes than any other party twenty years later in the general elections of 1890. In 1912, at the last prewar elections, more than one voter in three cast his ballot for the SPD, which thus received more votes than any two other parties combined. Yet the history of the rise of the labor movement in German politics is far more dramatic than a bald recitation of the figures would imply. It is truly a saga, a story of the organization and rallying of the oppressed and disinherited in the face of continuous persecution and harrassment from the state, including twelve years, from 1878 to 1890, when the party was outlawed; threats and intimidation on the part of employers; and contempt and hostility from the churches, the educational system and the vast majority of intellectuals and educated people. More than that, a quick look beyond the great election victory of 1912 reveals the story ultimately to be a tragedy, since it includes the outbreak of the First World War; the deep split in the labor movement that it caused between reformists and radicals, Social Democrats and communists helped to destabilize and destroy the Weimar Republic and was perpetuated in the division of Germany after 1945. For all these reasons, the history of the Social Democrats has attracted the attention of historians. There has probably been more written on them than on all the other political parties in Imperial Germany put together.

Perhaps surprisingly, this proliferation of scholarly inquiry has produced a striking consensus on the nature of the Social Democratic electorate and the sources of its growth. This consensus has two main elements. One was best expressed by the late Werner Conze, one of the pioneering social historians in the Federal Republic of Germany, who asserted that the SPD vote increased primarily because the party mobilized previous non-voters. On the face of it, this assertion looks plausible when one considers that in 1871 the Social Democratic parties received 2% of votes cast, but just 50% of those eligible actually voted, while in 1912 35% of those voting chose the SPD, and turnout amounted to 85% of eligible voters. Just the close identification of an increase in turnout of 35 percentage points and an increase in Social Democratic votes of 33 percentage points seems to clinch the argument.[1]

The second main element in the dominant consensus is that the SPD was the party of the labor movement. The vast majority of its voters, like the vast majority of its members, were urban, blue-collar workers. The bourgeoisie, the lower middle class and the peasantry were ultimately outside the circle of SPD voters. This assertion that the SPD was a workers' party, picking up on debates from the turn of the century, generally includes a confessional qualification: the SPD was a party of Protestant workers, their Catholic counterparts far more likely to cast their votes for the Center and the French or Polish nationalists than for the SPD. Urban, blue-collar and Protestant: these three charcteristics defined all levels of the labor movement before the First World War in Germany, typifying the SPD's electorate and its membership, as well as the membership of the "free" (that is, pro-SPD) trade unions and the various cultural and recreational organizations tied to the Social Democratic labor movement. This judgement is the broad consensus of scholars, endorsed both by the Marxist-Leninist historians of the former East Germany and their counterparts in the West, one of the few points of

---

[1] Werner Conze, "Politische Willensbildung im deutschen Kaiserreich als Forschungsaufgabe historischer Wahlsoziologie," in Helmut Berding (ed.) *Vom Staat des Ancien Regimes zum modernen Partiestaat* (Munich and Vienna: R. Oldenbourg Verlag, 1978), pp. 331–47, here pp. 342–43.

agreement in a branch of historical studies particularly divided by the Cold War.[2]

It is not logically necessary to hold to both elements of this consensus, to see the SPD as the party of urban Protestant workers and as the party of the previous non-voters.[3] However, the two elements of the consensus are both necessary for and implied by Rainer Lepsius's conception of sociomoral milieus. It was precisely urban Protestant workers who belonged to none of the three milieus already existing at the introduction of universal suffrage in Germany – the urban Protestant middle-class, the rural Protestant, and the Catholic. Since in Lepsius's theory voting for a party is a function of belonging to a milieu, individuals not in a milieu must have been non-voters, and since the rise of the labor movement involved the creation of a new, urban working-class Protestant milieu, the growth of the SPD must have been due to the political mobilization of previous non-voters from the Protestant working class.

This summary suggests three main questions that might be posed of the regression results. (1) What was the political pre-history of the SPD voters? Were they mostly previous non-voters, as most historians suggest, or did they come from elsewhere? (2) Were the SPD voters mostly or entirely Protestants? (3) Was the Social Democratic electorate composed largely or entirely of blue-collar workers, or might other social groups have been involved as well? Just as a preliminary discussion of the questions I can note in advance that the statistical analyses have led to some conventional but more unexpected conclusions. While some previous non-voters did choose the Social Democrats, they were, as a group, more likely to vote for other parties and their support does not explain the rapid

---

[2] Typical of this consensus (in the German literature) is Gerhard A. Ritter, "Die Sozialdemokratie im Deutschen Kaiserreich in sozialgeschichtlicher Perspektive," *Historische Zeitschrift* 249 (1989): 295–362, esp. p. 351; Dieter Fricke, *Handbuch zur Geschichte der Deutschen Arbeiterbewegung 1869 bis 1917* 2 vols. (East Berlin: Dietz Verlag, 1987) 2: 718–44, esp. pp. 743–44; Adelheid von Saldern, "Wer ging in die SPD? Zur Analyse der Parteimitgliedschaft in wilhelmischer Zeit," in G. A. Ritter (ed.) *Der Aufstieg der deutschen Arbeiterbewegung*, pp. 161–83, esp. p. 164; and Jürgen Schmädeke, *Wahlerbewegung im Wilhelmischen Deutschland.* (Berlin: Akademie Verlag, 1995) vol. 1, p. 537. Note that Jürgen Winkler (in *Sozialstruktur politische Tradition und Liberalismus: Eine empirische Längsschnittstudie zur Wahlentwicklung in Deutschland 1871–1933.* Opladen: Westdeutscher Verlag, 1995, p. 252), working in a statistically more systematic way with the same materials as Schmädeke, is more cautious in his judgement. In the English-language literature, see W. L. Guttsman, *The German Social Democratic Party, 1875–1933: From Ghetto to Government* (London: Allen & Unwin, 1981), pp. 87–112. While this is the dominant view, there have been some dissenters; cf. n. 40, below.

[3] Cf., for instance, Rohe, *Wahlen und Wählertraditionen*, p. 104; or Gerhard Ritter and Merith Niehuss, *Wahlgeschichtliches Arbeitsbuch: Materialien zur Statistik des Kaiserreichs 1871–1918* (Munich: Beck, 1980), p. 24.

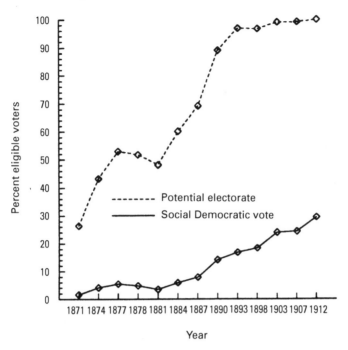

1.1 Social Democratic vote, 1871–1912

growth of the Social Democrats in 1890 and afterwards. The SPD was indeed a party of Protestants, although the percentage of Catholics supporting it and the proportion of Catholics among its voters both rose in the Wilhelmine era. Finally, in so far as their electorate was concerned, the Social Democrats were not exclusively a workers' party but enjoyed the support of a broad range of the urban, Protestant population.

Charting the rise of the Social Democrats

Let us begin the analysis with a graphical overview of the Social Democratic party's electoral results in Imperial Germany.

In figure 1.1, the solid line gives the vote for the Social Democratic Party (for 1871 and 1874, the two Social Democratic parties) as a percentage of eligible voters, while the dotted line gives the percentage living in constituencies where Social Democrats put up candidates.[4] At a very

---

[4] By putting up a candidate, I mean that the Social Democrat standing for the Reichstag received the minimum of twenty-five votes required to be listed in the official election returns under the party label and not in the rubric "scattered." Particularly for the first elections in the 1870s, when the Social Democrats were still a very small group, and when

early date, the Social Democrats sponsored an impressive number of candidacies. In the 1877 elections, the first following the unification of the two Social Democratic parties at the Gotha Congress of 1875, the newly unified party offered more than half the German electorate the opportunity to vote for its candidates. The reach of Social Democratic candidacies declined somewhat over the next two elections, a result of repeated official persecution, culminating in the passage of a law prohibiting the party in 1878. Yet even this "anti-socialist law," did not prevent the party from addressing an ever greater proportion of the electorate.[5] As early as 1884, Social Democratic candidacies covered a greater proportion of the electorate than at the previous high point in 1878, and increased their coverage continuously over the following decade. The single sharpest jump in this period was from 1887 (when 69% of the eligible electorate could vote for the Social Democrats) to 1890 when 89% could. From 1893 onwards, over 95% of the eligible voters had the opportunity to cast their ballot for a candidate of the SPD.

From 1871 to 1890, support for the party among the voters moved in parallel with the range of Social Democratic constituencies, rising from 2% of votes cast in 1871 to 5.5% in 1877, declining under the impact of vigorous governmental persecution to a little over 3% in 1881, to reach new highs in the two subsequent elections – albeit even in 1887 at 7.8% of eligible voters, not that much above the party vote in 1877. Another way to put this would be to say that between 1874 and 1887 in those constituencies where Social Democrats stood for election, a fairly constant 10% of eligible voters supported them, the figures ranging from a low of 9.3% in 1878, to a high of 11.3% in 1887. The only general election somewhat outside of this range was in 1881, the high point of state persecution, when just 7.1% of eligible voters in constituencies with Social Democratic candidates cast their ballot for the party. During these years, changes in the Social Democratic vote largely reflected greater or lesser opportunities to vote for Social Democratic candidates, circumstances determined by the organization of the party and the extent of repression from the state and the powerful elements in German society.

The elections of 1890 marked a turning point. As against 1887, the party's voted doubled, reaching 14% of eligible voters that year, or 20% of

the compilers of election returns were not always entirely conscientious about noting relatively small numbers of votes, this procedure may somewhat underestimate the extent of Social Democratic candidacies.

[5] Under the Imperial constitution and electoral legislation, it was not parties who stood for the Reichstag but individuals. Thus, representatives of an illegal party could and did run for parliamentary office, quite legally.

Table 1.1 *Previous voting of Social Democratic voters (percent)*

	Election year pairs				
Vote at previous elections	1871/74– 1874/77	1877/78– 1878/81	1881/84– 1884/87	1887/90– 1893/98	1898/03– 1907/1
Conservatives	0	2	2	7	4
Liberals	5	7	6	16	6
Minority parties	0	2	1	4	3
Social Democrats	31	66	46	59	64
Non-voters	44	23	31	7	11
Net new voters	19	—[a]	15	7	12
Total	99	100	101	100	100

Note:
[a] The electorate hardly increased in size at all between 1877 and 1881, so there is no figure for net new voters for the 1878 and 1881 elections.

votes cast. For the first time, this expansion was not just the result of a growing number of candidacies. The Social Democrats broke the 10% barrier in 1890, receiving the votes of 16% of the eligible electorate in constituencies in which the party put up candidates. From the 1893 elections onward, the SPD had achieved virtual blanket coverage of the electorate, so that an increase in vote totals could only come from a greater proportion of voters in individual constituencies supporting the party's candidates. While the proportion of eligible voters casting their ballots for the SPD increased at every single election between 1890 and 1912, most of the increase (about 70%) came in two sharp upturns, at the 1903 elections, when the SPD vote jumped to 24% of the eligible electorate as against 18% in 1898; and in 1912, when the SPD received over 29% of the eligible votes, climbing from the 24% of 1907.

Party voters, non-voters and the SPD

These considerations suggest that a study of the previous political affiliations of SPD voters might look to 1890 as a dividing line, and that such a study might want to pay special attention to the breakthrough elections – those of 1890, 1903 and 1912 – when the party's vote increased particularly rapidly. Table 1.1 gives the composition of the Social Democratic electorate for each of the given groups of pairs of general elections in terms of its vote at the first of each of the pairs. The column for 1887/90–1893/98, for instance, was calculated by breaking down the SPD's 1890 electorate in terms of its 1887 vote, the SPD's 1893 electorate in terms of its 1890 vote and the SPD's 1898 electorate in terms of its 1893 vote, and then averaging the three figures together. The results do indeed show a sharp break around 1890. Prior to the elections of that year, a substantial proportion of Social Democratic voters had not voted in the previous general elections. The contribution of these mobilized non-voters to the total Social Democratic vote was always greater – usually much greater – than that of voters switching from other parties. The situation changed fundamentally after 1890, that is to say in the years when the SPD's vote increased at a rapid pace. Voters switching from other parties, particularly the liberals but also the conservatives and the minority parties, played the major role in the success of the Social Democrats in that decade, while the importance of previous non-voters declined sharply. Even in the first decade of the twentieth century, when the proportion of Social Democratic voters coming from other parties declined, these voters still outnumbered previous non-voters among the Social Democratic electorate.

These figures do not confirm the assertion that the Social Democrats were the party of the previous non-voters. Someone trying to save the thesis might say that table 1.1 does not show changes among Social Democratic voters but in the overall electorate. Voter turnout was on the increase throughout the history of Imperial Germany, so that non-voters were becoming an ever smaller proportion of the electorate. Thus the proportion of Social Democratic voters who were previous non-voters would have had to decline. It is certainly true that turnout increased, but a look at the figures on non-voters further minimizes their importance for the Social Democratic vote. Between 1874 and 1881, non-voters made up about 40% of the German electorate; between 1884 and 1898 they averaged about 30%, and between 1903 and 1912, a bit under 20%. In other words, before 1890, previous non-voters were represented among the Social Democratic voters about in the same proportion as they were in the electorate as a whole, but after 1890 they were substantially under-represented among the Social Democratic electorate. Table 1.2, giving the composition of the Social Democratic electorate at the party's three breakthrough elections in 1890, 1903, and 1912, only confirms the importance of those voters switching parties and minimizes the significance of previous non-voters.

The results of 1890, the Social Democrats' *annus mirabili*, were only made possible by large-scale vote switching, carried out across the entire party spectrum. Changes in party affiliation on this massive scale would never be repeated, but vote switching still played a substantial role in the SPD's two subsequent victories. The contribution of the net new voters might be emphasized as well, reflecting the way that generational turnover

Table 1.2 *The Social Democratic vote in three breakthrough elections (percent)*

Vote at previous general election	Year		
	1890	1903	1912
Conservatives	12	6	5
Liberals	21	6	6
Minority parties	7	3	4
Social Democrats	45	58	66
Non-voters	7	12	9
Net new voters	8	15	10
Total	100	100	100

Table 1.3 *Subsequent votes of Social Democratic voters (percent)*

Vote at next general election	Election year pairs			
	1871/74–1877/78	18878/81–1884/87	1887/90–1893/98	1898/1903–1907/12
Conservatives	4	5	6	2
Liberals	18	12	8	12
Minority parties	0	0	1	1
Social Democrats	55	71	77	81
Non-voters	22	11	8	4
Total	99	99	100	100

of the electorate and movement of population from rural to urban areas both favored the Social Democrats.[6]

This discussion of the composition of the Social Democratic electorate is still missing one element, namely the long-term Social Democratic voters. Table 1.2 shows that the proportion of the Social Democratic electorate made up of previous voters for the party increased steadily from the mid-1880s onwards, but one might still wish to know about the loyalty of Social Democratic voters from one election to the next. To ascertain this, we need to interpret the regression results in the other direction. Instead of asking about the composition of the Social Democratic electorate in terms of voting in the first of a pair of elections, table 1.3 shows how Social Democratic voters at one election voted in the subsequent one. As

---

[6] Using somewhat different methods and data, Winkler, *Sozialstruktur*, pp. 222–33, sees a lesser if still noticeable effect of urbanization and increasing population on the the Social Democratic vote.

in the previous table, figures for each pair of elections were calculated and then averaged across a decade.

Over the entire history of the *Kaiserreich* relatively few Social Democratic voters switched to the conservative parties from one election to the next, and virtually none went from the SPD to the Center or the parties of the national and regional minorities.[7] There were, however, some who defected to the liberal parties, the greatest proportion in the 1870s, but a considerable number throughout the history of the empire. The largest change apparent in this table is the growing party loyalty of Social Democratic voters. Unlike the movements from other parties or previous non-voters to the Social Democrats, presented in table 1.1, where the 1890 elections marked a major change in voter behavior, the decisive change in voter movements away from the Social Democrats appeared in the mid-1880s. Before then, only half of the party's voters at one election supported it at the next, the other half equally divided between those who chose another party and those who did not cast a ballot. From the 1884 elections onwards, party loyalty substantially increased, with most of this increase attributable to a decline in the percentage of Social Democratic electorate not voting in subsequent elections.

Tables 1.1 and 1.2 showed which voters came to support the Social Democrats and table 1.3 showed which left the party, or which stayed loyal to it. As a final measure of the change in the Social Democratic vote, we can combine both these approaches to consider the relative size of vote switchers – in both directions, to and from the Social Democrats – and of persistent voters in the Social Democratic electorate. Table 1.4 does this. All figures in it are as a percentage of all eligible voters. In the first four rows, the number before the slash shows the voters from that party (or from the non-voters) at the previous elections who switched to the Social Democrats, while the number after the slash shows the Social Democratic voters at the previous election, who switched to that party. The figures in the fifth row are the party loyalists, the voters who voted for the Social Democrats in both of a pair of elections. The final row is the most complicated, showing that portion of the net new voters supporting the SPD greater than the average vote for the party, in other words the extent to which turnover in the electorate favored the SPD.

A concrete example may help make these categories clearer. Taking the column 1881/84–1884/87, in those two pairs of elections an average of

---

[7] Note that these figures relate to voter movements between one general election and the next; they say nothing about how voters at the first round of one election voted in the runoff round of that same election. There were many instances when Social Democratic voters supported Center candidates in runoffs.

Table 1.4 *Voter swings and the Social Democratic electorate,*
1871/74–1907/12 (percent)

	Election year pairs				
Vote at previous election	1871/74– 1874/77	1877/78– 1878/81	1881/84– 1884/87	1887/90– 1893/98	1898/03– 1907/12
Conservatives	0/0.4	0.1/0.4	0.1/0.2	1.2/0.8	1.1/0.4
Liberals	0.2/0.7	0.2/0.9	0.4/0.6	2.5/1.1	1.4/2.5
Minority parties	0/0.1	0.1/0	0/0	0.7/0.1	0.8/0.2
Non-voters	2.1/0.4	0.1/1.1	2.1/0.4	1.1/1.2	2.8/0.8
Social democrats	1.6	2.7	3.2	9.8	16.8
Net new voters	0.7	—[a]	0.7	0.3	1.2

Note:
[a] The electorate hardly increased in size at all between 1877 and 1881, so there is no figure for net new voters for the 1878 and 1881 elections.

0.1% of the electorate consisted of conservative voters at the first election switching to the Social Democrats and 0.2% of the electorate consisted of Social Democrats switching to the conservatives; 0.4% of the total electorate were former liberal voters choosing the Social Democrats while 0.6% were Social Democrats choosing the liberals, and so on through the first four rows. In the fifth row, one finds that an average of 3.2% of the electorate at those two pairs of elections were Social Democratic voters who had supported the party in both elections of the pair. To understand the figure in the sixth row, let us note that in 1884 5.9% of eligible voters chose the Social Democrats. I took the total number of net new voters who supported the Social Democrats and subtracted 5.9% of them, thus arriving at the proportion of the electorate consisting of those net new voters in that year supporting the Social Democrats above the average for all voters. Doing the same for the 1887 elections (this time subtracting 7.8% of net new voters, since 7.8% of all voters cast their ballots for the Social Democrats in 1887) and averaging the two figures gave the results in row six.

These figures amplify but also modify somewhat the results in tables 1.1–1.3 concerning the place of previous non-voters in the Social Democratic electorate. Between 1874 and 1887, the Social Democrats persistently lost more voters to the other parties than they gained from them. Almost all the increase in Social Democratic votes was attributable to attracting and keeping previous non-voters. In the 1878 and 1881 elections, the party lost to abstention more of its voters than it was able to obtain from previous non-voters, making these the only two elections in

Table 1.5 *Voter swings in three SPD election victories (percent)*

Voters at previous election	Election years		
	1890	1903	1912
Conservatives	1.7/0.3	1.5/0.3	1.4/0.2
Liberals	3.0/0.6	1.4/1.9	1.7/1.7
Minority parties	0.9/0	0.6/0.1	1.3/0.2
Non-voters	1.0/0.3	2.9/0.6	2.7/1.0
Social Democrats	6.3	14.0	19.5
Net new voters	0.6	1.5	0.6

the history of the empire at which the Social Democratic vote as a percentage of the eligible electorate declined.

As might be expected from the results above, the 1890s show a quite different pattern. In that decade, for the first time the SPD gained noticeably more votes from other parties than it lost to them. Previous non-voters contributed not at all to the party's success; in fact, more voters left the SPD for abstention than went from non-voting to the Social Democrats. In the three general elections of the twentieth century, a third pattern emerged. The party had built up a group of loyal voters who now substantially outnumbered the swing voters, whether from the other parties or from the previous non-voters. However important loyal voters were, they did not help to increase the party's vote totals, especially in a period when turnout was increasing, going from 68% of eligible voters in 1898 to 84% in 1912. Over the entire period, voters from other parties did not do much for the SPD, the net gains from the conservatives and the minority parties just compensating for the net losses to the liberals. Rather, it was both previous non-voters and net new voters who accounted for the party's increase in votes.

We can specify these results for the Wilhelmine era a bit more exactly by looking at the voting swings for the three big election victories of the SPD in 1890, 1903, and 1912. Table 1.5 presents results for those years along the same lines as in table 1.4.

In 1890, the SPD gained all around, with substantial net swings from all the other parties, and more modest ones from the previous non-voters and the new entrants to the electorate. The year 1903 was the year of the non- and new voters, who accounted for much of the SPD's success. Swing votes from other parties were less, and the SPD actually lost votes to the liberals. Finally, in 1912, the SPD's increases were about equally attributable to previous non-voters and new entrants to the electorate on the one hand, and voters from the conservative and minority parties on the other.

In all three of these election victories, the SPD obtained consistent if modest gains in votes from adherents of the conservative and minority parties, while the exchange of voters with the liberal parties fluctuated strongly: very much to the Social Democrats' favor in 1890, against them in 1903, and about equal in 1912. There were similar fluctuations in the importance of voters not before affiliated with any party – previous non-voters and net new voters: only a minor factor in the great breakthrough of 1890, most of the reason for the party's success in 1903, and accounting for about half the increase in 1912.

Organization, agitation, and persecution

Let use see if we can put all these results in the context of the history of the Social Democratic movement in Imperial Germany. From its very beginnings the German labor movement placed an enormous weight on parliamentary elections. It was not parliament or parliamentarianism as such that inspired socialist activists. They were very much of two minds about the desirability or usefulness of taking part in the work of the Reichstag – and not unjustifiably so, in view of the constitutionally and factually weak position of the body.

Elections, however, were another matter. They were the one main way that the party had to agitate, to bring its views to a wide circle of supporters. More than that, they provided a public display of the of the extent of the movement's support, a "review of the troops" (*Heerschau*), as the Social Democrats liked to say. The relationship between parliamentarianism and parliamentary elections, might be exemplified by an article in the party's main newspaper in 1876, noting that Social Democratic deputies had missed significant roll-calls in the Reichstag, because they were doing something much more important – giving speeches in the election campaign.[8]

Describing national elections as the main arena of the Social Democrats' agitation presupposes that agitation was important to the party. It was; the Social Democrats were a party of political mass agitation from the very first instant of their existence. An example of just how organized such agitation could be appears in the plans of the Social Democrats in the 19th Saxon Reichstag constituency for the 1874 Reichstag elections. Local committees in every major town in the con-

[8] Pracht, *Parlamentarismus und deutsche Sozialdemokratie*, pp. 119–20, 189–90 and passim.

stituency were to be formed, each of which would act as an agent for the central Saxon election committee. Four weeks before the election, the campaign would begin. Two weeks after that, 8–10,000 copies of an election appeal were to be sent to the committees to be distributed, using reliable comrades who would be paid for their work. The following week, a second pamphlet would appear, denouncing opposing candidates and exposing their "machinations," as well as offering any necessary emendations of the original appeal. A third pamplet would be distributed one week later, shortly before the elections, containing further replies to opponents' campaigning; along with it, the ballots were to be distributed. "Four good speakers" were to be sent by the central committee to the appropriate constituencies in the four days preceding the election, for pre-election rallies. Finally, the local committees were to monitor public opinion, reporting any changes back to the central election committee, and then send in the results as soon as the votes had been counted.[9]

Even today's politicians might be impressed by the combination of the presentation of the party's own program with attacks on its opponents and the shaping of the campaign to fit public opinion, to say nothing of the carefully targeted use of different media. For the 1870s, this kind of campaigning was nothing short of sensational.[10] Of course, Saxony in general and the nineteenth electoral district in particular, were strongholds of the labor movement. Elsewhere, the Social Democrats did not necessarily have the supporters and the corresponding organizational spinal chord to carry out such organized mass agitation. Yet they certainly aspired to it. The 1874 congress of the Social Democrats of Bavaria – then as now, not precisely prime terrain for the party – divided the kingdom into seventeen agitation districts, each district's committee working under the direction of the Bavarian central agitation committee in Nuremberg. The party conference laid out an ambitious program for these committees, including gathering industrial and electoral statistics and preparing for agitation among the peasants.[11]

Much of the growth of the Social Democratic electorate, from the 1871 to the 1877 elections, can be understood in terms of the interaction

[9] Georg Eckert (ed.) *Wilhelm Liebknecht: Briefwechsel mit deutschen Sozialdemokraten* vol. 1, 1862–1878 (Assen: Van Gorcum & Comp. B.V., 1973), pp. 514–16; cf. also pp. 561–62, 672–73. A similar example of agitation by the other Social Democratic party in Berlin during the 1874 elections can be found in Arno Herzig, *Der Allgemeine Deutsche Arbeiter-Verein in der deutschen Sozialdemokratie: Dargestellt an der Biographie des Funktionärs Carl Wilhelm Tölcke* (West Berlin: Colloquium Verlag, 1979) p. 93.

[10] For one example of how it struck contemporaries, see Willi Breunig, *Soziale Verhältnisse der Arbeiterschaft und sozialistische Arbeiterbewegung in Ludwigshafen am Rhein 1869–1919* (Ludwigshafen: Stadtarchiv Ludwigshafen a. Rh., 1976), pp. 166–69.

[11] Heinrich Hirschfelder, *Die bayerische Sozialdemokratie 1864–1914*, vol. 2, (Erlangen: Verlag Palm & Enke, 1979), pp. 210–11.

between electoral agitation and party organization. Successful agitation centered on elections – distributing leaflets and fliers, but above all holding mass meetings with well-known speakers – increased the party's membership, strengthening its organization and allowing it to expand its agitation further.[12] It produced the structure of voting support that the quantitative results suggest for the 1870s: an expansion of the proportion of the eligible electorate that could cast votes for Social Democratic candidates, and the mobilization of previous non-voters to do so.

There were two limitations to this process. One was the lack of resources. Outside of its strongholds, the party often lacked the activists needed to carry out its agitation and the funds to support them. The few paid, professional agitators in the early Social Democratic movement were stretched far too thin. If they went to start agitating in a new location, then efforts in the area where they had previously been active would come to an end.[13] Thus, it is not entirely surprising that voters having once supported the party would drift away from it at a subsequent election.

The second limitation was much more serious, a major obstacle to the development, becoming at some points, a threat to the very existence of the Social Democratic party. For the first twenty years of the German Empire, the party was at best semi-legal, and government persecution severely hampered its activities. The Social Democrats' big plans for agitation in Bavaria never got off the ground because the Nuremberg city government dissolved the central agitation committee – and Nuremberg was far from the only locality where the party organization was prohibited. The authorities would refuse the Social Democrats permssion to hold public meetings or would break up the meetings once they had started. Activists distributing fliers and leaflets for the Reichstag elections would be arrested and their material confiscated.

A more drastic and effective measure was for the authorities to confiscate the party's ballots. The Australian ballot, one that lists all the candidates and allows voters to check the one they prefer, was not used in German elections before the First World War; rather the candidate's name, place of residence and occupation had to be written on a blank piece of paper, and brought by the voter to the polling place. (It was only in 1903 that voters were allowed to write up their ballots at the polls, and curtained-off rooms provided, so they could do so in secrecy.) All the

---

[12] See, for instance, *Wilhelm Liebknecht Briefwechsel*, vol. 1, pp. 609–10.
[13] Wolfgang Schmierer, *Von der Arbeiterbildung zur Arbeiterpolitik: Die Anfänge der Arbeiterbewegung in Württemberg 1862/63–1878* (Hanover: Verlag für Literatur und Zeitgeschehen, 1970), pp. 191–94.

parties distributed preprinted ballots for their supporters. If the Social Democrats' ballots were confiscated, then they could not receive any votes.[14]

All these forms of repression were practised sporadically by local and state governments in Germany throughout most of the 1870s. They peaked in the 1878 elections, which were largely over the issue of whether or not the Reichstag should pass a law prohibiting the Social Democratic movement. Just one example of circumstances in that year might suffice, taken from the liberal kingdom of Württemberg, where the party had previously been able to agitate with little official hindrance. On the eve of the election in Stuttgart, the police arrested the Social Democratic candidate for the constitutency, all the members of the party's election committee and all the workers at the party's cooperative printing plant. An additional feature of the 1878 elections was that employers, working hand in hand with the authorities, announced they would dismiss all Social Democratic activists – a threat that really put a crimp in the Social Democrats' election campaign. The repression exercised at the local level was so great that the Social Democrats were for all intents and purposes outlawed, even before the elections were held to decide whether they should be.[15]

In this respect, the passage of a law, following the elections, prohibiting Social Democratic organizations, publications, meetings, and agitation, did not create a fundamentally new situation at the local level. Rather, the determining factor for the party was the way the law was enforced in the twelve years (1878 to 1890) that it was on the books. The years between 1878 and 1881 were characterized by a maximalist interpretation and strict enforcement so that the Social Democrats' campaign during the 1881 general elections was even more restricted than it was in 1878. The party was unable to hold public meetings, or even to distribute ballots, the authorities defining them as examples of prohibited Social Democratic literature. Not only was persecution at its most intense, the party's

[14] On the practice of balloting in Imperial Germany, see Anderson, "Voter, Junker, *Landrat*, Priest," pp. 1456–57.

[15] On repression before the anti-socialist law of 1878, see Günther Bergmann, *Das Sozialistengesetz im rechtsrheinischen Industriegebiet* (Hanover: Verlag für Literatur und Zeitgeschehen, 1970), pp. 22–26; Volker Eichler, *Sozialistische Arbeiterbewegung in Frankfurt am Main 1878–1895* (Frankfurt: Verlag Waldemar Kramer, 1983), pp. 23, 26–29; Guttsman, *The German Social Democratic Party*, pp. 58–59; Hirschfelder, *Die Bayerische Sozialdemokratie*, pp. 210–11, 222–27, 232; Klaus-Michael Mallmann and Horst Steffens, *Lohn der Mühen: Geschichte der Bergarbeiter an der Saar* (Munich: Verlag C.H. Beck, 1989), p. 54; Bernhard Parisius, *Vom Groll der 'Kleinen Leute' zum Programm der kleinen Schritte: Arbeiterbewegung im Herzogtum Oldenburg* (Oldenburg: Heinz Holzberg Verlag, 1985), pp. 147–49, 150–51; Schmierer, *Anfänge der Arbeiterbewegung in Württemberg*, p. 248.

response was at its weakest, socialist activists having only begun to figure out ways to organize and agitate illegally.[16] Once again, a consideration of the organizational circumstances of the party suggest a plausible connection with the results of the quantitative analysis of the election returns. In 1878 and 1881 the Social Democrats could put up fewer candidates and had far fewer chances to solicit votes for them, or even give their supporters the opportunity to cast their ballots. It is not surprising that under these circumstances, as tables 1.1 and 1.4 show, virtually no non-voters were mobilized to support the Social Democrats and many of the party's previous voters either sat the two elections out – whether voluntarily or not – or cast their ballots for other parties.

The five or six years after 1881 were the era of the "mild practice" of the anti-socialist law. A Reichstag committee, set up under the anti-socialist law to adjudicate disputed issues, declared that both campaign meetings and the distribution of ballots for Social Democratic candidates were legal. Although the police and mid-level state authorities did not always pay attention to such niceties, the party was sometimes able to mount legal election campaigns in some constituencies in the 1884 and 1887 elections. Wilhelm Liebknecht's comments on the 1884 elections give some idea of what could be managed in these circumstances: "The election campaign is glorious. But work, work, work! In the past week I had nine meetings, one conference and twenty-five hours travelling on the railroad or in a carriage on country roads!"[17]

At the same time that the party had more possibilities for legal action, it was figuring out more effective ways to act illegally. Clandestine cells were set up, each consisting of just a few members, with only one knowing how to contact other levels of the party. An alternative option was to use choral

[16] This and subsequent paragraphs on the anti-socialist law are based on the following accounts: the general discussion in Vernon Lidtke, *The Outlawed Party: Social Democracy in Germany 1878–1890* (Princeton: Princeton University Press, 1966); and local and regional accounts of the works cited in the previous footnote, especially the work of Eichler, *Arbeiterbewegung in Frankfurt am Main*, the best local study. In addition, see Breunig, *Arbeiterbewegung in Ludwigshafen am Rhein*; Jürgen Jensen, *Presse und politische Polizei: Hamburgs Zeitungen unter dem Sozialistengesetz 1878–1890* (Hanover: Verlag J.H.W. Dietz Nachf., 1966); Christof Rieber, *Das Sozialistengesetz und die Sozialdemokratie in Württemberg 1878–1890* (Stuttgart: Müller & Gräff, 1984); Helga Kutz-Bauer, *Arbeiterschaft, Arbeiterbewegung und bürgerlicher Staat in der Zeit der Großen Depression* (Bonn: Verlag J.H.W. Dietz Nachf., 1988); Marianne Schmidt, "Die Arbeiterorganisationenen in Dresden 1878 bis 1890. Zur Organissationsstruktur der Arbeiterbewegung im Kampf gegen das Sozialistengesetz," *Jahrbuch für Geschichte* 22 (1981): 175–226; Karl A. Hellfaier, "Die Sozialdemokratische Bewegung in Halle/Saale (1865–1890)," *Archiv für Sozialgeschichte* 1 (1961): 69–108.

[17] *Wilhelm Liebknecht Briefwechsel mit deutschen Sozialdemokraten* vol. 2, 1878–1884, ed. Götz Langkau (Frankfurt and New York: Campus Verlag, 1988), pp. 716–17.

societies, social clubs, or other seemingly innocuous groups as fronts for forbidden activities, or simply to meet informally in a tavern or at a picnic in the countryside. Funerals of comrades became occasions for large public demonstrations, bringing together thousands of sympathizers, following a casket decked with red cloth. Even when the Social Democrats could not hold their own election meetings, they could and did attend en masse those of other parties, to provide a public forum for their views. The party's newspaper, published in Zurich, was smuggled into Germany in ever larger numbers, as were leaflets and pamphlets designed for electoral agitation. At one point, frames were set in type in Switzerland, and then smuggled into Germany, so material could be printed secretly at several different locations around the country.

To maintain a broader level of contacts, Social Democratic Reichstag deputies toured the country. Sometimes they received permission to give public speeches, but even when they did not, they would meet informally with local activists and discuss strategy with them. These activists in turn would hold clandestine regional party congresses. The upshot of all these efforts, both legal and illegal, was an increasing presence of the prohibited party at the general elections. Throughout the 1880s, more Social Democratic candidates ran for office, and their campaigns were increasingly elaborate, the money financing such efforts coming both from the clandestine collection of dues, and, more importantly, from large sums raised among radical German immigrants in the United States.

At first, some of this activity was tolerated by the authorities, acting on the behest of Bismarck, who hoped to make use of the Social Democrats to weaken the liberal political opposition. Yet even without the nod from Berlin, the police lacked the possibilities of political repression found in twentieth-century totalitarian regimes, or even the more modest but still stringent methods used to suppress radical movements in the aftermath of the revolution of 1848, and so were unable to cope with the clandestine labor movement. They could neither stop the distribution of prohibited printed materials, nor successfully penetrate and disrupt the combination of formal and informal, legal and illegal structures, set up by activists to maintain and expand the party's organization. The proclamation of the "lesser state of siege" allowed the authorities to expel Social Democratic activists from cities that were party strongholds, a measure frequently employed, disrupting the lives of hundreds of leading activists and their families. Yet even these expulsions did not suffice to destroy party organization and agitation. Sometimes they backfired when expelled activists settled in an area which had known little Social Democratic agitation, thereby spreading the reach of the party. The ineffectiveness of official efforts was demonstrated when public policy changed in 1887, the era of "mild practice" giving way to a return to a more intense level of persecution in the years 1887–89, characterized by several large large trials of activists, accused of forming illegal secret societies. These trials had little effect on the movement and mostly resulted in embarassing legal defeats for the state.

Here as well, we can see a congruence between organizational history and analysis of election returns. The proportion of the electorate having the opportunity to vote for Social Democratic candidates expanded greatly over the decade of the 1880s. Tables 1.3 and 1.4 show that the party once again attracted substantial numbers of previous non-voters, as might be expected from increased electoral efforts. However, the years of tolerated illegality in the 1880s were not simply a return to the years of poorly tolerated legality in the 1870s, either organizationally or electorally. The party developed a firmer, better structured, more effective and more widespread national organization during the 1880s, and this improved organization was reflected in the greatly enhanced loyalty of Social Democratic voters. Over 70% of the party's voters at any one election in the 1880s supported the party at the subsequent one, as against just 55% in the previous decade. In this way, the dramatic electoral breakthrough of 1890 was prepared by a period of consolidation and expansion of the party's organization and its base of voting support.

The Reichstag refused to renew the anti-socialist law in 1889, and although it did not actually expire until after the 1890 elections, it was already at least in part a dead letter during the campaign of that year. Consequently, the Social Democrats were able to organize and carry out their electoral agitation on an unprecedented scale. Thirteen regional party congresses, some of quite spectacular size and publicity, were held in 1889. The congress for Rhineland-Westphalia, for instance, met openly in Elberfeld with 2,500 delegates in attendance. The chief topic of discussion there, as at the other congresses, was the forthcoming elections. A very large number of candidates were put up, so that almost 90% of the electorate would have the opportunity to vote for a Social Democratic candidate. Candidacies were both more widespread and more intensively pursued than ever before. Over 100 "workers' electoral associations" were formed to direct the campaigns in major cities – a tactic that had been tried earlier in the decade, but with little success, since the groups had usually been prohibited shortly after being formed. This time, such prohibitions were the exception and the members of each of these associations were able to hold public meetings and distribute literature and ballots on a much larger scale than the much smaller number of semi-clandestine activists had been able to achieve earlier in the decade. Perhaps the characteristic moment of the campaign was the appearance of Social Democratic leader August Bebel in Hamburg, on January 20, 1890. Some 50,000 people crowded the streets to greet him and thousands cheered him for hours at the election rally where he was the featured speaker.[18]

This account would suggest that the 1890 elections were a culmination of the Social Democrats' efforts in the previous decade – an 1884 or 1887 style election, only bigger and better. From an organizational point of view, this probably was the case, but when the changes in voters' behavior are considered, it becomes clear that 1890 also marked a new departure. Really for the first time, the Social Democrats attracted a large number of voters from the other parties; they would continue to do so, admittedly with interruptions at certain elections and for certain parties, throughout the Wilhelmine era. One might say that the 1890 elections marked the change from an era of extensive growth in Social Democratic support – that is, improved vote totals achieved primarily by running more candidates and attracting previous non-voters – to an era of intensive growth, where party candidates covered the vast majority of the electorate and increasing the vote occurred mostly by winning voters away from other parties.

There thus seems to be a paradox of cause and effect in the great Social Democratic election victory of 1890, a continuation of and expansion in previous organizational and agitational developments leading to a new departure in voting behavior. Even without the statistical apparatus used here, historians have been aware that the socialist victory of 1890 was unprecedented and not entirely explicable.[19] Study of the Social Democratic vote with the tools of ecological inference does provide an answer to the question of how the party succeeded in 1890 – by attracting voters from other parties – but not why such voters, after not doing so for almost two decades, suddenly chose the Social Democrats. An answer to this question will have to be adjourned, pending analysis of the electorate of the other parties and a more detailed consideration of the individual elections. Let me just say for the moment that much of the explanation for the extraordinary results of the 1890 general elections lies in the preceding general elections of 1887, which also produced quite extraordinary results, although in very different ways.

With the lapse of the anti-socialist law in 1890, the Social Democrats

---

[18] Besides the sources cited in the previous notes, Wilfried Henze, in "Die politische Massenarbeit der Sozialistischen Arbeiterpartei Deutschlands in Vorbereitung der Reichstagswahl 1890," *Beiträge zur Geschichte der Arbeiterbewegung* 27 (1985): 29–49, provides a handy overview of the campaign.

[19] See, for instance, Anderson, "Voter, Junker, *Landrat*, Priest," p. 1470; or Lidtke, *The Outlawed Party*, pp. 299–301.

were able to work as an open and legal political party. To be sure, in the eyes of the authorities, they were not a party like any of the others. The SPD faced constant harassment and persecution, from police surveillance of meetings to prohibitions on civil servants from becoming members, to repeated trials of party journalists and public speakers for lèse-majesté and slandering the state. The possibilities for petty (and not so petty) chicanery on the part of police, local officials, employers and other powerful elements in society were endless: even when they contravened the law, legal remedies against them were hard to get and slow to work. Yet in contrast to the years of prohibition, or even to the 1870s when the party had been legal but fiercely persecuted, the Social Democrats had a much easier task in the Wilhelmine era.[20]

Consequently, in the years 1890–1914, the SPD was able to expand its membership enormously, reaching 1 million dues-paying adherents on the eve of the First World War; to develop a large-circulation party press; and to create an elaborately organized and well-financed organizational structure, supporting thousands of professional politicians, and a whole galaxy of affiliated organizations, from trade unions, to bicycling clubs, to free-thinkers' burial societies. National elections remained a central concern of the party: the key level in its organizational structure was the Reichstag constituency organization (*Wahlkreisverein*); party activities, whether organizational, agitational or educational in nature, were centered on the Reichstag elections, with preparations for the forthcoming campaigns begun as much as two years in advance.[21]

[20] The literature on the state and the Social Democrats is endless. Two good summaries, with useful bibliographical references, are in Gerhard A. Ritter, *Staat, Arbeiterschaft und Arbeiterbewegung in Deutschland* (Berlin and Bonn: Verlag J.H.W. Dietz Nachf., 1980), pp. 41–43, and Guttsman, *The German Social Democratic Party*, pp. 133–41. A long-term discussion in a regional context is provided by Inge Klatt, "Sozialdemokratie und Obrigkeit vor dem ersten Weltkrieg in Schleswig-Holstein – Aktion und Reaktion," *Demokratische Geschichte* 3 (1988): 97–116.

[21] Fricke, *Handbuch zur Geschichte der deutschen Arbeiterbewegung*, offers an exhaustive account of the development of the organization of the German labor movement. My general discussion of the SPD and elections in Wilhelmine Germany draws primarily on several excellent local studies: for the early years (until 1895) see Eichler, *Arbeiterbewegung in Frankfurt am Main*; and Karl-Ernst Moring, *Die Sozialdemokratische Partei in Bremen 1890–1914* (Hanover: Verlag für Literatur und Zeitgeschehen, 1968); Mary Nolan, *Social Democracy and Society: Working-Class Radicalism in Düsseldorf, 1890–1920* (Cambridge and New York: Cambridge University Press, 1981); Rainer Paetau, *Konfrontation oder Kooperation: Arbeiterbewegung und bürgerliche Gesellschaft im ländlichen Schleswig-Holsteiun und in der Industriestadt Kiel zwischen 1900 und 1925* (Neumünster: Karl Wachholtz Verlag, 1988); and Adelheid von Saldern, *Auf dem Weg zum Arbeiter-Reformismus: Parteialltag in sozialdemokratischer Provinz Göttingen (1870–1920)* (Frankfurt: Materialis Verlag, 1984). The most recent work of this kind, Karl Heinrich Pohl, *Die Münchener Arbeiterbewegung: Sozialdemokratische Partei, Freie Gewerkschaften, Staat und Gesellschaft in München 1890–1914* (Munich: K.G. Saur, 1992), offers less for the concerns of this book.

Yet this extraordinary organizational effort – all the more remarkable, in that it was accomplished by working people with low incomes, little free time and a meager formal education, and in spite of endless hindrances on the part of the state and the socially and economically powerful – did not pay off directly in voting support. Each modest organizational step forward before 1890 was matched by an increase in the number of previous non-voters supporting the party (and, conversely, each organizational setback produced a decline in this form of electoral support), but this direct link between organization, mobilization of previous non-voters and rising vote totals no longer existed in the Wilhelmine era. One reason is that the easiest way of attracting previous non-voters, namely putting up candidates in constituencies where the party had not done so in the past, was exhausted. From 1893 onwards, at least 95% of the electorate had the opportunity to vote for Social Democratic candidates.

The great possibility of 1890, attracting voters from other parties, proved impossible to repeat on quite so large a scale because the other political parties began developing their own versions of mass campaigning, holding on to their own voters and even attracting some supporters of the SPD. The increasingly elaborate organization of the SPD in the Wilhelmine era, the ever more expensive election campaigns with more and larger mass rallies, with more leaflets, fliers and ballots distributed, was countered by similar efforts on the part of the other parties, so that the labor movement was just able to hold its ground with the voters, and to make some modest progress. To expand on the martial metaphor of the election "campaign," one might say that the general elections of the Wilhelmine era, particularly the three twentieth-century elections of 1903, 1907, and 1912, were like the great battles on the Western Front during the First World War: each side threw in ever larger amounts of men and material, and had to do so, lest the opponents make a decisive breakthrough, but the upshot was ever more effort, at best for the gain of relatively little terrain.[22] To get a further notion of the nature of the Social Democratic electorate we need to turn away from the interwoven discussion of the organization and agitation of the Social Democratic party and the previous political affiliations of the party's voters, and go on to consider their other characteristics, in particular their class and confession.

Protestants, Catholics, and Social Democrats

The figures on the confessional composition of the SPD electorate are straightforward and easy to explain. Figure 1.2 gives the proportion of

---

[22] Bertram, *Die Wahlen zum Deutschen Reichstag vom Jahre 1912* gives a good picture of the universally practised mass electioneering at the last general elections in the *Kaiserreich*.

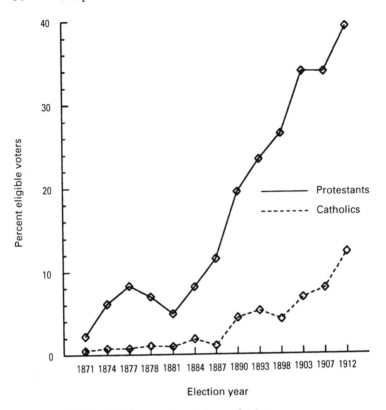

1.2 Social Democratic vote by confession

eligible Protestant and Catholic voters casting their ballot for the Social Democrats at each general election during the empire.

Protestant support for the SPD rose from 1871 to 1877, declined until 1881 and then increased steadily at every general election until 1907, and resumed its upward climb in 1912. That year, 39% of eligible Protestant voters supported the SPD, as did 45% of Protestants who actually voted, thus making the Social Democrats very close to being the party of the absolute majority of Protestant voters. Throughout the history of Bismarckian Germany, on the other hand, a tiny proportion of Catholics cast their ballot for the Social Democrats, Catholic support for the party never breaking the 2% mark in all the general elections from 1871 to 1887. As we have seen, 1890 was a breakthrough year for Social Democrats in general, and in a modest way, it was for Catholic voters in particular. The 4.4% of them who endorsed the Social Democrats at the ballot box that year were more than twice the previous maximum propor-

Table 1.6 *Confessional composition of the Social Democratic electorate (percent)*

	Election years			
Confession	1871–78	1887–87	1890–98	1903–12
Protestant	93	91	90	88
Catholic	7	9	10	12
All	100	100	100	100

tion, but new high or not, it was still an insignificant portion of the Catholic electorate. Catholic support for the SPD remained at the 5% level throughout the 1890s, to rise at each of the general elections of the twentieth century, finally breaking double digits – 12.3% of eligible Catholic voters – in 1912.

Table 1.6, giving the confessional composition of the Social Democratic electorate throughout the history of the *Kaiserreich*, reinforces these observations.

German voters were about 35% Catholic and 65% Protestant (plus the smaller confessional groups), a figure that changed little between 1871 and 1912. Protestants were thus noticeably over-represented and Catholics heavily under-represented among Social Democratic voters. To be sure, the Roman Catholic proportion of the Social Democratic electorate did increase steadily, but even at the beginning of the twentieth century there were only one-third as many Catholics among SPD voters as there were among all eligible voters. To a great extent, the Social Democrats of Imperial Germany were a Protestant party.

In and of itself, this is not a particularly new finding; both contemporaries and historians have been well aware that the SPD had many more Protestant than Catholic sympathizers. Yet this observation is one that calls for a little reflection. Strong Protestant support for the SPD – by 1912, bringing the party within a hair's breadth of being the majority party of German Protestants – went along with violent hostility of the German Protestant churches to the Social Democrats. Pastors preached against the party; in the countryside, they organized peasants to beat up Social Democratic agitators appearing in the village. Both revivalists and adherents of what Americans would call the "social gospel" directed their efforts against the socialist labor movement, forming Protestant workers' associations to keep the working masses from falling victim to the radicals.

Protestant pastors and devout laymen were pious and monarchist; the

Social Democrats were atheistic (in spite of the party giving lip-service to neutrality in religious matters) and republican. Most devout Protestants, both clergy and laypeople, supported the existing social order, which the Social Democrats wished to overthrow, or at least change drastically. That minority of German Protestants favoring social reform generally threw their support to the anti-Semitic Christian Social Welfare movement, rather than to the godless SPD, whose leadership, to boot, included a suspiciously high proportion of Jews.[23]

The usual, and I would say, correct explanation of this state of affairs is that "Protestant" Social Democrats were Protestants in name only. They were de-Christianized, no longer going to church and having an increasingly anti-clerical, rationalist, and materialist view of the world. If the Social Democrats were stronger among Protestants than Catholics, it was in large part because there were many more such de-Christianized Protestants than Catholics.

However, the anti-clericalism and irreligion that was rife in the Social Democratic Party, rather like the anti-clericalism and irreligion present more generally in nineteenth-century German society, had a strong anti-Roman Catholic tinge to it. The SPD party press attacked the Catholic Church and the Center Party, which represented it in the political realm, with a special vigor. The party's polemics against religion – frequent, in spite of efforts of the leadership to tone them down – focused, in the Enlightenment tradition, on the Jesuits and other Catholic priestly representatives of medieval ignorance and superstition. Favorite reading matter of the party faithful was *Der Pfaffenspiegel* (rather inadequately translated into English as "The Mirror of those Damned Priests"), a book that thundered against the corruption, deceit and questionable sexual practices of the Catholic clergy. In short, while breaking with the Protestant church, the Social Democrats had retained much of the Protestant hostility to Catholicism.[24]

---

[23] On Protestantism and politics in Germany before 1914, see Thomas Nipperdey, *Religion im Umbruch: Deutschland 1870–1918* (Munich: Beck, 1988), pp. 92–117 and passim. An insightful local study of the Protestant church and the labor movement is Eckehart Lorenz, "Protestantische Reaktion auf die Entwicklung der sozialistischen Arbeiterbewegung. Mannheim 1890–1933," *Archiv für Sozialgeschichte* 16 (1976): 371–416, esp. pp. 371–88.

[24] Konrad Elsässer, *Die badische Sozialdemokratie 1890 bis 1914: Zum Zusammenhang von Bildung und Organisation* (Marburg: Verlag Arbeiterbewegung und Gesellschaftswissenschaft, 1978), pp. 176–77; Karl Rohe, "Die Ruhrgebietssozialdemokratie im Wilhelmischen Kaiserreich und ihr politischer und kultureller Kontext," in Ritter (ed.) *Der Aufstieg der deutschen Arbeiterbewegung*, pp. 317–44, esp. pp. 341–44; Nolan, *Social Democracy and Society*, pp. 48–49; Alfred Kelly, *The Descent of Darwin: The Popularization of Darwinism in Germany 1860–1914* (Chapel Hill: University of North Carolina Press, 1981), p. 128 and p. 161 nn. 22, 24.

The political scientist Karl Schmitt, in his excellent study of confession and voting in the Federal Republic of Germany, has found that Protestants who were regular churchgoers were more likely to vote for the CDU and less likely to vote for the SPD than voters who were nominal Protestants, but seldom or never went to church (although with the passage of time, the differences in voting behavior between regular Protestant churchgoers and more nominal Protestants have declined). Protestants, on the other hand, who were not conventionally religious, and did not go to church, but did identify themselves as Protestants – that is, in opposition to Catholics – were strong supporters of the SPD and overwhelmingly rejected the CDU.[25]

I wonder if there might not have been a similar relationship between Protestantism and politics in Imperial Germany, with nominally Protestant SPD voters rejecting the Protestant churches while retaining a Protestant/anti-Catholic confessional identity. We could test this suggestion, in a very crude way, by considering how Protestants voted in those constituencies where the Center Party put up candidates, in those areas, one might say, where Ultramontanism showed itself most directly, and where Protestant confessional identities might have been most directly expressed at the voting booth. From 1898 onwards, the SPD was the favored party of Protestants in such constituencies, receiving more of their votes than either all the liberal parties, or all the conservative parties, put together. Indeed, at the last prewar general elections of 1912, when 39% of all eligible Protestant voters chose the SPD, in constituencies with Center Party candidates a remarkable 51% of eligible Protestant voters – 59% of all Protestants who turned out to vote – cast their ballot for the Social Democrats. The party of atheists and materialists had become the party of the Protestants in confrontation with the Papist enemy. Martin Luther must have been spinning in his grave.

This same combination of de-Christianization and confessionalism that helped the Social Democrats among Protestants hindered them among Catholics. Hindered is far too mild a word for the difficulties the SPD had in predominantly Catholic areas. The clergy vigorously denounced the godless socialists from the pulpit and threatened the party members, or even subscribers to its newspapers, with eternal damnation. Priests carried out this threat by refusing Social Democrats the sacraments; the Munich SPD noted that subscriptions to its newspaper fell off every year after Easter.

---

[25] Karl Schmitt, *Konfession und Wahlverhalten in der Bundesrepublik Deutschland* (West Berlin: Duncker & Humblot, 1987), pp. 136–38, 284–92, 313. Schmitt's work is based on survey data and some of his arguments, admittedly, involve interpretation of quite small sub-samples.

Protestant pastors could and did engage in similar sorts of hostile actions, but a much larger proportion of Catholic laypeople went to church and listened to what the clergy told them. Perhaps the most dramatic contrast between Protestants and Catholics could be seen in an eminently spiritual area, funeral processions. As noted above, these were a major form of Social Democratic public demonstration during the years of the anti-socialist law, a dramatic sign of the party's strength, in spite of its prohibition. These demonstrations, however, occurred in such predominantly Protestant cities as Hamburg, Stuttgart, Frankfurt or Breslau. In Catholic areas, things were quite different. Funeral processions of Social Democrats became occasions for mass demonstrations against the party, as pious Catholics lined the routes and jammed the cemeteries, screaming curses and consigning the godless leftists to hell.

Catholic hostility could be seen in more earthly political matters as well. The SPD found it hard to hold meetings in heavily Catholic areas because tavernkeepers were too frightened of clerical reprisals to allow their locales to be used. As late as 1912, in the Dortmund constituency, the very stronghold of the SPD in the Ruhr industrial area, the party was unable to find any place to meet in the predominantly Catholic towns and villages outside the city of Dortmund.[26]

In these circumstances, the Social Democrats found it extremely hard to make headway. Storming right back at the church and the Center Party, and denouncing clerical power in no uncertain terms was the favored response of Social Democratic activists and party leaders from a Catholic background, who had only joined the party after a painful break with the church. With the bulk of the pious voters, though, such an approach was generally counter-productive. But attempting to downplay religious issues or insisting on the piety of Social Democrats and the compatibility of socialism with Christianity, proved equally ineffective,

[26] On Catholic, especially clerical, opposition to the Social Democrats, see Ilse Fischer, *Industrialisierung, sozialer Konflikt und politische Willensbildung in der Stadtgemeinde: Ein Beitrag zur Sozialgeschichte Augsburgs 1840–1914* (Augsburg: Verlag Hieronymus Mühlberger, 1977), pp. 270–72; Goch, *Sozialdemokratische Bewegung und Arbeiterkultur im Ruhrgebiet*, p. 118; Hiery, *Reichstagswahlen im Reichsland*, p. 322; Hirschfelder, *Die bayerische Sozialdemokratie*, p. 563; Ralf Lützenkirchen, *Der sozialdemokratische Verein für den Reichstagswahlkreis Dortmund-Hörde* (Dortmund: Verlag des Historischen Vereins Dortmund, 1970), p. 93; Nolan, *Social Democracy and Society*, pp. 47, 215; Norbert Pies, *"Hetzer wohnen hier verhältnismäßig wenige." Geschichte der Arbeiterbewegung am linken Niederrhein.* ed. Günter Pätzold and Karl-Heinz Schlingmann (Marburg: SP-Verlage Norbert Schüren, 1989), pp. 53–54, 65–66, 73, 74; Schadt, *Die Sozialdemokratische Partei in Baden*, p. 121; Pohl, *Die Münchener Arbeiterbewegung*, pp. 87–89, 171, 201–2. The best work on the trials and tribulations of the socialist labor movement in a Catholic region of Germany is Michael Klöcker, *Die Sozialdemokratie im Regierungsbezirk Aachen vor dem 1. Weltkrieg* (Wentorf: Einhorn-Presse Verlag, 1977). On funeral processions, see pp. 353–62.

Table 1.7 *Support for the Social Democrats by region and confession (percent)*

| | Election years | | | | | | | |
| | 1871–78 | | 1881–87 | | 1890–98 | | 1903–12 | |
Region	Prot.	Cath.	Prot.	Cath.	Prot.	Cath.	Prot.	Cath.
Prussia	4	2	6	2	20	5	32	8
Non-Prussian Germany	9	0	12	1	29	4	41	11
All Germany	6	1	8	1	23	5	36	9

especially as the clergy were quick to point out to the faithful the prevelance of irreligion in the socialist labor movement. Until the 1890s, the Social Democrats oscillated between these two tactics in addressing Catholics, neither with much success.[27]

The only way the SPD could hope to gain Catholic voters would be if they were removed from the influence of the church. Such voters were not necessarily won for the Social Democrats: they might continue to vote for the Center or choose one of the other political parties. But at least the Social Democrats could address them.[28] We can see something of this development in the analysis of election returns. Table 1.7 gives the proportion of eligible Protestant and Catholic voters supporting the Social Democrats, broken down very crudely by region, separating Prussia from non-Prussian Germany. This distinction is particularly useful in discussing the Catholic population, because it coincides very closely with one of the classic regional contrasts in Germany, that between the areas north and south of the Main River. Non-Prussian Germany included south German states, such as Bavaria, Baden or Saxony, as well as the north German Hanseatic cities, Braunschweig or Mecklenburg, but virtually all the Catholics who lived in northern Germany lived in Prussia.

[27] The sources cited in the previous note generally contain discussions of Social Democratic efforts to appeal to Catholic voters. On the importance of breaking with the church and anti-clericalism for Social Democratic activists from a Catholic background, see Pies, *"Hetzer,"* pp. 71–72; Jochen Lorek, *Wie man früher Sozialdemokrat wurde* (Bonn-Bad Godesberg: Verlag Neue Gesellschaft, 1977), pp. 147–51; *Wilhelm Liebknecht Briefwechsel 2*: 735–37.
[28] On the importance of Catholics with loosened ties to the church for the Social Democrats, see Nolan, *Social Democracy and Society*, pp. 116–17, and Goch, *Sozialdemokratische Arbeiterbewegung und Arbeiterkultur*, pp. 172–73. In the Federal Republic, those Catholics who do not go to church are much more likely to vote for the SPD than those who do, and this contrast in voting behavior between churchgoers and non-churchgoers is much more marked among Catholics than Protestants. Schmitt, *Konfession und Wahlverhalten*, p. 137,

The Social Democrats persistently received greater support from Protestant voters living outside of Prussia than they did from their co-religionists in the Prussian kingdom. For Catholics, the picture is somewhat more mixed. In Bismarckian Germany, a slightly greater proportion of Catholics in Prussia voted for the Social Democrats than did Catholics in southern Germany, but the party received little support from any Catholics. The figures show that a disproportionate share of the post-1890 growth in Catholic support for the SPD came from southern Germany, to the point that in the last three prewar elections the Social Democrats did noticeably better among the Catholics in the south than they did among Catholics in the north. Explanations of this development in terms of de-Christianization occurring as a result of urbanization or industrialization are not very convincing, since the heavily industrialized regions with a large Catholic population – the cities of the lower Rhine and the Ruhr industrial area – were in the north. Munich, Würzburg and Mainz, to take three predominantly Catholic cities in southern Germany where the SPD did quite well among the voters, were far from being as industrialized as, say, Essen, Aachen or Düsseldorf, where the Social Democrats had noticeably less success.

A more plausible explanation must be sought in terms of the differing religious history of the two regions of Germany, and the greater prevalence of anti-clericalism and religious indifference among Catholics in the southern part of the country.[29] As will be seen below, in Bismarckian Germany it was primarily the liberal parties which capitalized on this; after 1890, the SPD increasingly appeared as the heir to the liberal, anti-clerical tradition south of the Main River. An additional factor to be considered is the effect of the national minorities on German politics. Non-Prussian Germany included Alsace-Lorraine, a region which in part shared the French tradition of anti-clericalism, and where the Social Democrats did quite well among Catholic voters after 1890. In the 1912 elections, Social Democratic candidates were elected in just twelve of the 146 majority Catholic constituencies in Germany; five of those Catholic constituencies represented by the SPD were in Alsace-Lorraine. Of the thirty predominantly Catholic constituencies in the German Empire where the SPD received its best vote totals, ten were in Alsace-Lorraine, with one of them, Mulhouse city, in first place.[30] Conversely, in the eastern, predominantly Polish portions of the Prussian monarchy, the Social Democratic Party did extremely poorly, obtaining its worst vote

---

[29] On this point, see Jonathan Sperber, *Popular Catholicism in Nineteenth Century Germany* (Princeton: Princeton University Press, 1984), pp. 290–92.
[30] Hiery, *Reichstagswahlen im Reichsland*, pp. 359, 398.

Table 1.8 *The German electorate according to the censuses of 1895 and 1907 (percent)*

Social/confessional group	1895	1907
Protestant farmers	21	16
Protestant middle class	23	24
Protestant workers	21	24
Catholic farmers	15	11
Catholic middle class	10	11
Catholic workers	11	14
Total	101	100

totals in the heavily Polish province of Posen (Polish: Poznàn), where, even in 1912, less than 4% of votes cast were for the German labor party. This is hardly a suprising result, given the interlocked strength of Polish nationalism and the Catholic church

Throughout the history of the empire, the Social Democrats received far more votes from Protestants than Catholics; the gap between the confessions did close a bit after 1890, but even in Wilhelmine Germany it remained very large. Such a confessional difference was produced, as I have suggested above, by both the decline in and the persistence of religious traditions. Confession, in short, was a major factor determining the vote for the labor party. It will need to be taken into account when considering the influence of occupation and class on the vote for the SPD.

People's party or labor party?

In contrast to the results of the influence of confession on the Social Democratic electorate, which largely reinforce the dominant scholarly opinion, the findings on the role of class and occupation go strongly against it. Indeed, at first glance, they might seem so implausible as to cast serious doubts on the method used to arrive at them. Consequently, I will present the results of my analysis step by step, offering suplementary evidence as I go along. To begin with, table 1.8 gives the composition of the German electorate by class and confession according to the occupational censuses of 1895 and 1907.

Crucial to understanding the whole line of argument is noting that the blue-collar workers were a much smaller portion of the electorate than they were of the population. Depending on how you define the categories, blue-collar workers made upwards of 60% of the labor force in

Table 1.9 *Support for the SPD in the 1912 elections, by class and confession (percent)*

	Confession		
Class	Protestant	Catholic	All
Farmers	8	0	5
Middle class	45	13	35
Workers	54	22	42

Wilhelmine Germany, but they were only one third of those eligible to vote in 1895, and under 40% of them in 1907.[31] The reason for this discrepancy was the high voting age (25 years) and the very different age structures of different social classes. Of male blue-collar workers 40% were under the age of twenty-five and hence ineligible to vote. By contrast, less than 5% of independent businessmen or farmers and between 20 and 25% of salaried employees were twenty-five or younger. Thus, in spite of the relatively democratic franchise, the German electorate before the First World War was older, and more property-owning than the male labor force. Historians confuse the two at their own risk.[32]

A labor party, that is one whose votes came largely from the working class, would be at a severe disadvantage in such an electorate. But in addition, the SPD, as the previous section as shown, received relatively few votes from Catholics. Protestant workers made up less than one quarter of the electorate, so one has to wonder if there were enough of them to account for the successes of the SPD in Wilhelmine Germany. At this point, let me introduce table 1.9, which gives my estimates of the percentage of eligible voters in each social and confessional groups voting for the SPD in the last prewar elections of 1912.

What is striking about these figures is the very high proportion of middle class voters, particularly Protestant ones, who cast their ballots for candidates of the labor party. If the estimates are anywhere near to being correct, than the pre-1914 SPD, at least in so far as its voters are con-

---

[31] For a typical set of figures on the German labor force, see Guttsman, *The German Social Democratic Party*, p. 86.

[32] This difference between the electorate and the labor force was noticeable in the Weimar Republic, where the voting age was twenty, as has been pointed out by Falter and Hänisch, "Die Anfälligkeit von Arbeitern," p. 192; this difference was much more distinct in Imperial Germany, given its higher voting age. For an embarrassing example of confusing the electorate and the labor force, see Dieter Groh, *Negative Integration und revolutionärer Attentismus: Die deutsche Sozialdemokratie am Vorabend des Ersten Weltkrieges* (Frankfurt: Ullstein, 1973), p. 279, n. 62

cerned, was not a labor party, but a people's party attracting support from different sectors of the non-agricultural population.

Since these results directly contradict the standard picture of the SPD as the party of skilled Protestant workers, let me offer a supporting argument, mostly not based on regression procedures, to underscore my conclusions. In 1912, a little over 29% of eligible voters supported the SPD. Going by the 1907 census, 24% of the electorate were Protestant workers. Thus, even if all the Protestant workers in Germany had turned out to vote and had voted for the SPD, together they could not have accounted for the party's success. However, every Protestant worker did not vote for the Social Democrats. Assuming an enormous, if not implausible turnout rate of 90%, about 10% of Protestant workers did not appear at the polls. Additionally, a certain number – at a minimum, 25% of them – voted for the candidates of other parties.

How can I justify this 25% figure, the crux of the argument? It was certainly the case, later in the century. Jürgen Falter's estimates are that between 30 and 40% of eligible Protestant workers voted for parties other than the Social Democrats or the Communists in the general elections of the Weimar Republic, between 1920 and 1932.[33] Of course, in the Weimar Republic, the electoral system was different, the voting age was lower than during the *Kaiserreich*, and women had the vote. Additionally, Falter's "workers" include agricultural laborers, who are grouped with farmers in my estimates. Still, these figures from the 1920s are at least suggestive of the pre-1914 political universe.

Falter's estimates are derived from ecological regressions similar to the ones used in this book. For those who mistrust such methods, I can point to the results of survey research from the post-1945 Federal Republic. These show that between 24 and 38% of the votes cast by Protestant workers (in this case, not including farm laborers, of whom there were very few in any event) in the general elections to the Bundestag from 1953 to 1983 were for either the CDU/CSU or the FDP.[34] Besides the qualifications about who had the franchise and the nature of the electoral system which applied to the Weimar Republic, the pre-unification Federal Republic also encompassed a quite different territory than did the German Empire. Nonetheless, once again we can see a significant minority of Protestant workers who voted for liberal or conservative parties.

Given that there were many such workers present after 1914, it seems plausible to assume that they were around before the First World War. We

[33] Falter and Zintl, "The Economic Crisis of the 1930s and the Nazi Vote," p. 75.
[34] Schmitt, *Konfession und Wahlverhalten*, p. 315.

need not, however, just remain with this argument by analogy, since a number of studies have clearly identified groups of Protestant workers who voted for parties other than the Social Democrats in the first decade of the twentieth century. Working-class adherents of forms of evangelical Protestantism – pietism, religious revivalism, and the "free" (unestablished) churches – such as the cigar-makers of the Minden-Ravensberg region, or the workers in the Siegerland iron industry, were persistent and loyal supporters of the conservative parties. Many Protestant coalminers and steelworkers of the Ruhr industrial area voted for the National Liberals. These included but were definitely not limited to Polish-speaking but Protestant Masurians, closely tied to the party via the church and Protestant workers associations, and workers at the Krupp enterprises, loyal to their employer. While SPD vote totals in the Ruhr Basin constituencies were increasing in the early twentieth century, and the party was emerging as the dominant force among Protestant coalminers – less so among steelworkers – in the Saar Basin of south-western Germany, the Social Democrats remained basically a splinter party down through 1914, with the industrial working class voting along religious lines, Catholics for the Center, Protestants for the National Liberals. Even in SPD strongholds, such as Thuringia, or the city of Kiel, there were pockets of working-class support for the liberals, and all these examples do not include Protestant blue-collar voters in the small towns and villages of East Elbian Germany, or those who supported the Hanoverian particularists or the French nationalists in Alsace-Lorraine (also, probably, primarily in villages and small towns), or who were strongly nationalist and rejected the Social Democrats for their supposed lack of patriotism. Considering all this, 25% of Protestant workers voting for parties other than the SPD seems like a quite modest estimate. The actual figure was probably closer to the 36% that I have obtained from ecological regression.[35]

For caution's sake, let us stay with 10% of Protestant workers not

[35] Frank Nipkau, "Traditionen der Erweckungsbewegung in der Parteipolitik? Die Christlich-Konservativen und die Christlich-Soziale Partei in Minden-Ravensberg 1878–1914," in Josef Mooser et al. (eds.) *Frommes Volk und Patrioten: Erweckungsbewegung und soziale Frage im östlichen Westfalen 1800 bis 1900* (Bielefeld: Verlag für Regionalgeschichte) pp. 368–90, esp. p. 379; Helmut Busch, *Die Stoeckerbewegung im Siegerland* (Siegen: Forschungsstelle Siegerland, 1968) pp. 134, 137–41 and passim; Goch, *Sozialdemokratische Arbeiterbewegung und Arbeiterkultur im Ruhrgebiet*, p. 172; Karl Rohe, Wolfgang Jäger and Uwe Dorow, "Politische Gesellschft und politische Kultur," esp. pp. 459–60; Bajohr, *Zwischen Krupp und Kommune*, pp. 69, 79–81, 83, 108; Mallmann and Steffens, *Lohn der Mühen*, pp. 103–4; Ulrich Hess, *Geschichte Thüringens 1866 bis 1914* ed. Volker Wahl (Weimar: Verlag Hermann Böhlaus Nachfolger, 1991), p. 385; Paetau, *Konfrontation oder Kooperation*, p. 182; Klaus J. Mattheier, "Drei Führungsorganisationen der wirtschaftsfriedlichen-nationalen Arbeiterbewegung," *Rheinische Vierteljahrsblätter* 37 (1973): 244–75, esp. pp. 254–55. Another possible source of Protestant working-class voters opposed to the SPD would have been those workers

voting and 25% voting for non-socialist parties. That means that 65% voted for the SPD, and since Protestant workers were 24% of eligible voters, their SPD votes made up roughly 16% of the electorate ($0.65 \times 0.24 = 0.156$). In 1912, the SPD received over 29% of the vote, so 13% of the electorate, voting for the SPD, but not Protestant workers, remains to be accounted for. Regression results presented above, quite close to contemporary estimates, suggest that 12% of all eligible Catholic voters chose the SPD. Catholics were 36% of eligible voters, so Catholic SPD voters were 4% ($0.36 \times 0.12 = 0.043$) of the electorate. Together Protestant working-class and Catholic SPD voters made up 20% of the electorate, leaving 9% of the electorate SPD voters who must have come from the Protestant middle class and farming population. If we assume, as contemporaries did, and as the weakness of the party in rural areas suggests, that just a small proportion of Protestant farmers voted for the party, making up, say, just 1% of the electorate, we are left with 8% of the total electorate Protestant middle-class voters supporting the SPD.[36] Protestant middle-class voters were 24% of the electorate, so one-third of them must have voted for the Social Democrats. This figure is a minimum, dependent on the assumption that 65% of Protestant workers supported the SPD in 1912. If that figure was less, as the regression estimates suggest, then a greater proportion of Protestant middle class chose the SPD, perhaps as high as the 45% given in table 1.9.

Many of these voters may have been master craftsmen, running their own businesses as far as the census-takers were concerned, but in reality were proletarianized outworkers, in debt to and controlled by merchant capitalists. Evidence of this state of affairs might be seen in the success of Social Democratic slates in elections for the employers' representatives on industrial conciliation courts in predominantly Protestant cities such as Frankfurt or Nuremberg.[37] Others were former workers, recipients of social insurance disability pensions, who were quite numerous before 1914. They were counted with rentiers in the census records and cannot be separated from them.[38] These groups may have made up as much as

employed by the postal service or state-owned railways who were not tenured civil servants, and were thus counted by the census as workers in transport and communication rather than with the state servants. On this census practice, see Bleek, *Quartierbildung*, p. 144.   [36] Suval, *Electoral Politics*, p. 81.

[37] Hirschfelder, *Die Bayerische Sozialdemokratie*, p. 582; Eichler, *Sozialistische Arbeiterbewegung in Frankfurt*, pp. 354–55.

[38] Volker Hentschel, *Geschichte der deutschen Sozialpolitik 1880–1980* (Frankfurt: Suhrkamp, 1983), p. 24 Before 1914, there were just one-tenth as many old-age pensioners as disability pensioners, so the former were not a very sizeable group. To give a local example, in 1909 there were 50 recipients of an old-age pension in the city of Frankfurt am Main, and 600 of a disability pension. If they were all men, they would have been 0.8% of the 1907 electorate. Ralf Roth, *Gewerkschaftskartell und Sozialpolitik in Frankfurt am Main* (Frankfurt: Verlage Waldemar Kramer, 1991), p. 190.

Table 1.10 *Support for the SPD in Wilhelmine elections, by class and confession (percent)*

| | Confession | | | | | |
| | 1890–98 | | | 1903–12 | | |
Class	Protestant	Catholic	All	Protestant	Catholic	All
Farmers	5	1	3	6	0	4
Middle class	24	6	19	43	9	33
·Workers	40	8	29	48	16	36

15% of the "middle class," although they were in part balanced out by others contemporaries understood as middle class, such as retail sales clerks, who were counted with workers in the census.[39]

After all these adjustments are taken into account, there remains a substantial proportion of Protestant businessmen, professionals, civil servants and salaried employees who voted for the SPD. Local studies have identified them in Hamburg, Frankfurt and Ludwigshafen; Jürgen Winkler's national-level study of the SPD vote in 1912, using a different ecological inference procedure than the one I employed, also suggests substantial middle-class Protestant support for the Social Democrats.[40] Nor is this finding something new and unprecedented. The arithmetic argument presented in the previous paragraphs is a refined version of one first proposed by the German sociologist Robert Blank in 1905. His conclusion, that the SPD drew votes from a wide variety of social groups besides the working class, has often been criticized, but the criticisms do not touch the essentials of his argument, which, I would say, is basically correct.[41]

At this point, let me introduce some broader figures on support for the SPD by class and confession. Table 1.10 gives decadal averages for the

[39] Carole Elizabeth Adams, *Women Clerks in Wilhelmine Germany: Issues of Class and Gender* (Cambridge and New York: Cambridge University Press, 1988), p. 11. Admittedly, a very large proportion of sales clerks were women, who were not eligible to vote in any event (p. 12).
[40] Eichler, *Sozialistische Arbeiterbewegung in Frankfurt am Main*, pp. 223–24; Kutz-Bauer, *Arbeiterschaft, Arbeiterbewegung und bürgerlicher Staat*, pp. 162–64; Rolf Wender, *Wahlen und soziale Strukturen in Ludwigshafen am Rhein 1871–1914. Unter besonderer Berücksichtigung der Reichstagswahlen*, (Ludwigshafen a. Rh.: Stadtarchiv, 1984), pp. 632–36; Winkler, "Die soziale Basis der sozialistischen Parteien," p. 169.
[41] Robert Blank, "Die soziale Zusammensetzung der sozialdemokratischen Wählerschaft Deutschlands," *Archiv für Sozialwissenschaft und Sozialpolitik* 20 (1905): 507–53. (One of the few authors to agree with him is Lorek, *Wie man früher Sozialdemokrat wurde*, pp. 88–90, with some interesting additional remarks.) A criticism of this argument which is

percent of eligible voters in each group voting for the Social Democratic Party in the Wilhelmine era. The table suggests a difference in the interaction of class and confession in the development of the SPD vote. The major long-term trend among Protestants was an increase in the proportion of middle-class voters casting their ballots for the SPD, to the point that their support levels had just about reached those of the working class in the three twentieth-century general elections of the *Kaiserreich*. For Catholics, on the other hand, the trend went in the opposite direction. Catholic support for the SPD increased primarily among workers and the difference in Social Democratic support between workers and the middle class widened in the quarter century before 1914, rather than narrowing as it did among Protestants. To exaggerate just a bit, we might say that on the eve of the First World War, as far as the voters were concerned the SPD was a Protestant people's party, and a Catholic labor party.

To the extent that the SPD was either a labor party or a people's party, it was an urban – more precisely, a non-agricultural – party. Table 1.10 makes all too clear the SPD's Achilles heel – its inability to attract farmers' votes. It was not for lack of trying. From the very outset, Social Democrats had agitated vigorously in rural areas, scoring some remarkable successes among agricultural laborers in Schleswig-Holstein during the 1870s. These efforts were redoubled in the late 1880s, with the waning of the anti-socialist law, and reached a crescendo in the following decade. Indeed, the agrarian question was the main issue of intra-party debate in the Social Democrats' first decade of legality, as both the leadership and ordinary rank-and-file members tried to figure out how to attract rural support without alienating the party's urban constituency.[42]

Its chances were not too bad either. As will be discussed in the chapter on the Wilhelmine elections, the 1890s were a period of economic crisis in the countryside, and there were substantial swings in farmers' votes. Both the agricultural laborers on large farms and landed estates in northern

actually no criticism at all, is in Fricke, *Handbuch zur Geschichte der deutschen Arbeiterbewegung*, pp. 742–43. To be taken more seriously are the remarks by Ritter, *Die Arbeiterbewegung im Wilhelmischen Reich*, pp. 77–78, but his criticisms contain a number of mistakes, primarily in substantially overestimating the number of Catholic workers who chose the SPD.

[42] On early Social Democratic efforts in the countryside, Holger Rüdel, *Landarbeiter und Sozialdemokratie in Ostholstein 1872 bis 1878: Erfolg und Niederlage der sozialistischen Arbeiterbewegung in einem großagrarischen Wahlkreis zwischen Reichsgründung und Sozialistengesetz* (Neumünster: Karl Wachholtz Verlag, 1986). On rural agitation and the great debate over agrarian policy in the 1890s, see Hans Georg Lehmann, *Die Agrarfrage in der Theorie und Praxis der deutschen und internationalen Sozialdemokratie* (Tübingen: J. C. B. Mohr, 1970) and Helmut Hesselbarth, *Revolutionäre Sozialdemokraten, Opportunisten und die Bauern am Vorabend des Imperialismus* (East Berlin: Dietz Verlag, 1968).

Germany, and the small farmers in the south-west, among whom the radical traditions of the revolution of 1848 were still alive, would seem to have offered good prospects for the Social Democrats. But the party could not take advantage of this situation. With a few local and regional exceptions, most noticeably among the workers on estates and in the forests of Mecklenburg, the SPD was unable to extend its organizational network out beyond the immediate vicinity of large cities, or to gain and retain farmers' electoral support. This weakness in agricultural areas was to be a permanent feature of the SPD, and a brake on its prospects at the ballot box, until the later twentieth century when the farm population was no longer a significant portion of the labor force.[43]

Rather like the support of Protestants for the SPD, the hostility of farmers to it has been taken for granted by historians, without too much further reflection. Yet a number of the more obvious reasons do not provide a sufficient explanation. One could say that farmers, with their strong interest in private property (even those who did not have it aspired to it) could not vote for a socialist party committed to its abolition. This would not explain why substantial numbers of farmers and agricultural or forest laborers supported socialists in early twentieth-century Sweden, France, Italy, or even Oklahoma, to say nothing of what would happen later in the century in Africa, Asia or Latin America.[44] Powerful and effective repression of the socialists' rural agitational efforts is certainly part of the story, particularly apt for the areas of large landed estates in East Elbian Germany, where even the left-wing liberals were deemed subversive by the agrarian power elite. It does not explain, though, why repression at least as determined failed to wipe out the Social Democrats in the 1880s, or how the SPD achieved its best agrarian results in Mecklenburg, the very epitome of noble landlord power.[45] It is also an

---

[43] Scattered examples of pre-1914 successes of the SPD among agricultural voters are offered in Sepainter, *Reichstagswahlen im Großherzogtum Baden*, pp. 243–44; Suval, *Electoral Politics*, pp. 83–84; Frank, *Die Brandenburger als Reichstagswähler*, pp. 133–34; and Klaus Saul, "Der Kampf um das Landproletariat: Sozialistische Landagitation Großgrundbesitz und preußische Staatsverwaltung 1890 bis 1903," *Archiv für Sozialgeschichte* 15 (1975): 163–208, esp. pp. 175–76. They all note the exceptional character of these successes.

[44] Tony Judt, *Socialism in Provence, 1871–1914 : a Study in the Origins of the Modern French Left* (Cambridge and New York: Cambridge University Press, 1979); Leif Lewin, Jansson and Sörbom, *The Swedish Electorate*, pp. 142–45; Mattei Dogan, "Political Cleavage and Social Stratification in France and Italy," in Seymour Martin Lipset and Stein Rokkan (eds.) *Party Systems and Voter Alignments: Cross-National Perspectives* (New York: The Free Press, 1967), pp. 129–95; Garin Burbank, *When Farmers Voted Red: The Gospel of Socialism in the Oklahoma Countryside, 1910–1924* (Westport: Greenwood Press, 1976).

[45] The article by Saul, cited in n. 42 above, offers a detailed discussion of the repression of the efforts at repression of the SPD in rural areas of large estates and also the relative lack of such success in Mecklenburg.

explanation that does not apply to southwestern Germany, where noble landlords, or any kind of large landowners, were few, and where democratic traditions were tenacious and long established. Perhaps most convincingly, one might see the Social Democrats' failures in the countryside as a special case of the more general hostility of Germany's churchgoers to the party's godless radicalism. Farmers were the most devout of Germans and the image of Hessian peasants greeting Social Democratic agitators in 1893 with calls of "Go home and read the Bible; that's the smart thing to do," is suggestive of the SPD's difficulties in this respect.[46] Yet given the declining piety of Protestant farmers, and the successes of the anti-clerical Bavarian Peasant League among their Catholic counterparts, religious ties cannot be the whole story either.

The missing piece in this puzzle is the efforts of the other political parties, their responses to the great agrarian crisis of the 1890s. As was the case with the SPD's greatest success in the elections of 1890, we must adjourn the discussion of the socialists' greatest failure until the other parties are considered. Provisionally, I would suggest that a necessary part of the explanation lies in a consideration of the two non-proletarian elements among SPD voters. The party's successes with craftsmen, small businessmen, civil servants, and professionals (largely urban and consumer oriented) and its failures among the rural, food-producing population, were two sides of the same coin, a coin minted by the responses of the Social Democrats and the other political parties to the discontents, both real and imagined, of German farmers at the end of the nineteenth century.

The Social Democratic electorate and the Social Democratic movement

At the end of this discussion of the SPD electorate it might be appropriate to pause and take stock of the findings. Those most easily expressed are the negative ones. Contrary to the dominant historical opinion, the Social Democrats were not the party of the previous non-voters and their electorate was not composed predominantly of urban Protestant blue-collar workers. The positive results of the statistical analysis, on the other hand, are more complex. They cannot be expressed in a few brief sentences but require more elaboration and qualification.

Up to 1887, the increase in Social Democratic votes came almost exclusively from the reservoir of previous non-voters, although the labor

---

[46] Quoted in Lehmann, *Die Agrarfrage*, p. 57.

party was hardly unique in that respect. Non-voters still made up a large minority of the electorate, so that all political parties drew on them for support. In the elections of Wilhelmine Germany, on the other hand, the origins of the growth in the SPD's support were more diverse. At different times between 1890 and 1912, the Social Democrats captured voters from all the other political parties, as well as gaining the support of previous non-voters and profiting from the renewal, both biological and migrational, of the electorate. This overall increase in the SPD vote in Wilhelmine Germany was, of course, not uniform, but composed of interchanges, both positive and negative, with other segments of the electorate. Of these interchanges, one stands out – voter movements between the Social Democrats and the liberals. There was more movement of voters from election to election between the SPD and the liberal parties than between the Social Democrats and any other party grouping, including the non-voters. In addition, these movements differed sharply from decade to decade. In the 1890s, the attraction of previous liberal voters was the single greatest factor in the election victories of the Social Democrats, while in the post-1900 general elections, the party suffered a noticeable net loss of votes to its liberal competitors, a longer-term setback which it never encountered with any other party or group of parties in the Wilhelmine era.

Turning from the political characteristics of the Social Democratic electorate to their social and confessional ones, we can say that the single most important determinant of SPD voting was occupation: the ratio of the percentage of non-farm voters choosing the SPD to that of agricultural voters doing so was about 8:1. It remained that way throughout Wilhelmine Germany, and was largely constant across confessional groups.[47] Confession provided the second most important determinant: Protestants preferred the SPD to Catholics by about 7:1 in Bismarckian Germany. The gap narrowed to 4:1 after 1890, but remained quite substantial. In comparison to these factors, social class did not play a major role in the SPD vote. Workers did support the SPD more than did the

---

[47] Since farmers lived in rural areas, it might be suggested that occupation was acting as a proxy for residence; it was really people of all occupations living in the countryside who rejected the SPD, while urban voters, of all occupations, supported it. The available material does not allow a breakdown of occupation by residence, as it does by confession, so this assertion cannot be fully tested. Election results by size of community, however, do not support this assertion. From 1898 to 1912 (the only years for which such results are available), the ratio of SPD percentages in cities of over 500,000 to SPD percentages in villages of under 2,000 was about 3:1 (Suval, *Electoral Politics*, pp. 80–81), thus making the urban–rural differential in the party's vote substantially less than the gap between farmers and non-farm occupations.

urban middle class in the 1890s, by about 1.5:1; after 1900, the middle class voted for the labor party to almost as great an extent as did the working class.[48] In conjunction with confession, class was somewhat more significant in determining voting behavior: the results show that after 1890 the percentages of Protestant workers and of the Protestant middle class voting for the SPD were converging, while they were diverging among the same social groups in the Catholic population. Yet even this gap did not get very wide. In the elections of 1903, 1907, and 1912, Catholic workers' support for the SPD exceeded that of the Catholic middle class by a ratio of 2:1, a difference noticeably less than that between the confessions, or between farmers and other occupations.

In considering the social composition of the SPD's membership, though, one searches in vain for the Protestant urban middle-class, seemingly so prominent in the Social Democratic electorate. Available local statistics show that blue-collar workers were usually around 90% of the dues-paying members.[49] Historians have often taken these membership figures as evidence of the nature of the SPD electorate; I would say that the disjunction between the two reflects the place of the Social Democratic movement in Imperial Germany.

I use the word movement advisedly, because it is the nexus between the party and the labor movement and between the public act of joining the party, whose membership lists had to be turned over to the police, and whose meetings were under police surveillance, and the private act of voting, that is crucial in this connection. For skilled blue-collar workers, the party and the free trade unions so closely affiliated with it offered a chance to improve their working and living conditions, possibilities that more than outweighed the disapproval of the authorities and the wealthy and powerful. In contrast, for the middle class – unorganized white-collar workers (or at least unorganized by Social Democratic unions), civil servants threatened with dismissal for joining the party, businessmen and professionals facing ostracism, or loss of clients and customers – there was nothing to be gained and everything to be lost by publicly affiliating

---

[48] These measures of class are very crude and separating out the upper bourgeoisie from the lower middle class, as can be done in finer studies of individual cities (for Hamburg, see Kutz-Bauer, *Arbeiterschaft, Arbeiterbewegung und bürgerlicher Staat*, pp. 143–62) would probably probably show that the well-to-do were less likely to support the Social Democrats than the more modestly affluent. Still, in a regime of universal manhood suffrage, where the upper classes make up at most 5–10% of the electorate, a class-based approach must be able to explain more than just their vote.

[49] The sources cited in n. 2 above all have local membership statistics. The first (albeit approximate) nationwide breakdown of party membership by social class dates from 1930.

with the SPD.[50] The (relative) privacy of the secret ballot, on the other hand, made it possible to express sympathies with the SPD without needing to fear the consequences.

Historians have frequently stressed the connection between the SPD's character as a mass membership political party and its successes at the ballot box. Nothing in the analysis I have presented refutes this contention and much in it strongly supports it. But one needs to remember that while the party's mass membership may have helped create its mass electorate, its mass membership was not identical to its mass electorate, or even necessarily representative of it. In this respect, the focus on the party's membership for understanding the party's vote is misleading. It underestimates the SPD's ability to gain (and also to lose) voters from different political and social backgrounds and also tends to divert attention from the occupational and confessional limitations on the party's electoral appeal.

---

[50] This was also true for unskilled workers in large industrial enterprises, such as those in the Saar and Ruhr basins, where the trade unions had no power. Social Democratic membership was also low in those areas, both as a percentage of the population and as a percentage of the party's vote. Conversely, innkeepers and small retailers with a working-class clientele, were the chief middle-class groups to join the party.

2 The minority parties

Opposition or affirmation

The history of the parties of the religious, national, and regional minorities in Imperial Germany is, in part, a story of a resistance to oppression
and struggle against the ruling powers thoroughly comparable to that
waged by the Social Democrats. These minority parties represented
groups who were at best reluctant participants in the German Empire of
1871 and apprehensive about its future development: the French, Danes,
and Poles with different national loyalties, the Hanoverians, conquered
and annexed by the Prussians, and, above all, Germany's Roman
Catholics, turned into a permanent minority following the exclusion of
the Habsburg monarchy from German affairs as a consequence of the war
of 1866. The initial decade of the empire's history showed that their fears
and apprehensions were thoroughly justified. No sooner was the new
empire created than its government began a policy of vigorous harassment and persecution of the Catholic Church, the *Kulturkampf*. The
Jesuits were expelled from Germany, priests arrested by the hundreds,
bishops forced to flee the country. Among the predominantly Roman
Catholic national minorities in Alsace-Lorraine and Prussian Poland, the
struggle between church and state quickly became intermingled with
national antagonism and so was carried out with a special bitterness and
vehemence.[1]

In the face of such policies, the leaders and activists of the minority
parties, themselves often men of basically conservative opinions, had no
choice but to employ the democratic strategies of popular political agitation

---

[1] On the *Kulturkampf*, see Sperber, *Popular Catholicism*, pp. 207–52; Lech, Trzeciakowski,
The Kulturkampf in Prussian Poland, trans. K. Kretkowska (New York: Columbia
University Press, 1990); Hiery, *Reichstagswahlen im Reichsland*, pp. 136–75. Even though
the party leaderships and most of their voters were Protestants, the Hanoverian and
Hessian particularists strongly opposed the *Kulturkampf*, among the few German
Protestants to do so. Aschoff, *Welfische Bewegung*, pp. 131–35; Enno Knobel, *Die
Hessische Rechtspartei: Konservative Opposition gegen das Bismarckreich* (Marburg: N.G.
Elwert Verlag, 1978), pp. 96–101, 201–2.

via the press, public meetings, and mass membership organizations. Their activities were strikingly similar to those of the contemporary Social Democrats, albeit on a larger scale, the 75,000 members of the Association of German Catholics in the early 1870s at least triple the membership of the two Social Democratic parties. The 5,300 members of the electoral association of the Hanoverian particularists were a similarly impressive accomplishment, given that they were all in just one Prussian province.[2]

The state authorities responded to these efforts with political persecution. A blizzard of criminal libel charges descended on the Catholic, French, and Polish press; public meetings sponsored by the minority parties were placed under police surveillance, closed down as they were under way, or simply prohibited; mass organizations of the minority parties were dissolved by court order. Measures taken against the church in the course of the *Kulturkampf* blended together with actions against the Center Party or the Polish and French nationalists into one campaign of official repression. While not reaching the degree of persecution seen with the anti-socialist law, this campaign was substantially greater in extent, directed against a much larger movement of political opposition.[3]

However, these heroic years of persecution and mass response gradually came to an end, to a greater or lesser extent for the different minority groups, in the decade of the 1880s. In Wilhelmine Germany, the minority parties faced a quite different problem, namely legitimating their continued existence even when the groups they represented were no longer the object of official persecution, or, at the very least, when this persecution had been substantially mitigated. Indeed – and here the growing difference between these parties and the Social Democrats emerges most clearly – all the minority parties were faced at some point with the question of whether or not to support the government, even the Polish nationalists, the party whose very existence put into question the German Empire in its boundaries of 1871.[4] At the same time that politicians of

[2] Membership figures from Fricke, *Handbuch zur Geschichte der deutschen Arbeiterbewegung*, p. 141; Sperber, *Popular Catholicism*, p. 212; Aschoff, *Welfische Bewegung*, p. 113. Regional Catholic associations in Silesia and Bavaria were not affiliated with the Association of German Catholics, so its membership understates the extent of Catholic political organization in the 1870s.

[3] Besides the sources cited above (n. 1), see Hans-Wolfgang Wetzel, *Presseinnenpolitik im Bismarckreich (1874–1890): Das Problem der Repression oppositioneller Zeitungen* (Frankfurt: Peter Lang, 1975), pp. 297, 304–5 and passim.

[4] On the development of "loyalism" among Polish nationalists in the late 1880s and early 1890s, see Richard Blanke, *Prussian Poland in the German Empire (1871–1900)*, (New York: Columbia University Press, 1981) pp. 109–41 and esp. Ted Kaminksi, *Polish Publicists and Prussian Politics (1890–1894): The Polish Press in Poznan during the Neue Kurs of Chancellor Leo von Caprivi 1890–1894* (Wiesbaden: Franz Steiner Verlag, 1988), pp. 57–71, 234–35 and passim.

these parties were negotiating with the government and simultaneously with their voters over the possibilities of opposition and support, the electoral universe was rapidly changing, as a result of the rapid rise of the SPD and due to the growing importance of economic interest groups with the concurrent saliency of economic issues to voters.

This is the point at which much of the historical literature on the minority parties sets in. Its basic organizing principle is to pose the question, first raised by contemporaries in the 1890s, of whether ethnic, confessional, or regional identities could continue to bind voters to a political party without continuous governmental persecution of the respective groups to reinforce it. Or, would voters tend to wander off towards other parties, more clearly delineated on the left–right political spectrum, and more clearly oriented towards specific social classes or economic interests? One version of this literature asks directly about the continued support for the minority parties, generally in the form of a narrative of political decline that can, at best, be delayed. Could the Center Party retain the loyalty of Catholic voters or would their support weaken over time? How many inhabitants of Alsace-Lorraine voted for a regional or French nationalist party and how many for one of the German political parties? How long would Hanoverians continue to vote for a party whose chief issue was the restoration of the dynasty overthrown by the Prussian army in 1866?

Some historians, while accepting the idea that in the long run ethnic, confessional or regional identities would not be a viable basis for a political party, have nonetheless rejected the narrative of decline. Rather, they have suggested that minority parties really never were ethnically, confessionally or regionally based, or that after 1890 they developed away from such loci. In these interpretations, the Center was not a Catholic political party but a Christian-democratic one, or a party representing liberal or constitutional principles, or one increasingly standing for the economic interests of the lower middle class. [5]

The assumption underlying both versions of the scholarly literature does have an empirical basis. The vote for a number of the regional political parties did decline in Wilhelmine Germany, and by the eve of the First World War the Hanoverians, and the French and Danish nationalists

---

[5] Examples of the first line of interpretation (and they naturally overlap): Schauff, *Das Wahlverhalten*; Lepsius, "Parteisystem und Sozialstruktur," esp. p. 69; Hiery, *Reichstagswahlen im Reichsland*; Loth, *Katholiken im Kaiserreich*; Aschoff, *Welfische Bewegung*. For the second, see Anderson, *Windthorst*; Blackbourn, *Class, Religion and Local Politics*, or Winfried Becker, "Die Deutsche Zentrumspartei im Bismarckreich," in Winfried Becker (ed.) *Die Minderheit als Mitte – Die Deutsche Zentrumspartei in der Innenpolitik des Reiches 1871–1933* (Paderborn: Ferdinand Schöningh Verlag, 1986), pp. 9–45.

were all quite close to being reduced to the fringes of political life in areas where they had once enjoyed overwhelming or even unanimous support. The Center Party did not disappear before 1914, or even 1933, in spite of frequent hopes and fears that it would, but continued to be the choice of a substantial proportion of Catholic voters. In the very long run, however, it gave way after 1945 to the Christian Democratic Union, a conservative party that has largely retained the Catholic electorate of the Center while attracting Protestant voters as well, thus bringing to an end the episode of a confessionally oriented political party.

This viewpoint, however, obscures as much as it illuminates. At the simplest level, it does not tell the whole story of politics in Wilhelmine Germany. The decline of the Danish, French and Hanoverian parties was matched by the growth of the Polish nationalists and the emergence of a new regional party, the Bavarian Peasant League. More importantly, though, the assumption that confession or region were doomed to decline in importance as compared to social class or economic interest as a basis for voting behavior is simply not borne out by the developments of the late nineteenth and twentieth centuries. Whether considering the SPD vote at the end of the Wilhelmine era, the Nazi vote during the Weimar Republic, or the support for the interconfessional CDU in the Federal Republic, differences between the confessions are a more important determining factor than those between classes and even if regional parties as such have gradually disappeared after 1945 (although the Bavarian CSU is certainly a very large exception to this rule), regional differences in voting have remained perceptible in postwar Germany, even before unification in 1990 created newer and much larger ones. Confession or region have remained key features determining voting behavior after the decline of confessional or regional parties.

These considerations do suggest some outlines for conveying the results of the quantitative analysis. The idea of decline vs. persistence in the minority parties needs to be considered, to see whether these parties' support did peak in the 1870s, the period of the most intense governmental persecution and then declined, either sharply or gradually. However, we also need to get away from this version of posing the question, to go from net losses and gains to a broader consideration of the interchange between the minority parties and the other parties, or the non-voters. It might be that a consistent proportion of the vote concealed a pattern of losses and gains to different parties. Finally, the transition from persecution to toleration, from opposition party to at least potential supporter of the government needs to be evaluated, suggesting that the decade of the 1890s might come in for particular scrutiny.

Once again, without giving away all the conclusions in advance, I can

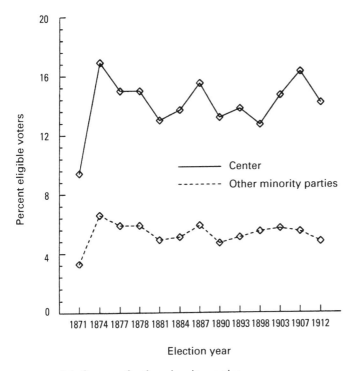

2.1 Support for the minority parties

make some preliminary observations about these issues. The decade of the 1890s was a period when the minorty party electorate was more unstable than at any other point in the history of the empire, with voters switching both among these minority parties and between them and other parties to a greater extent than they had previously or would do in the empire's twentieth-century general elections. This turmoil did ultimately have an effect on the ability of individual minority parties to retain consistent levels of support throughout the Wilhelmine era. Overall, though, this is little evidence of a long-term decline in support for these parties as a group, and a good deal to show that any losses among some groups of voters – and such losses certainly occurred after 1890 – were compensated for by gains from other groups.

A dynamic stability: the minority parties and the voters

Figure 2.1 provides a first consideration of global support for the minority parties.

The general election of 1874, held while the *Kulturkampf* was at its peak, and also the first time that voters in Alsace-Lorraine could cast ballots in Germany, marked the high point of the regional and national minority party vote, at 6.6% of the electorate. There was a second peak in 1887, at 5.9% of eligible voters. If you look hard, you can perceive a drop off in the minority vote after 1890. This decline, however, was not continuous; it was partially offset by a lesser fluctuation in the vote from election to election; and it is not very great in extent, the regional and national minority vote averaging 5.7% of eligible voters between 1874 and 1887 and 5.2% between 1890 and 1912. Individual minority parties may have had their ups and downs, but the proportion of German voters supporting such parties as a group changed little.

The figures for the Center certainly demonstrate the mobilizing effect of the *Kulturkampf*. The year 1871, when 9.4% of eligible voters chose the Center, was the party's electoral low point in the history of the empire, while 1874, when 16.9% did choose the party was its maximum. As a proportion of eligible voters, the Center vote rose 80% from 1871 to 1874, a percentage increase equivalent to the Social Democrats' great leap forward between 1887 and 1890. However, developments after 1874 do not fit a pattern either of decline or of persistence in support. One way to consider the curve would be to avoid looking for long-term trends and instead to point to three three peaks in voting support, in 1874, 1887, and 1907, that stand out against the other elections. Another way to look at the figure would be to suggest that the Center vote declined after 1874, with an interruption of this trend in the mid-1880s. This decline continued through the decade of the 1890s to a low point in 1898, with support picking up again in the empire's three twentieth-century general elections.

Refining these global figures means remembering that the minority parties were parties of minorities, that is to say they only appealed to certain, delineated groups of voters. This was most clearly the case with the Center Party, which was very closely tied to the Catholic Church. At the local level, the two were hard to distinguish. Clergy headed the local party organization or played a major role in it. They acted as campaign workers, giving speeches for the Center and, especially in its early years, handing out the ballots for it on election day. Even in Wilhelmine Germany, when the Center began to develop a more formal and elaborate party organization, local units tended to be based on parishes. Above all, the clergy made it known, formally and informally, that all good Catholics had a religious obligation to vote for the Center. Voting for another party, or even reading its newspaper, the faithful were given to understand, could mean a journey to hell, with turncoats sometimes sped on their way by the refusal of the sacraments. (If priests were handing out ballots at the polling place, it was not hard to identify Catholics voting for parties other than the Center, in spite of the nominal secrecy of the elections.) Such a stringent attitude was most common and most understandable during the *Kulturkampf*, when the church really was under attack and needed to rally all the faithful in its defense, but it began at the first elections in 1871, before the *Kulturkampf* had commenced, and continued to a greater or lesser extent throughout the entire history of the empire.[6]

This close connection between the clergy and the party was an obvious plus for the Center in receiving votes from Germany's devout, church-going Catholics, but it also ensured that the party, officially interconfessional, could not hope for any Protestant votes.[7] The proportion of Protestants voting for the Center was as high as 1% only in the 1871 elections, and that primarily because several of the Hanoverian particularists, whose supporters were primarily Protestants, ran as Center candidates (or at least votes for them were tallied as such) in that year.

Figure 2.1 thus tracks both the percentage of Catholics voting for the Center and the turnout of Protestants. Since Protestants voted for parties other than the Center, an increase in the turnout of Protestant voters would lower the Center percentage of all voters and a decline in Protestant turnout would increase the Center percentage of all voters, regardless of what Catholic voters did. To gain a more exact idea of the Center's support among its actual clientele, we should see the percentage of Catholic voters supporting it. There is, however, another point that needs to be considered, arising from the single member constituency, majority vote system of elections to the Imperial Reichstag.

---

[6] Besides the sources cited above (ch. 1, fn. 25), see Sperber, *Popular Catholicism*, p. 190; Sepainter, *Die Reichstagswahlen im Großherzogtum Baden*, pp. 206–8, 210–11; Ernst Otto Bräunche, *Parteien und Reichstagswahlen in der Rheinpfalz von der Reichsgründung 1871 bis zum Ausbruch des Ersten Weltkrieges 1914* (Speyer: Verlag der Pfälzischen Gesellschft zur Förderung der Wissenschaften, 1982), pp. 129–66; Peter Hattenkofer, *Regierende und Regierte, Wähler und Gewählte in der Oberpfalz 1870–1914* (Munich: Kommissions-buchhandlung R. Wölfe, 1979), pp. 94–104, 181, 201–4; Hiery, *Reichstagswahlen im Reichsland*, p. 419; Herbert Lepper, "Vom Honoriatiorenverein zur Parteiorganisation: Ein Beitrag zur 'Demokratisierung' des Zentrums im Rheinland 1890–1906," *Rheinische Vierteljahrsblätter* 48 (1984): 238–74, esp. pp. 271–74; *Mit Gott für Wahrheit, Freiheit und Recht: Quellen zur Organisation und Politik der Zentrumspartei und des politis-chen Katholizismus in Baden 1888–1914* ed. Hans-Jürgen Kremer (Stutgart: Verlag W. Kohlhammer, 1983), pp. 179–84, 188–89, 256–60; Hochberger, *Der Bayerische Bauernbund*, pp. 181–82, 186–87, 213; Christoph Weber, *"Eine starke, enggeschlossene Phalanx": Der politische Katholizismus und die erste deutsche Reichstagswahl 1871* (Essen: Klartext Verlag, 1992), passim; Bertram, *Die Wahlen zum Deutschen Reichstag im Jahre 1912*, pp. 194–96.

[7] Weber, *"Eine starke, enggeschlossene Phalanx"*, pp. 12–41, 123–39, provides good discus-sions of the gap between the Center's claim to interconfessionality and its Catholic con-fessional basis.

A number of heavily Catholic constituencies were the domain of the French or Polish national minorities, where the clergy called on the faithful to vote for the parties representing these groups and the Center often did not put up candidates. In addition, there were many constituencies where Catholics were a substantial minority so that the Center could have a strong presence but could generally not hope to elect a candidate on the first round of balloting. One option in these circumstances was to put up a candidate anyway, either with the intent of getting into a runoff (and hoping that enough Protestant voters would find the opposing party in the runoff even less palatable than the Center), or just to show the flag and collect the maximum number of votes. Another option, though, was for the Center politicians to renounce putting up a candidate and calling on Catholic voters to support another party's choice – depending on the political situation typically either one of the conservative or left-liberal parties.[8] The upshot was that the proportion of Catholic voters who had the possibility of voting for Center candidates varied considerably from election to election, from a high of 85% in 1907 to a low of 71% in 1887. Consequently, we need to consider not just the proportion of Catholics voting for Center candidates, but the proportion of Catholics choosing the Center in those constituencies where there were Center candidates for whom they could vote.

Figure 2.2 provides this distinction. The solid line gives the proportion of eligible Catholic voters in all Germany supporting the Center, the dashed one the proportion of eligible Catholic voters choosing the Center in those constituencies where the party put up candidates.

The lines in figure 2.2 bear a strong family relationship to their predecessor in figure 2.1, with the peaks of support for the Center in 1874, 1887, and 1907, a low point in 1898, and little evidence of a long term decline. The *Kulturkampf* elections of 1874 no longer appear as the very high point of the Center vote. In all of Germany, a greater proportion of Catholics voted for the Center in 1907 than in 1874, and in constituencies with Center candidates 1887 was clearly the maximum. We might follow the dashed line (marking Catholic support for the Center in those constituencies where it put up candidates) a bit further since it marks most clearly the relationship between the party and its clientele. The line

---

[8] For some examples of these strategies, see Carl Zangerl, "Courting the Catholic Vote: The Center Party in Baden 1903–1913," *Central European History* 10 (1977): 220–40; Thomas Mergel, "Christlicher Konservatismus in der Provinz: Politischer Katholizismus in Ostwestfalen 1887–1912," in Joachim Meynert, Josef Mooser, and Volker Rodekamp (eds.) *Unter Pickelhaube und Zylinder: Das östliche Westfalen im Zeitalter des Wilhelmismus 1881 bis 1914* (Bielefeld: Verlag für Regionalgeschichte, 1991), pp. 283–301; Bernd Liebert, *Politische Wahlen in Wiesbaden im Kaiserreich (1867–1918)* (Wiesbaden: Selbstverlag der Historischen Kommission für Nassau, 1988), pp. 163, 176–78.

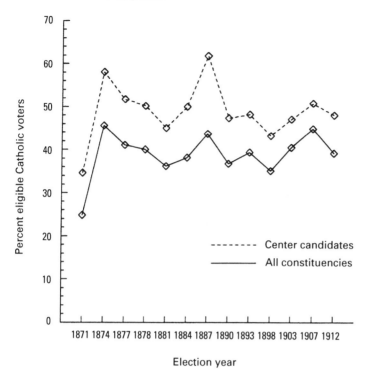

Election year

2.2 Catholic support for the Center

shows neither a pattern of stability nor decline, but rather indicates a bifurcation in Catholic voting patters between Bismarckian and Wilihelmine Germany. From 1871 to 1887, the percentage of eligible Catholic voters casting their ballot for the Center varied quite sharply from election to election, while in Wilhelmine Germany their support tended to be more stable, if overall at a slighly lower level than in the previous two decades.[9]

This contrast between volatility and stability also existed in regional terms. Figure 2.3 compares Catholic support for the Center in non-Prussian Germany (which, for Catholics, basically means Germany south of the Main River) with that in Prussia.

Prussian Catholics were much more consistent in voting for the Center than their co-religionists in the south. The decline in Center support during the 1890s and the revival of this support after the turn of the

[9] In constituencies with Center candidates, an average of 50.2% of eligible Catholic voters supported the party between 1871 and 1887, with a standard deviation of 8.2, while between 1890 and 1912, the average was 47.4%, with a standard deviation of 2.2.

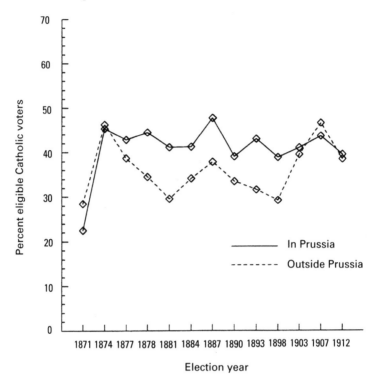

2.3 Catholic Center voters by region

century were both primarily voter movements of the Catholics of south-ern Germany. Not only were Prussia's Catholics more consistent about voting for the Center, they were generally more loyal to it as well, support-ing it more strongly than their south German counterparts in ten of the thirteen general elections in the history of the *Kaiserreich*.[10]

The national and regional minority parties also had a limited clientele, albeit one limited in a different way than was the Center's. One way to refine a consideration of their votes is to look at their potential electorate, the proportion of German citizens who had the opportunity to vote for these parties, and then at the proportion of voters in those constituencies who cast their ballot for the minority parties. Figure 2.4 does this, the

[10] Figure 2.3 gives Center support of all Catholic voters in the two regions, and not support in just those constituencies where the Center nominated candidates, because that would have reduced the number of observations to the point of unreliability. However, the pro-portion of Catholic voters having the opportunity to vote for the Center did not differ materially between Prussia and non-Prussian Germany, so differences in support cannot be explained in that way.

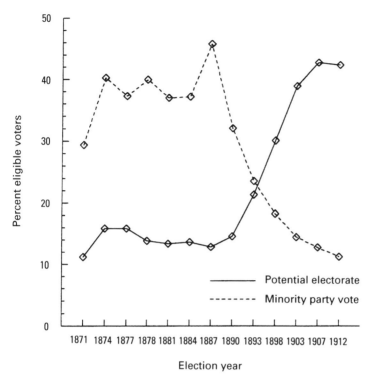

2.4 Regional/national minority vote

solid line giving the potential electorate of the national and regional minority parties, and the dashed line the vote they received in those constituencies where they put up candidates.

The contrast with figure 2.1 is quite striking. While the national and regional minority parties received a more or less constant proportion of all votes cast throughout Germany, this constant proportion conceals very considerable changes in the number and range of candidacies of such parties. From 1874 to 1890, a steady 13 to 16% of the electorate had the opportunity to vote for the candidate of a national or regional minority party. In constituencies with such candidates, the parties did quite well, their share of eligible voters taking two sharp jogs up, in 1874 and in 1887.

After 1890, a completely new pattern of minority party candidacies developed. An ever-growing proportion of the electorate had the opportunity to vote for these parties but their share of voters declined in all the constituencies where they nominated candidates. There are two interrelated reasons for this trend. One is the growth of new minority parties, which did not exist before 1890, above all the Bavarian Peasant League, but also including more exotic groups, such as the Lithuanian and Masurian nationalists. The new parties meant more candidacies, and thus a greater proportion of the electorate with the chance to vote for such a minority party candidacy, but in contrast to the Polish or French nationalists, they were less likely to receive very large numbers of votes, thus producing a decline in the overall proportion of votes cast.

The second reason is the changing nature of the Polish nationalist movement. In Bismarckian Germany, the Polish nationalist party was largely confined to the Prussian province of Posen, and some areas in neighboring West Prussia. Unlike the French nationalists, who put up candidates across Alsace-Lorraine, their Polish counterparts renounced campaigning in other areas with an ethnically Polish population, particularly Upper Silesia, conceding these constituencies to the Center, with whom they cooperated closely. Beginning tentatively in the 1890s, and more aggressively after the turn of the century, the Polish nationalists broke out of both the geographic limitations on their movement and their tacit agreement with the Center. They put up their own candidates in Upper Silesia, gaining the support of a good portion of the (Polish speaking) Catholic clergy and aggressively challenging the Catholic political party. Of the twelve constituencies in Upper Silesia, the Polish nationalists took the five heavily Polish constituencies in 1907, the high point of their success. As Polish-speaking German subjects left their impoverished agricultural homelands in the eastern part of the monarchy to look for work in the rapidly growing urban and industrial centers, such as Berlin, Hamburg, and particularly the Ruhr Basin, nationalists organized Polish trade unions, savings banks, choral societies, and social clubs, founded Polish newspapers, and nominated Polish candidates for the Reichstag. Unlike the circumstances in Upper Silesia, the Polish nationalists could never hope to obtain a majority in these constituencies, but they could show the nationalist flag, with results between 1 and 6% of votes cast.[11]

These global accounts of the minority party vote offer at best an extremely modest confirmation of the thesis that their support peaked early on in the history of the empire, during the 1870s, and declined after that. The minority vote was slightly lower in Wilhelmine than in Bismarckian Germany, but the difference between the two eras was

---

[11] Helmut Neubach, "Parteien und Politiker in Oberschlesien der Bismarckzeit," *Jahrbuch der Schlesischen Friedrich-Wilhelms Universität zu Breslau* 13 (1968): 193–231; Ronald Ross, *Beleaguered Tower: The Dilemma of Political Catholicism in Wilhelmine Germany* (Notre Dame and London: University of Notre Dame Press, 1976), pp. 68–74, 180; Christoph Kleßmann, *Polnische Bergarbeiter im Ruhrgebiet* (Göttingen: Vandenhoeck & Ruprecht, 1978); Schmädeke, *Wählerbewegung*, pp. 525–39.

Table 2.1 *Subsequent votes of minority party voters (percent)*

	Election year pairs			
Vote at next General election	1871/74– 1877/78	1878/81– 1884/87	1887/90– 1893/98	1898/03– 1907/12
Conservatives	3	4	5	3
Liberals	5	4	7	8
Minority parties	79	77	68	78
Social Democrats	0	0	4	4
Non-voters	13	15	17	6
Total	100	100	101	99

extremely small, and there was definitely no steady downward trend in support from election to election. Consistency or fluctuation without any long-term trend seems to be a more apt description of voting patterns for these parties. Yet just because the percentage totals of a party or parties remain fairly constant in the long run, it does not follow that the party vote is identical in this period. Instead, what the minority parties seem to demonstrate is a series of changes that balance each other out, leaving largely the same results. The proportion of Catholic voters supporting the Center stayed virtually the same over the decades, but in Bismarckian Germany this support fluctuated considerably, while in the Wilhelmine era it remained more constant. The national and regional minority parties enjoyed a substantial share of a fairly constant and narrowly delineated proportion of the electorate before 1890. After then, new minority parties emerged, some older ones lost votes, and others launched more frequent candidacies, but the average percentage support for each candidacy declined, the upshot being that the national and regional proportion of the entire electorate remained almost constant at around 5%. Overall, one might speak of a dynamic stability in the minority parties' vote; the further analysis of this vote will elucidate more carefully its components and place them in different periods of the empire's history.

The party loyalty of the minority electorate

Table 2.1, constructed along the lines of table 1.3, gives the votes of minority party voters, averaged by decade, for the second of each pair of general elections in the *Kaiserreich*.

Minority party voters were loyal to their choices, staying with their parties from one election to the next, this loyalty clearly demonstrating the strength of ethnic, religious or regional identities for the electoral process. The figures show no long-term decline in such loyalties, but the decade of the 1890s clearly stands out as the period when these voters were least likely to stay with their previous choice. Minority party voters switching to the Social Democrats, something they had never done before 1890, were the reason for much of this change. The most spectacular example of this was the election in 1890 of a Social Democrat to represent Strasbourg in the Reichstag, an unprecedented victory for a German political party on French terrain. The rest of the decade saw the steady growth of the SPD in Alsace-Lorraine and in Hanover, gaining ground at the expense of the particularists.[12] Minority party voters also switched in modestly growing numbers to other party groupings during the 1890s and to non-voters as well.

In another respect, the 1890s represented a turning point. In the two previous decades, the chief option for minority party voters who did not continue to support their party was non-voting. A very small percentage switched to other parties, a number of whom were probably Catholic voters who would usually have supported the Center, had that party not renounced its own candidate in favor of a conservative or progressive. In effect, the options for Catholics and the regional and ethnic minorities were either their party or none. In the 1890s, the proportion of minority party voters choosing other parties at a subsequent election doubled in comparison to the two previous decades, and this in a period when there were more minority party candidates then ever before. Even after 1900, when voter loyalty to minority parties returned to levels it had experienced in Bismarckian Germany, those minority party voters who were not loyal were more likely to switch to another party than to abstain, by a margin of about 2.5:1.

Voters were thus drifting away from the minority parties in Wilhelmine Germany, yet these parties were able to maintain their vote totals, an example of the dynamic stability mentioned above. Table 2.2, which gives averages by decade of the previous votes of minority party voters for each pair of elections (along the lines of table 1.1), shows how this was possible.

These figures demonstrate that there was a considerable amount of voter movement to the minority parties, both from the other parties – with the exception of the Social Democrats – and from non-voters and new entrants to the electorate. In the first decade of Imperial Germany, it was the other parties which provided a substantial number of minority party voters; after the mid-1880s, such contributions were clearly out-

---

[12] Hiery, *Reichstagswahlen im Reichsland*, pp. 248–80; Aschoff, *Welfische Bewegung*, pp. 186, 191–94.

Table 2.2 *Previous votes of minority party voters (percent)*

Vote at previous elections	Election year pairs				
	1871/74–1874/77	1877/788–1878/81	1881/84–1884/87	1887/90–1893/98	1898/03–1907/12
Conservatives	7	5	1	3	2
Liberals	11	9	2	9	4
Minority parties	64	79	71	65	71
Social democrats	0	0	0	0	1
Non-voters	15	7	22	13	10
Net new voters	4	—[a]	3	10	12
Total	101	100	99	100	100

Note:
[a] The electorate hardly increased in size at all between 1877 and 1881, so there is no figure for net new voters for the 1878 and 1881 elections.

Table 2.3 *Voter swings and the minority party electorate 1871/74–1907/12 (percent)*

Vote at previous election	Election year pairs				
	1871/74–1874/77	1877/78–1878/81	1881/84–1884/87	1887/90–1893/98	1898/03–1907/12
Conservatives	1.4/0.3	0.9/0.7	0.2/1.0	0.6/0.9	0.5/0.7
Liberals	2.3/1.1	1.6/0.5	0.5/0.8	1.7/1.2	0.8/1.5
Minority parties	13.5	15.1	14.2	11.8	14.4
Social Democrats	0.1/0	0/0.1	0/0	0.1/0.7	0.2/0.8
Non-voters	3.2/2.3	1.4/4.2	4.5/1.7	2.4/3.0	2.1/1.2
Net new voters	−0.2	—[a]	0	0.9	0.9

Note:
[a] The electorate hardly increased in size at all between 1877 and 1881, so there is no figure for net new voters for the 1878 and 1881 elections.

weighed by the mobilization of previous non-voters and new entrants to the electorate. This was particularly the case in the twentieth-century general elections, when support drawn from previous non-voters and net new voters outweighed support drawn from the other parties by about three to one.

Finally, table 2.3, by tallying voter swings to the minority parties allows us to consider the relative proportions of voters going to the minority parties, leaving them and staying loyal to them. As with table 1.4, which gave similar information for the Social Democrats, all figures in this table are percentages of the entire electorate.

The network of gains and losses for the minority parties is complex, varying substantially from period to period, but some general conclusions can be drawn from these figures. The earliest elections of the *Kaiserreich* (during the 1870s, when the *Kulturkampf* raged fiercely and the government's hostility to the Catholic church spilled over onto the national minorities and even the Protestant particularists in Hanover) were good ones for the minority parties. Official persecution clearly helped mobilize voters and win over those who had voted for other parties.

From the late 1870s onward, the ability of the minority parties to gain support from the voters of the other parties declined as these parties reached their "natural" limits. The Center, for instance, could win over a large majority of the previous Catholic voters of the liberal parties, but the confessional appeal needed to gain the Catholic votes ensured that none of the Protestants in the liberal electorate would join them. Similarly, the Polish, French or Danish nationalists could not hope to gain any voters who identified themselves as Germans. Of all the minority parties in this period, the one with the potentially most expandable electorate was the Hanoverian particularists, who could often pick up voters from other parties who wished to cast a protest vote against government policies and the parties supporting them. Even here there were limits, particularly among those voters in the province of Hanover who lacked, as many of them did, fond memories of the pre-1866 kingdom.[13] Having thus attracted about as many voters from other parties as they could by the end of the 1870s, after about 1880 the minority parties had nowhere to go but down. Table 2.3 shows this balance of party switchers running, with occasional exceptions, from neutral to increasingly negative from the 1880s until the First World War.

Returning to the theme of dynamic stability, we need to balance these voter interchanges between the minority parties and the other parties with those between the minority parties and the non- and new voters. In the decade 1878–87, it was the mobilization and demobilization of non-voters that largely determined the change in the vote for these parties, particularly the Center. The pattern of peaks and valleys in the Center vote during the decade 1877–87 (as shown in figures 2.1–2.3) reflects previous Center voters no longer going to the polls and then being persuaded to come out and vote again.

[13] Aschoff, *Welfische Bewegung*, p. 45. Probably the main reason that the Hessian particularists never achieved the success of their Hanoverian counterparts was that the pre-1866 Principality of Hessen was a rotten, corrupt, oppressive, and deeply unpopular state, thoroughly lacking in nostalgia appeal.

Table 2.4 *Support for the regional and national minority parties by confession (percent)*

	Election years			
Confession	1871–78[a]	1881–87	1890–98	1903–12
Protestant	2.6 (3.0)	2.4	2.7	2.1
Catholic	10.1 (11.3)	10.6	9.3	10.9
All	5.4 (6.0)	5.3	5.1	5.3

Note:
[a] Figures in parenthesis are averages for the election years 1874–78

The increasing steadiness in the Center Party's vote after 1890 was a result of the decline in the large swings between minority parties and non-voters in Wilhelmine Germany. Particularly after 1900, when the minority parties persistently lost voters to the other parties, the ability to mobilize previous non-voters and new entrants into the electorate were crucial factors in stabilizing the minority party vote. The above average support of the net new voters enjoyed by the minority parties at the beginning of the twentieth century – new voters entering the electorate, and voters moving to large industrial centers, in Upper Silesia, the Ruhr and Saar basins and Lorraine – is testimony to the continuing significance of ethnic and religious identities for the electoral process in a period when historians have often seen them as declining in importance.[14]

The calculations of voter transition probabilities on which these remarks are based unfortunately do not allow us to consider the movement of voters within the minority parties, although on a regional level in some of the Wilhelmine elections they were clearly considerable. In 1898, for instance, the Center Party was the choice of 41% of the eligible voters in the twelve Upper Silesian constituencies, while the Polish nationalists received no votes at all.[15] By 1907, on the other hand, the Center and Polish nationalists each received the votes of about 24% of eligible voters. In the 1890s and 1900s, there were shifts of votes of comparable magnitude among the minority parties in Lower Bavaria and Alsace-Lorraine.

If we consider the confessional bases of support for the minority parties we can gain some indirect information about these vote shifts. Table 2.4

[14] A comparable, if briefer and more vaguely stated argument is to be found in Schmädeke, *Wählerbewegung*, pp. 265–67, 643; see also, Winkler, *Sozialstruktur*, pp. 331–32.
[15] Admittedly, in one constituency, there were two opposing Center candidates, one of whom was closer to the Polish nationalists. But even including those votes would bring the Polish nationalist total to just 4% of votes cast.

Table 2.5a *Catholic vote in constituencies with Center Party candidates*
(percent)

Party	Election year 1871–78[a]	1881–87	1890–98	1903–12
Center	49 (53)	52	46	49
Other minority parties	0 (0)	0	3	7
Other parties	20 (19)	12	15	23
Non-voters	31 (28)	36	36	22
Total	100 (100)	100	100	101
Percent Catholic electorate	77 (79)	76	79	85

Note:
[a] Figures in parenthesis are averages for 1874–78

gives the proportion of different confessional groups supporting the national and regional minorities, averaged by decade.

Not surprisingly, given the confessional composition of the minority groups, a substantially greater proportion of Catholic voters supported the regional and national minority parties than did Protestants. Although the numbers are very small, and conclusions drawn from them are necessarily speculative and unreliable, it would seem that Protestant support for the minority parties was declining in the first decade of the twentieth century, while Catholic support was increasing. The declining voting totals in this period of the chief Protestant minority groupings, the Hanoverian particularists and the Danish nationalists, while the regional and national minority party vote overall was slightly increasing, certainly supports the supposition.

Protestant voters deserting the regional and national minorities for other party groupings went off to the Social Democrats, or one of the liberal or conservative parties; like other Protestant voters, they never chose the Center. Consequently, if we want to consider vote switching within the minority parties, we need to focus on Catholic voters. Table 2.5 does this by giving the preferences of Catholic voters, averaged by decade, and separated into two groups of constituencies: those with Center Party candidates and those without.

Two patterns emerge from these tables, both important to understanding the dynamic stability of the minority parties' vote.

First, there is the relationship between the Center and the other minority parties. In Bismarckian Germany, they did not compete for Catholic

Table 2.5b *Catholic vote in constituencies without Center Party candidates (percent)*

	Election year			
Party	1871–78[a]	1881–87	1890–98	1903–12
Minority parties	47 (55)	44	32	37
Other parties	29 (23)	26	31	43
Non-voters	25 (22)	31	36	21
Total	101 (100)	101	99	101
Percent Catholic electorate	20	24	21	15

Note:
[a] Figures in parenthesis are averages for years 1874–78

voters: no minority party candidates were put up in constituencies where a Center candidate was running. This state of affairs reflected an implicit and often open cooperation between the Center and the other minority parties, especially the Polish and French nationalists.[16] Indeed, in the elections during the *Kulturkampf* era of the 1870s, the pattern of the Catholic vote was virtually identical in the two groups of constituencies: for Catholic voters, the Center and the other minority parties were interchangeable. In Wilhelmine Germany, on the other hand, the Center and the other minority parties increasingly went head to head. In the 1890s, just 3% of eligible Catholic voters chose these other minority parties in constituencies with Center candidates, but those 3% helped reduce the Center share of eligible Catholic voters to its lowest level in the history of the empire. Between 1903 and 1912, an average of 7% of eligible Catholic voters in constituencies with Center candidates voted for the regional and national minorities, as against the 37% of Catholic voters choosing these parties in constituencies without Center candidates. However, 85% of all Catholic voters resided in constituencies with Center candidates, so more than half of all the votes cast by Catholics for the regional and national minority parties were in constituencies where those parties stood in opposition to the Center. While cooperation between the Center and the other minority parties had not been completely abandoned after 1890, the two were increasingly rivals for the Catholic vote.

[16] This was also true in the Prussian Province of Hanover, where the Hanoverian particularists conceded to the Center the one heavily Catholic constituency and the Center called on the Catholic minority elsewhere to vote for the particularists. Aschoff, *Welfische Bewegung*, pp. 101–3, 108, 143–47.

The second point concerns the Catholic non-voters. As one might expect, Catholic turnout was very high in the 1870s, as the faithful came to the polls to defend their endangered religion (or the national cause closely associated with that religion), but it dropped off noticeably in the two subsequent decades. Catholic turnout then rose again in the empire's three twentieth-century general elections, exceeding even the quite high figures seen in the 1870s. The result of this increasing turnout was that all parties – the Center, the national and regional minorities, conservatives, liberals and Social Democrats – received a higher proportion of Catholic votes.

Organization and orientation of the minority parties

Let us now try to combine the results from the analysis of voter transition probabilities with those obtained from considering the confessional basis of the minority party votes and integrate these with the historical scholarship on the Center and the other minority parties. In general, the conclusions reached from the quantitative analysis and from the scholarly literature on the minority parties in Bismarckian Germany tend to converge. For the post-1890 period, on the other hand, the statistical results, if not completely upsetting the standard picture, at least suggest the need for some qualifications and revisions.

Intransigent opposition to Bismarck's regime

The returns from the 1870s certainly underscore the importance of the *Kulturkampf*, or to put it more broadly, the struggle of the government of the German Empire, a government influenced by liberal-nationalist ideals (with both liberalism and nationalism understood in a strongly Protestant way) against what the regime and the political parties endorsing it saw as the internal enemies of the newly created national unity: religious and national minorities, and particularist adherents of the state of affairs as they existed before the events of 1866–71. Voters belonging to these groups were not impressed by the campaign against them; they rallied in large numbers to the political parties representing the minority interests, these parties mobilizing both previous non-voters and the supporters of other party groupings, particularly the liberals. Just as the authorities made relatively little distinction between German Catholics who voted for the Center, and Polish or French Catholics, who voted for their minority nationalist parties – for Bismarck and the liberals, they were all *Reichsfeinde*, enemies of the nation – so the voters for these parties treated them as close to interchangeable. The different minority parties did not put up candidates in the same constituency and Catholic voters, in particular, were as likely to support Center candidates in constituencies where they ran as they were to vote for candidates of the other minority parties in constituencies where they stood for office.

Moving on to the less well-studied terrain of the 1880s, we might begin by noting that this decade saw no new organizational initiatives on the part of the minority parties. If anything, their early efforts at mass organization were followed by a period of stagnation and decline. The Catholic mass associations created in the early 1870s and prohibited by the authorities during the *Kulturkampf* were not revived. Hanoverian particularists made no special effort to expand their organization, and while there were efforts in that direction among the Polish nationalists, they proved abortive.[17] Of course, new organizational initiatives were really not needed, since, as the electoral analysis suggests, the voting patterns for the minority parties created in the 1870s remained the same in the subsequent decade. The minority parties neither gained many voters from other parties nor lost many to them. Changes in the minority party vote from 1878 to 1887 were due primarily to these parties' voters either dropping out of the electorate, as they did in the late 1870s and early 1880s, or returning to it, as they did in the second half of the 1880s.

Such a continuity of voting patterns lends credence to the contention that the basically oppositional stance of the minority parties, first adopted during the the 1870s, continued into the following decade. Even when Bismarck began gradually dismantling at least some of the apparatus of religious and ethnic persecution erected in the previous decade and turned governmental policy away from liberalism, and even when the minority parliamentarians supported his government on some social and economic questions (such as the imposition of protective tariffs), a sharp difference between these parties and the government remained.[18] The different minority parties continued their cooperation and their leaders continued to be able at crucial moments to mobilize their supporters in large numbers. Indeed, if we just consider the clientele of the minority parties – Catholic voters in constituencies with Center candidates, the electorate in constituencies where regional and national minority party candidates stood for office (figures 2.2 and 2.4) – we find that the

[17] Cf. Nipperdey, *Organisation der deutschen Parteien*, p. 274; Aschoff, *Welfische Bewegung*, pp. 242–44; Blanke, *Prussian Poland*, pp. 102–4. There were no organizational initiatives among the French nationalists in Alsace-Lorraine, but they had always been a loose grouping of local notables, with little in the way of formal organization. Hiery, *Reichstagswahlen im Reichsland*, pp. 136–75, 200–19 and passim.
[18] On this point, cf. Anderson, *Windhorst*, pp. 296–358; Hiery, *Reichstagswahlen im Reichsland*, pp. 200–19.

elections of 1887 marked the very highest point of support for these parties in the entire history of the empire. In many ways, one could understand the entire Bismarckian era as a period when the minority parties successfully rallied their clientele against the government, the chief difference between elections during these years being the extent of the feelings of urgency the parties created among their supporters and their consequent willingness to turn out and vote.

A difficult reorientation after 1890

These aligning features of the minority vote of Bismarckian Germany did not vanish after 1890, but they became less consistent. The clash between a centralizing, nationalist regime and its supporters – at some times and places both supporters and regime were more liberal, at others more conservative – against national, regional and religious minorities could continue to be a main theme of general elections, as was the case in 1907, but other issues were increasingly competing for voters' attention. Distributing the growing burden of taxation, or the vexed and linked issues of protection for agriculture and cost of living in urban areas, cut across the old alignment between the central government and the minority opposition, often dividing supporters of the minority parties among themselves and opening possibilities for other parties, particularly the Social Democrats, but also the liberals, to gain votes from the previous minority clientele. This former alignment was also no longer an efficient mobilizing axis of politics because the minority parties themselves were no longer always in opposition to the government.

This was primarily a result of the changing position of the Center. In Bismarckian Germany, the party had acted as a sort of parliamentary big brother for the smaller regional and national groupings, leading a joint oppositional bloc. After 1890, Catholic politicians sought and often (once again with exceptions for specific times and places) obtained cooperation with the executive branch of government. The other minority parties, after some internal division, generally rejected this policy of cooperation and remained in opposition. The Bavarian Peasant League was in fact a regional minority party that came into existence at least in part because the Center had abandoned its oppositional politics.

The upshot was that the Center and the minority parties were increasingly at odds, and ever more likely to run candidates against each other, a development that began in the 1890s in Bavaria. By 1898, the the Bavarian Peasant League was going head to head with the Center in all the predominantly Catholic constituencies, winning three of six in Lower Bavaria (the peasant movement's stronghold). The three elections of the twentieth century saw this development continue and expand in extent, as the Polish nationalists were increasingly aggressive about their campaigning, abandoning their former tacit agreement with the Center. However, this was also the period in which the Center itself expanded the range of its candidacies, reaching the highest proportion of the Catholic population of the empire, and, in particular, expanding into Alsace-Lorraine, successfully campaigning against the French nationalists. Even in the Prussian province of Hanover, where the Center had long lived amicably with the predominantly Protestant Hanoverian particularists, the two parties began competing in some constituencies and were on increasingly hostile terms.[19]

All these developments – the declining salience of the previous main campaigning themes for the minority parties, the growing importance of issues dividing the minority electorate and offering more possibilities to competing parties, and the growing competition among minority parties who were, in effect, cannibalizing each other's voters – would seem to make the Wilhelmine era a period of at least incipient decline for the minority parties, as most of the scholarly literature suggests. Yet this decline does not seem to show up in these parties' vote totals, which suggest a dynamic stability over the years 1890–1912, with votes lost at one election regained later on. Tables 2.3 and 2.5 offer an explanation of how this could happen. Overall, minority parties lost voters to other parties and voting support shifted from one minority party to another, but these losses could be made up by mobilizing new voters and previous non-voters. To do this, the minority parties needed to retain as much as possible their former strengths, their close connection with religious, regional or ethnic identities, while at the same time reorganizing themselves for an era of more aggressive election campaigning, a more varied palette of issues and a substantially greater turnout.

The party accomplishing this on the most massive scale and with the greatest effect was the Center. The 1890s saw the creation or the expansion and the centralized organization on a national level of a wide variety of Catholic social and economic organizations. Heading the list were those associations speaking to the largest social groups, whose disaffection from the Center would have been politically the most dangerous: the Christian Peasant League, the Catholic Workers Associations and the Christian Trade Unions (this last technically interconfessional, but with Protestants just a very small minority of its members). In addition, there

---

[19] On these developments, see the sources cited above (n. 11) and Hochberger, *Der bayerische Bauernbund*; Hiery, *Reichstagswahlen im Reichsland*, pp. 92–96, 331–32, 338–45; Aschoff, *Welfische Bewegung*, pp. 195–96, 222–39.

were a wide variety of organizations for small business and other elements of the urban middle class.

In a sense capping this pyramid of socioeconomic organizations was the People's Association for Catholic Germany, a group whose membership exceeded 800,000 by the eve of the First World War, not far from the 1 million members of the SPD. The modest dues paid by the members enabled the organization's central office in the Rhenish textile town of Mönchengladbach to issue a constant stream of pamphlet literature supporting the Center Party's position on social and economic issues, and attacking its enemies, above all the Social Democrats. Having, in effect, created a permanent election campaign for the Center, the People's Association also trained its campaign workers, with its yearly courses covering important social, economic and political questions, as well as social insurance and trade-union law. There were thousands of participants in such courses, many of whom went on to become officials of the Christian Trade Unions, and as such to play a major role in retaining support for the Center.[20]

This was an impressive organizational effort, yet in many ways the most impressive part of it is that it was accomplished without loosening the close ties between the clergy and the Center and without fundamentally altering the party's leadership or organizational structure. Rather than pushing priests aside politically, the new associations offered them an additional arena of activity, the clergy playing an important role in the founding and leading of such groups, at both the national and the local level. We can follow this point a bit further by noting that these Catholic social and economic organizations were not formally affiliated with the Center, but were started and directed by Center politicians, both lay and clerical.

A few regional and local exceptions aside, before 1914 the Center never developed a party organization with a dues-paying membership, a party leadership elected by it, or a full-time, paid party staff. The electoral business of the party, the nomination of candidates for the Reichstag and the planning of election campaigns, continued to be, with some regional exceptions, as it had been since 1871, largely the work of local and regional committees of Catholic notables. After the turn of the century it was enhanced on an ad hoc basis by the cooptation of individuals representing

---

[20] Horstwalter Heitzer, *Der Volksverein für das katholische Deutschland im Kaiserreich 1890–1918* (Mainz: Matthias Grünwald, 1979); Hans-Jürgen Kremer, "Der Volksverein für das Katholische Deutschland in Baden 1890–1933," *Freiburger Diözesan-Archiv* 104 (1984): 208–80; Eric Brose, *Christian Labor and the Politics of Frustration in Imperial Germany* (Washington: Catholic University of America Press, 1985); Loth, *Katholiken im Kaiserreich*, pp. 39–98; Mittmann, *Fraktion und Partei*, pp. 164–94.

the peasant leagues, the People's Association and other Catholic organizations. Such an arrangement allowed these groups to provide at least part of
the financing and manpower required in the increasingly expensive and
elaborate national election campaigns at the beginning of the twentieth
century, while at the same time minimizing the internally divisive consequences of the social and economic questions they addressed.[21]

It is tempting to understand the rebound of the Center Party vote in the
first decade of the twentieth century as the result of these organizational
realignments, which preserved the previous strengths of the Center – its
close connection to the clergy and to Catholic religious identity – while
adding on the ability to deal with social and economic issues and to
engage in more encompassing and aggressive electioneering. Both the
electoral analysis and the literature on the Center and its competitors
point in this direction. As figure 2.3 shows, the rebound in Catholic
support for the Center, like the decline in the preceding decade, occurred
primarily in non-Prussian Germany, and developments in Alsace-
Lorraine and Bavaria – two areas where the Center did well in this period
– certainly support this notion. The rapidly growing vote totals of the
Center in Alsace-Lorraine reflected the activities of the People's
Association and the Catholic Workers Associations, which inspired the
younger Catholic clergy there, moving them away from their elders'
support of French nationalism (the victory of anti-clericalism in French
politics in the wake of the Dreyfus Affair also helped in this regard) and
enabling them to challenge the political power of the Francophile
industrialists of Lorraine, one of the long-term pillars of the French
nationalist party. Center politicians in Bavaria aggressively founded
Christian Peasant Leagues, led by the secondary school teacher Georg
Heim, who, to the astonishment of the authorities, pedalled his bicycle up
and down mountainous country roads, going from the founding meeting
of one local group to the next. Parish clergy readily endorsed his work and
chaired the organizations. This combination of the associations and clerical support for them played a major role in driving back the influence of
the Bavarian Peasant League and reviving a rural Center vote that by
1898 had seemed seriously endangered.[22]

---

[21] On these points, see more generally, Nipperdey, *Die Organisation der deustchen Parteien*,
pp. 268–85; and three good case studies: Lepper, "Vom Honoriatiorenverein zur
Parteiorganisation," Manfred Friedrich, "Die Parteitage des Zentrums in Bayern,"
Zeitschrift für Bayerische Landesgeschichte 36 (1973): 834–76, and Werner Chrobak,
"Politische Parteien, Verbände und Vereine in Regesnburg 1869–1914," *Verhandlungen
des Historischen Vereins für Oberpfalz und Regensburg* 119 (1979): 137–223; 120 (1980):
211–384 and 121 (1981): 183–284, here 120 (1980): 257–58, 261–71, 304–6.

[22] Hiery, *Reichstagswahlen im Reichsland*, pp. 338–45, 353, 423–24; Hochberger, *Der
Bayerische Bauernbund*, pp. 180–90; Hattenkofer, *Regierende und Regierte*, pp. 180–84.

The point of these remarks is not to replace the narrative of stagnation or decline with one of advance and triumph. In many urban and industrial areas – Munich, Augsburg, Würzburg, the Rhine-Main region, the lower Rhine Valley, the Ruhr Basin and Upper Silesia – the Center Party continued to lose ground after the turn of the century. Here, the new Catholic social and economic organizations were able to moderate and slow the decline of the Center, not prevent or reverse it.[23] If these organizations helped the Center to compete successfully in elections centering on social and economic issues, the party still did best when such questions did not come to the fore. The peak of the Center revival came in the general elections of 1907, in which political alignments (discussed in chapter 5) were closer to the elections of Bismarckian Germany, pitting minority groups against nationalist initiatives from the government and its supporters, than they were to other Wilhelmine elections, whose campaigns were oriented more toward questions of taxation, farm prices, and the cost of living.

Much of what was said about the Center applies to the Polish nationalists as well: the expansion of the range of candidacies and the creation of subsidiary social and economic organizations supporting the party without disruptively restructuring it, with the simultaneous retention of earlier bases of support, particularly the involvement of the clergy. In some ways unique to the Polish nationalists, though, was an intellectual reorientation that accompanied the organizational one, and provided the basis for their single greatest success after the turn of the century – the advances in Upper Silesia. Prior to the 1890s, the Polish nationalist movement in Germany had worked within the nineteenth-century tradition calling for the revival of the pre-partition Polish kingdom in its boundaries of 1772. Upper Silesia had then been part of Prussia, indeed had not been part of Poland since the Middle Ages, so Polish nationalists had renounced any political activity there, in spite of the region's large Polish-speaking population.

The last decade of the nineteenth century saw the growth and rapid development of a "national democracy," a new, ethnically oriented (and frequently racist and anti-Semitic) Polish nationalism in Germany and throughout the Polish-speaking areas of Europe. Coupled with and closely related to the increasing influence of an urban, Polish middle class on a political party previously dominated by the nobility and the Catholic clergy, this nationalism rejected notions of historically based rights, whether the boundaries of the pre-partition Polish kingdom or the guar-

---

[23] On this point, cf. Rohe, Jäger and Dorow, "Politische Gesellschaft und politische Kultur," pp. 461–62, 469.

antees to the Polish minorities made in the Treaty of Vienna. After embittered political infighting lasting through much of the 1890s, national democrats increasingly gained the upper hand in the Polish nationalist party, largely because of the failure of the policy of cooperation with the German government proposed by the more traditionalist and moderate wing of the party. With a return to intransigent opposition and an increasingly confrontational political stance around the turn of the century, Polish nationalists laid claim to representation in all areas with a Polish-speaking population – and not without success and popular endorsement, as the election results demonstrated.[24]

Here as well, however, we can see the preservation of older forms of political alignment within a new political orientation. Polish nationalists may have rejected their previous close cooperation with the Center Party, but they continued to play on the Catholic loyalties of the Polish-speaking population, as is apparent from the comments of the *Wiarus Polski* (*The Polish Messenger*), the Polish nationalist newspaper in the Ruhr industrial area. Attacking the Center Party, it announced "The Polish people know these German and Catholic gentlemen very well and say of them: Every German is a hidden Lutheran."[25]

In contrast to the successful reorientation and reorganization of the Center and the Polish nationalists, the two other main minority parties, the French nationalists and the Hanoverian particularists, seemed stuck in the past. Refusing to create any permanently existing party organization or engage in the mass electioneering of the early twentieth century, and instead continuing to rely on the influence of the informally organized Francophile notables, the French nationalists steadily lost votes in this period, dropping from 33% of eligible voters and ten of Alsace-Lorraine's fifteen constituencies in 1898, to 21% of eligible voters and just three seats in 1912.[26]

The Hanoverians, in contrast, did try to improve their political organization, if belatedly (their efforts only really getting going after 1900), founding both particularist social clubs and constituency-level party associations, sometimes including a paid, full-time party secretary. At one point, they even created a party school, to train members in public speaking. Their example shows that organization alone did not suffice, that issues counted decisively as well. For younger voters who had grown up under Prussian rule, the resurrection of the pre-1866 Hanoverian kingdom seemed an increasingly irrelevant issue. Social and economic

---

[24] Blanke, *Prussian Poland*, chs. 6 and 8; Kaminski, *Polish Publicists*, pp. 234–35 and passim.
[25] Cited in Rohe, Jäger and Dorow, "Politische Gesellschaft und politische Kultur," p. 470.
[26] On the decline of French nationalist politics in Alsace-Lorraine after 1890, see Hiery, *Reichstagswahlen im Reichsland*, pp. 248–402.

concerns were ever more important to voters, as can be seen from the growth in the province of both the Social Democrats and the main farmers' special interest group, the Agrarian League. Efforts of the particularists to modernize their ideology, to create a nationwide federalist-conservative party led to nothing, above all because there were few Germans outside of Hanover interested in such schemes.[27]

Of course, the revival of an eighteenth-century Polish kingdom was an even more anachronistic demand than the call for the return of the Hanoverian royal family. Neither issues nor organization fully explain the electoral decline of the Hanoverian particularists, from 23% of the eligible voters in the province in 1890, to 12% of them in 1912. The changing strength and relevance of confessional loyalties also need to be taken into account. After 1890, Catholic confessional allegiance remained a strong force in determining the minority party vote, both for the Center and the Polish nationalists. The decline of the French nationalist vote also exemplified continuing confessional loyalties, since a good deal of it resulted from Catholic priests in Alsace-Lorraine and the lay public who followed their lead, switching political allegiances from the French nationalists to the Center.

The Hanoverians were the one major heavily Protestant minority party, closely connected to traditionalist and orthodox Lutheranism, a religious tradition fast losing popular support. The decline in the party's vote followed the lines of religious identity closely. It was least in areas with a tradition of revivalism or particularly strong Lutheran identity, and indeed, the party's very strongest supporters were those Lutherans who had seceded from the Hanoverian state church when it merged Calvinists and Lutherans early in the nineteenth century. More generally, the particularists lost fewest votes in the countryside, where church going remained more common, while their decline was greatest in large urban areas where both the working and middle class had abandoned the church in substantial numbers.[28]

Social groups and the minority party electorate

These observations about the Hanoverians suggest another way to look at the minority party vote in Wilhelmine Germany, namely by social class. We could ask how the parties' different efforts at reorganization and realignment were accepted by different social groups. This is really a

---

[27] Aschoff, *Welfische Bewegung*, pp. 186, 189–90, 216–17, 240–58, 264–71.
[28] Ibid., pp. 203–5, 208, 218–19. Just about the only supporters of the Hessian particularists were such Lutheran separatists. Knobel, *Die Hessische Rechtspartei*, pp, 69, 174–77.

Table 2.6 *Catholic vote in Wilhelmine Germany by social class (per cent)*

	Social class					
	1890–98			1903–12		
Party grouping	Farmers	Middle class	Workers	Farmers	Middle class	Workers
Minority parties	50	37	49	55	50	52
Other parties	18	19	18	22	25	29
Non-voters	33	44	32	22	25	20
Total	101	100	99	99	100	101

question about Catholic social groups, since the analysis of Protestant supporters of minority parties makes the limits of the procedure apparent. The regression results for the elections of the 1890s are that an average of 4% of Protestant farmers, 4% of Protestant workers, and none of the Protestant urban middle class supported the minority parties; for 1903–12, the figures are 4% Protestant farmers, 3% Protestant workers, and, once again, none of the Protestant middle class.

Such results would imply that there were absolutely no Protestant master craftsmen or small businessmen in Hanover voting for the particularists, and no Protestant businessmen in Alsace-Lorraine supporting the French nationalists. Put so starkly, such an assertion is evidently incorrect and demonstrates some of the specific problems, mentioned in the introduction: namely working with both larger aggregates, as is the case in developing estimates by class and confession, and considering smaller groups, since Protestants supporting the minority parties made up just some 2% of the entire electorate. Consequently, I would not push the results much further than to say that the minority parties attracted few Protestant voters and fewest among the urban middle class.

Catholics supporting the minority parties were of course a much larger group within the electorate. Table 2.6 gives figures on the Catholic vote in Wilhelmine Germany, divided by social class, and averaged by decade. These figures confirm and amplify the results of tables 2.4 and 2.5. Catholic turnout increased in the first decade of the twentieth century and both the minority parties and the other parties profited from it. This statement is also true about each individual Catholic social group. But specific party groups profited to a different extent from the newly mobilized voters of the different social classes. Among both farmers and the urban middle class, the minority parties gained more than the other parties put together.[29] For the working class, this relationship was reversed, and strongly so, with gains to other parties outnumbering those for the minority parties by almost four to one, gains for the SPD alone (see table 1.10) outweighing those for the minority parties by two to one. From this long-run view, we would have to say that Catholic workers were the group among whom the minority parties' efforts at reorganization and realignment were by far the least successful.

Unfortunately, the data does not allow us to distinguish between the Center and the other minority parties in deriving estimates for vote by class and confession. If we could, I strongly suspect that this unique position of the working class would also appear in vote switching among the minority parties. The Center's successes after 1900 in winning votes from the Bavarian Peasant League occurred in heavily agricultural areas; in Alsace-Lorraine, on the other hand, the Center probably got more farm voters from the French nationalists, although also counting successes among blue-collar voters, especially those employed in heavy industry in Lorraine. Voters shifting from the Center to the Polish nationalists, on the other hand, were mostly found in the heavily industrial constituencies of Upper Silesia and the Ruhr Basin. If these speculations are correct, we might want to speak of a growing proportion – albeit, still a minority – of the Catholic working class rejecting an exclusively confessional political orientation, in favor of different ones, at least partially influenced by nationalist or socialist ideas.

Changing to stay the same

In summing up the results of this section, let us return to the concept of dynamic stability to describe the minority party vote. The percentage of the whole German electorate and of the minority parties' specific clientele voting for these parties changed relatively little over the history of the *Kaiserreich*, but there were many changes in voter behavior – movements between the minority parties and the other parties, among the minority parties themselves and between the minority parties and non- or new voters – needed to keep these percentages so constant. Religious, ethnic and regional/dynastic loyalties remained the basis of the minority party vote, but these parties' politicians had to find new ways to articulate these loyalties and new organizational forms in which they could be expressed, so that voters would continue to support the minority parties.

[29] For farmers, these figures understate the extent of this development, since about half the farmers' votes for "other parties" went to the conservative parties, in whose favor the Center often renounced candidacies in this period. In contrast, less than 3% of Catholic workers or urban middle class cast ballots for these parties of the right.

We can specify these changes more precisely by time and place. In Bismarckian Germany, the minority parties represented the opposition, coming from Germany's Roman Catholics and a few (regionally sharply delineated) groups of Protestants to a centralizing and nationalist regime. This opposition was most sharply and drastically expressed during the *Kulturkampf* of the 1870s, but it persisted throughout the period and in some ways reached its peak in the general elections of 1887. During these years, ties between clergy, political parties organized and run by local notables, and the ordinary voters – sometimes members of mass organizations, sometimes not – were close and immediate, making party loyalties very powerful. Minority party voters in some elections and some regions (southern Germany in particular) might not always turn out to vote, but they rarely switched to other parties.

All these circumstances changed in the 1890s. The confrontation between the regime and the minorities disappeared, or at least was weakened and lost its centrality; other political issues came to the fore. The minority party politicians were uncertain and divided about how to deal with the new situation, and while they experiemented with different options voters began deserting their parties, the 1890s marking the low point for minority party voter loyalty and for these parties' vote totals, whether understood as a proportion of the entire electorate or as a proportion of the parties' specific clientele. Crisis is a grossly overused word in historical explanation and it would be an exaggeration to talk of the 1890s as a period of crisis for the minority parties, but it was certainly a time when the future of these parties depended on their reorganization.

The results of the three twentieth-century general elections underscore this point. Those minority parties whose reorganization and reorientation was either non-existent or ineffective – the French nationalists and the Hanoverians – saw their vote drop by a good 50%, while the Center and the Polish nationalists, who did carry out such a reorganization, were able to increase their vote totals, albeit to a more modest extent. These reorganizations, it should be understood, did not change the nature of the parties' appeal away from national and religious loyalties to socioeconomic or constitutional issues; rather, they made it possible for these loyalties to continue having a resonance with voters at a time when social and economic issues were becoming ever more central to politics.

Nor did these reorganizations stop the flow of voters away from the minority parties. Instead, they allowed these parties to replace their lost voters with previous non-voters and new entrants into the electorate overall coming out a bit ahead on the transaction. To put this another way, and to focus on the Center (the largest of the minority parties), the first decade of the twentieth century did not see a decline in the proportion of eligible Catholic voters supporting the Center. Quite the opposite, the proportion of eligible Catholic voters supporting the Center increased by about 10% over the previous decade, and in the 1907 elections reached levels comparable to the glory days of the *Kulturkampf*. What did happen, though, is that the proportion of Catholic voters casting their ballots for parties other than the Center also increased and reached an all time high. These two developments were both possible because the proportion of eligible Catholic voters going to the polls increased from an average of 64% in the general elections of the 1890s to 78% between 1903 and 1912.

Regrettably, ecological inference does not allow us to combine these two forms of observations. We cannot ascertain the extent to which the increase in Catholic votes for parties other than the Center at the beginning of the twentieth century came from Catholic voters who had previously supported the Center or from Catholics who had previously not voted or were new voters. What we can say is that the pattern of an increasing proportion of Catholic voters supporting the minority parties and the other parties as well had a class dynamic: the increase in the percentage of Catholic blue-collar workers supporting parties other than the minority parties was much larger than among farmers or the middle class, while the increase in the proportion of Catholic proletarians voting for the Center and the other minority parties was smaller than among other Catholic social groups.

These results do not quite fit the two versions of understanding minority voting patterns offered in the historical literature: long-term decline, as the popular religious and ethnic loyalties and the political confrontations associated with them gradually softened and weakened; or, continued stability, often seen as based on something other than these ethnic and religious loyalties. The overall minority party vote did not decline, although it did not stay the same from election to election and from decade to decade either; religious and ethnic loyalties remained the basis of the minority parties' ties to the electorate, even after the end of the political confrontations of Bismarckian Germany. Yet the results do not exactly contradict these two forms of explanation; working with the concept of a dynamic stability in the minority party vote, they can both be reconciled and used in a differently structured account.

In retrospect, the decade of the 1890s appears as a critical period when religious, ethnic-national and regional-dynastic ties did seem to be loosening, when previously central issues for minority party voters were losing their force and when the minority party vote was declining. These trends continued after 1900 among the French nationalist and Hanoverian particularist electorate, so that the decline thesis works well for them. However, this was not the case for the other minority parties, largely because their politicians found ways to repackage their basic appeal, not abandoning it for new issues, as some adherents of the stability thesis might suggest, but successfully incorporating it into their approach to these new issues. For the minority parties to stay the same in Wilhelmine Germany as they had in the previous two decades they had to change; it is a tribute to the quality of their leadership that, overall, they were able to accomplish this difficult task.

3   The "national" parties

Parties of government / parties of the "nation"

If the Social Democrats were the party of opposition to the national government in Imperial Germany, and the minority parties consistently in opposition – indeed, the leading element of the opposition – in Bismarckian Germany and sporadically oppositional afterwards, the liberal and conservative parties, by contrast, were the parties of the government. To be a governmental party in the *Kaiserreich*, though, had a particular meaning in view of the independent position of the executive. In nineteenth-century parliamentary regimes, a party became governmental as a result of the election returns and the construction of a majority parliamentary coalition, but in the *Kaiserreich* the government was formed independently of the political parties and their appeal to the voters. "Governmental" parties thus agreed to support a government not of their own making and in return received the endorsement and support of the authorities at election time.

Now, not all the liberal and conservative parties were supporters of the government all the time. However, every single one of these parties campaigned in at least one general election as a supporter of the government; and at every individual election at least one of the liberal and one of the conservative parties appealed to the voters as a party of the government. Two such parties, the National Liberals and the Free Conservatives, were consistent supporters of governmental policy through all its twists and turns across the history of the empire.[1] Even the left-liberal parties, which were frequently in opposition to the national government, retained a governmental orientation. They were, at least in part, reluctantly driven into opposition at the end of the 1870s and saw themselves for much of the following decade as a governmental party in waiting, counting on a change in the executive, via the accession of a new monarch to the throne.

---

[1] At the very last general elections, in 1912, there were elements of opposition in the National Liberals' election campaign, but these were mixed with elements of support for the government.

The split of the left-liberals in 1893 centered on whether or not to be a party of government and the question of a pro-governmental orientation was important to their reunification after 1907. There were groups at the extremes of the ranks of the liberal and conservative parties – on the left, the democratic German People's Party, while on the right, the various anti-Semitic parties – who were usually vociferously in opposition to the government and the authorities were likely to return the hostility and suspicion they received from these parties. Yet even they could occasionally act as parties of the government. Moreover, they were both small fringe groups, with a regionally very limited electoral appeal.[2]

In much of the historical literature, the liberal and conservative parties are usually seen as having another common element, namely a primary base of support among property-owning Protestants. To be sure, these were not a homogeneous group and the different parties might have regional or social strongholds – the farming population of east Elbia, say, for the Conservatives, and the middle class of large urban areas for the Progressives – but overall this was an electorate common to all the liberal and conservative parties, sometimes amiably shared among them, sometimes bitterly competed over. Karl Rohe has articulated this idea most explicitly in his concept of a "national" camp in the German electorate, a group of voters who could move among the liberal and conservative parties, from one election to another but generally did not vote for any of the other parties.[3]

Rohe's concept is particularly useful in this context, because it brings to mind three important issues connected with the history of the liberal and conservative parties, which can help frame the analysis of their voters. First, "national," as the term was used by contemporaries, referred to partisans of the German nation-state, Bismarck's empire of 1871.[4] The liberal and conservative parties affirmed the government as the minority parties opposed it. But, as we have seen in the section on the minority parties, a politics centered on opposition to the government ended in the

---

[2] On these parties, see Klaus Simon, *Die württembergischen Demokraten: Ihre Stellung und Arbeit im Parteien- und Verfassungssystem in Württemberg und im Deutschen Reich 1890–1920* (Stuttgart: W. Kohlhammer Verlag, 1969); James Clark Hunt, *The People's Party in Württemberg and Southern Germany, 1890–1914* (Stuttgart: Ernst Klett Verlag, 1975) and Richard S. Levy, *The Downfall of the Anti-Semitic Political Parties in Imperial Germany* (New Haven and London: Yale University Press, 1975).

[3] Rohe, *Wahlen und Wählertraditionen*, pp. 69–73, 92–97; cf. Sheehan, *German Liberalism*, p. 223.

[4] "Nationalist," a word one might expect in this context, only entered the German political vocabulary in the 1920s. Otto Dann, *Nation und Nationalismus in Deutschland 1770–1990* (Munich: Verlag C.H. Beck, 1993), p. 270.

1890s, both as these parties and the government experimented with cooperation rather than conflict, and as new issues gained greater resonance among the electorate. One must wonder whether the "national" parties experienced a similar disorientation, albeit from the other side. Perhaps for them and their voters as well, support for the government was no longer the key political issue, but social and economic questions came to be ever more significant. In this respect, we might want to know whether the 1890s saw a change in voting patterns for the conservative and liberal parties, as they did for their minority counterparts, and if these changes persisted into the twentieth century, or gave way to other trends.

Second, there is the question of the gap between these parties' claim to be "national," to represent the entire population, and the reality of their voting support. If they were, as the literature tends to suggest, the parties of the Protestant middle and upper classes, then their "national" status could only be achieved by excluding a majority of the population – Catholics, minorities, the working class – from the nation, a procedure with a distinctly sinister side to it. On the other hand, this description of the social and confessional composition of the liberal and conservative electorate might be no more accurate than the one identifying Social Democratic voters with urban Protestant workers. Or, of course, the social and confessional composition of the supporters of these parties might be subject to fluctuation or to change in some consistent direction over the history of the empire.

Finally, the whole notion of a "national" camp itself needs some study. Both Karl Rohe and his critics have wondered about the extent to which the progressive parties and their voters were part of such a grouping. The idea seems least applicable to the 1880s, when the left-liberals were both persistently in opposition to the government – and thus persistently stood against both the conservative parties and the pro-Bismarckian National Liberals – and also made up a substantial proportion of the total liberal vote.[5]

Here, a study of voter movements would be particularly helpful. One could see whether a "national" camp actually existed among voters, that is whether voters moved back and forth among the liberal and conservative parties more than they did between these parties and the minority parties or the Social Democrats. We can also note the circumstances under which voters moved between the liberal and conservative parties, seeing whether such movements were the result of cooperation, a liberal or conservative voluntarily renouncing a candidacy in favor of a member

---

[5] Rohe, *Wahlen und Wählertraditionen*, p. 93 and n.8, pp. 203–4; Kühne, "Wahlrecht – Wahlverhalten – Wahlkultur," pp. 519–21.

of the other party group, or if they were the result of the two party groups going head to head in the same constituency, competing with each other for voters. A comparison of such voter movements with the positions of the liberal and conservative parties toward the government would enable us to bring together two levels of political life – the orientation of the parties and the orientation of the voters – and provide some firmer notion about the continued and uninterrupted existence of a national camp in German politics.

All things considered, the results of the electoral analysis presented in this chapter tend to contradict the standard picture of the "national" parties found in the literature. The voters of these parties were not exclusively from the Protestant middle class, but were spread out over a wider social and confessional field, albeit in different ways among individual parties and party groups, and to a different extent at different times in the history of the empire. While voters did move back and forth between the liberal and conservative parties – sometimes as a result of cooperation, more often as a consequence of conflict – they also moved in comparably large numbers between these "national" parties and other party groups as well as the non-voters. Finally, the 1890s were a critical decade for the electorate of the national parties, although in different ways than for the minority parties and different consequences for liberals and conservatives.

Liberals, conservatives, and the voters

Once again, let us start the analysis quite simply with a view of the development of the conservative and liberal vote in the general elections of the empire. Figure 3.1 gives the percentage of eligible voters casting their ballot for these parties.

The movement of the liberal vote is remniscent of the support for the liberals' antagonists, the minority parties (see figure 2.1), albeit with more distinct peaks and valleys. Reaching a first peak in 1874, the liberal vote as a percentage of the electorate declined modestly after that, only to shoot up to a new high in the elections of 1887, and then to fall very sharply to a low point in 1898. This initial impression suggests that the liberals, even more so than the minority parties, had troubles with their voters in the decade of the 1890s. But also like the minority parties, the liberal vote revived in the three twentieth-century general elections, although also remaining below its 1870s levels.

The long-term trend in the conservative vote was quite different from that of the liberal or minority parties. The percentage of the electorate choosing the conservatives rose, with interruptions, from the first general

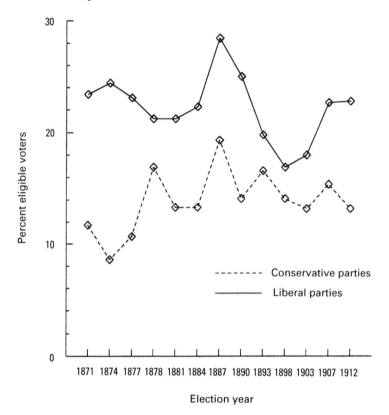

3.1 The conservative and liberal vote

elections of the empire until 1887, and then fell off again, although also not in a straight line, through the outbreak of the First World War. However, the conservative vote is remniscent of that of the minority parties in another respect, the presence of clear high points, set off from the previous or subsequent general elections. There were two clear, sharp peaks in the conservative vote in 1878 and 1887, and two smaller ones in 1893 and 1907. Even with these peaks, the conservative parties were consistently outpolled by their liberal counterparts, the two party groupings coming closest together in the elections of 1893 and 1898.

Figure 3.2 provides a breakdown of the liberal vote, distinguishing between the National Liberals and the left-liberal and bourgeois democratic parties.[6]

---

[6] In these, and all following figures and tables, the smaller, ephemeral moderate and right-wing liberal groupings, such as the Liberale Reichspartei, are counted with the National Liberals.

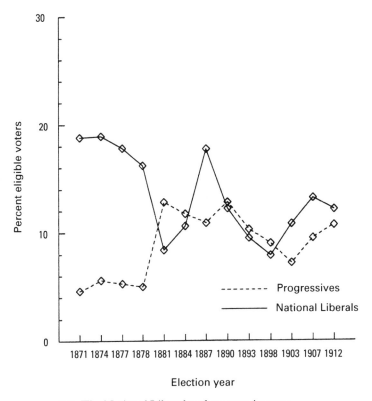

Election year

3.2 The National Liberal and progressive vote

The movement of the National Liberal vote followed quite closely that of the liberal vote as a whole, declining from the mid-1870s, picking up sharply in 1887, declining to 1898 and rising again afterwards. Before 1890, the progressive vote showed a different pattern. It was consistently low throughout the 1870s, and then jumped at the elections of 1881. Preceding the elections that year, the National Liberal party split, and its dissident left wing, the Secessionists, ran its own candidates, thus materially improving the left-liberal vote totals. As a percentage of the electorate, the progressive vote changed relatively little in the following decade, only to decline after 1890 and to pick up again in the two general elections preceding the First World War. In sum, the movements of voter support for the National Liberals and the left-liberal parties went in quite different directions in Bismarckian Germany, but were much more synchronized in the Wilhelmine era.

As we have noted in the discussion of the Social Democratic and

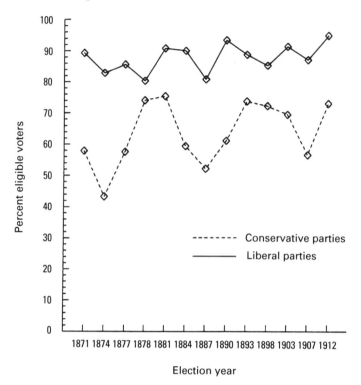

3.3 Liberal and conservative candidacies

minority parties, vote totals depended to an important extent on the number of candidates that parties or groups of parties ran. This was also the case with the conservative and liberal parties. Figure 3.3 gives the proportion of the electorate with the opportunity to vote for candidates of the liberal and conservative parties respectively.

The liberal parties were present always and almost everywhere. At least 80% of the electorate had the opportunity to vote for some liberal candidate at all the general elections, and in five of them the figure was over 90%, peaking at 95.2% in 1912. Although the extent of candidacies for the individual liberal parties differed considerably, taken together they had a national presence, consistently available to a very large majority of the voters in the empire.

Conservative candidacies were consistently less common than liberal ones, and the proportion of the electorate with an opportunity to vote for a conservative candidate varied considerably from one general election to the next. The pattern of peaks and valleys in Figure 3.3 corresponds

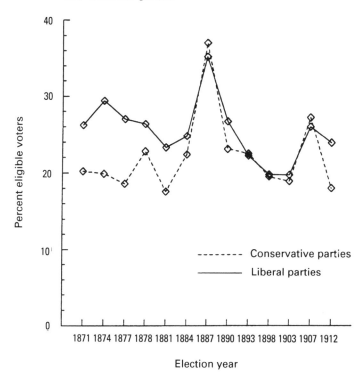

Election year

3.4 Conservatives, liberals, and the voters

closely to political alignments among the "national" parties. There were a maximum of conservative candidacies in 1878, 1881, the 1890s, and 1912, all years when conservatives and liberals were generally at odds in the electoral arena. Conservatives were least likely to stand for office in 1874 (the one year that the liberal parties enjoyed a greater governmental support than did the conservatives), and in 1887 and 1907, which were both general elections in which the conservatives and at least some of the liberals were campaigning on the same side.

We can combine the approaches used in figures 3.1 and 3.3 by calculating the percentage of eligible voters supporting a given party or parties in those constituencies where those parties put up candidates. Figure 3.4 does this for the conservative and liberal parties.

Up through 1881, not only did the liberal parties run more candidates than the conservatives, each candidate they nominated received, on the average, the support of a greater proportion of eligible voters than his conservative counterpart. From 1884 through 1907 this distinction disappeared. The liberal and conservative vote, expressed as a proportion of

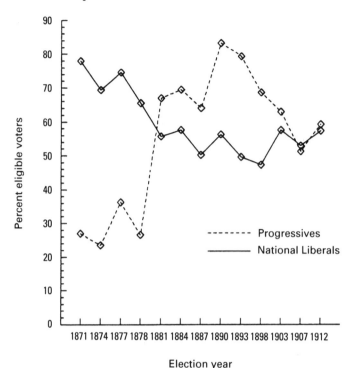

3.5 National Liberal and progressive candidacies

the eligible voters having the opportunity to vote for each of these party groups, was almost identical. Any difference between the liberal and conservative vote in those years (and a look at figure 3.1 shows that it was sometimes considerable) was solely the result of liberal parties running more candidates or candidates in more populous constituencies.[7] At the very last prewar elections the proportion of eligible voters received by conservative candidates in the constituencies where they stood for election declined to a level not seen since the 1870s, and the gap between the conservative and liberal parties opened up once again.

Continuing this overview, let us consider the extent of the candidacies of the different liberal groupings. Figure 3.5 gives the proportion of the German electorate who had the opportunity to vote for National Liberal and progressive candidates.

---

[7] Naturally, if the conservative parties put up fewer candidates than their liberal counterparts, this might have been because they had fewer supporters throughout the country or could not count on much of a vote in many constituencies, suggesting in a different way a broader lack of support.

The consistent and almost complete coverage of the electorate by the liberal parties as a whole, shown in figure 3.3, turns out to conceal very different trends among the more right wing and the more left wing of the liberal parties. In the early and mid-1870s, the National Liberals were truly a nationwide party, their candidates available to a good three-quarters of the electorate. In a twenty-year period beginning in 1878, the party's reach steadily declined. At the low point in 1898, the National Liberals presented candidates to just 47% of German voters. In the empire's three twentieth-century general elections, National Liberal candidacies once again became more extensive, although covering a much smaller proportion of the electorate than they had in the 1870s.

For the progressive parties, on the other hand, the 1870s were a decade of marginality, their candidates reaching no more than one-third of the eligible voters. The split of the National Liberals in 1880 and the candidacies of its secessionist left-wing completely reversed the situation. Now it was the left-liberal groups who could claim to be a nationwide party while the National Liberals were increasingly downgraded to a regionalized existence. The merger of the secessionist wing of the National Liberals with the older Progressive group in 1884 to form a united left-liberal party, only contributed to this move toward a national presence, a presence which peaked in 1890 when the left-liberal and bourgeois democratic parties offered candidates to over 80% of eligible voters. Even the split of the united left-liberal party in 1893 into two separate groups did not do much damage to this coverage of the electorate. Then, from 1898 through 1907, the extent of left-liberal candidacies declined, increasing only very modestly in 1912, following the merger of the three main left-liberal and bourgeois democratic parties. In the empire's three twentieth-century general elections, the National Liberals and the left-liberals each put up candidates for between 50 and 60% of the electorate.

When we look at the candidates' success in the two liberal groupings, a still different picture emerges. Figure 3.6 gives the proportion of eligible voters casting their ballot for the National Liberals or the left liberals in those constituencies where they put up candidates.

Once again, the curve for the National Liberals follows very closely that for the liberals as a whole (cf. figure 3.4). The 1870s were a successful decade for the party, when a high proportion of eligible voters chose the National Liberals in those constituencies where the party put up candidates. The 1881 elections, on the other hand, were a catastrophe, since the party put up fewer candidates than before (cf. figure 3.5) and they each were chosen, on average, by a smaller percentage of eligible voters. In contrast, 1887 was the National Liberals' best year ever in constituencies where it put up candidates, although by that year only half the

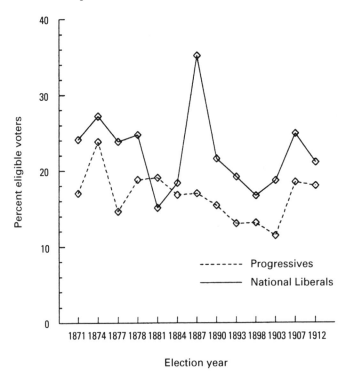

3.6 National Liberals, progressives, and the voters

electorate had the opportunity to vote for the party, a far cry from the 70–80% of the 1870s. Both the percentage of eligible voters who had a chance to vote for the National Liberals and the percentage of those who actually did so when they had the chance dropped off sharply after 1887 to a low in 1898, and then both the party's coverage of the electorate and its success with the voters increased in the general elections of after 1900.

Figure 3.6 shows a different picture for the left-liberal parties, a pattern of long-term decline. With some fluctuations from the first general elections in the empire, and directly from 1878 for a quarter century onward, the percentage of voters choosing the left-liberal parties in those constituencies where they put up candidates declined. Here, a comparison with the Social Democrats is helpful. In the 1880s and early 1890s, both the Social Democrats and the left-liberals steadily expanded the range of their candidacies, moving toward nationwide coverage of the electorate. For the Social Democrats, this expansion of candidacies also expanded their electorate, the party's percentage of eligible voters in those constituencies where it put up candidates staying constant through the 1880s and then rising in 1890 and afterwards. The left-liberals, on the other hand faced a situation of diminishing marginal returns. Expanding the range of their candidacies diluted their base of support: the more left-liberal candidates, the smaller the percentage of voters choosing the left-liberals in those constituencies where left-liberals stood for office. To put it simply, the Social Democrats' aspirations to be a nationwide political party were successful; the left-liberals' were not.

Even as the reach of left-liberal candidacies moved downward in the late 1890s, the slide in left-liberal votes per candidacy continued. It was only reversed in the general elections of 1907 and 1912. Having given up pretentions to a nationwide presence, and so just running candidates for a little over 50% of the electorate, the left-liberals received the support of just under 20% of the eligible voters in the constituencies where they stood for office, among the best results they had ever achieved, reversing a quarter-century slide in voter support.

A "national camp?" Party loyalty of liberal and conservative voters

These initial results suggest several issues to be considered in the analysis of the voter transition probabilities. As was the case with the minority parties, the 1890s appear as a decade of disorientation and decline, when the liberal and conservative parties had difficulties with their voters. Neither a governmental nor an oppositional orientation (and both could be found in that decade among the liberals and the conservatives) seems to have helped the situation. At least for the liberals, this decline was reversed at the beginning of the twentieth century. However, unlike the minority parties, voter trends in Bismarckian Germany were not continuous for the liberals and conservatives. There were very sharp swings in support for the different parties, both from election to election and between the two decades of the 1870s and 1880s.

The equally sharp swings in the proportion of the electorate covered by the different parties and the way that the liberal and conservative vote sometimes moved in tandem, sometimes in opposite directions (to say nothing of the voter movements of the two main liberal groupings), suggest a need to keep a sharp eye on the non-voters. Their mobilization and demobilization manifestly played a large role in the successes and failures of the liberal and conservative parties. In this respect, it would be interesting to see if the experience of the Social Democrats and the minority parties – a great influence of non-voters on swings of support before 1890, a decreasing influence after that – was also the case.

Table 3.1 gives the composition of the electorate of the liberal and

Table 3.1a *Previous voting of liberal voters (percent)*

Vote at previous elections	Election years				
	1871/74–1874/77	1877/78–1878/81	1881/84–1884/87	1887/90–1893/98	1898/03–1907/12
Conservatives	6	12	4	11	11
Liberals	63	63	66	70	56
Minority parties	4	3	3	6	7
Social Democrats	3	4	2	6	12
Non-voters	19	18	23	4	9
Net new voters	5	—[a]	2	3	4
Total	100	100	100	100	99

Note:
[a] The electorate hardly increased in size at all between 1877 and 1881, so there is no figure for net new voters for the 1878 and 1881 elections.

Table 3.1b *Previous voting of conservative voters (percent)*

Vote at previous elections	Election years				
	1871/74–1874/77	1877/78–1878/81	1881/84–1887/87	1887/90–1893/98	1898/03–1907/12
Conservatives	50	53	59	60	61
Liberals	22	18	11	18	22
Minority parties	3	4	6	6	5
Social Democrats	0	3	1	5	3
Non-voters	22	22	21	9	9
Net new voters	3	—[a]	1	2	1
Total	100	100	99	100	101

Note:
[a] The electorate hardly increased in size at all between 1877 and 1881, so there is no figure for net new voters for the 1878 and 1881 elections.

conservative parties, averaged by decade, in terms of previous voter affiliation, that is their votes in the first of each pair of general elections (as in tables 1.1 and 2.2).

In some ways, these figures support Karl Rohe's idea of a national camp or voting bloc in Imperial Germany. Former liberal voters made up between 10 and 20% of the conservative electorate at all periods in the history of the empire, a good deal more than previous supporters of all the other parties put together. The contribution of one-time adherents of the

conservatives to the liberal vote, on the other hand, was not quite so pronounced, but was larger than than of any other party grouping at all elections before 1900.

Overall, however, the results suggest that Rohe's concept is rather too
narrow to encompass the history of the empire. While not denying that
there was a good deal of voter interchange between the liberal and conservative parties, I would suggest that there are three modifications needed
to the idea of a national voting bloc. One is simply to note that the switching of votes between the liberal and conservative parties did not have sym-
metric effects: former liberal voters were always a larger portion of the
conservative electorate – and usually substantially so – than one-time
conservative voters were of the liberal electorate.

The second point has to do with the role of new entrants into the electorate – previous non-voters and net new voters – for the electoral fortunes of the liberal and conservative parties. Here, we can see a familiar
distinction between Bismarckian and Wilhelmine Germany. Before 1890,
these new entrants were the second largest group among both liberal and
conservative voters, after voters staying loyal to their party groupings.
After 1890, they were a much smaller component of the liberal and conservative electorate. Since turnout was much higher in Wilhelmine
Germany than it had been in the previous two decades, one would expect
non-voters to be a smaller proportion of any party's electorate, and their
representation among minority party and Social Democratic voters also
declined in this period. However, the post-1890 electorate was fed by a
new source, net new voters, a result of both rapid increases in the voting-
age population and movements from rural to urban areas. Both the
minority parties and the SPD were able to tap this source of voters, but
the conservative and liberal parties were not. Turnover in the electorate
worked strongly against them.

The third point concerns the interchange between the conservative and
liberal parties in the decade of the 1880s and after 1900. In the elections
of 1884 and 1887 the proportion of former liberal voters in the conservative electorate and former conservative voters in the liberal electorate
were both at much lower points than either before or after. These were
years when a large portion of the liberal electorate supported the left-
liberal and bourgeois democratic parties in open opposition to Bismarck's
government and the conservative and National Liberal parties who supported it. The idea of a liberal-conservative "national" camp explains
neither the alignments of politicians nor of voters in this still relatively
little studied period of the empire's history.

The empire's three twentieth-century general elections only partially fit
the picture of a national voting bloc. Between 1903 and 1912, former

Table 3.2a *Subsequent votes of liberal voters (percent)*

Vote at next general elections	Election years			
	1871/74–1877/78	1878/81–1884/87	1887/90–1893/98	1898/03–1907/12
Conservatives	11	9	11	16
Liberals	64	73	58	67
Minority parties	9	4	7	5
Social Democrats	1	2	11	8
Non-voters	14	12	13	4
Total	99	100	100	100

Table 3.2b *Subsequent votes of conservative voters (percent)*

Vote at next general election	Election years			
	1871/74–1877/78	1878/81–1884/87	1887/87–1893/98	1898/03–1907/12
Conservatives	56	66	63	65
Liberals	12	14	14	17
Minority parties	11	4	4	4
Social Democrats	0	1	8	8
Non-voters	20	16	11	6
Total	99	101	100	100

liberal voters remained the main source of the conservative electorate (outside of conservative loyalists), outnumbering for the first time all other sources of support put together. The liberal electorate of the early twentieth century, on the other hand, was quite different. Former Social Democratic voters were as important to the liberal parties as conservative voters; if we add the contributions to the liberal vote made by former Social Democrats, former minority party voters, non-voters and net new voters, we find that they outweighed the contribution of former conservative voters by a ratio of three to one.

All these points suggest that the idea of a national voting bloc is a bit shaky. The results of table 3.2, giving the subsequent votes of liberal and conservative voters, their votes in the second of each pair of general elections, averaged by decade (as in tables 1.3 and 2.1), help stabilize the concept somewhat.

Party loyalty among conservative voters was lowest in the 1870s but stayed at a reasonably high and fairly constant level thereafter. Between one-sixth and one-eighth of conservative voters at any one election voted for the liberals in the subsequent one, making the liberals the persistent main choice for conservative voters switching parties. However, a substantial number of conservative voters switched to the minority parties in the 1870s and to the Social Democrats in the Wilhelmine elections, so the liberals were not the only choice for ex-conservatives. Finally, the conservative parties had increasingly greater success in keeping their voting support intact, as the proportion of conservative voters lapsing into abstention at the subsequent elections declined steadily over the history of the empire.

The picture for the liberals is in many respects complementary. Overall, the conservatives were the main option for liberal voters switching to another party, although, as was the case with conservative voters, a fair number of liberal voters defected to the minority parties in the 1870s and to the Social Democrats after 1890. Liberals' losses to non-voters remained at a consistent level from the 1870s through the 1890s, which meant that the liberals were unusually successful at keeping their supporters coming to the polls at the beginning of the empire, but were only average at this two decades later (cf. tables 1.3 and 2.2).

Indeed, table 3.2a underscores and suggests the reasons for what the global accounts of the liberal vote show (see figures 3.1–3.2). The 1890s were a disaster for the liberal parties, when their support among eligible voters declined to a good one-third below the level of 1887. In the elections of that decade, the liberals gave up substantial numbers of voters in all directions. They lost supporters to the Social Democrats on a large scale for the first time, continued to lose voters to the conservatives, and to abstention, and lost quite a few to the minority parties as well. The liberals continued to lose substantial numbers of voters to other parties after 1900, increased losses to the conservatives compensating for slighly less substantial losses to the minority parties and to the SPD. If the liberal vote recovered after 1900, it was above all because the liberal politicians found ways to bring previous non-voters to the polls.

As one additional way to look at the liberal and conservative electorate, let us consider the total pattern of gains and losses of these parties. Table 3.3 gives the same information on voter swings to and away from the liberal and conservative parties that was provided for the Social Democrats in table 1.4 and for the minority parties in table 2.3.

The first point to make about this table concerns the core electorate of the two party groups, voters who voted for their respective parties from one election to the next. In the early years of the empire, the conservative core electorate was very small, under 5% of all eligible voters. From the

Table 3.3a *Voter swings and the liberal electorate, 1871/74–1907/12 (percent)*

Vote at previous election	Election year pairs				
	1871/74–1874/77	1877/78–1878/81	1881/84–1884/87	1887/90–1893/98	1898/03–1907/12
Conservatives	1.5/2.3	2.6/2.7	0.9/1.6	2.3/2.8	2.3/3.0
Liberals	15.1	13.5	16.6	14.5	11.8
Minority parties	1.1/2.3	0.5/1.6	0.8/0.5	1.2/1.7	1.5/0.8
Social Democrats	0.7/0.2	0.9/0.2	0.6/0.4	1.1/2.5	2.5/1.4
Non-voters	4.7/2.8	3.8/4.1	5.9/1.9	0.9/3.3	2.0/0.7
Net new voters	−0.1	—[a]	−0.3	−0.4	−0.6

Note:
[a] The electorate hardly increased in size at all between 1877 and 1881, so there is no figure for net new voters for the 1878 and 1881 elections.

Table 3.3b *Voter swings and the conservative electorate, 1871/74–1907/12 (percent)*

Vote at previous election	Election year pairs				
	1871/74–1874/77	1877/78–1878/81	1881/84–1884/87	1887/90–1893/98	1898/03–1907/12
Conservatives	4.9	7.8	9.4	8.7	8.5
Liberals	2.3/1.5	2.7/2.6	1.6/0.9	2.8/2.3	3.0/2.3
Minority parties	0.3/1.4	0.7/0.9	1.0/0.2	0.9/0.6	0.7/0.5
Social Democrats	0.3/0	0.4/0.1	0.2/0.1	0.8/1.2	0.4/1.1
Non-voters	2.1/1.8	3.4/2.4	3.8/2.2	1.4/1.6	0.8/0.7
Net new voters	−0.3	—[a]	−0.3	−0.5	−0.9

Note:
[a] The electorate hardly increased in size at all between 1877 and 1881, so there is no figure for net new voters for the 1878 and 1881 elections.

1878 elections onward, it increased to the 8 to 9% level, where it remained for the further general elections of the empire. In contrast, the core liberal electorate was very substantial, along with the persistent supporters of the minority parties, the largest element among voters in Bismarckian Germany. In the 1890s, however, this group of steady liberal supporters declined in size, and continued to do so after 1900, even though the overall liberal vote increased. During the last three general elections of the empire, persistent liberal voters took third place in the electorate, behind reliable supporters of the Social Democrats and of the minority parties, thus making the liberals increasingly dependent on swing voters for their success at the polls.

Table 3.3 also confirms what was apparent in the previous figures on the liberal and conservative vote. Persistently – not, as will be seen in the next two chapters, at every single general election, but averaged across every group of general elections – the liberal parties lost more voters to the conservatives than vice-versa. If there was a national voting bloc composed of voters switching back and forth between the liberal and conservative parties, the vote-switching ran primarily in one direction. The elections of 1884 and 1887, when the interchange between liberal and conservative supporters was noticeably less than at any other period in the empire, was also the time when the switching was most heavily in favor of the conservatives.

We can look at the liberal-conservative national voting bloc from another angle, clearing up an ambiguity inherent in different discussions of its existence. The regression estimates confirm that there were a considerable number of voters who switched between the liberal and conservative parties from one general election to the next, but were these switches the result of cooperation between the parties or conflicts among them? Karl Rohe, in his formulation, seems to suggest that they were a consequence of candidates from one party stepping down in favor of another. To put it a little differently, Rohe describes a situation in which the same group of notables would nominate and the same group of voters support a candidate calling himself a liberal at one general election and another candidate – or even the same one – calling himself a conservative the next time around. An alternative explanation for the vote-switching between liberals and conservatives is that there existed a considerable group of swing voters, accessible to the arguments from two competing groups of parties, who could be convinced at different times by one or the other. Both situations might be seen as demonstrating the existence of a national camp in German politics, a group of voters who could chose either the liberal or the conservative parties, but were much less likely to vote for any other party. However, the two situations would have quite different implications for the meaning of the relationship between the liberals and the conservatives.[8]

Needless to say, it is possible that both kinds of vote-switching occurred in different areas. In regions where the minority parties were active and popular – the Rhineland and Westphalia, for instance, or Prussian Poland – liberal and conservative voters might have formed a cooperative national voting bloc, while in other, predominantly Protestant regions,

---

[8] For these different lines of interpretation, see n. 3, above.

such as East Prussia, Lower Silesia, Saxony or Thuringia, voter movements between the liberal and conservative parties could have been the
result of efforts by each of these party groups to win over the other's
supporters. Nonetheless, we might like to explore which of these two
possibilities was more common and at what time.

It is possible to develop a very approximate estimate of the extent of
cooperative and competitive vote-switching among the conservative and
liberal parties. I have done this by identifying all the constituencies where
the two party groups "switched off" (i.e. the candidate of one party
stepped down in favour of the candidate from another) from one election
to the next – as, for example, in constituencies where there was a liberal
but not a conservative candidate in 1874 and a conservative but no liberal
candidate in 1877. I have then assumed that all the voters made the
switch as well – so that, continuing the example above, all the 1874 liberal
voters in those constituencies voted for the conservatives at the next elections. By then comparing these voters with the estimates of all the voters
who switched between the liberals and the conservatives in the two elections, I can calculate the percentage of vote-switches that reflect cooperation between the two party groups. This figure is a maximum estimate
since, of course, not all the liberal voters might have made the switch:
some might have preferred not to vote, or to vote for another party rather
than support the conservatives.[9]

Figure 3.7 gives the results of these calculations, for each election
between 1874 and 1912.

Three points emerge from consideration of this graphic. First, a majority, usually a considerable majority of the voters who moved between the
liberal and the conservative parties did so in a competitive environment.
Cooperative vote-switching was the exception; there were rarely as many
as thirty, and often less than ten of the 397 Reichstag constituencies
where liberal and conservative parties stood down for one another from
one general election to the next. Second, and perhaps not very surprisingly, cooperative vote-switching was most common when liberals and
conservatives worked together in support of the government, in 1877, and
at the Kartell elections of 1887, with their alliance between the
Conservatives, the Free Conservatives and the National Liberals. At elections where the two party groups were more likely to be in conflict – 1881,
1890, 1893, and 1912 – and at which the conservatives put up an usually
large number of candidates (cf. figure 3.3) there was relatively little in the
way of cooperative vote-switching. Finally, a noticeably greater propor-

---

[9] Clagget et al., "Political Leadership and the Development of Political Cleavages,"
attempted to develop regression estimates of voting behavior in these situations, but their
conclusions seem to me suspect, since the regressions are based on too few cases.

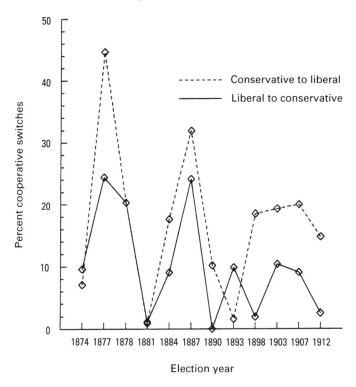

3.7 Liberal–conservative vote-switching

tion of the voters switching from the conservative to the liberal parties did so in situations where the two party groups were cooperating than was the case in the other direction. Conservative voters were more likely to cast a ballot for one of the liberal parties as part of a broad cooperation of the two groups against the "enemies" of the nation (the minority parties and, to a lesser extent, the Social Democrats), than was the case for liberal voters who were noticeably more likely to be won over by the parties of the right in a competitive voting situation. All these results confirm the previous modifications of Karl Rohe's notion. A "national" voting bloc only existed at some times in the history of the empire and not at others, and movements within this bloc were not equally balanced but tended to go in favor of the conservative parties.

Both the liberal and conservative parties overall lost voters to the minority parties in the 1870s, as the *Kulturkampf* and related struggles impelled Catholic and Hanoverian voters (neither liberals nor conservatives had much of a presence in Alsace-Lorraine in the 1870s) away from the "national" parties and towards the enemies of Bismarck's empire. From the 1880s onward, this movement of voters reversed itself, and both the liberals and the conservatives gained voters from the minority parties, albeit with an exception for the liberals in the 1890s and overall to a more modest extent than they had lost voters to these parties in the first decade of the empire. The voter loyalties – and hostilities – forged during the *Kulturkampf* may have weakened with time but they did not disappear. In fact, it may well be that the voters won by the liberal and conservative parties away from the minority parties later in the history of the empire came from different groups of voters than were lost by the liberals and conservatives to the minority parties earlier on. Certainly, the advances of the "national" parties in Alsace-Lorraine after 1890 are striking, especially considering that they had essentially no presence there in the Bismarckian elections.[10]

There is a similar story, though one moving in the other direction, concerning voting exchanges between the liberal and conservative parties on the one hand, and the Social Democrats on the other. Throughout Bismarckian Germany, the former parties gained more voters from the Social Democrats than they lost to them. In the Wilhelmine elections, this relationship was reversed, the SPD now clearly profiting on the exchange with the national parties, with the exception of the liberals in the elections of 1903–12. Reversing the 1890s trend of losing voters to the Social Democrats played a significant role in the liberal electoral revival at the beginning of the twentieth century.

Overall, mobilizing previous non-voters and losing supporters to abstention became the single largest factor determining the voting results of the liberal and conservative parties in the general elections of Bismarckian Germany. Voters either moving to one of these party group from the ranks of the non-voters or leaving the support of the liberals and conservatives for abstention were one-half to two-thirds the size of the liberal and conservative core electorates before 1890. Such exchanges with the non-voters were of great importance for the minority parties and the Social Democrats in this period as well, so that we might say the elections of Bismarckian Germany took place in the era of non-voters. The extent of swings between non-voters and the liberal and conservative parties declined after 1890, both overall and in relation to the size of the two party groups' core constituency, but the net losses to abstention in the 1890 played an important role in the liberal decline in that decade, as the mobilization of previous non-voters did in the liberals' resurgence after 1900.

---

[10] On this point, see Hiery, *Reichstagswahlen im Reichsland*, pp. 136–237, 248–65, 304–5, 366–402 and passim.

On the whole, exchanges with the non-voters were more important to the liberal than the conservative parties. Both in periods when the total exchange between the conservative parties and the non-voters was larger – the 1880s – and smaller – before and after – the net result was generally not too substantial. Over a group of elections the conservatives' losses to and gains from abstention balanced themselves out. This was very definitely not the case with the liberal parties, for whom both the overall interchange with non-voters and the net swings – positive in the 1870s, 1880s, and after 1900; negative in the 1890s – were much larger and a good deal more important for the parties' successes or failures at the ballot box.

Turnover in the electorate worked consistently against both the liberal and conservative parties, this negative effect increasing in size with the growth in the proportion of net new voters after 1890. This inability to recruit net new voters was particularly pronounced for the conservative parties and explains how their proportion of eligible voters could decline, even though they gained more votes than they lost to the other parties and from the non-voters. Although generational change was probably involved, a good deal of the conservative weakness with regard to turnover of the electorate reflected the rapid rural–urban population movement after 1890. Figures on Reichstag voting by size of community were collected from 1898 to 1912, and in those years the conservative support among eligible voters increased in areas with a population of less than 2,000 and declined in all more populous communities, most dramatically in large cities of over 500,000, where the right-wing parties had 9.4% of eligible voters in 1898 and just 4.2% in 1912.[11] In other words, as voters moved from the country to the city (or young men left the countryside and came of voting age in urban and industrial areas), they left the orbit of the parties of the right.

Liberals, conservatives, and the authorities

Now let us put some of these results into the context of the historiography of the conservative and liberal parties in the German Empire. In the 1870s, almost all of these parties were supporters of the government and enjoyed official support and favor. Civil servants were reminded by their superiors of their duty to vote for these parties at election time and were often pressed into service as their campaign workers, with gendarmes, village mayors, and other low-level state officials passing out the ballots for their candidates. An example of how this worked would be the 1871

[11] Figures from Suvall, *Electoral Politics*, pp. 80–81. See also the more elaborate and sophisticated discussion of the political effects of urbanization in Winkler, *Sozialstruktur*, pp. 222–33.

campaign of in the Schweinfurt constituency, of Winfried von Hörmann, a textile manufacturer and the District Governor of Swabia. This liberal candidate noted, "Sentiment is very good here, and every thing has been arranged. Bailiffs, postmen, administrators of [Bavarian] government property and [village] mayors, as well as my weavers, who work for me, are all inspired for our cause and instructed not to let any other opinion appear in the various localities."[12]

Under these circumstances, liberal and conservative party organizations and activities were at best rudimentary. A few weeks or at most a few months before the elections, self-appointed committees of local notables would meet and discuss, sometimes after consultation with the authorities, whom to nominate. Their chosen candidate would then be presented to the general public for ratification at an open meeting, although even here sometimes an entry fee would be charged, or admission cards distributed in advance to keep out unwanted elements, such as the Social Democrats. In the areas of large landed estates in east Elbian Prussia, even this modest effort might not be necessary, the county commissioner simply proclaiming himself, or another important official or estate-owner, as the candidate. The election campaign itself would be equally modest, perhaps including a speech or two by the candidate – if indeed he ever visited his potential constituency – and notices in the newspaper. Following the election, the committee would dissolve, only to reappear with pretty much the same membership at the next general election. The liberal and conservative notables counted on government influence to bring through their candidate, sometimes to the point that the authorities became annoyed at being expected to do all the campaigning for them.[13]

There were some exceptions to this picture of informal organization, reliance on the authorities and a passive approach to politics. The left-liberal parties, the Progressives in Prussia, and the German People's Party south of the Main River, less likely to enjoy official favor (the latter, in fact, the object of governmental hostility), created a modest network of local political clubs that campaigned more energetically and continued to exist between general elections. These efforts were probably most extensive in Berlin, which, as the national capital, offered unusually good opportunities for parliamentarians to stay in touch with their voters. On

[12] Cited in Grohs, *Die Liberale Reichspartei*, p. 20.
[13] On these points, see Nipperdey, *Die Organisation der deutschen Parteien*, pp. 42–74, 241–45; Sepainter, *Die Reichstagswahlen im Großherzogtum Baden*, pp. 193–95, 204, 208–10; Aschoff, *Welfische Bewegung und politischer Katholizismus*, pp. 102–3; Frank, *Die Brandenburger als Reichstagswähler*, p. 21, 54–56, 87; Grohs, *Die Liberale Reichspartei*, pp. 9–12, 16–20; Liebert, *Politische Wahlen in Wiesbaden*, pp. 71, 90–93, 110–11; Rüdel, *Landarbeiter und Sozialdemokratie in Ostholstein*, pp. 170–71; Bräunche, *Parteien und Reichstagswahlen in der Pfalz*, pp. 56, 59–60, 210.

election day in the capital city, the Progressives did not count on the authorities to distribute their ballots – which they would not have done in any event – but instead hired the unemployed to stand in front of each polling place and hand ballots to the voters. In western Germany, conservatives could not count on official support, that was more likely to go to the National Liberals (indeed, in Baden during the 1870s, the authorities openly opposed the conservatives, treating them no better than the Center), nor on the influence of a large landowning aristocracy, which did not exist. Consequently, they were forced to organize themselves more efficiently than their counterparts in the more favored territory east of the Elbe River. Neo-orthodox Protestant pastors were a guiding force in both the organizations and activities of these conservatives in the western part of the country.[14]

The liberals and to a lesser extent the conservatives were most active in the 1870s in those regions where they faced substantial opposition, either from the Social Democrats or, more commonly, from the minority parties. The mass campaigning style of these parties forced the adherents of the government to follow suit. They organized local political clubs and mobilized associations of sharpshooters or veterans of the Franco-Prussian War, as did the liberals in the heavily Catholic areas of the Rhineland or the National Liberals of Baden, who were locked in a sharp struggle with the Center in the 1870s and throughout the history of Imperial Germany. Such activities, however, did not replace government support, but supplemented it, and the liberals could count on most leading officials to join their organizations, endorse their campaigning and public demonstrations, and pressure their subordinates to do so as well.[15]

Both liberals and conservatives celebrated triumphs at the polls in the 1870s – the former in the earlier part of the decade, the latter in its final general elections, for reasons to be discussed in the next chapter. The close cooperation with the government during the 1870s enabled these parties to bring previous non-voters to the polls and to intimidate or to

[14] Nipperdey, *Die Organisation der deutschen Parteien*, pp. 78–79, 176, 245–47; Frank, *Die Brandenburger als Reichstagswähler*, pp. 56–57; Simon, *Die württembergischen Demokraten*, pp. 18–20; Siegbert Wolf, *Liberalismus in Frankfurt am Main:*, pp. 39–42, 48, 194 n.31; Sepainter, *Die Reichstagswahlen im Großherzogtum Baden*, pp. 73–76.
[15] Norbert Schloßmacher, *Düsseldorf im Bismarckreich: Politik und Wahlen Parteien und Vereine*, 77–87, 89–94, 108–16; Nipperdey, *Die Organisation der deutschen Parteien*, p. 78; Hans-Jürgen Kremer, "Die Krieger- und Militärvereine in der Innenpolitik des Großherzogtums Baden (1870–1914)," *Zeitschrift für die Geschichte des Oberrheins* 133 (1985): 302–36, esp. pp. 305–7; Rose Kermann, "Das Pfälzische Kriegervereinswesen nach der Reichsgründung. Aspekte seiner Entwicklung und seiner politischen und gesellschaftlichen Bedeutung," *Mitteilungen des Historischen Vereins der Pfalz* 85 (1987): 302–36, esp. pp. 305–7.

convince Social Democratic voters to support them. On the other hand, this strategy proved unsuccessful against the main enemy of the national parties and the new central government, the parties of the religious, regional and ethnic minorities. Far from winning over the voters of these parties, liberals and conservatives lost voters to them, thus demonstrating the limits of their hold on the electorate.

This situation came to an end with the reorientation of German politics at the end of the 1870s, following Bismarck's turn to protectionism and a more generally conservative socioeconomic and political course. While this shift in policy enhanced the governmental status of the conservative parties, it created a new situation for the liberals, forcing them to choose between being governmental and being liberal. The right wing of the National Liberal Party followed the former option, supporting Bismarck's protectionism, his efforts at reinstating the guilds, and his early moves towards a social insurance system, while dropping the party's former insistence on a gradual transition towards parliamentary government. In effect, the National Liberals went from being an independent partner of the executive, as they had been in 1870s, to its subordinate. The left wing of the party, on the other hand, chose the opposite course, going into opposition, running candidates on their own (the so-called "secession") in 1881 and then merging with the main left-liberal group, the Progressives, to form a united Radical (*Deutsch-Freisinnige*) Party. Allied with the democrats of southern Germany, this Radical Party was in determined opposition to Bismarck's social and economic policy and raised the anti-Bismarckian demand for a parliamentary regime.[16]

In the 1870s, the distinction between a more left-wing Progressive Party and a more right-wing National Liberal one, had been confined to the parliamentary caucuses. With relatively few exceptions – and those mainly in those areas of southern Germany where the democratic People's Party was active – the ad hoc nominating and electioneering committees that made up local-level liberal political organization in that decade included both left-wing and right-wing liberals. The split in the National Liberal parliamentary caucus and the subsequent creation of a Radical Party fundamentally changed this state of affairs. By the mid-

[16] On Bismarck's change of policy and its consequences for the political parties, see Michael Stürmer, *Regierung und Reichstag im Bismarckstaat 1871–1880* (Düsseldorf: Droste Verlag, 1974), pp. 183–288; Heinrich August Winkler, "Vom linken zum rechten Nationalismus: Der deutsche Liberalismus in der Krise von 1878/79," *Geschichte und Gesellschaft* 4 (1978): 5–28; Retallack, *Notables of the Right*, pp. 28–34 (which tends to exaggerate the extent to which the conservatives did not support the government); Sheehan, *German Liberalism*, pp. 179–216.

1880s, the previous local liberal unity was the exception; separate National Liberal and Radical committees or associations were the rule.[17] It would be fair to say that the Radicals and their various predecessors and offshoots were the dominant group in liberal electoral politics in Germany during the 1880s and 1890s. The left-liberal parties outpolled the National Liberals at every general election in those two decades, with, admittedly, the important exception of 1887. Unlike the latter, who were content with an increasingly regionalized existence, the Radicals strove to become a truly nationwide party with a presence and a candidacy in as many constituencies as possible (cf. figures 3.2, 3.5). Overall, these two decades were the oppositional era of German liberalism in the empire.

This opposition was embodied by Eugen Richter, the acknowledged leader of the Radical Party and the dominant figure in German left-liberal politics for a good quarter century from the late 1870s onward. Richter was firmly committed to political opposition, although his opposition was quite different from that of the minority parties or the Social Democrats. Very much a classic nineteenth-century liberal, Richter believed in a weak state, with a government limited by constitutional guarantees of civil liberties and controlled by a parliamentary majority. He stood for low taxes and low government expenditures, including a modestly sized state bureaucracy and armed forces, and opposed state interference in the economy, whether – to name three of the main economic issues of the 1880s and 1890s – in the form of protective tariffs, the reintroduction of the guilds or the creation of a social insurance system. In many ways, his views might best be compared to those of a Victorian era radical, a Richard Cobden or John Bright.

Perhaps more significant than his ideas was Richter's political style. He strove to create a disciplined party caucus, that would vote as a bloc according to the caucus leadership's (i.e. Richter's) will. He was an energetic and active publicist, founding a national newspaper for the party, and authoring many political brochures, including his *ABC Book* of German politics, that offered pithy explanations of important issues in alphabetical order. Not content with just newspapers and pamphlets as connecting links between parliamentarians on the one hand, and local activists and the voters on the other, he strove to create a centralized party organization, that would tie together a nationwide network of political clubs with a corresponding national reach for the party's Reichstag

---

[17] Nipperdey, *Organization der deutschen Parteien*, pp. 31–36; Bräunche, *Parteien und Reichstagswahlen in der Rheinpfalz*, pp. 59–68, 113–117; Liebert, *Politische Wahlen in Wiesbaden*, pp. 130–31; Schloßmacher, *Düsseldorf im Bismarckreich*, pp. 89–103, 108–16; Frank, *Die Brandenburger als Reichstagswähler*, pp. 21–22.

candidacies, all supported by special fundraising campaigns. These were upsetting notions for many of his left-liberal colleagues, anchored in the traditions of notables' politics. They were scandalized, for instance, when Richter paid some less affluent deputies' expenses from party funds, thus enabling them to attend the Reichstag sessions, but also ensuring that they would vote as Richter told them to.[18]

The historians' verdict on Richter is that while he was a man of zeal, energy, and deep devotion to principle, he was also dogmatic, inflexible, and politically unsuccessful. After considering the election results, there is no reason to doubt this conclusion. Over the general elections of 1884, 1887, and 1890 – the era of a strong polarization in campaigns between the Radical Party and the pro-governmental alliance of the conservative parties and the National Liberals that contemporaries called the Kartell (when politics came closest to fitting Richter's world view) – the left-liberal parties were able to maintain just about the same share of the electorate. They did this, though, only by increasing the number of candidates they put up for office; their share of votes per candidate declined steadily.

With Bismarck's fall from power in 1890 and the development of a new relationship between the political parties and the government, and the coming to the fore of different issues in the subsequent decade, Richter's strategy completely collapsed. The Radical Party split over whether or not to support the government's proposed military appropriations in 1893. Richter was in favor of opposing the government, and he and his followers had by far the larger and more influential of the two parties that emerged from the split.[19] However, in the new political universe of the 1890s, neither opposition to nor support of the government could do the trick for the left-liberal parties; their share of the eligible voters fell by 40% from 1890 to the general elections of 1903 (cf. figures 3.2 and 3.6).

Richter's experience suggests that issues mattered in the electoral politics of the German Empire, that a solid organization, successful fundraising, and an extensive press and pamphlet literature were not enough for a party to succeed if the party's positions did not appeal to the voters. The same point, albeit from the other direction, can be made about the National Liberal Party. As a result of the secession of its left wing in 1880, it had become the party whose program was above all supporting the

[18] Nipperdey, *Die Organisation der deutschen Parteien*, pp. 32, 177–81, 198–224; Ina Susanne Lorenz, *Eugen Richter: Der entschiedene Liberalismus in wilhelmischer Zeit 1871 bis 1906* (Husum: Matthiesen Verlag, 1981).
[19] On the split, see Sheehan, *German Liberalism*, pp. 265–66.

actions of Chancellor Bismarck. What was to become of such a party when Bismarck was no longer chancellor? The voters delivered the verdict, the National Liberal share of the total electorate dropping by over 50% from 1887 to 1898 (cf. figure 3.2).

In the general elections of 1884 through those of 1890, when a left-liberal opposition had stood against the pro-governmental Kartell, an increase in the proportion of eligible voters supporting the left-liberals went along with a decline in the proportion of those who cast their ballots for the National Liberals, and vice-versa. In the 1890s, on the other hand, both right-wing and left-wing liberal parties lost votes, their supporters deserting them for parties across the political spectrum, who spoke to their interests more effectively. Many liberal voters who did not switch to other parties were clearly unconvinced by the liberal election campaigns, since they just stopped voting (cf. tables 3.2a and 3.3a).

The picture for the parties of the right was not quite as dismal as it was for the liberals. Indeed, the conservatives came closest to matching liberal vote totals in the decade of the 1890s. This, however, was not a result of the increase in the conservative vote but of the decline in the liberal one. Conservatives came closer to the liberals because they were better able to limit their overall losses.

Thus the main question the liberal and conservative parties faced in the 1890s was one similar to that faced by the minority parties: how to adopt to a new political situation, where the contrast between parties supporting the government and those opposing it was no longer the main axis of political life. The minority parties that were successful at the polls after 1900 did this by incorporating new issues into their basic political appeal and developing new forms of political organization – mostly not involving the parties themselves, but associations affiliated with them – to bring their new approach to the issues to the electorate. Facing similar problems to the minority parties, the liberal and conservative parties found similar solutions.

As was the case with the minority parties, changes in the organization of the liberal and conservative parties were the least of the solution to the dilemmas of the 1890s. Particularly among the liberal parties, one can observe a gradual movement away from the informal, locally oriented committees, existing only at election time, and towards nationally organized mass political parties. The National Liberals, having the most ground to make up, moved the furthest in this direction. The number of local National Liberal political clubs increased more than fourfold in the years between 1900 and the First World War, reaching a total of some 2,200 clubs with perhaps 200,000 members after 1910. After the turn of the century the party's central office in Berlin employed a full-time general secretary, with a paid staff of seventeen.[20] The other conservative and liberal parties could not match this effort. Long possessing the best political organization among these parties, the left-liberals were unable to keep up the pace after 1900 and were clearly overshadowed by the National Liberals. Each of the three left-liberal groupings attempted to create a broader and better organized political structure in the early years of the twentieth century; their merger into the Progressive People's Party in 1909 only encouraged these efforts. By the outbreak of the First World War, this party could count some 1,500–1,600 local political clubs with some 120,000 members.[21]

This was a less than impressive effort, especially since almost one-seventh of these clubs were former affiliates of the German People's Party, the south German democrats who had always been well organized. Neither the Progressive nor the National Liberal Party organizations could compare with that of the SPD and its over 1 million members or with the 800,000 of the People's Association for Catholic Germany, and certainly did not provide the substantial campaign funds raised by the latter groups' dues.[22] Yet these modest successes were a lot more than the conservatives ever accomplished, or even attempted. Conservative party organization after the turn of the century was little different from what it had been twenty or thirty years earlier: largely autonomous committees of notables, with a substantial representation of the landed nobility and neo-orthodox Protestant clergy, loosely tied together by a parliamentary caucus, lacking any centralized party structure.[23]

Both in extent and in the degree of organization the new initiatives taken by the liberal and conservative parties after the turn of the century

[20] Nipperdey, *Die Organisation der deutschen Parteien*, pp. 86–109, 149–58; two regional studies reaching similar conclusions are Bräunche, *Parteien und Reichstagswahlen in der Rheinpfalz*, pp. 94–113; and Karl Heinrich Pohl, "Ein zweiter Emanzipationsprozeß des liberalen Unternehmertums? Zur Sozialstruktur und Politik der Liberalen in Sachsen zu Beginn des 20. Jahrhunderts," in Klaus Tenfelde und Hans-Ulrich Wehler (eds.) *Wege zur Geschichte des Bürgertums* (Göttingen: Vandenhoeck & Ruprecht, 1994), pp. 231–48.
[21] Nipperdey, *Die Organisation der deutschen Parteien*, pp. 176–87; Simon, *Die württembergischen Demokraten*, pp. 21–27, 81–90.
[22] On the inability of liberal parties to finance themselves from membership dues and their dependence on outside contributions, see Siegfried Mielke, *Der Hansa-Bund für Gewerbe, Handel und Industrie 1909–1914: Der gescheiterte Versuch einer antifeudalen Sammlungspolitik* (Göttingen: Vandenhoeck & Ruprecht, 1976), pp. 150–51, 214–15.
[23] Nipperdey, *Organisation der deutschen Parteien*, pp. 241–64; the main English language account, Retallack, *Notables of the Right*, pp. 179–90, adds little. The extreme right-wing anti-Semitic political parties were better organized than the other conservative parties, but these groups led a mostly sectarian existence, never achieving more than a regionally limited importance.

remained relatively modest.[24] They certainly provided neither the funds nor the manpower for the remarkable expansion of the election campaigns of these parties. In a pronounced break with the practices of notables' politics, liberal and conservative candidacies increasingly included elaborate preparation with intensive canvassing of voters months or even years in advance, the distribution of tens or hundreds of thousands of fliers and leaflets in each constituency, an ever-increasing number of election mass meetings and organized get-out-the-vote drives, climaxing on election day when volunteers would climb into their automobiles and bring voters to the polls. Indeed, the automobile became both a symbol of this new political style of the national parties, and a primary instrument of it, as liberal and conservative candidates would drive or be chauffeured around their constituencies, going from one meeting to the next. The National Liberal Eugen Schiffer noted of this practice in 1912:

Previously, there was at most one meeting per day; on the following day, you were driven in a coach at a leisurely pace to another place to speak. Now, you have scarcely had the opportunity to climb down from the trapeze where you have been performing acrobatics all morning, when you are packed into an auto and driven to another circus, to put on a show there, and on the evening of the very same day come to yet a third locality to stand in the ring.[25]

In view of the previous remarks on the weakenesses of even the reformed liberal and conservative party organizations, the reader might wonder how this new style of mass politics was possible. The answer lies in the development of ancilliary mass organizations, not formally affiliated with the political parties, but founded and led by prominent party members. This was the same solution to the problem of mass politics that the politically successful minority parties, especially the Center and the Polish, had found at about the same time; the minority parties unable or unwilling choose or implement such solutions – above all, the Hanoverians and the French nationalists – declined at the polls. There

---

24 Cf. the remarks of one frustrated activist in 1906 that the National Liberals "had not the slightest idea how to handle an election by organizing the contact-men, distributing leaflets, supervising the electoral lists and working on the non-voters." Cited in Eley, *Reshaping the German Right*, p. 231.
25 Cited in Bertram, *Die Wahlen zum Deutschen Reichstag*, p. 186. For other examples of this new campaigning style, ibid., pp. 173–93; Hans-Dieter Loose, "Der Wahlkampf des liberalen Reichstagskandidaten Carl Braband 1911/12," in *Aus der Arbeit der Archive: Beiträge zum Archivwesen, zur Quellenkunde und zur Geschichte* ed. Friedrich P. Kahlenberg (Boppard: Harald Boldt Verlag, 1989), pp. 727–45; Hiery, *Reichstagswahlen im Reichsland*, pp. 321, 361; Liebert, *Politische Wahlen in Wiesbaden*, pp. 186–88, 209–10, 228–29, 242–43, 258–62, 275–77, 279; Wolf-Arno Kropat, "Der Beamte und Politik in wilhelmischer Zeit," *Nassauische Annalen* 83 (1972): 173–92, esp. 186–90; Suvall, *Electoral Politics*, p. 131; Mielke, *Der Hansa-Bund*, p. 160.

was also a dichotomy in the relationship of the liberal and conservative parties to the ancilliary mass organizations; not between those who successfully adapted them and those who did not (all the liberal and conservative parties used such groups successfully at least to some extent), but between parties' ties to ancilliary mass organizations that were economic special interest groups and those that were for more general nationalist ideas. The different conservative and liberal parties had ties to these groups to different extents, with resulting consequences for their relationships with the voters.

The one great special interest group – which, in membership, finances and political influence, far surpassed all others – was the Agrarian League. Founded in 1893 by large estate-owners of east Elbian Germany, in protest against the post-Bismarckian government's move to reduce agricultural protective tariffs, the organization quickly acquired over 300,000 members, mostly Protestant farmers of all sorts, throughout the entire country. Tightly and efficiently organized, with a centralized leadership able to mobilize members for all kinds of activities, and enjoying the benfits of both a dues-paying mass membership and the influence of prominent and powerful adherents – noble landlords and senior Prussian civil servants – the Agrarian League was extraordinarily effective at pressuring the government to act on behalf of farmers' interests, above all by taking measures to raise farm prices.

The League's founders included a number of Conservative politicians and the group soon came to exercise a dominant influence on the Conservative Party. The mass agitation of Conservative election campaigns after the turn of the century, the public meetings, the distribution of campaign literature and of a popular political press, were all carried out by the League, whose lucal groups were aggregated into some 250 Reichstag constituency associations, itself led by conservative politicians. There was no need for the Conservatives to create a better and more effective party organization, when they had the agrarians to do it for them, provided the Conservatives went along with the agrarians – and considering the close ties between the leadership of the special interest group and of the party it is no surprise that they did.

By the first decade of the twentieth century, the Agrarian League thus dominated the Conservative Party and was also quite influential in the affairs of the smaller Free Conservative Party. The League also ran candidates for the Reichstag under its own name and sometimes in alliance with one of the anti-Semitic parties of the extreme right. However, its influence on the political parties did not end there; in predominantly rural areas of central and western Germany, including Hanover, parts of Hessen and the Rhine-Palatinate, areas where there was no tradition of conservative politics, the League endorsed and actively supported National Liberal candidates. It was, more generally, a major force on the right wing of the National Liberal Party. In other words, the Kartell parties of the 1880s were strongly influenced or indeed completely dominated by the Agrarian League two decades later.[26] This close connection between a farmers' interest group and the political right could not be matched, either by other special interests or by the liberal parties. While there existed a profusion of different special interest groups for various elements of the business community, as well as still more groups for small business and the crafts, none of them could claim the combination of mass membership and elite influence of the Agrarian League. No one group could therefore dominate any of the liberal parties the way the Agrarian League ruled the conservatives, but, conversely, the liberals could not count on any one effectively organized interest group to do their campaigning for them.[27]

Liberals had to look elsewhere for effective campaign workers, finding them in the nationalist mass organizations that developed in the 1890s, among the largest of which were the Navy League, the Protestant League, and the national federation of veterans' associations.[28] These groups, and others that developed after the turn of the century, such as the National Association against Social Democracy, were not so exclusively tied to the liberal parties as the agrarians were to the conservatives. Their political orientation brought them into the field against the Social Democrats and usually against the minority parties, but this activity could be and often was as easily in favor of the conservatives as of the liberals.

This asymmetrical relationship between the parties and the ancilliary mass organizations helps us to understand the different trends in voting behavior between the liberal and conservative parties in Wilhelmine Germany. The greater steadiness of conservative vote totals over the period reflect the early and effective organization of the Agrarian League

---

[26] On the Agrarian League and its activities, see the classic study of Hans-Jürgen Puhle, *Agrarische Interessenpolitik und preußischer Konservatismus im wilhelmischen Reich (1893–1914)* (Hanover: Verlag für Literatur und Zeitgeschehen, 1966).

[27] On the ultimately unsuccessful attempt to create a businessman's version of the Agrarian League, see Mielke, *Der Hansa-Bund*, passim. More generally on special-interest groups and politics in Wilhelmine Germany, see Dirk Stegmann, *Die Erben Bismarcks: Parteien und Verbände in der Spätphase des Wilhelmischen Deutschlands* (Cologne: Kiepenheuer & Witsch, 1970).

[28] On these groups, see Eley, *Reshaping the German Right*; Helmut Walser Smith, *German Nationalism and Religious Conflict: Culture, Ideology, Politics, 1870–1914* (Princeton: Princeton University Press, 1995); Klaus Saul, "Der 'Deutsche Kriegerbund.' Zur innenpolitischen Funktion eines 'nationalen' Verbandes im kaiserlichen Deutschland," *Militärgeschichtliche Mitteilungen* 5 pt. 2 (1969): 95–160. A brief regional example of the connections between such groups and liberal leadership is in Hess, *Geschichte Thüringens*, pp. 388–90.

and its close connection with the material interests of a substantial group of voters. The right-wing parties' difficulties with net new voters, demonstrating their increasing weakness in rapidly growing urban and industrial areas, document the response of such voters to a party ever more identified with a program of higher food prices.

The inability of the liberal parties, on the other hand, to develop such a close relationship with a powerful special interest group helps explain the more erratic course their vote totals took in the general elections of Wilhelmine Germany. As economic issues became more central to popular politics in the 1890s, but the liberal parties remained focused on other questions, a large proportion of their voters went off to other parties or lapsed into apathy. The active and exciting campaigns of the nationalist organizations brought previous non-voters back into the fold after 1900, and the siren-song of an aggressive nationalism also lured over to the liberals a portion of the Social Democratic electorate. This provides an explanation of why the National Liberal vote turned up in 1903, but the Progressive vote continued to decline. The left-liberal parties stuck to their themes of opposition to the government through the 1903 general elections; it was only after their defeat that year that they fundamentally changed course and moved toward a more nationalist stance in 1907 (a year after Eugen Richter's death), allying with both the National Liberals and the conservative parties in the general elections of that year, and so allowing them to profit from the particularly active campaigns of the nationalist associations.[29]

In Bismarckian Germany, both the political stance of the liberal and conservative parties and their relationship with the voters was largely determined by their attitude toward the government, either supportive or oppositional. In the 1890s, the authorities gradually withdrew from the close management of election campaigns characteristic of Bismarck's chancellorship and issues cutting across the previous lines of opposition and support – particularly questions of food prices and the distribution of the burdens of taxation – became politically more prominent. Circumstances changed faster than politicians did, and the voters repaid liberal and conservative party leaders' inattention with a withdrawal of support. Gradually, the parties managed to adapt to the new political environment, the Conservatives doing it most quickly, the left-liberals taking the longest. The three twentieth-century general elections saw the development of a different set of forces, no longer a contrast between

---

[29] On the changing postions of the left-liberals after 1903, see Ludwig Elm, *Zwischen Fortschritt und Reaktion: Geschichte der Parteien der liberalen Bourgeoisie' in Deutschland 1893–1918* (East Berlin: Akademie-Verlag, 1968), pp. 158–84; Simon, *Die württembergischen Demokraten*, pp. 81–90, 118–19; Wolf, *Liberalismus in Frankfurt am Main*, pp. 68–72.

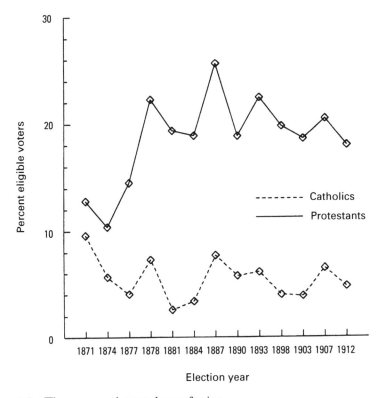

3.8a The conservative vote by confession

support and opposition, but an interplay of economic special interests and nationalist agitation. This new dynamic enabled the liberal and conservative parties to stabilize their voter support and make up part of the ground they had lost in the 1890s. To follow these changes more closely, we now need to look at the confessional and class bases of these parties' voting strength.

Liberal and conservative voters by confession and class

Figure 3.8 gives the proportion of Protestant and Catholic voters supporting the liberal and conservative parties across the history of the empire.

There are two general conclusions that can be drawn from these charts. One concerns the 1870s. In that decade, both the liberal and the conservative parties had quite different experiences with voters of different

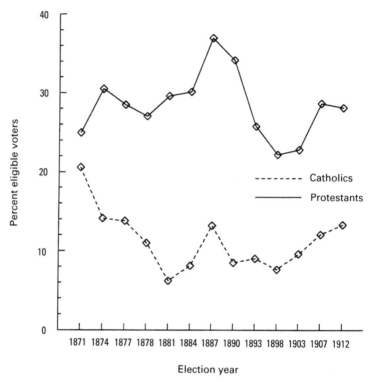

3.8b The liberal vote by confession

religious confessions. The Catholic vote for these parties fell sharply; the Protestant vote for them increased. This is consistent with what we have noted above about the flow of voters from the liberal and conservative parties to the minority parties in that decade (cf. table 3.3) and demonstrates the tremendous confessional polarization of the electorate brought about by the *Kulturkampf*. While this confessional polarization never came to an end, and Catholic support for the national parties continued to lag well behind that of Protestants down to the First World War, from the 1880s onwards movements of voters of different confessions to and away from the liberal and conservative parties were synchronized: support from Catholics and Protestants went up or down together.

The second point concerns the different attraction that the liberal and conservative parties had for voters of the two Christian confessions. Given the influence of various forms of orthodox Christianity in both the conservative parties and the Center, and the frequent instances of political arrangements between the parties, when the Center renounced nominating a candidate in favor of the conservatives, one might expect Catholics to have supported the conservatives in greater numbers than the liberals. Just the opposite was the case. As a percentage of eligible voters, Catholic support for the liberal parties outweighed Catholic support for the conservatives by about two to one. For the voters, confessional antagonism between Protestants and Catholics outweighed any possible joint Christian agreement against secularism. This greater support among Catholics is one important reason why the liberals had persistently higher vote totals than the conservatives. In the elections of Wilhelmine Germany, for instance, an average of 27% of eligible Protestant voters chose one of the liberal parties, as against 20% of Protestants voting for the conservatives; for Catholics, the figures were 10% liberal and just 5% conservative.

Catholic support for the conservative parties was steady and mediocre, averaging 7% of eligible Catholic voters in the 1870s, and 5% in each decade there after. The fortunes of the liberal parties among Catholic voters fluctuated considerably more: 15% of eligible Catholics cast their ballot for one of the liberal parties in the 1870s; 9% in the 1880s and a decadal low of 8% in the 1890s, but climbing back to 12% in the empire's three twentieth-century general elections. A good deal of the liberal revival after 1900 involved recruiting Catholic voters, some no doubt previous non-voters, others former supporters of the Center Party (cf. table 3.3a). The nationalist campaigns of the liberals attracted Catholic voters as well as Social Democratic ones.

We can look more closely at the relationship between confession and the vote for the national parties in two ways. One is to consider regional differences. Table 3.4 gives percentage of Protestant and Catholic eligible voters who supported the liberal and conservative parties in Prussia and in non-Prussian Germany.

The conservative parties obtained their best results in Prussia, the liberal parties outside of it. This held true for both confessions and at all general elections from 1871 to 1912. However, the party preferences of voters from the two Christian confessions varied in different German regions. In Prussia, from 1880 onwards, Protestant voters were about as likely to vote for one of the conservative parties as for one of the liberal ones. The same was true of Catholic voters, although, of course, the proportion of Catholic voters choosing one of these national parties was much smaller than their Protestant counterparts. Outside of Prussia, Protestants preferred the liberal to the conservative parties by a ratio of about 3:1 in the 1870s, declining to about 2:1 in Wilhelmine Germany. Catholic support for the liberal parties, on the other hand, was much stronger than for the conservatives, the ratio as high as 12:1 in the 1880s,

Table 3.4a *Support for the liberal parties by region and confession (percent)*

| | Election years | | | | | | | |
| | 1871–78 | | 1881–87 | | 1890–98 | | 1903–12 | |
Confession	Prussia	Not Prussia	Prussia	Not Prussia	Prussia	Not Prussia	Prussia	Not Prussia
Protestant	24	34	29	38	25	32	24	30
Catholic	11	21	7	12	7	11	10	14
All	19	29	21	28	18	24	19	24

Table 3.4b *Support for the conservative parties by region and confession (percent)*

| | Election years | | | | | | | |
| | 1871–78 | | 1881–87 | | 1890–98 | | 1903–12 | |
Confession	Prussia	Not Prussia	Prussia	Not Prussia	Prussia	Not Prussia	Prussia	Not Prussia
Protestant	17	11	25	15	24	16	23	14
Catholic	9	3	7	1	7	2	7	2
All	15	8	19	10	18	11	17	9

Table 3.5 *Support for the different liberal parties by confession (percent)*

| | Election years | | | | | | | |
| | 1871–78 | | 1881–87 | | 1890–98 | | 1903–12 | |
Confession	Nat-Lib	Prog	Nat-Lib	Prog	Nat-Lib	Prog	Nat-Lib	Prog
Protestant	21	7	15	17	12	15	14	12
Catholic	12	2	7	2	7	2	9	4
All	18	5	12	12	10	10	12	9

and 5.5:1 after 1890. One important, although not the only, reason for the greater strength of the liberal parties outside of Prussia was that Catholics there were substantially more likely to cast their ballots for them.

The second elaboration on the relationship between confession and voting concerns the different liberal parties. Table 3.5 offers figures on the percentage of eligible voters from each confession who cast their ballots for the National Liberals or the progressive parties. The numbers are unequivocal and not at all what one might expect. Among Protestant voters, the National Liberals and the progressives were about equally matched, following the secession of the former party's left-wing in 1880, but the National Liberals far outdistanced their left-liberal counterparts in gaining Catholic voting support. Although historians usually think of the National Liberals as a specifically Protestant political party, as the main proponent of the *Kulturkampf*, it had a steady Catholic clientele. Indeed, a consistent 25% of National Liberal voters were Catholic and 75% Protestant. In comparison, the electorates of the conservative, left-liberal and Social Democratic parties were between 85 and 95% Protestant, while the Center electorate was virtually entirely Catholic. Since about 65% of eligible voters in Imperial Germany were Protestant, and 35% Catholic, the National Liberals were the one major political party whose voters came close to matching the confessional composition of the entire electorate.[30]

Overall, the liberals and conservatives were Protestant parties, drawing their support to a differing extent from Protestants of different social classes, regions, and degrees of church attendance, but all at least nominally Protestant. There is one major exception to this rule, namely the minority of Catholics in southern Germany who regularly voted for the National Liberals and formed a significant portion of that party's electorate. Those smaller numbers of Catholics who voted for the conservatives or the progressives could have been doing so as part of a political arrangment between one of those parties and the Center, but the National Liberals were the Center's sworn enemies and a Catholic voting for it was making a clear statement about his relationship to the church and to political Catholicism.[31]

Those portions of Baden, Bavaria and the Palatinate, where the National Liberal Party enjoyed a substantial degree of Catholic support, were generally areas with a long tradition of anti-clericalism or where enlightened ideas had been influential in the Catholic Church, and had come into conflict with the neo-orthodox "ultramontanist" forms of religion that had become increasingly dominant in the second half of the

---

[30] Schmädeke, *Wählerbewegung*, 1: 292–93, 412–13, seems to be fumbling toward a similar conclusion, but his technically unsophisticated methods do not allow him to make any precise formulations.

[31] If we just consider those constituencies where the Center Party put up candidates, then we find that the National Liberals persistently received more votes from Catholics in them than the conservatives and progressives put together, and received more Catholic votes than any party outside of the Center, until the last prewar elections, when the SPD overtook them.

nineteenth century. Catholic voters sharing these ideas demonstrated their opposition to the official church by casting their ballots for the National Liberals, the party endorsing the Bismarckian unification of Germany, a unification excluding Catholic Austria and strongly opposed by the church and political Catholicism.[32]

There are two further points that can be made about this development. First, while among Protestants the progressives were generally seen as the more anti-clerical of the liberal parties, they were unable or unwilling to capitalize on Catholic anti-clericalism, and so were unable to gain much of a Catholic vote.[33] Second, this anti-clerical Catholic support for the National Liberals was in many cases a predecessor to Catholic support for the Social Democrats. We can see this most clearly in the earliest Social Democratic success in a predominantly Roman Catholic constituency, the spectacular victory of the Bavarian party leader Georg von Vollmar in one of the Munich election districts in 1884. Vollmar's election was only possible because of close cooperation between the Social Democrats and the National Liberals. The campaign and the candidate expressed an anti-clericalism so open and vehement that it upset a number of the party leaders accustomed at the time to seeing the Center Party as fellow oppositionists against Bismarck's rule.[34]

Mentioning the Social Democrats brings up the final issue for consideration in this section, the social composition of the liberal and conservative electorate. Since the SPD received votes from more than one social class (see tables 1.9 and 1.10) and managed only a narrow majority of the one social and confessional group most favorable to it, Protestant workers, one must wonder whether the liberal and conservative parties also had a varied electorate. Table 3.6, giving the percentages of different social and confessional groups voting for these parties suggests that they did.

Neither liberals nor conservatives drew their voters exclusively, or even primarily, from any one social and confessional group, as Lepsius's milieu theory suggests that they should have. Yet given that both party groups

---

[32] On these points, see Dietrich Thränhardt, *Wahlen und politische Strukturen in Bayern 1848–1953* (Düsseldorf: Droste Verlag, 1973), pp. 71–78; Sepainter, *Reichstagswahlen im Großherzogtum Baden*, p. 284; Rohe, *Wahlen und Wählertraditionen*, pp. 76–80. The smaller number of Catholics in northern Germany who voted for the National Liberals did so for similar reasons. Cf. Thomas Mergel, *Zwischen Klasse und Konfession: Katholisches Bürgertum im Rheinland 1794–1914* (Göttingen: Vandenhoeck & Ruprecht, 1994), pp. 263–71.

[33] On Protestant perceptions of the progressives' anti-clericalism, see Klaus Martin Hofmann, *Die Evangelische Arbeitervereinsbewegung 1882–1914* (Bielefeld: Luther-Verlag, 1988), pp. 134–36.

[34] *Wilhelm Liebknecht Briefwechsel*, 2: 735–37; cf., Hirschfelder, *Die bayerische Sozialdemokratie*, pp. 383–84.

Table 3.6a *Support for the liberal parties in Wilhelmine elections, by class and confession (percent)*

	Confession					
	1890–98			1903–12		
Class	Protestant	Catholic	All	Protestant	Catholic	All
Farmers	28	7	19	26	10	20
Middle class	42	13	33	27	13	28
Workers	11	7	10	26	12	21
All voters	27	8	21	27	12	21

Table 3.6b *Support for the conservative parties in Wilhelmine elections, by class and confession (percent)*

	Confession					
	1890–98			1903–12		
Class	Protestant	Catholic	All	Protestant	Catholic	All
Farmers	30	10	22	40	12	28
Middle class	6	0	4	14	3	11
Workers	26	3	18	10	1	7
All voters	20	5	15	19	5	14

were representative of a broad spectrum of Wilhelmine society, there are nonetheless distinct differences between their supporters and between trends in their development.

The conservatives were clearly a predominantly agrarian party, persistently showing more support among farmers than other social groups, a gap in support that grew between the elections of the 1890s and those of the early twentieth century. This observation, however, needs to be qualified by confession. Among Catholics, the conservatives were an almost exclusively agrarian party. The proportion of Catholic farmers voting for the conservatives outweighed that of other Catholic social groups by 5 or 6:1, and farmers made up more than 75% of Catholic conservative voters. For Protestants, on the other hand, the conservatives became an agrarian party: in the 1890s, the proportion of farmers supporting the conservatives was only slightly greater than that of blue-collar workers; in the three twentieth-century elections, Protestant farm support of the conservatives outweighed that of other Protestant social groups by a ratio of about 3.5:1.

This trend towards the agrarianization of the parties of the right is exactly what we might expect, in view of the other trends noted earlier in this section: increasing conservative votes in communities of under 2,000 people and a declining conservative vote everywhere else; the right-wing parties' persistent inability to attract net new voters, that is their poor showing in rapidly growing urban and industrial areas; the ever greater influence in conservative politics of the farmers' special interest group, the Agrarian League.[35] Yet a substantial proportion of farmers voted for other parties. Even if we assume that Catholic farmers were likely to be loyal to the minority parties and just focus on Protestant farmers, we find that while the conservative parties had a large minority of eligible voters and, by the early twentieth century, a majority of Protestant farmers who actually voted, a substantial minority of this core conservative electorate continued to vote for other parties. (Admittedly, many of the Protestant farmers who voted for the National Liberals were voting for candidates endorsed by the Agrarian League.) The conservatives were as much a party of Protestant farmers as the SPD was the party of Protestant workers.[36]

We can pursue this point one step further. While conservative support among the farmers was increasing, the place of farmers in the electorate was declining, from 36% of men eligible to vote, according to the 1895 census, to 27% by the count of 1907.[37] The result was that the proportion of farmers among conservative voters changed little over the elections of Wilhelmine Germany. In both the 1890s and the 1900s, about 53% of conservative voters were farmers. If the right-wing parties were able to maintain their place in the electorate it was not just due to their increasing support among farmers, but also a result of their growing vote totals in the Protesant middle class. Yet this development can, in part, be attributed to the long arm of the Agrarian League, which financed, supported and encouraged the formation of special interest groups for craftsmen and small businessmen, founded and led by politicians of the right and the extreme right. Unlike the case with Protestant farmers, where the Agrarian League dominated the field, other small businessmen's special interest groups with connections to the liberal parties contended with those supported by the right, so that in Wilhelmine Germany the liberals,

[35] Similar conclusions in Winkler, *Sozialstruktur*, pp. 262–70.
[36] Over the three general elections of 1903, 1907 and 1912, an average of 40% of Protestant farmers voted for one of the right-wing parties; 23% did not vote, so about 52% of Protestant farmers who voted cast their ballot for one of the conservative parties. In those same elections, some 48% of Protestant workers chose the SPD; 13% did not vote, so that about 55% of Protestant workers who voted, voted for the labor party.
[37] Winkler, who in *Sozialstruktur* bases his analyses of the relationship between occupation and voting exclusively on the 1907 census, does not take this development into account.

the conservatives and the Social Democrats could all claim some success with different portions of the Protestant middle class.[38] Unfortunately, the available information is not finely grained enough for us to say which elements within the Protesant middle class supported which of the political parties. Regional differences and size of urban areas – liberals and Social Democrats doing best in large cities, conservatives in towns of between 2,000 and 10,000 people – were clearly important factors, but in terms of the material on which this book is based such suggestions must remain speculative.

The liberal electorate developed quite differently in the Wilhelmine era from its conservative counterpart. In the 1890s, the liberals, while receiving votes from all social and confessional groups, had their strongest support in the urban middle class. Liberal support among Protestant farmers was also reasonably strong, almost as many of such farmers casting their ballot for the liberal parties as for the conservatives. The changes in the liberal vote in Wilhelmine Germany – the parties' steadily declining share of the electorate in the 1890s and their increasing proportion after 1900 – resulted in a quite different liberal electorate by the first decade of the twentieth century. Much of the liberals' previous core constituency, the Protestant middle class, had moved off to the conservatives or the Social Democrats, and the organizing efforts of the Agrarian League among Protestant farmers had primarily benefited the conservative parties and only helped the National Liberals to a lesser extent. As compensation for these losses, the liberals had done increasingly well among blue-collar voters, so that the liberal parties had close to equal support among all social groups.[39] The liberal electorate changed more in Wilhelmine Germany than that of any other party grouping; table 3.7 makes this point concisely, showing the share of each of these social groups in the liberal vote.

Liberal politicians were vaguely aware of their growing working class support; Anton Erkelenz, a leader of the small liberal trade union federation, suggested that about a half million workers had voted for the liberal parties in the 1907 elections; my estimates are larger, about twice as many. Yet Erkelenz noted, as did other contemporary liberal politicians, that while workers may have voted for the liberal parties, they did not join them. Scattered figures on the membership of liberal political clubs support these contemporary assertions. Over 80% of the members came

---

[38] On special interest groups for small businessmen, and the influence of the Agrarian League, see Puhle, *Agrarische Interessenpolitik*, pp. 153–54 and Stegmann, *Die Erben Bismarcks*, pp. 40–46, 143–45, 249–56.

[39] A similar conclusion about liberal support, albeit with different methods and from different data, in Winkler, *Sozialstruktur*, p. 250.

Table 3.7 *The composition of the liberal electorate in Wilhelmine Germany (percent)*

	Confession					
	1890–98			1903–12		
Class	Protestant	Catholic	All	Protestant	Catholic	All
Farmers	33	34	33	24	26	23
Middle class	54	42	52	38	34	42
Workers	13	25	15	38	40	34
All	100	101	100	100	100	99

from the middle class; working class representation was less than 10%.[40] Just as the SPD had a large middle-class vote and a small middle-class party membership, the liberal parties had a substantial working-class vote and a small working-class membership. We might say that party membership in Wilhelmine Germany ran along the lines suggested by Rainer Lepsius in his milieu thesis, but joining a party and voting for it were two different things. Historians ought to be cautious about drawing conclusions concerning a party's electorate from its membership, or vice versa.

The sources do not make it possible to distinguish between the voters for the National Liberals and the left-liberal parties. The former generally did a good deal better than the latter in communities of under 2,000 (between 1898 and 1912 by a ratio of about 1.5:1), while the left-liberals obtained their best results in cities with populations of between 100,000 and 500,000, outpacing National Liberals there by about 1.25:1.[41] These figures suggest, but do not prove that the National Liberals were stronger among farmers than the progressives, while the latter did somewhat better among urban workers and the middle class. On the basis of the sources used in the electoral analysis, there is simply no way to go any further, to say anything more exact about which of the two wings of the liberal movement had more support and when.[42]

We can speculate a bit more about the connection between the social

[40] Nipperdey, *Die Organisation der Deutschen Parteien*, p. 188, and see also pp. 102–5, 187–90; Pohl, "Ein zweiter Emanzipationsprozeß," pp. 329–40.
[41] The left-liberals had a similar margin over the National Liberals in the largest urban areas, with populations over 500,000, but such metropoli were the strongholds of the SPD. Figures from Suvall, *Electoral Politics*, pp. 80–81.
[42] Schmädeke, *Wählerbewegung*, 1: 371–74, 413–15, can also get no further on this point. (Winkler, on the other hand, always analyzes the liberal parties as a group, never distinguishing among them.) Perhaps the main distinction between the voters of the two liberal groupings was to be found in different regional political traditions.

composition of the different parties' electorates and the movements of voters between the parties (cf. table 3.3). Characteristic of the entire Wilhelmine era were net voter movements from the conservative parties to the SPD and from the liberal parties to the conservatives; in the 1890s, there was a substantial flow of voters from the liberals to the SPD; after 1900, the movement of voters went in the other direction. It is tempting, although ultimately unprovable, to connect these movements with the changes in the social composition of the conservative and especially the liberal parties discussed above. The voters leaving the liberals for the SPD in the 1890s might well have belonged to the Protestant middle class, given the way that group's support for the liberals declined as sharply as it increased for the Social Democrats. The small but steady overall transfer of votes from the liberals to the conservatives could have reflected losses of both farming and urban middle-class voters to the conservatives. Protestant workers could have left the conservative parties for the SPD throughout the Wilhelmine era, with some of them then turning to the liberals after 1900. This would explain both the persistent loss of conservative votes to the Social Democrats, the latter's loss of votes to the liberals after 1900 and how a fairly constant 35% of Protestant workers voted for the conservative and liberal parties together between 1890 and 1912, but over this whole period their preferences shifted from the conservatives to the liberals.

What does seem less speculative is the changes in voting patterns that resulted from the liberal parties' post-1900 reorientation and reorganization. Working from a new style of mass organization and agitation, increasingly utilizing aggressively nationalist appeals, the liberals were able to replace their losses in the decade of the 1890s by drawing voters from the SPD, the minority parties, and the previous non-voters. But the voters regained by the liberal parties after 1900 cannot have been the same voters that these parties lost in the previous decade: the liberal electorate in the empire's three twentieth-century general elections was more Roman Catholic, more working class, and less Protestant and middle class than it had been before. The liberal parties recovered from their crisis in the 1890s by finding a new base of support.

Liberal and conservative voters: change and stability

In summing up the results of this chapter, we might begin by accentuating the negative. It is difficult to see the conservative and liberal parties as representing and being supported by a national voting bloc. Liberals and conservatives did share something of a common electorate and there were, to be sure, periods (the 1870s, and the elections of 1907 come to mind) when the two groups of parties cooperated and voters followed their lead. Most of the time, though, the different parties competed for voters in common rather than amiably dividing them. The lines of division, however, generally did not run between the liberal and conservative parties, but rather among them. In the 1880s, oppositional left-liberals clashed with a Kartell made up of conservatives and National Liberals; after the turn of the century, conservative parties and some National Liberals sponsored by the Agrarian League were frequently at odds with the Progressives and other National Liberals who were not.

The idea that liberals and conservatives were the parties of Protestant property-owners needs some revision as well. Conservatives and progressives were heavily Protestant parties, but the National Liberals had a substantial Catholic vote, making them a party with a confessionally balanced electorate – a result not achieved by any other major political party before 1914. The voters of these parties were not all property owners either, over a third of Protestant urban workers choosing one of them in the Wilhelmine era. A substantial majority of Protestant agricultural laborers must have voted for the liberal and conservative parties as well. The liberals and conservatives may have had more support from Protestant property-owners than other parties, but other social groups played a major role in their electorate and at least some urban Protestant property-owners voted for other parties.

It is not so much that the idea of these parties as the parties of Protestant property-owners is wrong, as that it needs to be reformulated a bit. The liberals and conservatives were the parties of Protestant farmers – both agricultural proprietors and farm laborers: upwards of 60% of eligible Protestant agrarian voters, more than three-quarters of those who actually cast their ballot chose these parties. After the liberals and conservatives, the second choice for Protestant farmers was non-voting, with the minority parties and Social Democrats together generally not even reaching one-half the proportion of the Protestant agricultural population that did not vote.

Turning to the positive, I would suggest that the electoral history of the liberal and conservative parties in Imperial Germany falls into three phases. The first, in the 1870s, was a period when these parties were predominantly – with some individual exceptions – the parties of government, enjoying official favor and being understood by the voters as such. In the second phase, running from the beginning of the 1880s into the following decade, the orientation toward the government continued, but now these parties were split into two groups, the oppositional left-liberals and the pro-governmental alliance of the conservatives and National Liberals.

While this alignment seems to have satisfied the voters in the 1880s, it clearly did not do so in the following decade, the liberal and conservative parties generally losing supporters to non-voting and to the minority and Social Democratic parties. In a third phase, beginning in the mid-1890s and continuing until the eve of the First World War, these parties reorganized themselves and developed a different political thematic, stressing economic interests and nationalist agitation more, support for or opposition to the government less. Both conservatives and liberals did this, but the results of their efforts were quite different. The conservative parties largely shored up their existing base of support and kept their losses to a minimum. The liberals, on the other hand, started this process later, and so had a good deal of lost ground to make up. They did so, less by recovering voters previously lost than by gaining new supporters, above all from the working class, turning themselves electorally into quite different parties than they had previously been.

Part 2

The elections

4   The Bismarckian elections

The basic procedure used in Part 1 of this book, averaging out the results of elections over the course of a decade, has the advantage of bringing longer term trends into relief. However, it has a number of weaknesses as well, so that by itself it is inadequate for understanding the movements of voters in the general elections of Wilhelmine Germany. For one thing, averaging neglects the importance of swings in the vote from one election to the next. While in all the elections of the 1890s, for instance, the proportion of the electorate consisting of conservative voters switching to the liberals and of liberals switching to the conservatives was about equal, this was not true for each election: in 1890, there was a very sharp swing from conservatives to liberals; three years later, an even sharper swing back to the conservatives. Averaging over a decade also minimizes the significance of individual elections that stand out sharply from preceding and subsequent ones – 1878, for instance, 1907, or, above all, 1887 (a general election, I would argue, that proved to be a crucial turning point in the political history of Imperial Germany).

Consequently, in this and the following chapter, I will discuss the individual general elections. The focus will be on the specific circumstances of each election – the attitude and actions of the state authorities, the campaigns of the parties, and the issues presented to the voters, both by the parties and the government. I will compare these aspects of the elections with the results of the ecological analysis, allowing us to evaluate the effects of the campaigning on the voters. In this way, we will be able at least to get an impression of what issues and what forms of electioneering moved voters to stay with their respective parties, to switch parties, to come out to vote at all, or to reject going to the polls. We can also see the effects of the individual campaigns on the two major confessions, and for the post-1890 elections, on social and confessional groups.

Although these two chapters will proceed in narrative, chronological fashion, this one starting with the first nationwide general elections in 1871 and concluding with the elections of 1887, and the next beginning in 1890 and ending with the last general elections under the empire in

1912, I will also take the opportunity to make comparisons across time, contrasting the voter movements leading to the left-liberal election victory of 1881, for instance, with those that brought the Social Democrats their triumph in 1890, or comparing the three victories of the right in 1878, 1887, and 1907. At the conclusion of these observations we should be in a position to draw some general conclusions about voters and voter movements in Imperial Germany, and to evaluate and revise the existing explanations of them.

The elections of the 1870s

The German Empire of 1871, it should be remembered, was a nation-state born of warfare, emerging from a series of armed conflicts, reaching back to 1863. Electoral politics in the first decade of the empire's existence centered on the acceptance or rejection of the outcomes of these clashes of arms. On the one side were the political parties representing the victors. They affirmed the results of the battlefield that had made possible the creation of a unified German nation-state. The very names of these parties make the point clear: the National Liberals and the party (commonly known as the Free Conservatives) whose official title was the "Party of the German Empire" (*Deutsche Reichspartei*).

On the other side was a coalition of the defeated. One element in this coalition was the national and regional minorities. There were the Polish nationalists, many of whose leaders and all of whose sympathies had been with the anti-Russian Polish insurgents of 1863. Its supression by Czarist troops, with tacit Prussian support, had ended the possibility of creating a Polish nation-state by force of arms. The Danish nationalists had seen the ethnically Danish portions of Schleswig conquered in the war between Denmark and an allied Austria and Prussia in 1864; the Hanoverian particularists had lost their kingdom when its monarch made the fatal mistake of allying with Austria in its war with Prussia in 1866. The best known of these groups were the French nationalists of Alsace-Lorraine, the provinces torn away from their homeland as a result of the Franco-Prussian War.

The single largest element in the coalition was the Center, the political party representing the German Empire's Catholics, who had been the biggest losers of the most crucial of these series of wars, the Prussian–Austrian conflict of 1866. With the armed expulsion of Austria from Germany, Roman Catholics had gone from being a majority of the inhabitants of the German Confederation, the league of states under Habsburg leadership that had been the main factor in central European affairs from 1815 to 1866, to a minority of the citizens in the German

Empire, a much more closely knit form of government, dominated by the distinctly Protestant Prussian monarchy. The leading figure in the Center Party, the attorney Ludwig Windthorst, who also represented the deposed king of Hanover, both symbolized and led this oppositional coalition.

We can make out two elements within the opposition, best designated by the names given their representatives in Alsace-Lorraine. There were the "protestors," who rejected the entire state of affairs, announcing that a vote for them was a vote cast against the empire, or at least against Alsace-Lorraine's being a part of it, and the "autonomists," who reluctantly accepted the military *fait accompli*, but wished to make the best of it by reducing the influence of the German government in the conquered provinces to an absolute minimum. Similar divisions of opinion, if not quite so openly articulated, characterized the Polish nationalists, the Hanoverians particularists and could also be found among adherents of political Catholicism.[1]

The supporters of the German Empire feared that such a coalition of the defeated could be a serious threat to the integrity of their newly created nation-state. In retrospect, their fears were greatly exaggerated. While in the initial decade of the empire, opposition to its very existence was widespread and would continue to emerge sporadically as late as the 1890s, by the turn of the century the number of serious and determined opponents of its existence among the supporters of the minority parties, with the exception of the Polish nationalists, had become few in number and seemed increasingly like eccentrics and cranks.[2] However, in the 1870s, the friends of the empire could not know that it would prove to be a sturdy creation whose basic territorial integrity was only undermined by defeat in two world wars. In light of the events of 1989–91, and the rapidity with which a seemingly very powerful state based at least in part on military conquest vanished from the scene, we might today find the fears about the long-term prospects of a unified nation-state easier to understand. Supporters of the nation-state fanned these fears by conflating – both unintentionally and with cynical purpose – the distinction between

---

[1] Hiery, *Reichstagswahlen im Reichsland*, pp. 136–75; Aschoff, *Welfische Bewegung und politischer Katholizismus*, pp. 47–48, 126–30; Hattenkofer, *Regierende und Regierte*, p. 44; Blanke, *Prussian Poland*, pp. 6–7, 12–13, 109–10.

[2] For an example of hostility to the empire in the 1890s, see Dieter Brosius, *Rudolf von Bennigsen als Oberpräsident der Provinz Hannover 1888–1897* (Hildesheim: August Lax Verlagsbuchhandlung, 1964), p. 33 n. 22. An intriguing account of a resolute enemy of the empire, whose continued opposition to it well into the twentieth century made him into an eccentric and crank is Enno Knobel's book on the Hessian particularists, and their party's founder and dominant figure, Wilhelm Hopf (see Knobel, *Die Hessische Rechtspartei*, pp. 241–50 and passim).

autonomists and protestors among the minority parties.[3] The clash between friends and enemies of the empire, promoted by fears and illusions on both sides, gave the electoral politics of the 1870s an especially bitter character.

Whatever the extent of their resistance to the creation of the empire, the coalition of the defeated would be the main political alternative to the parties of the victors. In the four general elections of the 1870s, the parties representing this clash of opinion about the existence of the empire – the National Liberals and the Free Conservatives endorsing it, the Center and the other minority parties calling for its rejection or drastic modification – received almost three-quarters of the votes cast. Of these votes, in turn almost three-quarters fell to the leading parties of each group, the National Liberals and the Center. In 1874, these two parties accounted for 60% of votes cast between them.

The other political parties of the decade were divided on this existential question. The bourgeois left was split between the Progressives, in the north, who supported the empire, and the German People's Party in the south, which opposed it. There was a similar division between the two Social Democratic parties before their merger of 1875, separating the General German Workers' Association (the "Lassalleans"), with strongholds in Prussia and northern Germany, which endorsed Bismarck's work, and the Social Democratic Labor Party (the "Eisenachers"), centered in the south, which vehemently condemned it. The traditional Prussian Conservatives were not so much split as uncertain and vascillating on what position to take. The expansion of the power of the kingdom of Prussia that had gone along with the creation of the empire was certainly welcome to them; the overthrow of legitimate sovereigns in Hessen-Kassel or Hanover, the introduction of universal manhood suffrage, and the increasing cooperation between Chancellor Bismarck and the National Liberal politicians in legislation concerning social, economic, religious, educational and legal affairs was less enticing.

The elections of 1871

Although most historians would agree that the divisions between the political parties in the 1870s were along the lines I have described above,

[3] For fears of the empire's disintegration, both real and manufactured for political purposes in the early 1870s, see Anderson, *Windthorst*, pp. 53–62; Otto Pflanze, *Bismarck and the Development of Germany* 2nd edn, 3 vols. (Princeton: Princeton University Press, 1990), 2: 95–126, 179–202; on the continuation of such feelings into the 1890s, see the acute comments of John C. G. Röhl, *The Kaiser and his Court: Wilhelm II and the Government of Germany* trans. Terence F. Cole (Cambridge and New York: Cambridge University Press, 1994), pp. 112–13.

many would not see them as a consequence of the warfare leading to the creation of a unified German state. Rather, they would assert, there existed other possible political alignments – an alliance between the Center and the Conservatives, for instance, or a more oppositional liberalism that, by opposing Bismarck, gained the Catholic vote and rendered the Center Party unnecessary. These possibilities were eliminated by Bismarck's decision to launch the *Kulturkampf*, targeting the Catholics and offending Conservatives, and by the liberals' anti-clerical support of his decision, thus permanently alienating any Catholic support and driving the Conservatives into a temporary opposition to a government espousing policies they understood as anti-religious.[4]

Like all counter-factual assertions, these cannot be definitively tested, since we cannot rerun the Reichstag elections of the 1870s with the government or the liberal parties pursuing different policies. We can, however, have a closer look at the first general elections of the German Empire in 1871 that were held under somewhat different circumstances than those of their successors later in the decade. First, the polling took place just a few days after the signing of the Treaty of Frankfurt, bringing the Franco-Prussian War to a victorious conclusion, and in the aftermath of enthusiastic victory parades and victory celebrations held throughout the country. They were thus very much under the influence of the last (and admittedly the least controversial) of the wars of German unification. Second, the *Kulturkampf* had not yet begun, Bismarck not having decided whether or not to attack the Catholic Church. The clear distinction between support for friends of the new state and hostility to the clerical, particularist, and foreign "enemies of the Reich," which provided the basis for official actions in the general elections later in the decade, was missing. Political commentaries in the major government-owned newspaper and the Prussian state news service concentrated their fire on the left-liberals, denouncing both the Progressives and the German People's Party, calling for political cooperation between the Conservatives and the National Liberals. The Center played less of a role in these national-level, public pronouncements.[5]

At the local level, official attitudes were mixed, the state authorities in Prussia's western provinces of the Rhineland and Westphalia not at all

---

[4] See, for instance, Gustav Schmidt, "Die Nationalliberalen – eine regierungsfähige Partei? Zur Problematik der inneren Reichsgründung 1870–1878," in Ritter (ed.) *Die Deutschen Parteien*, pp. 208–23; Anderson, *Windthorst*, pp. 192–200; Rohe, *Wahlen und Wählertraditionen*, pp. 81–83.

[5] Steinbach, *Die Zähmung des politischen Massenmarktes*, pp. 283–92; *Wilhelm Liebknecht Briefwechsel* (ed. Georg Eckert), 1: 514–16; Michael Stürmer, *Regierung und Reichstag im Bismarckstaat: Cäsarismus oder Parlamentarismus*, pp. 38–39; Frank, *Die Brandenburger als Reichstagswähler*, p. 29.

unfriendly to the Center, while those in the monarchy's south-eastern province of Silesia generally hostile, supporting instead the Free Conservatives. There were even a few officials in the province of Hanover, willing to endorse the particularists against the National Liberals, seeing the former as true conservatives, the latter as crypto-revolutionaries. In the states of southern Germany with a large Roman Catholic population, such as Baden and Bavaria, governments vigorously supported liberal candidates and opposed their Center rivals – not surprisingly, since clashes between the state on the one hand and the Catholic Church and a nascent political Catholicism on the other had characterized the political scene for much of the 1860s.[6]

Liberal anti-clericalism and Catholic anti-liberalism were, however, quite pronounced, with the National Liberals and the Center at each other's throats. The national appeals of the former party, if directing much of its fire at particularists, such as the Hanoverians, or at the Prussian conservatives, also found space to denounce the "Ultramontanists . . . with their hypocritical cry of alarm that the rights of the Catholic church are endangered." In his pastoral letter on the elections, widely reprinted in the Catholic press, Bishop Ketteler of Mainz, the politically most prominent figure in the German episcopate, made no secret of his feelings about "parties existing widely throughout Germany, that in the name of free-thinking or liberal aspirations seek to transform all existing institutions according to the principles of godlessness and lack of belief. They are always talking about freedom but in reality practise the worst kind of tyranny." When the two parties actually campaigned against each other, much more strident accusations, denouncing opponents as tools of the Jesuits or the Freemasons, enlivened the election campaign.[7]

Clashes between liberalism and political Catholicism, or between liberals and particularists, thus predated Bismarck's taking up policies hostile to the church. The election of 1871 was, at least, one in which the authorities had not yet solidly lined up behind the liberals as they would later in the decade, so that we can partially separate out the effects on the voters of the wars of unification from those of the *Kulturkampf.* We can see the choices of Catholic voters under these circumstances (detailed in table

---

[6] Sperber, *Popular Catholicism*, pp. 189–90; Schloßmacher, *Düsseldorf im Bismarckreich*, pp. 200–1; Margaret Anderson, "The Kulturkampf and the Course of Germany History," *Central European History* 19 (1986): 82–115, esp. pp. 95–106; Aschoff, *Welfische Bewegung und politischer Katholizismus*, p. 102; Grohs, *Die Liberale Reichspartei*, pp. 4–7; Sepainter, *Die Reichstagswahlen im Großherzogtum Baden*, pp. 203–4.

[7] Both quotations cited in Steinbach, *Die Zähmung des politischen Massenmarktes*, pp. 305, 332; examples of election campaigns are given in Sperber, *Popular Catholicism*, p. 190; Schloßmacher, *Düsseldorf im Bismarckreich*, pp. 196–200; Weber, *"Eine starke, enggeschlossene Phalanx,"* pp. 75–99.

Table 4.1 *The Catholic vote in the 1871 elections (percent)*

Party group	All Germany	Region		
		Center candidates	Prussia	Non-Prussian Germany
Conservatives	10	8	13	5
Liberals	21	18	11	34
Center	25	35	23	28
Other minority parties	6	0	11	0
Social Democrats	0	0	1	0
Non-voters	38	39	42	33
All	100	100	101	100

4.1), giving the votes of the Catholic electorate for all of Germany, just in those constituencies where the Center Party nominated candidates in Prussia and in non-Prussian Germany.[8]

Only 31% of eligible Catholic voters supported the Center and the other minority parties in 1871, the very lowest level of support that these parties would ever have from Catholic voters and the only general election in the history of the *Kaiserreich* when other parties received as many Catholic votes as the minority parties did. Such a substantial level of support for the liberal and conservative parties, either open or at least half-hearted adherents of the new nation-state, would seem to demonstrate that the strong confessional polarization later in the decade did not yet apply, suggesting that these were at least in part the result of the government's anti-clerical measures and the liberal support they received.

However, the figures in Table 4.1 also offer some support for the role of the wars of unification in shaping lines of electoral allegiance. Non-voters made up 38% of the Catholic electorate, so that the turnout rate among Catholic voters, 62% of those eligible to vote, was much higher than the more modest 43% of their Protestant counterparts. Most Catholics voted in 1871; most Protestants did not, so something confessionally specific must have been influencing the voters, if not the *Kulturkampf*. Winfried Grohs, author of an interesting study of the *Liberale Reichspartei*, a short-lived parliamentary grouping of south German moderate liberals, has observed that in 1871 the hardest-fought elections with the highest turnouts were those between proponents and opponents of the new nation-state, between National Liberals and Hanoverian particularists, or

[8] Winkler, *Sozialstruktur*, p. 169, gives figures for the Catholic and Protestant vote in all of Germany from 1871 to 1878 that differ from my estimates by about one percentage point.

between liberals and those Bavarian Centrists, who were opposed to Bavaria joining a united Germany.[9] We cannot say that all Catholics cast a ballot opposing the nation-state, since many of them voted for the liberal and conservative parties endorsing it, but we might assert that the validity of the new empire was a more divisive issue among Catholics in 1871 than among Protestants.

The Center Party was not completely organized on a national scale in 1871, and there were a number of ethnically German constituencies with large Roman Catholic populations where it did not put up candidates. If we take just the constituencies where Center candidadates stood for office, we find that Catholics supported it over other parties by a ratio of about 4:3. Here, the Catholic preference for the Center was more pronounced, although there were still a substantial number of Catholics voting for parties opposed to it and the level of support for the Center as compared to the other parties was lower than at any other election during the empire.

A pronounced regional difference was also apparent in 1871. In Prussia, eligible Catholic voters preferred the minority parties over the liberals and conservatives by about 3:2. Outside of Prussia, for the first and only time in the history of the empire, the minority parties (in this case, the Center; since the Reichstag elections were not held in Alsace-Lorraine in 1871, there were no French nationalists on the ballot) were not the top choice for Catholic voters: 28% of them chose the Center, as against 34% for the liberals and 5% for the conservatives. One could argue that such a vote showed potential Catholic support for liberalism, had the liberals not abandoned their opposition to the government and taken up anti-clericalism, but this assertion would comport poorly with the regional structure of liberalism. Outside of Prussia the oppositional left-liberals – mostly, the democratic German People's Party, very oppositional and on the far left of the party spectrum – attracted just 3% of Catholic voters in 1871. The vast majority of Catholic liberal voters supported candidates of the National Liberals and the Liberale Reichspartei, groups that endorsed the creation of the empire, enjoyed the backing of the governments of the south German states and were strongly anti-clerical.

Indeed, the 1871 elections in southern Germany took place under unusual circumstances, with the liberal forces powerfully enhanced by the victorious conclusion of the Franco-Prussian War, and with their clerical opponents, especially in Bavaria, divided between those who rejected the accession of the south German states to the German Empire and

[9] Grohs, *Die Liberale Reichspartei*, p. 15.

those who wished to make the best of it. Catholic politics in southern
Germany was also disrupted by the controversy over the First Vatican
Council and its declaration of Papal Infallibility, that had stirred up a
surprisingly widespread if short-lived opposition.[10] All these considerations suggest that the 1871 elections might also be seen as reflecting the
contrast between friends and enemies of the new nation-state that would
be so dominant later on in the decade, only with special circumstances
offering the supporters of the new empire usually strong Catholic support
in southern Germany.

The Kulturkampf elections of 1874

The results of the 1871 elections thus offer evidence backing both assertions, that the wars of German unification, particularly the Austro-
Prussian War of 1866, were the dominant factor in creating voting
alignments in the first decade of universal manhood suffrage, but also that
the main determining factor was the *Kulturkampf*, and that the situation
in 1871 was more open than it would be later in the decade. A look at the
1874 elections, although it cannot allow us to decide between these two
options, might help clarify the arguments in support of each of them.

The polarization between friends and enemies of the empire was at its
most complete in the general elections of 1874. The main opposing
parties were the same as in 1871, the National Liberals with the Free
Conservatives as a subsidiary grouping on the one hand, and the Center,
flanked by the regional and national minorities – this time including the
French nationalists of Alsace-Lorraine – on the other. However, there
were several changes in this alignment, as a result of the policies of the
national and Prussian government – particularly the anti-clerical measures of the *Kulturkampf* – over the three previous years. First, the north
German left-liberals, the Progressive Party, gave up their previously
oppositional stance and portrayed themselves to the voters as a party
endorsing the liberal and anti-clerical actions of the German government. (In southern Germany, the People's Party continued in opposition
but received little support from the voters.) Second, the Conservatives,
embittered by what they saw as attacks on religion by Chancellor
Bismarck, their one time leader, and even more offended by the liberal

---

[10] Werner Blessing, *Staat und Kirche in der Gesellschaft: Institutionelle Autorität und mentaler
Wandel in Bayern im 19. Jahrhundert* (Göttingen: Vandenhoeck & Ruprecht, 1982), pp.
181–84; Fischer, *Industrialisierung, sozialer Konflikt und politische Willensbildung*, pp.
257–58; Sepainter, *Die Reichstagswahlen im Großherzogtum Baden*, pp. 87–92; Grohs, *Die
Liberale Reichspartei*, pp. 20–23; Hattenkofer, *Regierende und Regierte*, p. 44; Bräunche,
Parteien und Reichstagswahlen in der Rheinpfalz, pp. 209–12.

socieconomic and legal reforms his government was proposing, put themselves forward as a party of opposition.[11]

This realignment of the parties changed little for government attitudes in southern Germany, where the authorities continued, as they had in 1871, to endorse the National Liberals and to use their influence against the Conservatives and the Center. In Prussia, on the other hand, officials were mobilized against the Center and, at the very least, ordered not to work on behalf of the oppositional Conservatives. However, a number of county commissioners and other officials in the eastern provinces kicked over the traces and defied their superiors by supporting the right-wing opposition.[12]

The liberal election campaign in 1874, if still conducted within the borders of notables' politics, was more vigorous than three years previously and a good deal harsher. Not content with denouncing the Center parliamentarians as *"Reichsfeinde,"* as enemies of the nation, Badenese National Liberals went on to call them *"Franzosenvertreter,"* representatives of the French.[13] Whether expressing rhetorical excess, cynical calcuation, or fanatical hostility, such a remark exposed the connection between the wars of national unification and the new policies of the central government immediately following them. Ironically, the actual representatives of the French in the German Reichstag, the nationalist deputies from Alsace-Lorraine, were elected largely through the efforts of the Catholic clergy who informed the voting faithful of the linked dangers of foreign rule and religious persecution. Much the same occurred among the Polish nationalists in eastern Germany, the persecution of the Catholic Church – particularly vigorous in those regions – bringing together religion and nationality, somewhat to the embarrassment of a number of the leaders of the Polish nationalists, liberal and anti-clerical like their German nationalist counterparts.[14]

Interestingly, the Center Party conducted a much more modest election campaign in 1874 than it had three years previously. But it had little need to engage in vigorous appeals to the voters. Both the measures of the government in pursuing the *Kulturkampf*, which had put bishops in jail and left many parishes without priests, and the Catholic opposition to them, in the form of unorganized riots and demonstrations, as well as

---

[11] Generally, on public pronouncements by the parties, and broad lines of orientation, see Steinbach, *Die Zähmung des politischen Massenmarktes,* pp. 371–409. A concise discussion of legislation and government policy between 1871 and 1874, and their effects on the parties is in Stürmer, *Regierung und Reichstag,* pp. 42–117.

[12] Examples of this in Frank, *Die Brandenburger als Reichstagswähler,* pp. 116, 131.

[13] Cited in Sepainter, *Die Wahlen im Großherzogtum Baden,* p. 94.

[14] Hiery, *Reichstagswahlen im Reichsland,* pp. 136–75; Blanke, *Prussian Poland,* pp. 27–28; William Hagen, *Germans, Poles and Jews: The Nationality Conflict in the Prussian East, 1772–1914* (Chicago and London: The University of Chicago Press, 1980), pp. 144–46.

Table 4.2 *Composition of the minority party electorate of 1874 (percent)*

		Region	
Vote in 1871	Prussia	Non-Prussian Germany	All Germany
Conservatives	7	6	8
Liberals	4	24	13
Minority parties	51	43	49
Social Democrats	0	0	0
Non-voters	34	7	25
Net new voters	4	20	5
All	100	100	100

carefully conducted petitions and mass meetings, had made the period between the general elections into a sort of permanent election campaign. The organized opposition to the *Kulturkampf* had been filled with attacks on the government, cooperating with or being dominated by godless liberalism, thus preparing the way for the Center's theme for the 1874 election, as the Catholic newspaper in Regensburg noted, whether "Christianity in Germany [is] to be or not to be." The *Badische Beobachter*, chief newspaper of political Catholicism in that south German state brought this assertion into the context of the wars of German unification, saying: "The liberal leaders declare that the war is now just really starting; we have made peace with France; with Rome (that is, the Catholic Church), we will never make peace."[15]

The single most important result of the elections was the rapid growth of the minority parties, from 13% of eligible voters in 1871 to 24% three years later. Also noteworthy was the decline of the conservatives, whose share of the electorate fell from 12 to 9%, while the share of the liberal parties increased by the same three percentage points to about one-fourth of eligible voters. Table 4.2 gives the composition of the minority party electorate in 1874, in terms of its 1871 vote.[16] Please note that these

[15] Quotations from Chrobak, "Politische Parteien, Verbände und Vereine in Regensburg," pt. 3, p. 261 and Sepainter, *Reichstagswahlen im Großherzogtum Baden*, p. 94. More generally on these points, see Sperber, *Popular Catholicism*, p. 253; Bräunche, *Parteien und Reichstagswahlen in der Rheinpfalz*, pp. 212–14; Schloßmacher, *Düsseldorf im Bismarckreich*, pp. 207–8; Liebert, *Politische Wahlen in Wiesbaden*, pp. 101–3; Hattenkofer, *Regierende und Regierte*, pp. 51–54, 94–96.
[16] The estimates of voter transition probabilities for the 1870s given in Winkler, *Sozialstruktur*, pp. 125–28, are similar to mine although the discrepancies are greater than in the estimates of voting by confession. These differences are probably the result of the use of different forms of ecological regression, as is discussed in the appendix.

Table 4.3 *The Catholic vote in the 1874 elections (percent)*

Party group	All Germany	Center candidates	Prussia	Non-Prussian Germany
		Region		
Conservatives	6	5	9	2
Liberals	14	13	11	18
Center	46	58	45	46
Other minority parties	13	0	10	12
Social Democrats	1	1	1	0
Non-voters	21	23	23	21
All	101	100	99	99

results are for the 382 constituencies outside of Alsace-Lorraine, since elections were not held there in 1871.

The sources of the growth of the minority parties' vote were regionally quite distinct. In Prussia, this increase was fueled above all by previous non-voters; in southern Germany, by voters switching from the liberal parties. Another way of looking at this is to note that 8% of the voters in Prussia who had cast their ballots for the conservative and liberal parties in 1871, voted for the minority parties in 1874; while outside of Prussia, twice as great a proportion – 17% of liberal and conservative voters – went over to the minority parties.[17] The *Kulturkampf* may have mobilized the minority parties' clientele, but it did so quite differently in Baden than in Westphalia, in Bavaria than in Silesia.

To follow up and elaborate on this point, table 4.3 gives the Catholic vote in 1874, broken down by region.

Comparison with table 4.1 shows two quite distinct patterns. In Prussia, the proportion of Catholics supporting the Center doubled between 1871 and 1874, going from 23 to 45%, but the proportion of Catholic voters supporting the liberal parties remained unchanged, and the proportion voting for the conservatives declined slightly from 13 to 9%. Outside of Prussia, the Catholic Center vote also increased strongly, but the proportion of Catholics supporting the liberals took a nose-dive, dropping from 34 to 18%. Admittedly, the 1871 and 1874 figures for non-Prussian Germany are not entirely comparable because elections

[17] The reader will note that the figures for all of Germany are clearly not the average of those for Prussia and non-Prussian Germany, with the deviation being greatest for thè net new voters. This is the sort of case I mentioned in the Introduction, and is probably best explained by the possibility that the regression equations overestimated the proportion of net new voters among other minority party electorate in non-Prussian Germany.

were held in Alsace-Lorraine in 1874 for the first time, resulting in an overwhelming victory for the protesters and the autonomists, with the "German" political parties just receiving a handful of votes.[18] Nonetheless, the distinction between the two regions is clear. About 90% of the increase in Catholic support for the minority parties in Prussia between 1871 and 1874 can be attributed to the increase in turnout, while only 40% of this increase outside of Prussia was due to a rise in turnout, the rest resulting from voters switching to the Center from other political parties. If we take only those constituencies with Center candidates, we find that about two-thirds of the increase in the percentage of eligible Catholic voters casting their ballots for the Center resulted from increased turnout, and one-third from voters switching from other parties, similar proportions obtaining for all the minority parties in Germany as a whole.

These results demonstrate the paradox of the political effects of the *Kulturkampf*. In Prussia, the political situation changed drastically between 1871 and 1874: the authorities went from being sometimes favorable to the Center Party to completely hostile to it; the *Kulturkampf* was at its harshest, with bishops sent to jail and priests banned from their parishes. There, the proportion of Catholics voting for parties other than the Center or the closely allied national and regional minorities changed relatively little, those voting for the liberal enemies of political Catholicism changed not at all. The Catholic vote for the minority parties increased, and dramatically, but primarily because previous non-voters were mobilized to vote.[19] In states outside of Prussia with a large Catholic population – Hessen, Baden, Bavaria, Württemberg – the political situation had changed much less: the authorities were on the side of the National Liberals in 1874 as they had been in 1871, and the confrontation between church and state was nowhere near as severe as in Prussia. Bishops were not arrested, vacant parishes were filled, and the public exercise and practice of the Roman Catholic religion continued with little change. Yet the liberal parties suffered substantial losses among Catholic voters, these losses accounting for much of the Center's gains.

[18] If we imagine that elections had been held in Alsace-Lorraine in 1871 and that they had produced the same results – an overwhelming victory for the French nationalists – that they had in 1874 (hardly an implausible speculation), then liberals would have accounted for 28% of eligible Catholic voters in non-Prussian Germany, instead of the 34% that they actually did, and the Center would have been the choice of 23% instead of 28% of eligible Catholic voters. In other words, the addition of Alsace-Lorraine to non-Prussian Germany in 1874 accounts for about six of the sixteen percentage point drop in the Catholic liberal vote, as against the previous general election, but the other ten percentage points were still the result of Catholic voters switching to the Center.
[19] For a similar argument with regard to voting trends in the Prussian provinces of Rhineland and Westphalia, see Sperber, *Popular Catholicism*, pp. 254–56.

We can best resolve this paradox, if we understand the *Kulturkampf* as contemporaries did, as a continuation of the wars of German unification by other means. In 1871, at the beginning of mass politics in the German nation-state, both the parties of the victors in the wars of unification and the coalition of the defeated were organized and mobilized in Prussia; the lines of division between them were clearly and sharply drawn – in spite of, or perhaps because of the Prussian government's not speaking with one voice on whom to support. The *Kulturkampf* then continued and deepened these lines of division, the coalition of the defeated increasing its votes by mobilizing previous non-voters. In the political circumstances of southern Germany in 1871, on the other hand, the contrast between the parties of the victors and the parties of the defeated was less sharp. This was in part because of different initial conditions (the greater prevalence of anti-clericalism and religious heterodoxy among Catholics in southern Germany) but largely because the advocates of the victors were active and vigorous, enjoying official support, basking in the victories of German arms, while the losers were divided and uncertain. The *Kulturkampf* provided an issue around which the political coalition of the defeated could rally, mobilizing previous non-voters, as in Prussia, but also winning over voters it had lost to the opposing political coalition, due to the special circumstances existing three years previously.

The victory of the minority parties in the 1874 elections was thus the result of both a substantial increase in turnout (turnout of Catholic voters rose from 62% in 1871 to 79% in 1874, while turnout among Protestant voters increased over the same period more modestly, from 43 to 51%) and also of a substantial, if overall smaller movement of Catholic voters from the liberal and conservative parties to the Center and the other minority parties. This large influx of new voters into the minority party electorate from these two different sources occurring in 1874 would not be repeated in any subsequent election of Bismarckian Germany: at least 70% of the minority party voters at each general election from 1877 through 1890 would be those who had voted for the minority parties at a previous election.

The voter movements behind the modest liberal successes in 1871 were a mirror image of those of the minority parties and reflect the polarization of the electorate into national and oppositional camps. Of the 1871 liberal voters, 70% remained with the liberals in 1874. To be sure, 12% of the liberals' supporters of 1871 went over to the minority parties (a mere 4% chose the conservatives) but these defectors were more than balanced by the 24% of 1871 non-voters who cast their ballots for the liberals. While the liberal share of the Catholic electorate declined from 21% in 1871 to 14% three years later, liberal support among eligible

Protestant voters (and Protestant voters outnumbered Catholics by almost two to one) grew from 25 to 31%. Just as the minority parties mobilized Catholics against the new empire and its policies of religious and ethnic persecution, the liberal parties mobilized Protestants in favor of the newly created nation-state and its policies of cementing internally the external unity won on the battlefield.

This political polarization between governmental liberal parties, with strong Protestant support, and anti-governmental minority parties, with strong Catholic support, boded ill for the conservatives. The right-wing parties put up relatively few candidates: the 1874 general elections were the only ones in the history of the empire when conservative candidacies covered less than 50% of the electorate and the conservative vote dropped beneath 10% of eligible voters (figures 3.1 and 3.3). Where they did put up candidates, the voters deserted them in large numbers. Less than half of the conservative voters of 1871 – 46% is my estimate – voted for one of the conservative parties in 1874, with 17% choosing the liberals, 15% one of the minority parties, and 22% not voting. Smaller percentages of both Protestant and Catholic voters chose the conservative parties in 1874 as compared to 1871. While the vote for the pro-governmental Free Conservatives held steady, at about 4.5% of the electorate in both 1871 and 1874, the oppositional Conservatives saw their vote decline from 7 to 4% of eligible voters. In Bismarckian Germany, conservative parties were successful as parties of government, relying on the support and goodwill of the authorities; in opposition, they had few prospects.

The elections of 1877 and 1878

Much of the story of the two final general elections of the 1870s involves the resurgence of the conservative vote via a return of the conservative parties to a thoroughly pro-governmental position. The refounding of the Conservative Party as the German-Conservative Party in 1876 marked an important step in this direction. It involved no genuine organizational changes, the party continuing to be a loose coalition held together by parliamentary deputies and supported at the local level by large estate-owners and Protestant pastors. In a sense, what was most significant about the reorganization, in the context of the politics of the 1870s, was the party's new name. The Conservatives were to be a "German," a "national," party, endorsing the existence of the nation-state as Bismarck created it, no longer leaving the national label – and the concomitant support for and by the government – to the National Liberals and the Party of the German Empire. The politicians who reorganized the con-servative party had close ties with the Association of Tax and Tariff

Reformers, an economic interest group of large landowners who called for an end to a liberal, laissez-faire economic policy and government measures, such as protective tariffs, to raise farm prices that had fallen sharply in the second-half of the 1870s. If the Conservatives were moving toward the government, the government under Bismarck was moving closer to them. Disappointed that the liberal anti-clericalism of the *Kulturkampf* had neither caused the ecclesiastical hierarchy to cave in to official pressure, nor the clergy to drop their support for the minority parties, and worried that the economic liberalism of free trade was doing nothing to bring the German economy out of the depression it had entered following the crash of 1873, the Chancellor was growing disillusioned with his erstwhile liberal parliamentary allies, who had supported and encouraged his government to follow both of these paths.[20]

It was not so much that Bismarck intended to drop the liberal parties altogether and replace them with the conservatives – an electoral impossibility – but rather that he hoped to bring the National Liberals, in the 1870s by far the larger of the two major liberal groupings, along with him in his move toward more conservative policies. This was certainly how the state-run press organs portrayed the 1877 elections, denouncing the left-liberals and calling for cooperation between the government, the conservative parties, and the National Liberals for the creation of a "national majority from conservative and liberal circles."[21] The strategy behind such comments was not to give up the polarization of political life between the "national" parties, the friends of the nation as it emerged from the wars of unification, and the *Reichsfeinde*, the enemies of the nation. Rather, it was to redefine the specific policies associated with the nation, in doing so both upgrading the position of the conservatives vis-à-vis the liberals and changing positions that all the national parties would take on crucial issues.

The general elections of 1877 and 1878 followed along the lines suggested by this reorientation. In areas where the minority parties were influential, the election continued to be a struggle between them and the national parties, with the latter still enjoying the support of the authorities, and with both the issues and the style of the campaigns little changed from 1874.[22] Although the *Kulturkampf* was far from over, the

---

[20] On these developments, see Retallack, *Notables of the Right*, pp. 13–22; Stürmer, *Regierung und Reichstag*, pp. 137–79.
[21] Cited in Steinbach, *Die Zähmung des politischen Massenmarktes*, p. 428. More generally, on the government's attitude, see pp. 427–34.
[22] Sepainter, *Die Reichstagswahlen im Großherzogtum Baden*, pp. 98–113; Bräunche, *Parteien und Reichstagswahlen in der Rheinpfalz*, pp. 215–18; Sperber, *Popular Catholicism*, p. 253; Schloßmacher, *Düsseldorf im Bismarckreich*, pp. 217–20; Hattenkofer, *Regierende und Regierte*, pp. 94–96; Hiery, *Reichstagswahlen im Reichsland*, pp. 178–99.

sense of urgency characteristic of the 1874 elections, generated not so much by the election campaign itself as by the dramatic events of the two previous years, was no longer present. Catholic turnout in both 1877 and 1878 was ten percentage points lower than in 1874, and over the two elections the net losses of the minority parties to abstention about equaled the net gains these parties had obtained from previous non-voters in 1874.[23]

Of the two trends characterizing the minority party electorate in 1874 – the mobilization of previous non-voters and the gaining of votes from the national parties – the former was reversed but not the latter. A steady stream of voters continued to leave the conservative and, particularly, the liberal parties for the Center or the Hanoverians in 1877 and 1878; in fact, of the total net losses of the liberals to the minority parties throughout the decade, about 40% occurred after the 1874 elections. A fair speculation would be that these late defectors were voters who had previously been pressured by the authorities into supporting the liberals. As government policy moved in a more conservative direction and the futility of combatting the minority parties in their strongholds became more apparent, official pressures eased off, leaving these voters freer to vote according to their conscience.[24]

Losing voters to the minority parties was the least of the liberals' problems at the ballot box during the general elections of 1877 and 1878. Net liberal losses to the conservative parties outweighed losses to the minority parties by about 4:1. In each of these two elections, the liberals lost about twice as many voters to the conservatives as the latter had lost to the liberals in 1874. Although the conservative vote only increased modestly between 1874 and 1877, from 9 to 11% of eligible voters, this change reflected a pattern of losses among Catholics and more substantial gains among Protestants. Of eligible Protestant voters, 10% chose the conservative parties in 1874 and 15% three years later. Most of the total increase in the conservative vote went to the renamed German Conservative party, although its share of the electorate in 1877 at 6% was still modest.

The 1878 elections would bring a decisive change in the vote for the conservative parties, a result of the circumstances under which they were held. They have become known as the "attempted assassination elections" (*Attentatwahlen*) because they were preceded by two separate attempts on the life of Emperor Wilhelm I. Falsely attributing both

---

[23] An average of some 15% of previous minority party voters in Prussia moved to abstention in the 1877 and 1878 elections; outside of Prussia, the figure was higher (23%).

[24] On this point, see Schloßmacher regarding the cool calculations of the authorities in the Prussian Rhine Province in 1878 about the futility of supporting candidates opposing the Center in that party's strongholds (Schloßmacher, *Düsseldorf im Bismarckreich*, p. 220).

attempts to the Social Democrats, Chancellor Bismarck proposed to the Reichstag a law prohibiting the party. When all the parliamentarians, with the exception of the deputies of the two conservative caucuses, refused to go along with this measure, denouncing it as an assault on civil liberties, the Chancellor dissolved the Reichstag and ordered new elections, well ahead of the normal three-year cycle.

Although the Social Democrats had made gains in the 1874 and 1877 elections, largely by mobilizing previous non-voters and new entrants into the electorate, their vote totals in that latter year amounted to less than 6% of eligible voters, about 37,000 votes less than the parties of the regional and national minorities received, and less than three-eighths as many as the Center. Except perhaps in a few regions – one of which was admittedly in and around the national capital – the Social Democrats were not a major political presence in the second half of the 1870s; compared to the minority parties, they were a modest oppositional force. The assassins themselves were mentally unbalanced individuals with no particular connection to the Social Democratic party. Their dubious deeds provided Bismarck with a handy pretext to whip up fears of the red menace to accompany the new elections, called in order to complete the political realignment he had been planning, by increasing the strength of the conservative parties and intimidating the National Liberals into doing his bidding.[25]

The national government's public statements on the elections certainly demonstrated this strategy, concentrating their fire on the National Liberals and only occasionally mentioning the Social Democrats, whose ostensible threats to family, property, and society had been the official reason for the dissolution of the Reichstag and the call for new elections. Historians have pointed out the plebiscitary character of official pronouncements, their calling on the voters to support the executive branch of government, and its plans to prohibit the socialists and change economic policies by casting their ballot for one of the conservative parties. The conservatives were thus in the pleasant position of being able to coordinate their campaign slogans with those of the authorities. Sunning in official favor, the conservative parties ran a large number of candidates, offering about three-quarters of the German electorate the opportunity to vote for one, a very large increase over previous elections in the 1870s and close to the highest point ever obtained in all the general elections of the empire (see figure 3.3). Efforts of provincial and local officials against the liberals and in favor of the conservatives, already pronounced in 1877,

---

[25] Stürmer, *Regierung und Reichstag im Bismarckstaat*, pp. 191–230; Pflanze, *Bismarck*, 2: 392–403.

were stepped up a year later. In Berlin, the police even confiscated leaflets distributed by the Progressive Party.[26] In spite of these attacks – more likely, because of them – the National Liberals refused to go into opposition and give up their character as a "national" party, as the party supporting the government of the united German state. In the party press and in speeches and leaflets on the election, the National Liberals refrained from turning their fire on the executive. Sometimes they attempted to reach agreement with the conservatives, coming to terms on running joint candidates with them. Elsewhere, they furiously denounced conservatives, landed aristocrats, and the possibility of a reactionary turn in government policy. In Baden, a National Liberal stronghold where the party continued to enjoy the favor of the liberal Grand Ducal government even after Bismarck had changed his policies, activists attemped, apparently with some success, to physically disrupt conservative election meetings.

Everywhere, the party continued to emphasize its national character by launching attacks on particularist and Catholic *Reichsfeinde*, as it had done since 1871. As another part of the attempt to remain a "national" party, the National Liberals followed the government's lead and, for the first time, a focus of their campaigning was an attack on the Social Democrats. The informally organized committees of local notables in charge of nominating National Liberal candidates insisted, with few exceptions, that any nominee take a pledge to vote for a law prohibiting the socialists should he be elected to parliament.[27]

As this last point suggests, the party was under pressure from its rank and file, who were clearly agitated by the two attempts on the life of the emperor and the campaign by the government to play them up as a threat to the nation. As noted in chapter 1, the 1878 elections were accompanied by actions of businessmen, themselves generally liberal sympathizers, against Social Democrats in their employ. This combination of governmental propaganda and official legal steps against the Social Democrats, indignation at ostensible acts of radical terrorism, and the exploitation of these sentiments by leading businessmen and by conservative and National Liberal politicians encouraged patriotic voters to take

---

[26] Stürmer, *Regierung und Reichstag*, pp. 231–35; Pflanze, *Bismarck*, 2: 403–8; Steinbach, *Die Zähmung des politischen Massenmarktes*, pp. 542–581; Frank, *Brandenburger als Reichstagswähler*, pp. 58–59. Cf. Liebert, *Wahlen in Wiesbaden*, pp. 115–18; Wolf, *Liberalismus in Frankfurt am Main*, pp. 46–47; Hess, *Geschichte Thüringens*, pp. 156–57.

[27] Besides the sources cited in the previous note, see Steinbach, *Die Zähmung des politischen Massenmarktes*, pp. 593–627; Septainer, *Die Reichstagswahlen im Großherzogtum Baden*, pp. 106–11; Fischer, *Industrialisierung, sozialer Konflikt und politische Willensbildung*, pp. 259–60; Rieber, *Das Sozialistengesetz und die Sozialdemokratie in Württemberg*, pp. 155–61.

matters into their own hands. Social democratic election meetings in Frankfurt were disrupted by hundreds of conservative and National Liberal supporters singing the Prussian royal anthem, "Heil Dir im Siegerkranz," and the nationalist favorite, "Die Wacht am Rhein," and giving three cheers for the emperor. When the police came to terminate such meetings, they often found hundreds of patriots present, cheering "Bravo, Herr Police Commissioner!" Friedrich Payer, in 1878 a Reichstag deputy representing the German People's Party – no Social Democrats, but otherwise on the far left of the political spectrum and firm opponents of political persecution – noted in his memoirs about the 1878 election campaign:

It was a crazed election; in the shouting and screaming, it was made to seem as if I myself had been involved in the attempted assassinations. Because of very serious threats, we could not hold all the meetings we had scheduled and here and there were happy when we got out of the localities without being beaten up. The few Social Democrats around could scarcely appear in public.[28]

These examples might lead us to suspect that the campaigns of the authorities and the national parties reached the voters and that such an effect would be apparent at the polls. This is true, but only for very specific groups in the electorate. Overall turnout increased very modestly, from 60% of eligible voters in 1877 to 63% a year later. But turnout among all Catholic voters at the two elections was virtually the same (my estimates show a slight decline, from 70 to 69%) and outside of Prussia turnout of all voters actually fell, from 64 to 61%. The voter mobilization was concentrated almost entirely among Protestants in the kingdom of Prussia: their turnout jumped by ten percentage points, from 49% in 1877 to 59% in 1878. The voters' response to the assassination followed dynastic and confessional lines: Protestants in Prussia, the loyalists of the Hohenzollern monarchy, turned out to vote; other Germans were not impressed. Such a response demonstrates the extent to which the united German state did not yet have a united political life, and how the confrontations of the 1870s, far from creating such a national political scene had deepened the pre-existing divisions within Germany that had been exacerbated by the wars of German unification.

Given the nature of the newly mobilized voters, their party choices, noted in table 4.4, are not particularly surprising.[29]

In 1877 non-voters who turned out to vote in the assassination elec-

---

[28] Quotes from Eichler, *Sozialistische Arbeiterbewegung in Frankfurt am Main*, pp. 26–27, and Rieber, *Das Sozialistengesetz und die Sozialdemokratie in Württemberg*, p. 163.

[29] In this case, the estimates for all of Germany in Winkler, *Sozialstruktur*, p. 128, are very close to mine.

Table 4.4 *Choices of 1877 non-voters in the 1878 elections (percent)*

	Region		
Party group	Prussia	Non-Prussian Germany	All Germany
Conservatives	16	7	13
Liberals	14	8	13
Minority parties	4	6	4
Social Democrats	4	4	4
Non-voting	62	75	65
All	100	100	99

tions chose the liberal and conservative parties, particularly those in the kingdom of Prussia, who had made their disgust with the attempts a central theme of the election campaigns. Both the voters who were mobilized and the issues mobilizing them were not likely to do much for either the minority parties or the Social Democrats.

However, the nature of the elections did have a different effect on the supporters of these two groups of opposition parties. The minority parties were able to hold their supporters, over three-quarters of their 1877 voters choosing them again, while just 7% voted for the liberals and the conservatives. The Social Democrats, on the other hand, were badly defeated, with just a little more than half their 1877 voters (my estimate is 53%) staying true to the party and about one-third deserting it for the liberals and the conservatives, mostly the former. Naturally, the Social Democrats had borne the brunt of the agitation of the national parties, the persecution of the government, and the anger of Protestant nationalists. But the minority parties had suffered the same attacks in the elections of 1874, without suffering any such losses: indeed, a remarkable 87% of their 1871 voters had stayed true to them. The confessional, regional, and ethnic loyalties that brought minority party voters to the polls proved to be a much better protection against nationalist and patriotic appeals than the the social and political grievances motivating the supporters of the Social Democrats – a state of affairs not limited to the 1870s, but one that would be found in various forms throughout the electoral history of the *Kaiserreich*.

Since the conservative vote in 1877 was a bit less than half the liberal vote that year, attracting the same number of previous non-voters in 1878 meant a proportionately larger increase in votes for the conservative parties. But such a mobilization of non-voters was not the only reason that the conservative vote increased. Continuing and expanding on a trend begun in 1877, the conservative parties enjoyed substantial gains from liberal voters: 14% of 1877 liberal voters chose one of the conservative parties in 1878, as against just 5% of conservative voters switching to the liberals. In Prussia, the discrepancy was even greater, 20% of 1877 liberals going over to the conservatives, as against just 2% of conservatives choosing the liberals.[30]

The Conservative and Free Conservative parties profited equally from these voter movements, their combined vote increasing from 11% of eligible voters in 1877 to 17% in 1878. Partially compensating for defection of their voters to the conservatives by gaining the support of previous non-voters and Social Democratic supporters, the liberal parties held their losses (both the National Liberals and the left-liberals lost votes) to relatively modest levels, dropping from 23 to 21% of eligible voters. The total liberal vote thus remained ahead of the total conservative vote and the National Liberals continued to maintain their position as the political party with the most voters, but both by increasingly narrow margins.

As a result of this analysis, we can point to four main features of the 1878 elections. The campaign centered on nationalist and patriotic issues, guided in that direction by the national government, which set the terms for the election by the dramatic step of dissolving the Reichstag before the scheduled end of its session. Such a campaign had a strong mobilizing effect, bringing out previous non-voters to vote primarily for the candidates of the parties that supported the government's nationalist appeals. Besides mobilizing previous non-voters, the campaign also tended to move voters from the parties of the left to those of the right. Finally, the supporters of the minority parties were the voters least affected by the nationalist appeals of such a campaign.

These four features were all present to a greater or lesser extent in the future general elections that produced victories of the right – those of 1887, 1893, and 1907. In 1878, however, the four characteristics of right-wing election victories were most pronounced in the kingdom of Prussia, and were present to a much more modest extent in the rest of Germany. Subsequent general elections would see the pattern of 1878 reiterated throughout the entire country, testifying to a growing nationalization of political life and to a move from Prussian dynastic sentiment to an all-German nationalism.

---

[30] Outside of Prussia, 13% of 1877 liberals chose one of the conservative parties in 1877 as against 15% of 1877 conservative voters choosing the liberals. But since there were three-and-a-half times as many liberal voters in non-Prussian Germany in 1877·as conservatives, there were far more voters switching from liberal to conservative – 3.4% of the 1878 electorate – than from conservative to liberal, just 1.2% of the 1878 electorate.

If the 1878 elections can be seen as the precursor to future events, they were also part of a pattern of electoral politics that characterized the entire first decade of the German Empire. Central to this pattern was the sharp clash between the supporters of the empire and its enemies, a contrast ultimately derived from the wars that had created the empire and the united German nation-state it claimed to be. To be sure, there were political parties whose issues and voters did not entirely fit this pattern – the Conservatives in 1874, the left-liberals, except in 1874, and the Social Democrats, at all the elections of the decade. Yet all these parties were marginal to the electoral process, although the central government was willing to exaggerate the position of the Social Democrats for its own political purposes – and purposes that had relatively little to do with the Social Democrats.

Within this general pattern, two elections, those of 1874 and 1878, stand out, as mirror images of each other. Both brought large increases in turnout, in 1874 primarily among Catholics, in 1878 among Protestants in Prussia; the former benefitted the opposition minority parties, the latter the pro-governmental national parties. Both also saw substantial movements of voters among parties, from the national to the minority parties in 1874, and from the liberals to the conservatives in 1878. The changes in voter loyalties marked by these elections – the growth in the minority party vote in 1874 and the conservative vote in 1878 – remained permanent features of the electoral system for the remainder of the empire.

It is easy, though, to exaggerate the extent of these changes. All the elections of the 1870s retained certain common features. The liberals received the most votes of any party grouping, the minority parties the second most votes. Among individual parties, the National Liberals received the most votes, with the Center a close second. These features, a result of the underlying pattern of electoral politics, the contrast between the friends of the empire and its enemies, would only change as a consequence of the political realignment that occurred in Germany following the 1878 elections. This realignment would set the stage for a decade in which elections would retain some of the features of the 1870s, but would also show a different face.

Electoral politics in the 1880s

The voters had returned a Reichstag more right wing and more willing to do Bismarck's wishes in 1878, so that the parliamentary session of 1878–81 was characterized by cooperation between the executive and the legislature in setting a more conservative political course. The government introduced, and the Reichstag approved, an anti-socialist law, protective tariffs on agricultural and industrial products, and a substantial increase in indirect taxes. A majority for the tax and tariff measures was only to be had with the votes of the Center Party deputies. In return, the government proposed, and the parliament accepted, a series of measures temporarily suspending the harshest of the *Kulturkampf* legislation. Bismarck opened negotiations with the Vatican to resolve the conflict between the state and the Catholic Church. Dismissal of senior civil servants known for their liberal sympathies capped off this political reorientation.[31]

A majority of the National Liberal Reichstag deputies accepted these measures, choosing to be "national" (supporters of the national government) rather than liberal. For a left-wing minority of the caucus, this went too far. Accusing the majority of capitulation to "reaction" in religious and economic issues, they seceded from the caucus in 1880 and set up their own party, which ran candidates in the 1881 elections and merged with the Progressives three years later to form a united, liberal-oppositional party. These developments among parliamentarians were quickly seconded in the constituencies, where the united liberal committees and associations of the 1870s gave way to separate and opposing National Liberal and left-liberal ones.[32]

In contrast to the 1870s, with their clash between friends and enemies of the empire, the subsequent decade saw the development of three substantial groups of parties, each with a distinct attitude towards the government, contending for the voters' favor in the following decade: the parties of Bismarck's supporters, the Conservatives, Free Conservatives, and National Liberals, dubbed in the 1887 elections, the Kartell; the oppositional left-liberal parties; and the minority parties, less sharply aligned against the government than in the previous decade, but still far from being supporters of the executive and generally lacking official favor at election time. The Social Democrats would gradually increase their vote totals in that decade, but even in 1887, their best showing ever, they had the support of less than 8% of eligible voters.

The elections of 1881

The 1881 elections were the first in these new political alignments, and liberal politicians in particular were still tentative, feeling their way uncertainly after the previous legislative session. As the Prussian state news service noted about the general elections of that year, they were to be "a

---

[31] Stürmer, *Regierung und Reichstag*, pp. 236–88; Pflanze, *Bismarck*, 2: 445–89, 511–37.
[32] On the secession of 1880 and the subsequent left-liberal party formations, see above ch. 3, nn. 16–17.

kind of plebiscite on the [economic and fiscal] plans of the Chancellor."[33] Both the government's pronouncements and those of the conservative parties centered on this theme, the movement away from laissez-faire: praise for the measures taken after the previous elections, particularly the introduction of protective tariffs, and mention of future plans, such as the creation of a state-sponsored social insurance system and the reintroduction of the guilds. The voters were asked to support the government of the emperor and his chancellor that would grant them economic security.

The campaign of the left-liberal opposition was a mirror-image to that of the government and the conservatives. The opposition denounced the recent imposition of higher taxes and tariffs, called for the preservation of occupational freedom and vigorously condemned the official plans as "state socialism." Also, like the authorities and the conservatives, they called on the voters to ensure this economic choice politically, by strengthening the position of the Reichstag vis-à-vis the executive, ultimately by the introduction of a system of parliamentary government. The Progressives brought this common message of the different left-liberal groupings to the voters in more active fashion, by increasing the number of pre-election rallies and public meetings, and having their candidates speak directly to the voters. We might see this as a gradual move away from the notables' politics of the 1870s, or, perhaps more precisely, as an extension and wider use of the more aggressive campaigning techniques that some of the left-liberals had used in the previous decade.[34]

Because of the government's hesitation about setting a definite date for the forthcoming elections, the press discussed them for six months, easily three times as long as in the 1870s. The upshot of this situation was that the unusually long election campaign became increasingly an exchange of blows between the government and the conservative parties supporting it on the one hand, and the left-liberal opposition on the other. One new weapon in the arsenal of the authorities was the use of anti-Semitism to denounce the opposition. Capitalizing on the growth of anti-Semitic sentiment that had been expressed in both (relatively) peaceful petition campaigns and violent riots, the conservative parties, with the discreet encouragement of the Chancellor, announced that supporters of the free market or of parliamentary government were Jews or their lackeys. Proponents of the Christian Social Welfare movement within the

---

[33] Cited, in Liebert, *Politische Wahlen in Wiesbaden*, p. 129 n. 49.

[34] On pro-governmental and oppositional election campaigns in 1881, see Liebert, *Politische Wahlen in Wiesbaden*, pp. 131–34; Steinbach, *Die Zähmung des politischen Massenmarktes*, pp. 747–91, 847–89; Bräunche, *Parteien und Reichstagswahlen in der Rheinpfalz*, pp. 218–19; Peschke, "Die Bedeutung der liberalen Parteien und der Sozialdemokratie," pp. 85–86; Frank, *Die Brandenburger als Reichstagswähler*, pp. 79–80, 122–23; Hess, *Geschichte Thüringens*, p. 159.

Conservative Party were particularly active in this sort of anti-Semitic politics. On election day in Berlin, they paraded dogs through the streets bearing placards telling citizens "Don't vote for Jews!" They were, in other words, to reject the candidates of the oppositional Progressives, then the dominant political force in the capital city.[35]

As a result of this change in emphasis in political alignments, the two dominant parties of the previous decade, the National Liberals and the Center, found it difficult to develop an effective theme to reach the voters. They could and did continue to denounce each other every bit as ferociously as in the 1870s, but the political developments of the previous legislative session had decoupled such denunciations from the question of support for or opposition to the government. The *Kulturkampf* was not yet over, as Center newspapers and politicians, as well as the Catholic clergy, hastened to remind the voters: some of the anti-clerical legislation was still in force, while other items had been suspended, not repealed; negotiations with the Vatican had begun but had not been brought to a successful conclusion. However, the dramatic and immediately perceptible confrontations between state and church had come to an end; Center parliamentarians had cooperated with Chancellor Bismarck in his tax and tariff proposals; and the Chancellor had publicly abandoned his anticlerical policies and dismissed from office the liberal civil servants he made the scapegoats for them. Under these circumstances, it was difficult to maintain the sense of confrontation with a hostile and both godless and religiously alien national government that had been central to the mobilization of minority party voters in the previous decade.

Yet the Center politicians' dilemma was modest compared to that of their National Liberal counterparts. The party's leadership wanted to remain a "national" governmental party; that was, after all, what separated them from their colleagues who had seceded from their ranks to join the opposition. The problem was that the big issues of the 1870s, on which the National Liberals' leaders, the notables who represented the party in the provinces, and probably the rank and file of its voters could still agree – the promotion of national unity, and the concurrent attacks on the national, regional and religious minorities – were no longer decisive for a political party's relationship to the government. On the economic and political issues that were central to a pro- or anti-governmental stance – laissez-faire versus state intervention, unity of action among all liberal groups versus cooperation of the National Liberals with the con-

---

[35] Besides the sources cited in the previous note, see on anti-Semitism and its use in the elections, Peter Pulzer, *The Rise of Political Anti–Semitism in Germany and Austria* (New York: John Wiley & Sons, 1964), pp. 76–102; Frank, *Die Brandenburger als Reichstagswähler*, pp. 60, 122–23.

servatives – the National Liberal parliamentarians remaining in the party's caucus after the departure of the Secessionsists were divided. Trying to hold his followers together, party leader Rudolf von Bennigsen (a Hanoverian, whose political career in promoting a Prussian-dominated nation-state had involved many nasty clashes with the particularists) insisted, as the party's national appeal on the elections put it, "that questions of tariffs may not be made the basis for the formation of political parties, that the obligation to support one sole form of trade policy does not belong to the fundamentals of liberal opinion."[36] But if the National Liberals were to be a governmental party, as Bismarck defined it, and as Bennigsen wished them to be, then the party would have to take a single position on those issues.

Ultimately, with the Heidelberg Declaration of 1884, the party would choose this right-wing option – probably the one most of its activists and voters supported – and return to full support for the government. In 1881, the party had made no such clear choice and its campaign reflected the difficulties it had in this respect. The National Liberals insisted that they were a governmental party, yet they refused to endorse the government's plans on key economic issues. They consistently warned about the dangers of reaction – only where could such a danger come from, if not the government? Party journalists tried to subtly manipulate this issue by ignoring the policies of the executive and repeatedly attacking the conservative parties as the source of the dangers they warned about, but in 1881 those parties could legitimately claim to speak on behalf of the government. All such a campaign could accomplish would be to alienate the authorities without convincing the voters.[37]

After all this campaigning, the results of the general elections were quite different from what they had been three years previously. Turnout declined by seven percentage points to just 56% of eligible voters, its lowest level since 1871. The remaining voters showed no great inclination to support the conservative parties. In spite of a record number of candidacies, reaching the greatest proportion of voters of any general election in the history of the *Kaiserreich*, the conservative vote declined from 17% of eligible voters at the previous elections to 13% in 1881. The minority party vote also declined, from 21 to 18% of eligible voters. Of eligible voters, 21% chose one of the liberal parties in 1881, the same percentage

[36] Cited in Steinbach, *Die Zähmung des politischen Massenmarktes*, p. 840; more generally on Bennigsen and his strategy, see Sheehan, *German Liberalism*, pp. 198–99.
[37] On the National Liberal and Center 1881 election campaigns, see Steinbach, *Die Zähmung des politischen Massenmarktes*, pp. 792–846; Schloßmacher, *Düsseldorf im Bismarckreich*, p. 223–25; Liebert, *Politische Wahlen in Wiesbaden*, pp. 131–34; Sepainter, *Die Reichstagswahlen im Großherzogtum Baden*, pp. 113–19.

as three years previously, and an impressive result in view of the decline in turnout and the losses among the liberals' main rivals. If the overall liberal vote had not changed, the voters' choices among the liberals had, and substantially. In 1878, the National Liberals were the choice of 16% of eligible voters to just 5% for the left-liberals; in 1881, the proportions were almost reversed, with just 8% of eligible voters choosing the National Liberals and 13% the parties of the left-liberal opposition.

There are two points about the voters in 1881 that emerge immediately from these results. First, Bismarck's attempt to make the elections into a plebiscite on the government by calling on its supporters to vote for the conservative parties, a strategy employed with great success in 1878, was a failure three years later. Voters would turn out and vote for the conservatives in shock and horror at the news of the attempted assassinations of their emperor, in defense of family and property against the red menace. Public industrial accident insurance, to be financed by a state tobacco monopoly, on the other hand, lacked the same motivating force and even the use of anti-Semitism to spice up its appeal proved unavailing.

Second, the results of the elections demonstrated that the political alignments of the 1870s, the clash between the parties of the victors and the coalition of the defeated, had come to an end – not just among the politicians, but for the voters as well. The Center and the National Liberals, the two parties embodying this antagonism, who had persistently received over half the votes cast in the general elections of the 1870s (their low point in 1878 with 49% of votes cast), managed just 38% in 1881. A similar trend is apparent in the conservative vote. The entire decline in the vote for the conservative parties between 1878 and 1881 was a result of the losses of the Free Conservative Party, whose vote totals fell from 9 to 4% of eligible voters. Receiving almost as many or slightly more votes than the Conservatives in the elections of the 1870s, from 1881 onwards the Free Conservatives would just receive a fraction of the Conservative vote. Since the Conservatives had become a party endorsing the national government, and the existence of the empire was no longer the central political issue, the chief justification for the creation of a Party of the German Empire (a conservative and yet "national" party) no longer obtained. The Free Conservatives would not disappear from the German political universe but they would play an increasingly marginal role in electoral politics.

Using the results of the regression analysis can refine these initial impressions in several ways. First, we can determine more closely the voter movements that lay behind the decline in the conservative and National Liberal vote and the growth of support for the left-liberal opposition. Secondly, we can consider the confessional differences in

Table 4.5 *Liberal and conservative voters in the 1878 and 1881 elections (percent)*

	Vote in 1878		
Vote in 1881	Conservative	National Liberal	Left-Liberal
Conservative	51	9	19
National Liberal	11	33	3
Left-Liberal	15	27	56
Minority parties	8	9	4
Social Democrats	1	3	1
Non-voters	15	20	17
All	101	101	100

turnout, differences that are important for understanding the development of the minority party vote but also suggest the extent to which Catholic and Protestant voters in Germany lived in different political worlds. Putting all these results together, we can compare the 1878 and 1881 elections and in doing so move toward a typology of left-wing electoral victories.

Since the percentage of eligible voters choosing the liberal parties stayed constant between 1878 and 1881, while the proportions choosing the National Liberals and the left-liberals reversed themselves, it is tempting to understand these changes as solely the result of voter movements among the liberal parties. The creation of a new left-liberal party by parliamentarians seceding from the National Liberal caucus would seem to clinch this line of argument: if their voters chose the same candidate at two successive elections, then they would have switched from the National Liberals to the left-liberals. To test this proposition, I have performed an analysis for the 1878/81 pair of elections (not done for others) namely developing figures for the movements of conservative, left-liberal, and National Liberal voters separately. This seems justified because of the unique circumstances of the political alignments in those years, when the liberal unity of the 1870s was coming apart, but the pro-governmental alliance between the National Liberals and the conservative parties had not yet come into existence. Table 4.5 gives the results of this analysis.

As might be expected, voter loyalty to the National Liberal Party was very weak, with only one-third of the party's 1878 voters supporting it in 1881. It is tempting to see this as a consequence of the party's election campaign, which waffled between support of and opposition to the government. Both the conservatives and the left-liberals, parties that took a consistent stand in 1881, had more success in retaining their previous voters. A majority of those voters who deserted the National Liberals for another party went to one of the left-liberal parties, but a substantial minority (21% as opposed to 27% of 1878 National Liberal voters) chose the conservatives, the minority parties or the Social Democrats. However, the left-liberals did not just benefit from former National Liberal voters; 15% of those voting for one of the conservative parties in 1878 moved over to the opposition three years later.

The importance of these former conservative voters to the success of the opposition in the 1881 elections can be underscored by considering the composition of the left-liberal electorate in that year. Just 22% of the 1881 voters for one of the left-liberal parties had voted for one of those parties three years previously; 34% had chosen the National Liberals, and 20% – just about as many as the core left-liberal electorate – were former conservative voters. This is an unexpected finding; it certainly goes against Rainer Lepsius's milieu theory, as it involves substantial numbers of voters crossing over supposedly impermeable milieu boundaries. It does not really fit Karl Rohe's theory of a national voting bloc either, since conservatives and progressives took strongly opposed positions on the national government in the 1881 elections. Indeed, in that year the polarization between the conservative and all the liberal parties was at its height; none of the vote-switching between conservatives and liberals can be attributed to one party stepping down in favor of another (cf. figure 3.7).

To explain these results, we need to recall the circumstances of the 1878 elections, when substantial numbers of previous non-voters were mobilized to support the conservative parties. Such voters were not necessarily conservative loyalists, but were moved by the spectacle of the attempted assassinations and the subsequent campaigns by the authorities and the national political parties to convince the voters of the socialist dangers. After a cooler, longer, more cerebral election campaign, three years later, where economic issues were at stake, such voters, lacking firmer ties to the parties of the right, might have moved into support for the opposition.

Less than 2% of the oppositional left-liberal voters in 1881 had voted for the Social Democrats in 1878. As explained in the first chapter, the 1881 elections were a low point for the labor movement, the combination of persecution by the government and activities of employers and the notables deeply depressing the Social Democratic vote. That year, the Social Democrats lost the seventeenth Saxon electoral district, which had been theirs since the elections to the North German Reichstag of 1867. One activist described the scenes at the polling places:

Then there is the [precinct] election board, composed of nothing but our enemies. In the small towns and villages, everyone knows everyone else and the manufacturers are also sitting there [on the board]. They smile when someone comes in to vote and so the voters are intimidated, saying, they know that we will not vote for their candidates, so it is better to stay away.[38]

Staying away was exactly what many Social Democratic voters did in 1881. Half of the 1878 Social Democratic voters defied the powerful and supported their party at the polls in 1881; some 37%, on the other hand, abstained. The possible alternative – voting for the middle-class left-wing opposition if a vote for the Social Democrats was impossible, because of threats or the lack of a candidate – was the choice of only 4% of Social Democratic voters, about as many as voted for the National Liberals and the conservatives. The left-liberal opposition's denunciation of "state socialism," its advocacy of laissez-faire economics, was evidently not much to the liking of partisans of the labor movement, in spite of both groups' common opposition to Bismarck's authoritarian rule. Voters in 1881 did not switch to parties next to them on the political spectrum: former conservative voters were almost four times more likely to choose the left-of-center opposition than were former socialists.

If former Social Democratic voters thus contributed little to the victory of the opposition in 1881, former voters of the minority parties contributed even less. Minority party voters in 1878 made up approximately 1% of the left-liberal electorate three years later. Of minority party voters in 1878, 71% voted for the minority parties in 1881; 25% abstained and the remaining 4% were scattered across all the remaining political parties. This was a unique pattern: a majority of those leaving the liberal or conservative parties had switched to another party; even among the Social Democrats, those leaving the party for abstention outnumbered those going to another party by a bit less than 2:1, whereas for the minority party voters of 1878, the abstainers in 1881 outnumbered the switchers by 6:1.

This pattern coincides with some observations that can be made about differences in turnout by confession. Most of the decline in turnout between 1878 and 1881 was due to Catholic voters. Turnout among Protestants dropped slightly, from 59% in 1878 to 56% in 1881; but among Catholics, a gradual slide in turnout from 1874 to 1878 turned into a precipitous decline: turnout among Catholic voters, at 79% in 1874 had stood at 69% in the two subsequent elections of 1877 and 1878, only to fall by fourteen percentage points to just 55% of eligible voters in 1881. Outside of Prussia, just 47% of Catholic voters cast a ballot in 1881, the

---

[38] *Wilhelm Liebknecht Briefwechsel*, 2: 665–67

only time in the entire history of the general elections of the empire that just a minority of Catholic voters in any of the admittedly crudely drawn regions I have used in this study appeared to vote.

The 1881 elections marked a low point in Catholic support for the minority parties, only 46% of eligible Catholic voters casting their ballot for them. Catholic support for the minority parties in Prussia and outside of Prussia, as well as Catholic support for the Center in those constituencies where it put up candidates, was at similar, historically low levels. However, 1881 was the year when Catholic support for the liberals and for the conservatives was at its lowest level ever, and the proportion of eligible Catholic voters casting their ballots for the Social Democrats did not even reach 1%. In fact, among Catholics who actually voted, 1881 was the year when support for the minority parties was at its highest ever point: 82% of Catholics in Germany who cast their ballot in 1881 wrote on it the names of one of the minority party candidates. In constituencies where there were Center Party nominees, 85% of Catholics who voted, voted for the Center. This development was not confined to Catholics, but was more broadly typical of the entire minority party clientele. In the province of Hanover, for instance, the elections of 1881 marked a low point for the proportion of eligible voters who chose the allied Center and particularist parties, but a high point for those parties' share of votes cast.[39]

As the *Kulturkampf* wound down, or, to put it more broadly, as the confrontation between the winners and losers of the wars of national unification lost its place on the electoral center stage, the proportion of Catholics voting for the minority parties (the representatives of the coalition of losers) declined, but the proportion voting for the "national" parties (the representatives of the victors) declined even faster. Indeed, the drop in the Catholic vote for the liberal and conservative parties between the elections of 1877 and 1878, the last of the *Kulturkampf* era, and those of 1881 (from 18 to 9% of eligible Catholic voters) was even more precipitous than the decline in Catholic turnout over that period. The pressure the authorities had exerted in the 1870s not to vote for the minority parties was being directed in 1881 against another oppositional group altogether, the left-liberals, for whom Catholic support had always been minimal.[40]

Drawing all the threads of the argument together, we can make some observations about the 1881 elections as the prototype of a victory of the left. They followed directly on previous elections won by the parties of the

[39] Aschoff, *Welfische Bewegung und politischer Katholizismus*, p. 101.
[40] On the decline of officially supported liberal candidacies in heavily Catholic areas, see Thränhardt, *Wahlen und politische Strukturen*, p. 55.

right, largely the result of the mobilization of previous non-voters. Unlike the 1878 elections, those of 1881 were characterized by a decline in turnout; and the left-wing opposition was victorious by gaining the support of previous conservative and National Liberal voters, many of whom had been non-voters two elections previously and who had been mobilized by the parties of the right in 1878, but not necessarily permanently won over by them. The campaign that brought about the right-wing victory was centered on national issues, dramatic questions of patriotism that excited the electorate and brought the previously indifferent out to vote. In the subsequent victory of the left, the campaign was centered on economic issues and on political questions related to it, the sort of themes that drove indifferent voters away, but attracted those who had previously been motivated to participate in the political process.

The political mobilization in conjunction with the victory of the right in 1878 was a partial one, limited to Protestants, especially those living in the kingdom of Prussia. Catholics were less impressed by the assassination attempt and were not impelled to vote by it. Consequently, the successes of the left in 1881 were due to Protestant voters, who left the parties of the center and the right, the National Liberals and the conservative parties, for the left-liberal opposition. Having missed the first part of the cycle made up by voter mobilization/right-wing victory leading to voter switching and a victory of the left, Catholic voters missed the second part as well. They took almost no part in the switching of parties between 1878 and 1881; those not moved to support the minority parties just dropped out of the voting public altogether.[41] Future right-wing victories in the elections of 1887 and 1907 would see a broader mobilization of voters, one crossing regional and confessional lines. The victories of the left that followed hard on them, in the general elections of 1890 and 1912, would see a correspondingly broader switching of votes to parties of the left, benefitting above all the Social Democrats.[42]

The elections of 1884

The consequences of the 1881 elections showed most clearly the difference between the government and constitution of Imperial Germany and that of a parliamentary regime. Representatives of the parties supporting the government's program made up less than a third of the deputies

---

[41] The same point could be made about social democratic voters, although they were, of course, a much smaller proportion of the electorate.

[42] Admittedly, the elections of 1903, also a victory for the SPD, do not fit this pattern, since the previous elections in 1898 were neither a victory of the right nor ones in which voter turnout increased.

elected, even counting all the National Liberals as pro-governmental. The prime minister of a parliamentary government would have had to resign after such a defeat and give way to an opposition leader, or, at the very least, would only have have been able to stay in office by creating a fundamentally different political coalition. In either case, the upshot would be different policies followed by the executive branch of government.

Bismarck was under no such obligations. He remained in office and continued to propose to the Reichstag the policies that most voters had rejected. The parliament elected by these voters refused most of his proposals, so when its three-year term expired in 1884, the elections for its successor were in many ways a repeat of those of 1881. There were two differences worth noting. One was that the ambivalent position of the National Liberals, painfully apparent three years previously, had ended. In a series of regional meetings of National Liberal notables, most prominently one for south-western Germany held in Heidelberg in 1884, the party announced its support for Bismarck, in particular for the Chancellor's policies of protectionism, repression of the socialists, and state intervention in the economy. At about the very same time as these meetings were occurring, the former Secessionists from the National Liberal party were formalizing their merger with the Progressives, creating a unified left-liberal opposition party, denouncing the Chancellor, and calling for a return to laissez-faire. Thus the liberals had completely and definitively split into two blocs, one unequvuocably supporting, the other unequvuocably opposing the government's policies.[43]

The second main difference between 1881 and 1884 was that in the latter year there was no major central issue in the election campaign, as the ostensible threat from the Social Democrats had been in 1878, or the recently promulgated tax and tariff legislation had been in 1881. Bismarck had tried to create such an issue by playing up the question of the renewal of the anti-socialist law, hoping to get the left-liberals and the minority parties in the Reichstag to reject it, and then dissolving parliament and going to the voters in a renewed anti-socialist plebiscite. Fearing such an outcome, the opposition parties avoided it by voting against the measure, thus keeping their public promise to do so, but ensuring that enough of their deputies were absent so that the law was renewed in spite of their opposition.[44]

Thus, denied a powerful motivating issue, the campaign of 1884 was largely a case of _déjà vu_. The Center and National Liberals denounced each other as they had for a decade and a half; the left-liberal opposition

[43] On these developments, see Sheehan, _German Liberalism_, pp. 199–201, 212–14.
[44] Anderson, _Windthorst_, pp. 316–19.

called for a cheaper and less intrusive government under parliamentary control, while the pro-governmental parties praised state intervention in the economy and denounced the Semitic character of opposition to this. Summing the situation up from a left-of-center point of view, the great south German newspaper, the *Frankfurter Zeitung*, a supporter of the radical People's Party, ironically described the pro-governmental elements as "supporters of the guilds, colonial fanatics, enthusiasts for government subsidies for steamship lines, those thirsting for the blood of stockbrokers, Anti-Semites, and Heidelberger."[45]

Last in this cast of characters was the National Liberals, the party that with the Heidelberg Declaration had definitively moved into the government's camp. In adding the party to the list of governmental supporters, the *Frankfurter Zeitung* had caught an essential element of the campaign, and one that was different from its predecessor of three years previously. Then, the National Liberals had been ambivalent, wanting to support the government yet opposing its policies, unsure of whether to be a party with allies on the right or the left. Now, it had opted for the government and the right, aggressively supporting the Chancellor, denouncing the left-wing opposition, and largely sparing the Conservatives of any criticism.[46] Along with a clearer political orientation, the party seemed better organized at the constituency level in 1884, more able to run effective campaigns.

One final difference between 1881 and 1884 was a greater rapprochement between the Center and the parties of the left-liberal opposition. Although the parties did not cease to engage in polemics against each other, they moved increasingly toward a political rapprochement, brought together by a common opposition – albeit for different reasons – to the government. The Center Reichstag caucus even went as far as to suggest to its local activists that they not put up candidates in those constituencies where Catholics were a minority, but instead support the Radical opposition.[47]

If the election campaign of 1881 resembled its predecessor in 1884, so did the results of the polling. There was a modest increase in turnout,

---

[45] Quoted in Bendikat, *Wahlkämpfe in Europa*, p. 61.
[46] To be sure, the Conservatives did not entirely reciprocate, frequently criticizing the National Liberals. A look at the declining extent of conservative candidacies, however (see figure 3.3), shows that the parties of the right were, whatever their campaign rhetoric, in practice already beginning to cooperate with the National Liberals.
[47] In general, on the 1884 election campaigns, see Bendikat, *Wahlkämpfe in Europa*, pp. 25–79; Sepainter, *Die Reichstagswahlen im Großherzogtum Baden*, pp. 119–24; Schloßmacher, *Düsseldorf im Bismarckreich*, pp. 229–33; Bräunche, *Parteien und Reichstagswahlen in der Pfalz*, pp. 223–27; Frank, *Die Brandenburger als Reichstagswähler*, pp. 62–63; Liebert, *Politische Wahlen in Wiesbaden*, pp. 147–52; Peschke, "Die Bedeutung der liberalen Parteien," pp. 74–76.

from 56 to 60% of eligible voters, with increasing proportions of both Protestant and Catholic eligible voters casting their ballot. The vote for the parties hardly changed at all, the biggest swings being those of the National Liberals and the Social Democrats who each gained 2.5 percentage points over 1881. Both parties were better organized and enjoyed greater official favor – in the Social Democrats' case, less intense official persecution – than they had three years previously.[48]

There are two features of voter movements in this year worth noting, not so much for their effect on the 1884 elections, as for their implications for future polling. Both of these developments boded ill for the left-liberal opposition. First, there were noticeable changes in voter loyalty. In 1881, just about half the 1878 voters of the parties on the right wing of the political spectrum – the conservative parties and the National Liberals – continued to vote for one of these parties; only 42% of the 1878 National Liberal voters did so. In 1884, party loyalty on the right had improved considerably, with two-thirds of the right-of-center voters of 1881 casting their ballots for the parties of the right three years later. In contrast, party loyalty on the bourgeois left had changed little: 56% of 1878 progressive voters chose one of the left-wing parties in 1881, and 52% did so in 1884. Of the 1881 left-liberal voters, 29% had switched to one of the parties of the right, this change probably accounting for much of the success of the National Liberals in 1884. The right-wing parties had not been able to integrate many of the voters they mobilized in 1878, these voters playing a significant role in the victory of the left three years later. But the left-liberal opposition does not seem to have been able to keep their support either.

If the oppositionists of the newly united Radical Party were unable to mobilize and retain a core constituency, the decision of the Center to offer the support of Catholic voters does not seem to have done much for their cause. The percentage of minority party voters at one election casting their ballot for the left-liberals at a subsequent one went from 0.4% in 1881 to 0.6% in 1884. Of Catholic voters, 0.9% cast their ballots for the left-liberals in 1881, and 1.8% in 1884 – an improvement to be sure, but one that would not weigh very heavily on the scales, especially considering that the proportion of Catholics voting for the Center's enemy, the governmental National Liberals grew from 5.5% to 6.9% over the two elections. In fact, if we just take those constituencies where there were no Center candidates standing for office – and thus where a party decision to stand down in favor of the left-liberal opposition might best be observed –

---

[48] Only 8% of the social democratic voters in 1884 were switchers from other parties; previous non-voters and net new voters, on the other hand, made up about half of the social democratic electorate, with the previous non-voters alone accounting for a third.

we find that the proportion of eligible Catholic voters choosing the left-liberal parties was 3.8% in 1881 and just the same in 1884.

These figures suggest a state of affairs that would be typical for much of the remaining history of the empire: Center politicians' recommendation that their supporters vote for the candidates of another party do not seem to have had a large resonance with Catholic voters.[49] All those years of attacks on the left-liberals as godless and/or Protestant Freemasons could not be wiped away at once. If Catholic voters might provide help for the Progressive opposition in selected constituencies and, more significantly, offer the margin of victory in some runoff elections, they could not make up for the opposition's inability to retain the loyalty of its Protestant supporters.

The Kartell elections of 1887

The left-liberal parties did lose thirty-nine seats in the Reichstag elections of 1884, a loss completely out of proportion to the one percentage point decline in their share of eligible voters, and reflecting the idiosyncracies of a single-member constituency electoral system. Yet these losses did not fundamentally change the situation in the Reichstag, the pro-governmental conservative parties and the National Liberals remaining well short of a majority. Bismarck's search for a way to break the power of the opposition continued; it would reach a successful conclusion in 1887. The dissolution of the Reichstag in that year and the subsequent elections would mark both the climax and the end of the electoral politics of Bismarckian Germany.

The determining issue for the 1887 elections that year was the army bill of the previous year. It called for a substantial increase in the strength of the armed forces and, as was the case with previous military appropriation proposals, it would determine the budget of the armed forces for a seven-year period. Since about three-quarters of the total expenditures of the German central government at the time went to the armed forces, and since the authority to approve or reject proposed appropriations was one of the few constitutional powers the Reichstag had, the acceptance of this proposal would have weakened still further the position of the legislative vis-à-vis the executive. For that reason alone, the left-liberal and the minority party deputies were determined not to vote for it.

This rejection was precisely what Bismarck was looking for and had expected in advance, given that the previous seven-year arrangment for

---

[49] For similar difficulties in the Wilhelmine era, when Center politicians called on their supporters to vote for the conservatives, see Suvall, *Electoral Politics*, pp. 75–76.

army appropriations still had a year and a half to run when he submitted a new one to the Reichstag. The Chancellor dissolved the parliament and called for new elections at the beginning of 1887. The campaign was an unusually short one, with just thirty-seven days between the dissolution and the elections. However, the pro-governmental parties, informed in advance of the Chancellor's plans, were ready. With the assistance of the authorities, the Conservatives, Free Conservatives, and the National Liberals negotiated a joint campaign arrangement, the Kartell. They agreed to support each other's incumbents, to refrain from attacking each other in their campaigning, not to put up candidates against each other, if at all possible, and to support each other in runoff elections. Their agreement was quite effective. While at least two of these parties had stood against each other in 131 constituencies in 1881, and in 63 in 1884, the arrangement reduced competition among them to just 23 constituencies in 1887. The National Liberals and Conservatives, the two parties with the longest history of mutual hostility, had sponsored opposing candidates in 51 constituencies in 1884, but stood against each other in just 16 in 1887.[50]

Besides these favorable institutional arrangements, the Kartell parties and the governmental authorities supporting them had a powerful issue with which to run their campaign. They accused the opposition of undermining Germany's national security by refusing to agree to an increase in the strength of the army when in France nationalist elements, under the leadership of the Minister of War, General Boulanger, were aggressively re-arming and calling for a war of revenge against Germany. The National Liberals in their election manifesto accused the opposition of wanting to leave Germany "defenseless"; the Free Conservatives, in theirs, suggested that if the opposition had its way, the result would be the "decay and ruin of the fatherland." Alfred Krupp, the arms manufacturer, one of many businessmen in the Rhenish-Westphalian industrial area who aggressively supported the Kartell parties, explained in a personal appeal to his workers and the inhabitants of the city of Essen, where his factories were located, that "These elections are not about political controversies or differences of opinion, and least of all are they about differences with regard to religion. They are about the bases and the fundamental conditions of our national existence, about peace and the welfare of our realm!"[51]

---

[50] On Bismarck's strategy and the institutional arrangements of the 1887 elections, see Pflanze, *Bismarck*, pp. 228–32; Sepainter, *Reichstagswahlen im Großherzogtum Baden*, p. 125; Bendikat, *Wahlkämpfe in Europa*, pp. 294–96. I have defined two parties standing against each other as occurring when each receives at least 100 votes.

[51] Quotes from Bendikat, *Wahlkämpfe in Europa*, pp. 298, 300, 460 n.31.

The government and the parties supporting it thus described the elections as a struggle between the friends and enemies of the empire, as a return to the issues that dominated politics in the 1870s. In Augsburg, the National Liberals and conservatives formed a joint electoral committee of "voters true to the realm" (*reichstreuer Wähler*). The National Liberals of Baden asserted in their election appeal that "Ultramontanists, radicals and socialists, Poles and sympathizers with the French" had denied the government the "means necessary for [national] security."[52] Johannes Miquel, National Liberal leader explained in a campaign speech that the elections were between those who "spread discord, who endanger the constitution and those who wish to reinforce our armed might and stand up for the emperor and the realm." He hoped that in 1887, as in 1870, the people would do the right thing in the moment of national danger. This recourse to the wars of national unification was underscored by the place at which the speech was given, the wine town of Neustadt a.d.W. in the Rhine-Palatinate, whose inhabitants were strong supporters of the radical opposition but, living near the French border, were also susceptible to the appeal to memories of foreign danger and national unification.[53]

The left-liberal opposition had difficulty formulating an effective response to these appeals to stand by the fatherland in the hour of danger. On the defensive throughout the campaign, the opposition continued to stick to the themes it had emphasized throughout the decade. Eugen Richter personally condemned the proposed seven-year military appropriations as likely to lead to a major increase in the budget deficit, and thus to the promulgation of new indirect taxes, or to the imposition of a state tobacco monopoly. Opposition to a weakening of parliamentary power via a military budget that would not have to be renewed for seven years was also a main theme of the campaign. Increasingly aware that the Kartell's appeals were striking a responsive chord with the voters, while their own were not, the left-liberal politicians found nothing better to do than redouble their efforts to reach the voters, trying to hold more meetings, distribute more fliers and leaflets more systematically than they had before.[54]

The Center was faced with a different problem in these elections, namely Bismarck's attempts to cut off the party's appeal to its Catholic

---

[52] Quotes from Fischer, *Industrialisierung, sozialer Konflikt und politische Willensbildung*, pp. 266–67; Sepainter, *Wahlen im Grozßherzogtum Baden*, p. 127.

[53] Speech cited in Bendikat, *Wahlkämpfe in Europa*, p. 309; on the politics of Neustadt, see Bräunche, *Parteien und Reichstagswahlen in der Pfalz*, p. 223.

[54] On the oppositional election campaign, Bendikat, *Wahlkämpfe in Europa*, pp. 298–99, 301, 303–4, 306–7, 317–19; Sepainter, *Reichstagswahlen im Großherzogtum Baden*, p. 129; Peschke, "Die Bedeutung der liberalen Parteien," p. 79; Liebert, *Politische Wahlen in Wiesbaden*, pp. 164–65.

clientele to vote for it in defense of a religion threatened by a *Kulturkampf* still not officially concluded. The Chancellor went over the head of the party and the German episcopate by reaching an agreement with the Vatican to repeal most of the anti-clerical legislation of the 1870s, in return for which the Pope would call on the Center to support the government's seven-year military expenditure bill. Once this agreement became public – and the government made sure that it did – it would put the Catholic political party in the awkward position of defying the Pope. As part of this strategy, the Chancellor found a group of more conservative Catholics, previous supporters of the Center, who were willing to denounce it publicly as having "with the passage of time gone ever more in the direction of serving un-German goals, in alliance with the Guelfs [the Hanoverian particularists] and the Poles."[55]

Center Party leader Ludwig Windthorst was able to break out of the trap the Chancellor had for set him in a celebrated speech at a party rally in Cologne, where he grossly distorted the Pope's position, but, more importantly, he secured the loyalty of the vast majority of the German episcopate to the party. With the bishops' encouragement and approval, the Catholic clergy once again supported the Center. If priests in 1887 emphasized the dangers of militarism to the Faith and the political party supporting it, rather than anti-clerical legislation as was the case in the 1870s, we need to remember the close connection between the *Kulturkampf* and the wars of German unification in contemporaries' opinions. Just as the Kartell parties wished to portray the 1887 elections as a return to the period when creating and insuring the unity of the nation held the political center stage, the Center did so as well, albeit from the other side. However, unsure if stressing opposition to army expenditures would have quite the same effect on the Catholic electorate as calling on them to stand up in defense of endangered religion, Center politicians, like their left-liberal counterparts, seem to have redoubled their efforts at reaching the voters.[56]

This return to the politics of the previous decade was even more pro-

---

[55] Quote from Schloßmacher, *Düsseldorf im Bismarckreich*, p. 238. More generally, on the organization of Catholics in western Germany in support of the government, ibid. pp. 236–39 and, by the same author, "Erzbischof Philippus Krementz und die Septennatskatholiken," *Annalen des Historischen Vereins für den Niederrhein* 189 (1986): 127–42.

[56] For the Center campaign in 1887 and the politics surrounding it, see Anderson, *Windthorst*, pp. 335–56; Bendikat, *Wahlkämpfe in Europa*, pp. 298–99, 304–6, 309, 313–14, 317–19; Schloßmacher, *Düsseldorf im Bismarckreich*, pp. 240–42; Schloßmacher, "Erzbischof Philippus Krementz"; Herbert Lepper, "Die 'Septennantswahlen' 1887 im Raume Aachen," *Zeitschrift des Aachener Geschichtsvereins* 82 (1972): 77–110; Sepainter, *Die Reichstagswahlen im Großherzogtum Baden*, pp. 128–29; Wender, *Wahlen in Ludwigshafen*, pp. 382–85.

nounced for the other minority parties. In Hanover, supporters of the particularists understood the seven-year appropriation as meaning the introduction of a seven-year term of military service, thus raising again old grievances about the stringency of the military obligations as Prussian subjects, compared to the more lax handling of the matter in the pre-1866 Hanoverian kingdom. The Kartell's attack on the opponents of the military bill as those wishing to leave Germany defenseless before French aggression was only too welcome in Alsace-Lorraine, the campaign of the French nationalists being carried out in an atmosphere of widespread expectation of a new war and a glorious return of the lost provinces to France. On the day of the elections, there were pro-French street demonstrations in Metz, and the the news of the victory of the French nationalists was celebrated that evening in a number of villages by the singing of the Marseillaise.[57]

The campaign mobilized the voters to an unprecedented extent, turnout rising from 60% of eligible voters in 1884 to 77% three years later. It was the single largest increase from one election to another in the history of the empire. Unlike the case in 1874 or 1878, elections that had seen sharp jumps in turnout among some voters but not others, the increase in turnout between 1884 and 1887 was general and occurred to about the same extent among Protestants and Catholics, Prussians and non-Prussians. The Kartell parties were the big winners, the National Liberal vote increasing from 11 to 18% of eligible voters, the conservative parties from 13 to 19%. These increases translated into some seventy more seats in the Reichstag and an absolute majority for the supporters of the government. The minority parties increased their share of eligible voters by a more modest three percentage points to 22%, while the left-liberal opposition lost one percentage point falling to 11% of eligible voters.

It is difficult to tie the increase in turnout to any major organizational changes in the nature of electioneering. The 1887 elections were still held largely within the framework of notables' politics, informal committees organizing the campaign and newspapers providing the chief means – at least for the Kartell parties – of reaching the voters. The campaign certainly included a greater number of public meetings than in the 1870s, and more participants at each meeting than had previously been the case, but nothing in this respect marked a sharp break with the previous elections of the 1880s. If anything, it had been the defeated opposition parties, who made unusually great efforts in the 1887 election, not the victorious representatives of the Kartell.

<hr/>

[57] Hiery, *Reichstagswahlen im Reichsland*, pp. 219–40; Aschoff, *Welfische Bewegung*, p. 104.

The authorities had certainly supported the Kartell parties in the campaign, as had businessmen and other notables, such as Protestant pastors, although the pressure exerted by the government and social elites against their opponents was less than in the *Kulturkampf* or during the earliest and harshest phases of the anti-socialist law. Perhaps the most effective aspect of the cooperation between the government and the political parties supporting it lay, as might be expected in an era of notables' politics, in the coordination of press statements. The authorities leaked secret reports of French rearmament in conjunction with the Kartell parties' claims that Germany was in danger if the seven-year military appropriation were not approved. If there was any true organizational novelty in the election, it might have been in the use of the veterans' associations to support the government. Most studies of the politics of these groups center on their hostility to the SPD in the Wilhelmine era and occasionally mention their use against the Center during the 1870s, but a few scattered references suggest that they might have played a role in the Kartell campaign of 1887; the main issue of the elections, the government's call for an increase in the armed forces, would certainly have been an ideal one for their activity.[58]

As in the closely related question of the reasons for the lack of success of the left-liberal opposition, I can only conclude that the elections of 1887 showed that issues mattered to the German voters, that they could be more important in determining outcomes than organizational initiatives. Appeals to patriotism, to defense against the ostensible dangers of foreign aggression, to the maintenance of the unity of the nation, stock in trade of the Kartell parties, found a ready hearing. The mirror-image appeals of the minority parties to religious, regional or ethnic solidarity were also effective, if to a lesser extent, but the left-liberal opposition's reiterated insistence on cheap government and parliamentary power was not convincing, particularly to previous non-voters, whose mobilization determined the outcome of the elections.

Table 4.6, giving the choices of the voters of 1884 in 1887, confirms this viewpoint.

Both the Kartell and the minority parties were able to hold on to their voters to an impressive extent, some 84 or 85% of voters for the party group continuing to support it from one election to the next, which is among the best results in the electoral history of the empire. The left-liberals and the Social Democrats also did well in retaining their core con-

---

[58] Kremer, "Die Krieger- und Militärvereine in der Innenpolitik des Großherzogtum Baden," pp. 307–8.

Table 4.6 *The 1884 voters in the Kartell elections of 1887 (percent)*

Vote in 1887	Vote in 1884					
	Kartell	Left-Liberal	Minority parties	Social Democrats	Non-voters	Net new voters
Kartell	84	17	7	13	31	44
Left-Liberal	2	71	1	3	5	2
Minority parties	4	0	85	1	11	19
Social Democrats	1	4	0	76	6	16
Non-voters	8	8	6	7	47	20
All	99	100	99	100	100	101

stituency, but a certain minority of their voters were won over by the nationalist appeals of the government and its supporters.[59]

However, the real story of this election can be found in the last two columns of table 4.6. Over half of the non-voters of 1884 turned out to vote – an astonishingly large percentage, unmatched in any previous or subsequent election in Imperial Germany – and a very high figure by any standards, usually only seen in elections where the franchise has been changed, resulting in a substantial expansion of the electorate.[60] All the parties received some of these votes, but the lion's share, almost 60% of those so mobilized went to the Kartell.[61] Since almost 40% of those eligible to vote in 1884 had not actually voted, this meant that 12% of the entire 1887 electorate consisted of previous non-voters who voted for one of the Kartell parties. This is a remarkable figure, as one contrasting example will make clear. In the general elections of 1930 (the breakthrough elections for the Nazi Party, whose successes were widely attributed to the mobilization of non-voters), just 3.5% of the electorate consisted of previous non-voters who chose the Nazis.[62]

Turnover in the electorate also worked on behalf of the Kartell, with almost half the net new voters choosing one of the governmental parties.

[59] Since just 5% of all liberal voters (both National Liberals and left-liberals) of 1884 and 2% of social democratic voters in that year voted for the conservatives in 1887, most of the progressives and social democrats switching to the Kartell parties must have chosen the National Liberals.

[60] See, for instance, Ingemar Wörlund, Sten Berglund and Søren Risbjerg Thomsen, "The Mobilization of the Swedish Electorate (1911–1940)," in Berlund and Thomsen (eds.) *Modern Political Ecological Analysis*, pp. 78–90.

[61] Of these previous non-voters choosing the Kartell parties, about 55% voted for one of the conservative parties and 45% for the National Liberals.

[62] Falter and Zintl, "The Economic Crisis of the 1930s and the Nazi Vote," p. 79.

It would be reasonable to see this as reflecting a disproportionate prefer-ence for the Kartell parties among those newly eligible to vote, many of whom must have just recently finished their term of army service and, encouraged by the veterans' groups, wrote down the names of nationalist candidates (those supporting an increase in the armed forces). Among this category of voters – admittedly, a much smaller group than previous non-voters – both the minority parties and the Social Democrats enjoyed a fair amount of success, while the left-liberal opposition suffered a fiasco.

Figures on voting by confession underscore these results. The Kartell parties were the choice of 32% of eligible Protestant voters in 1884; in 1887, the figure was 47%, and 62% of all Protestants who actually voted. In contrast, the minority parties, choice of 48% of eligible Catholic voters in 1884, were supported by 57% of them three years later, 73% of Catholics casting their ballot. The elections thus saw the electorate polar-ized into two large blocs: Protestants voting for the Kartell and Catholics supporting the minority parties. These groups accounted for half of all eligible voters and 65% of all votes cast.

However, the nationalist campaign of the Kartell parties, if most successful among Protestant voters, was not limited to them. Of eligible Catholic voters, 18% supported these parties in 1887, a sharp increase from the 10% who had in 1884, reaching levels that had not been seen since the elections of the *Kulturkampf*. Although the Center worked more closely with the left-liberal opposition in 1887 than it had in 1884, and the two opposition parties' campaigns were synchronized to a greater extent than previously, both focusing on opposition to the proposed mili-tary appropriations, relatively few Catholics could be brought to cast their ballots for the parties of the bourgeois left. Just 2.6% of eligible Catholic voters did, a modest increase from the 1.8% of 1884.

The cooperation between the Center and the left-liberals included many instances of candidates from both parties stepping down in favor of the other. In fact, 1887 marked a low point of Center candidacies in the history of the empire, with just slightly over 70% of eligible Catholic voters having the option of voting for the Center, a figure even lower than in 1871, when the Catholic political party was still not completely orga-nized. In those constituencies where there were no Center candidates, about 7% of eligible Catholic voters chose one of the parties of the bour-geois left, about doubling the percentage obtained in 1884, and suggest-ing the greater degree of cooperation between the progressive and the minority party opposition in the year of the Kartell elections. However, in those constituencies without Center candidates, over 28% of eligible Catholic voters chose one of the Kartell parties in 1887, four times as many as voted for the Center's left-liberal allies, a result demonstrating both the nationalist appeal of the Kartell and also the extent to which the minority party vote was a result of religious, ethnic or regional loyalties that could not easily be transferred to other issues or political parties.

It is easy to use a whole range of superlatives to describe the 1887 elections. Both the conservative and the liberal parties received the support of a greater proportion of the entire electorate, a greater proportion of the Protestant electorate, and a greater proportion of the electorate in those constituencies where they put up candidates than at any other election in the history of the empire (see figures 3.1, 3.4, and 3.7). In those constituencies where it put up candidates, and in all constituencies in the kingdom of Prussia, the Center Party gained the support of a greater proportion of eligible Catholic voters than at any other election between 1871 and 1912 (see figures 2.2 and 2.3). The other minority parties won a greater share of eligible voters in those constituencies where they put up candidates in 1887 than at any other elections (see figure 2.4). As a proportion of eligible voters, 1887 marked a high point for the French nationalists, the Polish nationalists, and the Hanoverian particularists.[63] The year 1887 was also the year when participation in the political process, at least as indicated by voting, became the rule for a large majority of adult German men. Voter turnout in 1887 broke the 70% mark, reaching almost 80% – a remarkable figure for a democratic franchise, at any time and any place. Participation rates would never be below 70% afterwards, except in 1898, when they dipped to 68%.

Behind such superlatives lie four general characteristics of the Kartell elections. First, they were the climax of the Bismarckian system of electoral politics, marked by a contrast between governmental and oppositional parties, for whom the main issue was an existential one: the creation, preservation, and expansion of the German nation-state. This contrast between the parties reflected a confessional contrast between the voters with most, if not all Protestants lining up with the government, and most, if not all, Catholics with the opposition. The proportion of Protestants opposing the government was generally a good deal more substantial, though, than the proportion of Catholics supporting it, so overall it does seem fair to describe the Bismarckian electoral system as one with a very strong confessional polarity.

Second, the 1887 elections marked an end to the specific political circumstances of the 1880s, in particular to the challenge of the left-liberal political opposition. Not built on ethnic, regional or confessional loyalties, as was the minority party opposition, and generally accepting, sometimes even enthusiastically endorsing, the existence of the empire, this

[63] Hiery, *Reichstagswahlen im Reichsland*, pp. 239–40.

opposition represented the Central European example of classic nine-teenth-century liberalism, with its commitment to private property, laissez-faire, civil liberties, cheap government, and a parliamentary regime to ensure all these things. The left-liberal opposition never had an entirely secure and reliable clientele and it was simply swamped by the massive mobilization of non-voters and new voters in 1887, a result of the nationalist campaign of the government and the parties supporting it.

Third, the 1887 elections were a classic example of a victory of the right in the general elections of the empire. Such elections were characterized by a campaign centering on nationalist issues; a large-scale mobilization of previous non-voters, this mobilization benefitting primarily the right-wing, pro-governmental parties; a somewhat smaller number of voters switching from the parties of the left to those of the right; and a defeat for the left-wing opposition, while the minority parties usually were able to hold their voters, mobilize previously passive members of their clientele and successfully ride out the storm. The elections of 1878 had been a partial example of such right-wing victory, but the mobilization of non-voters and the switch from left to right had been limited primarily to Protestants in the kingdom of Prussia; in 1887, these features could be seen for both confessions and all parts of Germany.

However, such right-wing victories were self-limiting. Governmental policies made possible by the change in the make up of the Reichstag in the wake of right-wing successes created new political tensions, primarily related to economics, which in turn would allow for the emergence of other issues in subsequent elections. Those voters mobilized by right wing or governmental parties as a result of their nationalist appeals were not permanently tied to such parties; a different kind of election with different issues coming to the fore could lead them in unexpected direc-tions. This had certainly been the case in 1878 and 1881. The elections of 1887, a much greater victory for the right than those of 1878 would soon produce a comparably greater change in the electoral system, one so great, in fact, as to create a new political universe, the subject of the next chapter of this book.

5   The Wilhelmine elections

The elections of the 1890s

In Bismarckian Germany, elections had centered on the clash between oppositional and governmental parties. There were certainly other issues involved in the campaigns – the exercise of religion, taxes, tariffs, and social insurance, to name just a few – but they were brought to the voters' attention by governmental initiatives and discussed in the context of support for or opposition to them. The 1887 elections marked both the climax of these government-made elections and their end. In the general elections held between 1890 and 1912 the campaigns of the political parties and the initiatives of the government increasingly diverged; a strong polarization between governmental and oppositional parties determined the dynamics of just one general election, that of 1907.

It was not that the national government no longer had the intent of determining or at least influencing the nature and outcome of the Reichstag elections. After 1890, just as before, the authorities continued to provide useful information for the press and other campaign print media; to sift through the candidates, ascertaining which were deserving of official support; to implement or broker negotiations between different political parties in specific constituencies in order to ensure that the best candidate from the government's point of view could be elected; and to offer subsidies from secret discretionary funds to individual candidates or political parties.[1] However, if the state officials of Wilhelmine Germany were trying to run elections as they had done in Bismarck's day, they were having rather less success. One reason for this, certainly one that contemporaries cited, was that Bismarck's successors were no Bismarcks; they were made of rather more easily bendable elements than the Iron Chancellor, and lacked his ability to shape affairs to his will. Without

---

[1] For a good discussion of the government's role in Wilhelmine elections, see Brett Fairbairn, "Authority vs. Democracy: Prussian Officials and the German Elections of 1898–1903," *Historical Journal* 33 (1990): 811–38. See also Liebert, *Wahlen in Wiesbaden*, p. 281, or Bertram, *Die Wahlen zum deutschen Reichstag*, pp. 119–38.

denying the importance of individuals for historical developments, it does seem appropriate to point to other, broader influences, that could be summed up under the heading of the growing strength of civil society and its increasing independence from the state. Political parties, economic special interest groups, and nationalist mass organizations came to shape public affairs at least partially of their own accord, making it far less simple for the government to set the electoral agenda.

The elections of 1890

Ironically, it was Bismarck himself who began the dissolution of the electoral system that he had created and used to such great effect. Quickly coming into conflict with the young emperor Wilhelm II, following the latter's accession to the throne in 1888, the chancellor realized that his independence from the will of the majority of the Reichstag, previously so useful to him, left him with no constitutional recourse when he no longer had the favor of the emperor. Consequently, Bismarck resolved to establish his indispensability by bringing to an end the pro-governmental majority he had just created in the Imperial parliament. The emperor, he reckoned, would not dare to dismiss him if the Reichstag were dominated by the opposition parties. Bismarck began this policy by sabotaging the renewal of the anti-socialist law in 1889, proposing a version so extreme and so hostile to civil liberties that he could count on the National Liberals in parliament to reject it, which they did, breaking with their conservative allies in the Kartell. Having thus legalized the red menace, the chancellor then continued his disruptive campaign by ordering government officials not to intervene in the 1890 elections, as they had three years previously.[2]

The upshot of these decisions was that the Kartell parties entered the election campaign confused and divided. In some constituencies, the 1887 agreement between the conservatives and the National Liberals was renewed; elsewhere it was not.[3] Overall, there was a significant drop in the cohesion of the right-wing alliance: at least two of the three parties stood against each other in seventy-three constituencies in 1890, many more

[2] John C. G. Röhl, *Germany without Bismarck: The Crisis of Government in the Second Reich, 1890–1900* (Berkeley and Los Angeles: University of California Press, 1967), pp. 27–50; and by the same author, "The Disintegration of the *Kartell* and the Politics of Bismarck's Fall from Power," *Historical Journal* 9 (1966): 60–89.

[3] For examples of both the continuation and the collapse of the Kartell, see Sepainter, *Die Reichstagswahlen im Großherzogtum Baden*, pp. 131–32; Fischer, *Industrialisierung sozialer Konflikt und politische Willensbildung*, pp. 266–67; Aschoff, *Welfische Bewegung*, pp. 191–92; Schilling, "Politics in a New Key," pp. 38, 43; Busch, *Die Stoeckerbewegung im Siegerland*, pp. 65–68.

than the twenty-three in the previous general elections and a few more than the sixty-three constituencies where such opposition had existed in 1884. Also unlike 1887, economic rather than nationalist issues dominated the campaign, particularly the controversy over the decisions taken by the Kartell Reichstag to raise both indirect taxes and the tariff on grain. Lacking government support, increasingly disunited, and fighting on a terrain unfavorable to them, the Kartell parties, especially the National Liberals, were generally (with individual exceptions) unable to campaign in 1890 with the same energy and effectiveness as they had three years previously.[4]

The opposition parties of the previous decade, on the other hand, seem to have been more energetic, although there were individual exceptions here as well. For the left-liberals, the elections offered an opportunity to denounce protectionism, higher taxes and excessive government spending; a favorite target was Wilhelm II's yacht that had cost the taxpayers 3 million Marks. Along with these went, as in the past, demands for parliamentary government and the expansion of civil liberties. The Center Party ran its campaign along similar lines; in south-western Germany it even held joint election rallies with the bourgeois left. Although most of the Kulturkampf legislation had been repealed, Catholic politicians continued to point out that many of the religious orders had still not been allowed to return to Germany. The other minority parties also continued to emphasize their opposition to the empire, an issue that had worked well with the voters in the past.[5]

If the Kartell was weakening in 1890, its opponents seemed better united than before. On occasion, the union of opposition parties went beyond the Center and the left-liberals to include the Social Democrats, as happened in the south-west German industrial city of Ludwigshafen, where the three opposition parties agreed on a common size of paper for their ballots to ensure the secrecy of the franchise. The National Liberals, local representative of the Kartell parties, and favorite of the city's chemical manufacturers, refused to go along with this proposal, thus ensuring that the vote would not truly be secret, in the hope of intimidating workers in the chemical industry and others economically dependent on big business into voting for their candidate.[6] More often, though, the Social Democrats were excluded from the union of the opposition. The

---

[4] Besides the sources cited in the previous note, see Liebert, *Politische Wahlen in Wiesbaden*, pp. 176–78; Wender, *Wahlen in Ludwigshafen*, pp. 394–97.

[5] Besides the sources cited in the previous note, see Sepainter, *Die Reichstagswahlen im Großherzogtum Baden*, pp. 132–34; Seeber, *Zwischen Bebel und Bismarck*, p. 196; Kaminski, *Polish Press*, pp. 61–62; Brosius, *Rudolf von Bennigsen*, pp. 44–47

[6] Breunig, *Soziale Verhältnisse der Arbeiterschaft*, pp. 212–13.

Center Party in particular vigorously denounced the Social Democrats, condemning their atheism, republicanism, and hostility to the family. Sometimes, the attacks by Center activists and the Catholic clergy reached such an extreme that it seemed as if the Social Democrats were to replace the National Liberals as the main enemy of political Catholicism.[7]

In fact, such attacks, even if not typical for the Center campaign of 1890, did point toward future elections. If there was one party that was on the offensive in 1890, it was the Social Democrats. With the anti-socialist law scarcely enforced (technically, it did not expire until after the 1890 elections, but in fact it was little employed during the campaign), the labor party was able to practise the mass politics of public meetings, door-to-door agitation, and the passing out of enormous quantities of leaflets and fliers and ballots in a way and to an extent that put the efforts of the most enthusiastic of its competitors in the shade. During its period of illegality in the 1880s, the party had begun to prepare for such a mass agitation, developing organizations with which it could be carried out, such as constituency level "workers' election committees," but had only been able to engage in it on a local and sporadic basis, depending on the extent of the enforcement of the anti-socialist law. Now that the Social Democrats had been de facto legalized there were no barriers to the practice of this mass politics. Some of the issues raised by the Social Democrats in their campaign, such as opposition to high taxes, tariffs, and military expenditures, were common to all the opposition parties; others, such as the demand for a legally guaranteed eight-hour day, and other forms of labor protection legislation, were unique to the party of the labor movement. The party's agitation on these issues was helped along by the memory of the sensational 1889 strike of Ruhr Basin coal miners, in which hundreds of thousands of miners had walked off the job and had substantially helped their cause in public opinion with a dramatic appeal to the emperor. As the campaign continued, it became clear that the Social Democrats' aggressive efforts were making all the running; Wilhelm II, in a characteristically eccentric gesture, responded to it by drawing up the Berlin army garrison outdoors on Tempelhof Field on election day.[8]

Whether the emperor, in his typically bizarre fashion, was expecting a socialist uprising to coincide with the elections, or hoping to intimidate the labor movement with a show of armed force, his gesture (one that

---

[7] Sepainter, *Die Reichstagswahlen im Großherzogtum Baden*, p. 134; Schadt, *Die Sozialdemokratische Partei in Baden*, p. 121; Nolan, *Social Democracy and Society*, p. 47.
[8] This episode, according to Frank, *Die Brandenburger als Reichstagswähler*, pp. 65, 77. On the social democratic election campaign of 1890, see the sources cited above in ch. 1, nn. 16, 18, 21, and Sepainter, *Die Reichstagswahlen im Großherzogtum Baden*, pp. 134–37.

Table 5.1 *The 1887 voters in the elections of 1890 (percent)*

Vote in 1890	Vote in 1887					
	Kartell	Left-Liberal	Minority parties	Social Democrats	Non-voters	Net new voters
Kartell	60	11	10	7	5	10
Left-Liberal	13	60	1	4	7	2
Minority parties	9	3	62	0	3	21
Social Democrats	10	11	5	84	4	33
Non-voters	8	16	23	5	82	33
All	100	101	101	100	100	99

would be repeated throughout his reign) had little effect. In Berlin and throughout Germany, the 1890 elections were a major victory for the Social Democrats, their share of all eligible German voters going from 8% in 1887 to 14% three years later, making them the largest single party, just a fraction of a percentage point ahead of the Center in second place. The left-liberal parties also gained, but a more modest two percentage points, about as many as the minority parties lost. The conservative parties had similar, relatively modest losses, but the National Liberals suffered a true shipwreck, their share of eligible voters dropping from 18% to a little over 12%. Turnout, at 71% of votes cast, was high, but it was six percentage points beneath the record level of the Kartell elections, three years previously.

Table 5.1 shows the voter movements that had brought about this large-scale shift in the electoral landscape.

The party groups that were the three main protagonists of the 1887 elections, the Kartell parties, the left-liberals, and the minority parties, all suffered from poor voter loyalty in 1890, just about 60% of their voters repeating their choice. This was nothing new for the left-liberals, but typical of what they achieved in the 1880s; for the two other party groups it was a very significant decline of almost twenty-five percentage points from the voter loyalty rates they had reached at the previous election. Retaining close to 85% of previous voters was a feat that only the Social Democrats were able to achieve in 1890. These results, considered more closely, explain the main trends of the election: the large victory of the Social Democrats, the large defeat of the Kartell parties, the modest successes of the left-liberals, and the modest decline in the minority party vote.

The Social Democrats attracted votes from across the party spectrum, with 11% of the 1887 left-liberal electorate, 10% of the Kartell voters (this can be broken down to 9% of 1887 conservatives, and 11% of 1887 National Liberals) and 5% of the minority party voters supporting them. New entrants to the electorate were also strongly inclined to the Social Democrats, while previous non-voters – of whom there were very few in any event, as one might expect in an election where turnout had declined from the previous one – were not particularly favorable to the labor party. Now, while equal proportions of 1887 Kartell and left-liberal voters had switched to the Social Democrats, those elections had been a landslide victory for the Kartell, its parties receiving three-and-a-half times the vote of the Radical opposition. This means that many more former Kartell voters chose the Social Democrats in 1890 than did ex-left-liberals. The great breakthrough for the Social Democrats, therefore, came when they attracted voters from the parties of the right.

We can support this assertion still further by considering the Social Democratic electorate of 1890 in terms of its 1887 voting choices. Just a minority of Social Democratic voters in 1890 – about 45% of them – had supported the party in 1887. Of the Social Democratic voters, 25% had chosen one of the Kartell parties that year, 8% had voted for the left-liberals, and 7% for one the minority parties. Of the 1890 Social Democratic electorate, 9% were net new voters; last and least were the 6% of previous non-voters. The great stream of voters to the Social Democrats in 1890 did not follow the channels of ideological affinity: in the Social Democratic electorate that year, former voters from the Kartell and minority parties, on the center and right of the party spectrum, out-numbered former left-liberals and bourgeois democrats on the left, by four to one.

In his studies of the electorate in the Ruhr industrial area, Karl Rohe has found whole communities of coalminers, who went over virtually in a body from the National Liberals in 1887 to the Social Democrats in 1890. Rohe has suggested that the effects of the great coalminers' strike of 1889 were the motivating factor in such a switch.[9] However, since such switches were occurring throughout Germany in 1890, there must have been something wider at work. I would suggest that changes in voter loyalty between the elections of 1887 and 1890 were similar to what had occurred between 1878 and 1881, only on a much broader scale. In both cases, a nationalist election campaign had mobilized large – in 1887, extremely large – numbers of previous non-voters, in 1878 to vote for the conservatives, in 1887 to vote for the Kartell parties and for the minority party opposition. The subsequent elections dealt primarily with economic issues, and those voters, who had been mobilized but not yet won

---

[9] Rohe, Jäger and Dorow, "Politische Gesellschaft und politische Kultur," p. 457.

over, then switched to the party most able to address such economic
questions: in 1881, the left-liberals; in 1890, as a result of their spectacu-
larly successful and effective campaign, the Social Democrats. For the
coalminers of the Ruhr Basin, their strike of 1889 brought such economic
issues to the fore in most dramatic fashion, and their switching from the
Kartell parties to the Social Democrats may have occurred in the most
massive of ways. It was, however, not a unique regional pattern but part of
a national trend.[10]

This same development – voters brought into the electoral universe by
parties of the right in a nationalist election campaign, then moving to the
left in a subsequent election turning on economic issues – helps explain
the more modest victory of the bourgeois left in 1890. While about the
same percentage of 1887 left-liberal voters chose one of the Kartell
parties in 1890 as 1887 Kartell voters switched to the left-liberals, since
there were many more Kartell voters in 1887, the absolute number of
voters switching from the national parties to the bourgeois left-wing
opposition was much greater: the net flow of voters from the Kartell to
the left-liberals made up about 3.5% of the 1890 electorate. If the
Radicals did not obtain quite the same success as the Social Democrats, it
was in part because they lost votes to the labor party but, more importantly, because they were unable to gain support from new entrants into
the electorate and from former minority party voters as the Social
Democrats did. Still, the left-liberals and bourgeois democrats received
the votes of almost 13% of the electorate in 1890, putting them just one
percentage point behind the Social Democrats. Although subtle measures, such as the declining proportion of eligible voters choosing the left-
liberal parties in constituencies where they nominated candidates (see
figure 3.6), point toward future problems that the bourgeois left would
have with the electorate, such difficulties would only become manifest in
subsequent elections. The election of 1890 was a victory for all the parties
of the left, "bourgeois" as well as socialist.[11]

The minority parties occupied a different position in the movement of
voters from 1887 to 1890. These parties had not done well with voter
loyalty. The 62% of voters at the previous elections that they had been
able to retain was almost ten percentage points beneath their previous

[10] The importance of the voters mobilized by the Kartell elections for the later successes of
the Social Democrats has been noted by Aschoff, *Welfische Bewegung*, p. 186, but he is one
of the few historians to have done so.
[11] The 1890 elections were a remarkable point of almost perfect equality in success with the
voters for the major parties in Imperial Germany: the three right-wing parties
(Conservatives, Free Conservatives, and Anti-Semites) were the choice of 14% of the eligible voters; the National Liberals received the votes of 12% of them; the left-liberal
parties and the Center 13% each, and the social democrats 14%.

lowest figure. This sharp drop in voter loyalty between 1887 and 1890 parallels a similar decline among the voters in the Kartell parties and probably occurred for the same reason. Many of the previous non-voters brought out to vote for the minority parties in the dramatic elections of 1887, voters mobilized against the Kartell's nationalism by contrary appeals to regional, confessional and ethnic loyalties, then deserted these parties after an election campaign focused on quite different economic questions. If both the Kartell and the minority parties mobilized previous non-voters in 1887 and lost many of them in 1890, these voters departed in quite different directions. Voters leaving the Kartell parties for parties of the opposition – and they left in almost equal numbers for the left-liberals, the minority parties, and the Social Democrats – outnumbered those leaving for abstention by a ratio of 4:1. In contrast, most of the 1887 minority party voters who left off supporting them in 1890 dropped out of the electorate, the move to non-voting outnumbering the switch to other parties by about 1.5:1.

To be sure, the 16% of 1887 minority party voters who switched to another party in 1890 was something new and unprecedented. Never had so many voters deserted these parties for other party groups; the previous high was just 8%. The 1890 elections marked the beginning of a decade in which the minority parties, lacking the previous political alignments that found them in almost existential conflict with the German nation-state, would have the most difficulty in retaining their voters. Still, the ties of confession, region, and ethnicity remained strong; indifference to an election not centered around such loyalties was a more likely response from former minority party voters than switching to other parties.

Figures on voting by confession once again confirm these trends. In 1890, 75% of eligible Protestant voters turned out, just very slightly beneath the Protestant turnout rate in the Kartell elections of 77%. Catholic turnout, on the other hand, fell from 78% in 1887 to just 64% in 1890, returning to about its 1884 level. This decline in Catholic turnout was general, occurring roughly to the same extent in Prussia and in non-Prussian Germany, in constituencies with and those without Center Party candidates. Lacking the confessionally tinged confrontation with the hostile nation-state to motivate them, many Catholic voters were simply not interested in the elections.

Protestant support for the Kartell parties slipped by fourteen percentage points, putting them back to where they were in 1884. Protestant support for left-wing opposition, on the other hand, increased almost as much as it declined for the governmental parties. However, this increase in votes left the left-liberal parties at about their 1884 levels of support, while the Social Democrats (the choice of almost 20% of eligible Protestant voters in 1890) were way above their 1884 figure of just 8%. In some respects, the elections between 1881 and 1890 had been a seesaw for Protestant voters, who went from the conservatives and National Liberals to the left-liberals and back again, but the massive weight of the newly mobilized added in 1887 wobbled the seesaw and dropped a large number of voters off into the socialist camp three years later.

The proportion of eligible Catholic voters casting their ballot for both the minority and the Kartell parties declined between 1887 and 1890, from 57 to 45% for the former, and from 18 to 13% for the latter – bringing them back to about the levels of 1884. (About 3% of eligible Catholic voters chose the left-liberals in 1890, approximately the same as in 1887.) The only party gaining a higher percentage of eligible Catholic voters in 1890 was the Social Democrats, albeit just to 4%, from the 2% share they had received in 1884. We could see this as the beginnings of a new option for Catholic voters, who would no longer have to chose between clerical and particularist parties on the one hand, and governmental and anti-clerical ones on the other. If so, it was a very modest beginning for this new option; it would find relatively few additional takers in the further elections of the decade.

These considerations suggest two different ways of understanding the elections of 1890, both centered on the role of the voters mobilized in the Kartell elections of 1887. These voters played an important role in the victory of the left, just as the voters mobilized in the attempted assassination elections of 1878 had in the left-wing victory of 1881. In that year, however, it had been the left-liberal parties that had captured the voters previously brought to the polls by nationalist appeals. These parties had enjoyed a similar if more limited success with such voters in 1890: between 1878 and 1881, the left-liberal parties enjoyed a net gain of some 6% of the electorate from the conservatives and National Liberals; between 1887 and 1890, the net gain was only about 3%. The reason was of course the rise of the Social Democrats, who were co-victors in the triumph of parties of the left. In 1903 and 1912 (elections characterized by a swing to the left), the SPD would be the only party to profit.

The year 1890 also marked the first step in the political journey of the voters brought into the electorate in 1887. Many Protestants mobilized in 1887 moved to the left three years later; some Catholics did, but others moved out of the electorate altogether. However, these voters' journey was not over in 1890. The two subsequent elections of the decade would see quite a lot of voter-switching between the parties, until the elections of 1903 and 1907 brought a new stratum of previous non-voters into the arena.

The elections of 1893

If the dissolution of the Bismarckian clash between governmental and oppositional parties was begun by Bismarck himself in 1890, his successor as chancellor, General Leo von Caprivi, completed it – by trying to act like Bismarck. One of the acts of the Kartell Reichstag elected in 1887 had been to pass a law lengthening the term between elections from three to five years, the measure to come into force following the 1890 elections. Thus, the next regularly scheduled elections were due for 1895. In 1893, however, Chancellor Caprivi brought in a seven-year army bill, calling (like its predecessor) for a substantial increase in both military appropriations and size of the standing army.

This action posed a painful dilemma for the Center and the left-liberals. Following the defeat of the Kartell and Bismarck's dismissal in 1890, they had been willing to cooperate with the new chancellor, who, in turn, had proposed a number of measures that won their support, including the repeal of additional elements of the Kulturkampf legislation and a de facto reduction in tariffs via the negotiation of most-favored-nation trade treaties with Germany's major commercial partners. Continuing their cooperation in this arena, however, would have meant renouncing their opposition to higher taxes and greater military expenditures, issues that both parties had used among the voters with great effect. The left-liberals split over the issue, with a slim majority of the parliamentary deputies, but a much more substantial number of local election committees under the leadership of Eugen Richter, voting to continue their oppositional role, and a minority wishing to cooperate with the government and endorsing the military bill. The Radical Party united in 1884 now dissolved into the Radical People's Party (oppositional) and the Radical Alliance (governmental). The leaders of the parliamentary caucus of the Center wanted to vote in favor of the army appropriations, as did their counterparts among the Polish nationalists. While the Polish leaders were able to keep the caucus in line, a revolt of the Center backbenchers prevented its leadership from supporting the government. A large majority of the Center deputies opposed the bill and it did not pass.

Caprivi then took the logical Bismarckian step and dissolved the Reichstag, appealing to the voters to support the government in its efforts to protect vital national interests. 1893 was to be a rerun of 1887. However, there were a number of obstacles in the authorities' way. One of the secrets of Bismarck's electoral successes had been the "Guelf" or "reptile" funds. These were monies accruing from the property of the former Hanoverian royal family, which the Prussians had confiscated in 1866 and which Bismarck had used – without any parliamentary control or review, whatsoever – to purchase favorable coverage in the press for the government and the parties favorable to it. In a gesture of accommodation to the particularist opposition, and a proof of his endorsement of liberal ideas about parliamentary control over the budget, Caprivi had returned the property, thus putting him in the position of trying to influence public opinion in a nationalist direction without one of the key means to do so.[12]

More than that, Bismarck's successes in such plebiscitary elections had been based on his close cooperation with the parties of the right. In 1893, however, these parties, and their organized supporters, were far from rallying around the chancellor on nationalist issues. Instead, they were furious about his moves – even partial and gradual as they were – away from protectionism. There were three interrelated, partially complementary, partially competitive anti-governmental mobilizations on the right in that election year, all focused at least in part on agricultural interests and involving the use of anti-Semitism as part of a political appeal. The one that in some ways drove all the rest was the initiative of organized political anti-Semitism. An independent, organized anti-Semitic political party – as opposed to the use of anti-Semitic appeals in conservative election campaigns – made its first appearance in the 1887 elections (its candidates were noted in the official returns, in keeping with the dominant campaign theme, as supporters of the government's military appropriation), but the anti-Semites just put up candidates in five constituencies that year. That number increased to 31 in 1890 and jumped to 128 in 1893, giving some 38% of all German voters the opportunity to chose a candidate of the anti-Semitic party.

As had been the case with the anti-Semitic rhetoric in conservative politics of the 1880s, the organized anti-Semitism of the following decade was closely connected with opposition to free trade and laissez-faire. Northern Hessen, the anti-Semites' main political stronghold was also the home to the Central German Peasant League, founded and led by the political anti-Semites' leader Otto Böckel; his party blamed the government's trade treaties for farmers' problems almost as much as it condemned the Jews for them. In Saxony, another stronghold of the anti-Semites, the party worked closely with small businessmen and master craftsmen, who called for limitations on entry into the crafts and blamed Jews for both capitalist liberalism and working-class social democracy – the twin enemies of the lower middle class.

Fearing the loss of voters to the anti-Semites, and driven by anti-Semitic

[12] Röhl, *Germany without Bismarck*, pp. 56–84, 110–12; Loth, *Katholiken im Kaiserreich*, pp. 48–50; Kaminski, *Polish Publicists*, pp. 156–63; Sheehan, *German Liberalism*, p. 265; Seeber, *Zwischen Bebel und Bismarck*, pp. 197–205.

sentiment in their own ranks, delegates to the 1892 Conservative Party conference officially denounced the "disintegrative Jewish influence on the body of our nation" (Volkstum).[13] Simultaneously competing and cooperating with the independently organized anti-Semites in the six months between the adoption of the new program and the elections, the Conservatives increasingly took on an oppositional stance, placing the leading party of the right on the worst terms with the national government that it had been in two decades. The chancellor, the emperor, leading figures in the court, and senior civil servants came to see the Conservatives during the election campaign as more of an enemy than a friend of the government.

Finally, the 1893 elections were the maiden voyage of the Agrarian League. It was founded in February 1893, and still not fully organized by the time of the Reichstag elections in June of that year, but it was nonetheless able to throw itself into the campaign in at least some constituencies, supporting National Liberal, Free Conservative, Conservative, and anti-Semitic candidates, with a message of opposition to the government's trade policy. Politically active League members were sometimes friends of the organized anti-Semites, sometimes supporters of other right-wing parties that were in competition with them, but in either case the combination of anti-Semitism and hostility to free trade was typical of the campaigns supported by the organized agrarians.[14]

Rural discontent in 1893 was not limited to Germany's Protestant farmers who, as we will see, were the main supporters of these right-wing initiatives. Catholic agriculturalists were equally unhappy about declining farm prices and the government's move away from protectionism. Often, they were not too impressed with the Center's parliamentary leadership, who had supported the trade treaties farmers held responsible for their plight and had also been willing to endorse the government's plans for a larger army – meaning more peasants' sons drafted and higher taxes on hard-pressed farmers to pay for it. Some of this discontent, which was characteristic of both the 1893 and the 1898 elections, took the form of opposing or insurgent Center candidacies. In a number of heavily Catholic constituencies, where there was little danger that any other party could gain the seat, there were two Center candi-

---

[13] Quoted in Puhle, *Agrarische Interessenpolitik*, p. 119.
[14] On the mobilizations of the right in 1893, see Puhle, *Agrarische Interessenpolitik*, pp. 35, 167–68; Richard S. Levy, *The Downfall of the Anti–Semitic Political Parties in Imperial Germany* (New Have and London: Yale University Press, 1975), pp. 43–90; Retallack, *Notables of the Right*, pp. 91–105; Dan S. White, *The Splintered Party: National Liberalism in Hessen and the Reich 1867–1918* (Cambridge, MA: Harvard University Press, 1976), pp. 142–44; Schilling, "Politics in a New Key," passim.

dates, one endorsed by the party's parliamentary leadership, one opposed to it.[15]

In Bavaria, rural Catholic discontent took more drastic form with the formation of regional Peasant Leagues, which then ran candidates for the Reichstag against the Center. These leagues, consolidated in 1897 into a unified Bavarian Peasant League, asserted in their organizational meetings and in their electoral agitation that economic interests would have to come first in politics. They denounced higher taxes and government expenditures, the move away from agricultural protectionism, and specifically Bavarian problems such as limitations on the peasants' use of forest and mountain terrain, or the payments farmers were still making to finance compensation for the nobility's renunication of seigneurial dues a half century previously. The league politicians described theirs as a new political movement transcending the clash between liberal and clerical parties that had previously dominated electoral politics in Bavaria. However, league activists included many physicians and schoolteachers who made no secret of their anti-clericalism, as well as former supporters of the extreme, protest wing of political Catholicism in Bavaria, who had refused to accept Bavaria's belonging to the German Empire. The leagues were thus a triple threat to the Center's position among Bavarian voters, since they melded together a new insistence that economic issues had to take priority over past religious and regional ones, along with two issues of Bismarckian politics – opposition to the clergy and particularist opposition to the national government – that had previously been espoused by opposing political parties.[16]

One can speak, more generally, of an incipient mood of rural protest in the 1893 elections. Since the farmers' economic interest groups that would represent agrarian demands and channel them back to some of the established political parties were just in the initial process of formation, it was still unclear how this rural discontent would affect the elections. The SPD conducted an aggressive rural agitation in 1893, hoping to repeat its breakthrough at the previous elections with a new portion of the electorate. Social Democrat agitators turned up in the oddest places, such as the deeply Catholic and conservative Upper Palatinate of Bavaria; to the consternation of the authorities and the clergy some of the peasants were

---

[15] Loth, *Katholiken im Kaiserreich*, pp. 43–45; Klaus Müller, "Zentrumspartei und agrarische Bewegung im Rheinland 1882–1903," in *Spiegel der Geschichte: Festgabe für Max Braubach zum 10. April 1964* ed. Konrad Repgen und Stephan Skalweit (Münster: Verlag Aschendorff, 1964), pp. 828–57; Blackbourn, *Class, Religion and Local Politics*, pp. 44–45.

[16] Hochberger, *Der bayerische Bauernbund*, and Ian Farr, "From Anti–Catholicism to Anticlericalism."

actually listening to them, although the area's (admittedly few) industrial workers were not.[17]

The upshot of this situation was that there were three separate election campaigns being conducted in 1893. One was the campaign the government wanted, the attempt to make the elections into a referendum on the army appropriations. The only party willing to shape its appeal along those lines was the National Liberals, who told the voters that a vote for them was a vote for Germany's national security against French aggression. Although generally sympathetic to protectionism and other forms of government intervention in the economy favoring farmers and small business, the party tried to avoid becoming too closely identified with this issue, but to fight a campaign primarily on "national" questions.

But 1893 was not 1887; the government's support was not what it had been during the Kartell elections. The Kartell was also not all it had been either; in 1893, the National Liberals and the two conservative parties stood against each other in fifty-eight different constituencies. The rise of the anti-Semites disrupted the unity of the parties of the right and center even more; the extreme rightists stood against the National Liberals in sixty-two constituencies and against the Conservatives in thirty-seven.[18] The anti-Semites and the Conservatives, who were increasingly forced to imitate them, showed no interest in discussing the army appropriations, except to oppose them. Their campaigns turned on denouncing pernicious Semitic influences in the liberal parties and the Social Democrats, and in the government's practice of free trade and laissez-faire.

If the National Liberals concentrated their efforts on the army bill, the parties of the right and the extreme right on economic issues (as mediated via racial hatred), the parties of the opposition (the Center, the oppositional majority of the left-liberals and the SPD) ran a still different election campaign. They focused on the army bill, but in opposition to the government's plans, denouncing militarism and its high costs. Each of the opposition parties added its own individual touch. The SPD discussed labor issues, and denounced rumored changes the government was preparing to make the Reichstag franchise less democratic; the Center emphasized the continuing discrimination against the Catholic Church; and the left-liberals promoted laissez-faire and government non-intervention in the economy. The parties had different positions on the trade

---

[17] Walter Stelzle, "Die Wirtschaftlichen und sozialen Verhältnisse der bayerischen oberpfalz um die Wende vom 19. zum 20. Jahrhundert: Der Streit von Fuchsmühl," *Zeitschrift für Bayerische Landesgesch.* *hte* 39 (1976): 487–550, esp. pp. 520–25.

[18] On clashes between National Liberals and anti–Semites or Conservatives in 1893, cf. White, *The Splintered Party*, pp. 143–44; Sepainter, *Die Reichstagswahlen im Großherzogtum Baden*, p. 143.

treaties: the left-liberals and the Social Democrats in favor, the Center generally unfavorable but divided. Trade treaties, however, took a back seat to opposition to the government on the question of the armed forces and the taxes to pay for them.[19] The clear alignments of the Bismarckian era had definitely come to an end by 1893, with parties opposing the government from both the left and the right and with different parties agreeing with the authorities on some issues but not on others. The government's efforts to make the army bill the major issue of the campaign were, at best, partially successful, and even when the military was discussed, more often than not it was done in ways that did the interests of the authorities little good. Making the trade treaties a crucial issue was not something that the government had in mind, but many political forces, including the authorities' erstwhile right-wing allies went ahead and did so.

The clear victors at the elections were the conservative and anti-Semitic parties, their share of the electorate going from 14% in 1890 to 17% in 1893. While only about 15% of the votes cast for these right-wing parties went to the anti-Semites, almost all the increase in the right's vote was due to them. The vote totals of the anti-Semitic parties went from 50,000 in 1890 to almost 270,000 three years later, while the Free Conservative vote declined slightly between the two elections. The Conservatives did poll about 100,000 more votes in 1893 than in 1890, but if we deduct from them the 80,000 received by seven candidates who stood as anti-Semites and then joined the Conservative caucus in the Reichstag (and so were counted as Conservatives in the official election returns), we find that just about the entire increase in the right-wing vote was due to the aggressive, oppositional, racist campaign mounted by the anti-Semites.[20]

The big losers in 1893 were the liberal parties, whose share of eligible voters fell from 25% to under 20%. In other words, they lost about one-quarter of their 1890 voters; these losses affected the National Liberals and the left-liberal parties about equally, in spite of their different political

---

[19] On campaigns in 1893, besides the sources cited in n. 12–16, see Aschoff, *Welfische Bewegung*, pp. 192–93; Weidner, *Wahlen in Ludwigshafen*, pp. 406–9; Liebert, *Wahlen in Wiesbaden*, pp. 185–88; Schadt, *Die Sozialdemokratische Partei in Baden*, pp. 175–76; Moring, *Die Sozialdemokratische Partei in Bremen*, pp. 35–36; Bräunche, *Parteien und Reichstagswahlen in der Pfalz*, pp. 241–46; Sepainter, *Die Reichstagswahlen im Großherzogtum Baden*, pp. 140–47; Bajohr, *Zwischen Krupp und Kommune*, pp. 42–43; Kaminski, *Polish Publicists and Prussian Politics*, pp. 165–70; Christoph Reinders, "Sozialdemokratie und Immigration. Eine Untersuchung der Entwicklungsmöglichkeiten der SPD in einem überwiegend ländlich geprägten Reichtagswahlkreis auf der Grundlage der Wahlbewegung von 1893 bis 1912," in Wolfgang Günther (ed.) *Parteien und Wahlen in Oldenburg: Beiträge zur Landesgeschichte im 19. und 20. Jahrhundert* (Oldenburg: Heinz Holzberg Verlag, 1983), pp. 65–116, esp. pp. 75–79.

[20] Levy, *Downfall of the Anti-Semitic Parties*, p. 90.

Table 5.2 *The 1890 voters in the elections of 1893 (percent)*

Vote in 1893	Vote in 1890					
	Right or Extreme Right	Liberal	Minority parties	Social Democrats	Non-voters	Net new voters
Right or extreme right	73	16	6	12	10	4
Liberal	8	55	3	6	5	11
Minority parties	2	5	78	1	15	35
Social Democrats	5	7	2	70	6	32
Non-voters	12	17	12	11	65	19
All	100	100	101	100	101	101

positions and attitudes toward the government (see figure 3.2). The minority party share of the electorate, in contrast, held almost steady. The Social Democrats were also successful, although the three percentage point increase to 17% of eligible voters was a disappointment to party members, spoiled by their big victory in 1890 into expecting similar gains three years later. Turnout increased very slightly as against 1890, almost all of the increase due to a greater participation of Catholic voters.

Table 5.2, giving the 1893 choices of the 1890 voters, offers some indication of the voter movements behind these changes in party preferences.

There are two main trends shown in this table. First, we can see the disintegration of the liberal electorate. Just a little more than half the 1890 liberal voters chose one of the liberal parties three years later, with most of the voters defecting choosing either one of the right-wing parties or not turning out to vote. Neither the National Liberals' nationalist, pro-governmental campaign on the dangers of war, nor the left-liberals' perennial calls for lower taxes, smaller government, and the free market convinced former liberal voters. In contrast, the right-wing campaign not focusing on the army or government expenditures but instead appealing to specific economic interests in conjunction with a denunciation of Jews and the free market found a ready hearing. In a contest between the liberal parties who stuck with the old Bismarckian politics, and conservatives and anti-Semites who struck out in new directions, the voters had found the latter's appeals more convincing.

The second main trend apparent in 1893 is the further political wandering of the voters mobilized in 1887. Of the 1890 Social Democratic voters, 12% chose one of the right-wing parties in 1893, the single highest movement from the extreme left to the right at any two elections in the history of the empire. It is hard to avoid the impression that the aggressive and oppositional campaign, particularly of the anti-Semites, won over those Germans who had cast a protest vote for the Social Democrats as the leading opposition party in 1890, but had not been integrated into the SPD's ranks. Substantial regional differences in the choices of the 1890 Social Democratic voters support this assertion. In Prussia, where the parties of the right were primarily represented by the traditional conservatives, only 3% of the 1890 Social Democratic voters chose one of the right-wing parties; in non-Prussian Germany, where radical anti-Semitism set the pattern of the right to a greater extent, 16% of the Social Democratic voters of 1890 moved to the right. This would seem to be what party leader August Bebel was describing, when he wrote to the elderly Friedrich Engels in London about his campaigning experiences in 1893:

I heard artisans say: You [the SPD] explain in detail that you cannot help us; we do not wish to go under, so we vote for the anti-Semites, who promise to help us. It's the same with the small peasants. Use your finest language with these people and prove to them with the greatest clarity that it's [the anti-Semitic agitation] all a fraud and they stay with their opinions.[21]

The minority party vote in 1893 shows another aspect of the political path of voters brought into politics in 1887. A good quarter of those who cast their ballots for the Center, Hanoverians or Polish nationalists in 1887 did not vote in 1890. But at least two aspects of the 1893 elections – the familiar one of the minority parties' opposition to the national government, and the newer one of the growing controversies over economic issues – appealed to these non-voters, and brought them back to the polls to vote for the traditional minority parties or the new version of regional politics provided by the peasant leagues in Bavaria. New entrants to the electorate were successfully mobilized by the minority parties as well.

As was the case with past elections, we can continue our analysis by considering the voters' choice by confession. Since the elections of 1890 and 1893 are the first two for which we have figures on the vote by confession and social group, we can expand this analysis somewhat. Table 5.3 gives the Protestant vote at these two elections by social group.

It was the parties of the right who were able to capitalize on the angry mood of Protestant farmers in 1893, while the liberal parties were unable

---

[21] Cited in Lehmann, *Die Agrarfrage*, p. 61.

Table 5.3 *The Protestant vote in 1890 and 1893 by social group (percent)*

	Social group							
	1890				1893			
Party group	Farmer	Middle class	Worker	All	Farmer	Middle class	Worker	All
Right	27	3	28	19	33	9	27	22
Liberals	34	59	8	34	26	39	11	26
Minority parties	4	0	4	3	4	0	4	3
Social Democrats	2	20	36	20	5	24	42	23
Non-voters	33	18	24	25	31	29	17	26
All	100	100	100	101	99	101	101	100

to connect with them. The SPD also had some very modest success in its agrarian agitation, although the payoff was far less than the effort that the party had put into it, and fell well behind the socialist hopes. The Social Democrats achieved a good deal more with their core constituency, Protesant blue-collar workers.

The real story of the 1893 elections among Protestant voters, though, is the collapse of middle-class support for the liberal parties. Clearly the choice of a substantial majority of the Protestant middle class (admittedly very broadly defined) in 1890, the liberals suffered an utter fiasco three years later. Part of this change was due to the movement of middle-class Protestant voters to the parties of the right, exemplified, for instance, by the very successful campaign of the anti-Semites in Saxony. To a lesser extent, gains of the SPD with this social group also hurt the liberals. Much of the difference, however, was due to the sharp decline in turnout; it seems reasonable to conclude that many of the disappointed liberal voters of 1890 who did not come to the polls three years later belonged to the Protestant middle class. Unconvinced by the stale politics of both the National Liberals and the progressives, not attracted by the generally (with regional exceptions, such as in Saxony) agrarian orientation of the right and not yet ready to cast a ballot for the Social Democrats, these voters simply stayed home.

This decline in turnout meant that the liberal parties in 1893 no longer received the support of a majority of eligible Protestant middle-class voters, but they still could still manage 54% of the votes cast by this social and confessional group. However, 1893 was the liberals' last hurrah: when these non-voters emerged from their abstention, they would turn to other parties. The liberal parties would never again manage even a majority of the votes cast by the Protestant middle class; their share of its vote would shrink steadily in the subsequent general elections of the *Kaiserreich* – a state of affairs only briefly and very modestly reversed in 1907.

A comparable table detailing the Catholic vote by social group in 1890 and 1893 would show very little change. This result is in part an artifact of the procedure required to estimate voting choices by confession and social class, which requires all the minority parties to be lumped together. The percentage of eligible Catholic voters choosing one of the minority parties increased from 45% in 1890 to 47% in 1893. The particular minority party Catholics chose, however, was different, at least on a regional basis. In Prussia, the Center enjoyed a modest increase in its share of eligible Catholic voters – 39% in 1890, 43% in 1893, while the other minority parties dropped slighty from 10 to 9%. The picture was different in non-Prussian Germany. Here, the Center vote declined from 34 to 32% of eligible Catholic voters, while the other minority parties went from 6 to 11% – primarily because of the success at the polls of the peasant league candidates in Bavaria.

Among Protestant voters, the parties of the right profited from agrarian discontent, and the liberals suffered from it. This same agrarian discontent had relatively little effect on the voting of Catholics living in Prussia, who were often willing to follow the lead of the clergy and the Center politicians and vote on the basis of other issues, such as the defense of religion, or opposition to the military plans of the national government. Such discontent as did emerge tended to be expressed politically within the Center Party, in the form of competing Center candidates in the same constituency. In southern Germany, particularly in Bavaria, on the other hand, Catholic farmers' anger pushed them politically beyond the boundaries of the Center. A tiny piece of this anger may have been captured by the Social Democrats, who managed a grand total of 1% of the vote of eligible Catholic farmers (but probably most of that in southern Germany, so a higher percentage of Catholic agriculturalists there) and enjoyed some modest successes in a few predominantly Catholic rural areas of Baden and Bavaria.[22] Mostly, though, it was the Peasant Leagues that were the beneficiaries of

---

[22] Ibid., pp. 67–71; Schadt, *Die Sozialdemokratische Partei in Baden*, pp. 152–53. 1893 marked the highpoint of the SPD vote in rural and agricultural areas of the Bavarian Upper Palatinate: Stelzle, "Die wirtschaftlichen und sozialen Verhältnisse der bayerischen Oberpfalz," pp. 525–31; Hattenkofer, *Regierende und Regierte*, p. 232.

farmers' anger; on a regional basis, they would pose the greatest threat to the Center's leading role in the Catholic countryside that the party had ever experienced.

If the general elections of 1890 marked the transition from the Bismarckian to the Wilhelmine version of popular politics, those of three years later showed the full face of Wilhelmine politics. A number of aspects of these elections would be characteristic of subsequent ones, up to the First World War. The government would no longer be able to determine the main issues of the campaign by itself and the parties that oriented their campaigns primarily to the government's initiative, whether in support of or in opposition to it – as did the liberal parties and, to a lesser extent, the Center in 1893 – would not do particularly well with the voters. The 1893 election saw the introduction of the question of farm prices as a central campaign issue; in various forms, it would retain its central position. The realignments of Protestant voters in 1893 – farmers toward the right-wing parties, the middle class away from the liberals – would remain permanent features of the Wilhelmine political universe.

There were some anomalous aspects of the 1893 general elections that neither fit the pattern of other victories of the right nor were precursors of future developments. The 1893 election saw the only right-wing victory in the elections of the *Kaiserreich* not to be achieved by an increase in turnout, the mobilization of previous non-voters, and a nationalist election campaign supported and sponsored by the government. Rather, the parties of the right that year drew their increase in votes from the other political parties – the liberals, primarily, but also to some extent the Social Democrats – with a campaign centered on economic issues. Both of these developments were more typical of elections characterized by victories of the left. These atypical voter movements in 1893 were connected to the other anomalous aspect of that year's elections, the rapid rise of the radically oppositional anti-Semitic parties of the extreme right. Although they had firmly established a niche for themselves in the electorate in 1893, these parties would be unable to expand on it any further in the future. The ever more effectively organized Agrarian League, with its powerful and influential supporters, would take over the rural discontent exploited by the anti-Semitic parties, as well as their use of anti-Semitism for political purposes and channel it in the direction of the more establishment and more pro-governmental conservative parties and the right wing of the National Liberals. Quickly splitting into quarreling factions, unable to decide whether to cooperate with or oppose the conservative parties, the independently organized anti-Semitic movement would retreat after

1893 into a few provincial strongholds.[23] However, the effect of its political innovations would be felt throughout the Wilhelmine era.

The elections of 1898

Although Chancellor Caprivi was able to get the Reichstag elected in 1893 to pass both a military appropriations bill and additional trade treaties (though by the narrowest of margins), these were his last political successes. He was forced to resign in 1894, and under the regime of his weak successor, Prince Chlodwig zu Hohenlohe, government policy moved slowly and erratically toward the right. Mostly, this meant an end to some of the initiatives of Caprivi's chancellorship such as proposals for further labor protection legislation or social reform, or for continued liberalization of import restrictions. There were also abortive efforts at political repression, including legislatively unsuccessful proposals for new legal restrictions on the Social Democrats, or plans to abolish universal and equal manhood suffrage for the Reichstag elections. The one major positive proposal and accomplishment of this turn to the right in the five-year legislative session of the 1893 Reichstag was the Naval Law of 1898, which established the beginnings of a German high seas navy, as part of a move toward a more aggressive and imperialistic foreign policy.[24]

Some historians have asserted that this naval expansion can be seen as the centerpiece of a new political direction, Sammlungspolitik – a policy of rallying or coalition building that sought to reconcile the economic interests of business and agriculture, to unite the Kartell parties, the Center and at least some of the left-liberals, and in doing so aimed to ensure popular support for the regime and destroy that same support for the Social Democrats. There has been a good deal of scholarly debate about whether there actually was such a policy and, if so, whether it was successful.[25] For our purposes, we need not engage in that debate, but just ask whether the building of the navy, with its nationalist and imperialist implications, was a central issue in the 1898 elections.

The answer is quite clear: it was not. Burned by its lack of success in 1893, the national government refrained from trying to make the navy or any other theme central to the 1898 campaign. The authorities restricted their efforts to encouraging the election of candidates other than the

---

[23] See Levy, *The Downfall of the Anti–Semitic Political Parties*, chaps. 5–9.
[24] Röhl, *Germany without Bismarck*, pp. 112–270.
[25] A discussion of these ideas and a criticism of them can be found in Geoff Eley, "*Sammlungspolitik*, Social Imperialism and the Navy Law of 1898," in Eley, *From Unification to Nazism*, pp. 110–53.

Social Democrats or the national minorities. Of the major political parties, only the National Liberals stressed the issue of the fleet and denounced the "anti-national" Social Democrats opposing it (and rather less, the party's traditional enemy, the Center), in part doing so because on a key economic question (the raising of agricultural protective tariffs), the party was badly divided.

The fleet was not a major concern of the parties of the right and the extreme right. Following in the wake of the now well-organized Agrarian League, they centered their campaign on demands for the protection of agriculture, and, to a lesser extent, small business. Most of their fire was aimed at the ostensibly Semitic laissez-faire policies of the left-liberals, with the Social Democrats (the main target of Sammlungspolitik) playing a much lesser role as villain. These different campaign themes reflected continuing clashes between the right-wing parties and the National Liberals. To be sure, there was a good deal of harmony among the old Kartell parties, who put up candidates against each other in just twenty-three constituencies. However, independent anti-Semites or candidates of the Agrarian League stood against the National Liberals in sixty-six constituencies and against the Conservatives in thirty-six.[26]

Thus, both in the issues raised and in their political alignments, the 1898 campaigns of all the right-of-center parties were strongly reminiscent of the previous elections. To a great extent, this was also true of the 1893 opposition parties, the SPD, the oppositional left-liberals, and the Center. Once again, the radicals denounced higher taxes and excessive government military expenditures; they condemned the Junkers and their plans for higher tariffs. These were issues raised by the SPD as well, but more of the Social Democrats' fire was concentrated on the government's plans to repeal universal manhood suffrage and restrict civil liberties. The Center was in a more awkward position since the leaders of its Reichstag caucus and about two-thirds of its deputies had voted in favor of the navy law, a stance difficult to reconcile with being in opposition to the government. Still, the Center politicians followed the SPD in denouncing threats to civil liberties and defending the democratic suffrage. They downplayed their support for the fleet, or explained that the imperialist policies associated with it would make it easier for Catholic missionaries to convert the heathens. They also tried to dodge the issue of agricultural protective tariffs, making 1898 a record year for dissident Center candidacies in northern Germany and for the Peasant League in Bavaria.[27]

---

[26] For one example of such a campaign, see Frank, *Die Brandenburger als Reichstagswähler*, p. 141.

[27] On the 1898 campaign, see Fairbairn, "Interpreting Wilhelmine Elections," esp. pp. 33–40; Eley, "*Sammlungspolitik*, Social Imperialism and the Navy Law," pp. 116–17,

Table 5.4 *The 1893 voters in the elections of 1898 (percent)*

Vote in 1898	Vote in 1893					
	Right or Extreme Right	Liberal	Minority parties	Social Democrats	Non-voters	Net new voters
Right or Extreme Right	62	12	4	3	3	5
Liberal	14	56	11	11	1	9
Minority parties	4	6	63	0	9	44
Social Democrats	9	14	5	77	3	12
Non-voters	11	12	18	9	84	29
All	100	100	101	100	100	99

In sum, the 1898 elections lacked a unifying theme, a question on which all parties and the authorities took a position. The issues and the alignments were not ones that particularly excited the voters. A number of studies of different localities note that the 1898 elections were the dullest of the Wilhelmine era, with the least campaigning by the parties and the least public participation.[28] Since turnout, at 68% of eligible voters was the lowest at any general election between 1890 and 1912 – and this was true for both Catholics and Protestants – it is hard to doubt this assertion.

The decline in turnout was, in fact, the main result of the election. The right-wing parties, the liberal parties and the Center suffered modest losses of voter share when compared with 1893, while the SPD and the national and regional minorities made even more modest gains. The voter transitions from 1893 to 1898, given in table 5.4, show the dynamics that created this relative stability.

131–40; Liebert, *Wahlen in Wiesbaden*, pp. 209–10; Aschoff, *Welfische Bewegung*, p. 194; Moring, *Die Sozialdemokratische Partei in Bremen*, pp. 52–56; Wender, *Wahlen in Ludwigshafen*, pp. 418–33; Sepainter, *Die Reichstagswahlen im Großherzogtum Baden*, pp. 147–51; Schadt, *Die Sozialdemokratische Partei in Baden*, pp. 177–78; Hattenkofer, *Regierende und Regierte*, pp. 168–71; White, *The Splintered Party*, pp. 144–48; Bräunche, *Parteien und Reichstagswahlen*, pp. 252–67; Puhle, *Agrarische Interessenpolitik*, pp. 165–68, 189–90; Loth, *Katholiken im Kaiserreich*, pp. 68–69; Reinders, "Sozialdemokratie und Immigration," pp. 79–82, and the sources cited above, n. 15–16.
[28] Frank, *Die Brandenburger als Reichstagswähler*, pp. 68–69; Aschoff, *Welfsiche Bewegung*, p. 194.

Only 16% of the non-voters of 1893 voted in 1898, the lowest figure in any of the Wilhelmine elections and the second lowest in any general election between 1874 and 1912. This is what one might expect in view of the declining turnout and the generally dull nature of the campaign. In such an election, the most successful party would be the one that was best able to bring its supporters to the polls: the 77% of 1893 SPD voters who chose the party again in 1893 was fifteen to twenty percentage points ahead of the socialists' rivals and the main reason that the Social Democrats were the only major party to enjoy even modest improvements in vote totals.

The weak party loyalty shown by liberal voters in 1893 (see table 5.2) was repeated three years later; unlike 1893, however, in 1898 defections from the liberal party were as likely to be to the SPD on the left as to the conservatives, agrarians, and anti-Semites on the right. Although the liberal vote declined in 1898, the elections were not the disaster for the liberal parties that their predecessors had been. In 1893, the liberals had lost voters to all other party groupings and to the non-voters as well, but had received little from any of those in return. Five years later, the liberal parties lost voters to the other parties but these losses were balanced out overall by gains from previous supporters of the other parties. The liberal vote declined in 1898 because one-eighth of the liberal voters of 1893 did not appear at the polls, but virtually no previous non-voters found the lackluster election campaigns of the liberal parties attractive enough to get them out to vote.

If the party loyalty of liberal voters changed little between 1893 and 1898, that of the voters of the right-wing and the minority parties declined by ten to fifteen percentage points (see table 5.2). In 1898, an increased proportion of previous voters for the right-wing parties chose the liberals and Social Democrats. Part of this change reflected a greater cooperation between the Kartell parties; about one-fifth of the right-wing voters of 1893 who voted for the liberals in 1898 did so in situations where conservative candidates stood down in favor of a liberal one, typically a National Liberal (see figure 3.7). This does suggest that there was something in the idea of Sammlungspolitik. Under a more conservative government – even a weak and confused one – the traditionally pro-governmental parties of the right and center-right could work together better than at other times. Such circumstances do not, of course, explain the greater losses of the parties of the right to the Social Democrats; the less sharply oppositional campaign of the right-wing parties in 1893 probably encouraged protest voters to choose the SPD instead.

In 1898, as in the previous elections of the decade, a far greater proportion of voters who abandoned the minority parties did so for abstention than was the case with the other parties. The mobilizing effect for these voters of a clash between a central government and a particularist opposition, just vaguely present in 1893, was completely lacking five years later. The desire of Center politicians to dodge the tariff issue, the main economic question in the campaign, did little to motivate their clientele to come to the polls. The 1898 elections were a bit unusual in that a little over half the voters who left the minority parties switched to one of the other parties, mostly to their traditional rivals, the liberals. It is unclear whether economic questions (such as the tariff), nationalist issues (such as the navy), or the older theme of anti-clericalism – or any combination of these – encouraged them to do so. All these changes might have added up to fairly substantial losses for the minority parties had the turnover in the electorate not been so favorable to them, with 44% of the net new voters – over 3% of the entire electorate – choosing one of the minority parties. Even in an election that was otherwise difficult for them, the persistent appeal of the minority parties to new voters and to those moving to rapidly growing urban and industrial areas continued to be considerable.

As might be expected in elections where the movements of voters between the parties and in and out of the electorate tended to cancel each other out, the changes in voting by class and confession from 1893 to 1898 were not very great. Turnout declined among all social and confessional groups, with the exception of Protestant workers, among whom it increased by less than one percentage point. The single largest change was the continuing decline of support for the liberal parties from the Protestant middle class: 39% of these voters chose the liberals in 1893; just 29% did so five years later. The proportion of middle-class Protestant voters choosing the right-wing parties fell slightly compared to 1893; the proportion choosing the SPD increased a little; most of the change in the middle-class Protestant liberal vote can be accounted for by the seven percentage point decline in turnout among that social and confessional group.

My calculations of the Catholic vote, specified by social class, show even less change against 1893 than for Protestants. The most interesting feature of the Catholic vote was the differential decline in turnout. Turnout among all Catholic social groups fell from 1893 to 1898, but it fell least for farmers, by just three percentage points, as against eight to nine percentage points for urban social groups. In 1898, there existed the unusual situation that turnout among Catholic farmers, at 64% of eligible voters, was higher than among other Catholic social groups.

This higher turnout among farmers was not to be found among Protestants in 1898 and had not been the case among Catholics in 1893. Its existence points to a confessionally differentiated political response to agrarian discontent. Among Protestants, the 1893 elections were decisive

Table 5.5 *The Catholic vote in non-Prussian Germany during the 1890s (percent)*

Party group	Election year		
	1890	1893	1898
Right-wing parties	3	3	1
Liberals	12	12	9
Center	34	32	29
Other minority parties	6	11	14
Social Democrats	3	5	4
Non-voters	42	37	42
All	100	100	99

for the agrarian vote. The changes occurring that year – increased support by Protesant farmers for parties of the right, with their anti-free market and anti-Semitic appeals, and declining support of Protestant farmers for the liberal parties – set the pattern for the future. For Catholic farmers, on the other hand, the politicization of farmers' problems was just beginning in 1893; the changes set in motion then – agrarian Center candidacies in northern Germany, independent peasant leagues in Bavaria – would peak five years later.

We can best observe this situation by considering the Catholic vote in non-Prussian Germany in the decade of the 1890s, as given in table 5.5.

The Catholic vote for all the minority parties increased slightly over the course of the decade, and the vote for the liberals, the Center's anti-clerical rival, declined a little. But the figures show a steady realignment of Catholic voters among the minority parties, with support for the Center falling and support for the others, above all the Bavarian Peasant League, on the increase.[29] By 1898, less than a third of eligible Catholic voters in southern Germany were choosing the Center and almost half of those actually voting were casting their ballots for another party. The Center vote in southern Germany had often been at relatively low levels – as a percentage of eligible Catholic voters, it was lower in 1881 than in 1898. But previous lows had been a result of low Catholic turnout; the alternative to the Center had been non-voting. Catholic turnout in non-Prussian Germany was low during the 1890s in general, and at the 1898 elections in particular, but at those elections there was also a party offering (in some regions at least) an effective competition to the Center, one that was

[29] On this point, cf. the helpful regional analysis in Schmädeke, *Wählerbewegung*, pp. 237 n.53, 251.

effectively taking advantage of the waffling of the Center parliamentary leadership, both with regard to protection for agriculture and concerning its support for the government.

Nothing comparable was occurring in the kingdom of Prussia. There, the proportion of eligible Catholic voters choosing the Center fluctuated between 39 and 43% in the 1890s – thus, at a noticeably higher level than outside of Prussia – with support for the other minority parties constant at about 10% of the Catholic electorate. Although 1898 saw Catholic agrarian interests field a record number of candidates opposed to the official Center nominee, these candidates did very poorly with the voters, gaining under 1% of votes cast.[30] The Center would face parallel difficulties with other minority parties in Prussia only after 1900, when the Polish nationalists would oppose the Catholic party in the Upper Silesian and Ruhr industrial areas. Such clashes would be quite different from those of the previous decade among the Catholic farming population.

We cannot trace any comparable regional difference among Protestant farmers; north and south of the Main, east and west of the Elbe, in Prussia, and in non-Prussian Germany, the agrarian crisis moved them away from the liberal parties, primarily to the right and the extreme right, although a small fraction (at the high point in 1898, not quite 7%) went over to the SPD. The regionally differentiated effect on the Catholic vote suggests that for Catholic farmers, the political effects of agrarian discontent were mediated by other factors: the greater prevalence of anticlericalism among Catholics in southern Germany, their weaker ties to the Center (previously reflected not so much in voting for other parties as in a greater likelihood to abstain from voting), and, especially in Bavaria, a greater distance from the German nation-state, which the Center's parliamentary leadership was increasingly coming to support (as shown by its vote for the naval bill of 1898).

The 1898 elections in the Catholic areas of rural Bavaria were hard fought, and literally so, since they included several instances of brawling between adherents of the Peasant Leagues and supporters of the Center who had joined the newly organized Christian Peasant Leagues, which Catholic politicians and the clergy were promoting as an alternative to the insurgent agrarians.[31] Such vigorous confrontations were an anomaly in what was, in most of Germany, a relatively dull campaign, exciting comparatively little interest on the part of the electorate. Yet, for all their exceptional character, they show something of the unfinished nature of the 1898 elections. They confirmed the disruption of the Bismarckian

---

[30] Müller, "Zentrumspartei und agrarische Bewegung," p. 850.
[31] Hattenkofer, *Regierende und Regierte*, pp. 168–70.

political universe that had taken place in the two previous general elections of the decade, disruptions that made the 1890s a low point for party loyalty among German voters during the *Kaiserreich*. In the three twentieth-century general elections of the empire, turnout would rise and party loyalty would increase, suggesting the emergence of a new pattern of electoral alignments.

The twentieth-century general elections of the German Empire

Many of the characteristics of the general elections of 1903, 1907, and 1912 were also those of the elections of the previous decade. The government's inability to set the tone for the campaigns would continue after the turn of the century, with only a partial exception in 1907. The question of farm and food prices would remain a major issue for all the political parties; nationalist themes, particularly those relating to the German navy and Germany's position as a (potential) world power, would be significant for the electorate as well. Those economic special interest groups and mass associations, which had already begun to shape popular politics in the 1890s, would play an increasingly central role in the electoral process.

What differentiated the twentieth-century general elections from their predecessors was the use of all these post-Bismarckian elements of electoral politics that had developed in the 1890s. Two new developments deserve our attention. One is that the liberals and the Center, the parties that had had the most difficulty in the 1890s in adapting to the post-Bismarckian scene, proved more successful in doing so after 1900, that is, in integrating economic special interests and new styles of mass agitation into their election campaigns. The other is the centrality of the SPD to the electoral process. Even though the Social Democrats had been the only party to gain both votes and mandates consistently throughout the 1890s, the other parties, and even the government, had not always placed it at the center of their calculations but had, at least in part, continued to think in terms of the Bismarckian era, when the labor party had been at best of regional significance. After 1900, this would definitely change: issues raised by the SPD, issues raised against the SPD, and the relationship to this party, in both a friendly and and hostile form, would play an ever larger role in the calculations of the other parties and the authorities.

The elections of 1903

The empire's first general elections of the twentieth century would be a remarkable example of the centrality of the SPD. It would be the party to strike the dominant chord in the campaign, doing so by a clever combination of parliamentary and extra-parliamentary agitation, and by exploiting during the campaign political organization and activity carried out in off years. The other parties and the government struggled to counter the Social Democrats' initiative; their post-election planning would center around the SPD as well. The results of this planning would be apparent in 1907.

The 1903 election campaign grew out of one of the main themes of the politics of the 1890s, the agrarian issue. More precisely, it resulted from the ultimate success of German farmers – whether Catholic or Protestant, large landowners or small peasants – in bringing up the issue and refusing to let it go until they had obtained some satisfaction. The right-leaning German government, since 1900 under the energetic direction of the new Chancellor, Bernhard von Bülow, finally responded to the farmers' complaints by proposing to the Reichstag a new, substantially more stringent tariff on imported agricultural products.

This decision provided the SPD with its opportunity. The party launched a nationwide petition campaign, gathering millions of signatures condemning the measure; it held countless – and generally well attended – public meetings, incisively denouncing the measure for its effect on the cost of basic necessities. In the course of the thirteen months that the Reichstag considered the legislation, the Social Democratic deputies did not just oppose the measure in committees and on the floor: they obstructed the normal business of parliament, offering endless amendments, and, finally, filibustering, hoping to keep talking until the regular legislative period of the parliament elected in 1898 expired and the issue could be brought directly before the voters. For a while, it seemed that such a policy would succeed, since the left-liberal deputies joined the Social Democrats in their obstruction. Then, however, a majority of the left-liberal deputies – oddly enough, the groups that had been in opposition to the government when the Radical Party split in 1893 – ended their participation, enabling the Reichstag to vote to cut off debate and to pass the tariff.[32]

This decision on the part of the SPD to fight the tariff to the bitter end, to put itself forward as the party of cheap food, as the representative of urban consumers, has itself a history, and a significant one for the electoral developments in Wilhelmine Germany. As we have seen in

[32] Nolan, *Social Democracy and Society*, 157–60; von Saldern, *Auf dem Wege zum Arbeiter–Reformismus*, pp. 62, 89; Lorenz, *Eugen Richter*, pp. 183–93; Elm, *Zwischen Fortschritt und Reaktion*, pp. 84–95; Kenneth Barkin, *The Controversy over German Industrialization, 1890–1902* (Chicago and London: University of Chicago Press, 1970), pp. 211–52.

chapter 1, and briefly recapitulated in the sections above on the elections of 1893 and 1898, the SPD had made a very substantial effort to gain the support of agrarian voters in the 1890s, ultimately enjoying only very modest success. Confronting this issue in a protracted intramural debate in 1894–95, the party decided not to make any concessions to small farmers, in particular not to support measures to prop up farm prices. Hans Georg Lehmann has shown in his excellent study on the SPD and the agrarian question, that the party leadership – both the "reformists" and their "revolutionary" opponents – was largely in favor of making these concessions, but the rank and file rebelled against such an idea. They vigorously and furiously denounced any measures to raise the price of their daily bread, one comrade noting that there was no need to fry some "extra sausage," for the peasants.[33]

Having thus abandoned the agrarian issue to the parties of the right and the center, the SPD was in a position to make the call for cheap bread the heart of its agitation. Working with the slogan, "Down with the bread-usurers!" (die Brotwucherer) the party put aside virtually all other issues and devoted its 1903 campaign to denouncing the government and those political parties that had passed the tariffs and so ensured that the ordinary people would find it harder to make ends meet.[34]

The Social Democrats, of course, had not invented opposition to agricultural protective tariffs. The left-liberal parties were the original enemies of these measures and, as recently as the 1890 elections, had made significant gains by exploiting the issue. To some extent, this effort continued after the turn of the century. In conjunction with the Trade-Treaty Association, a group sponsored by wholesalers, export-oriented industry, and other businessmen with an interest in lower farm tariffs, left-liberal politicians had circulated petitions and held public meetings against the tariff. However, the decision of the Radical People's Party, by far the largest of the left-liberal parties to break off the parliamentary obstructionism against the tariff did little for the credibility of the bourgeois left on this issue. Since a fair proportion of the left-liberal electorate

[33] Lehmann, *Die Agrarfrage*, pp. 145–223; quote on p. 178. In an interesting and psychologically incisive argument, Adelheid von Saldern has suggested that deep-rooted fears of hunger, perhaps stemming from childhood experiences of not having enough to eat, determined the attitude of the party rank-and-file on this question. Von Saldern, *Auf dem Wege zum Arbeiter–Reformismus*, pp. 62–63.

[34] Nolan, *Social Democracy and Society*, pp. 161–62; Fairbairn, "Interpreting Wilhelmine Elections," pp. 38–39; von Saldern, *Auf dem Wege zum Arbeiter-Reformismus*, p. 81; Paetau, *Konfrontation oder Kooperation*, p. 175; Breunig, *Soziale Verhältnisse der Arbeiterschaft*, pp. 310–11; Moring, *Die sozialdemokratische Partei in Bremen*, pp. 72–73; Liebert. *Politische Wahlen in Wiesbaden*, pp. 225–26; Wender, *Wahlen in Ludwigshafen*, pp. 437–39; Aschoff, *Welfische Bewegung* pp. 195–96; Reinders, "Sozialdemokratie und Immigration," pp. 82–87.

consisted of Protestant small farmers – by 1903, sensitized to the importance of protection by a decade of agrarian agitation on the issue – these
parties could not afford to engage in the same sort of whole-hearted
attack on the tariffs that the SPD did. But another substantial proportion
of left-liberal voters were urban consumers with an interest in cheaper
food, so the bourgeois left could also not be unrestrained in endorsing
protectionism. Trying to balance free trade and protectionism, or to say
one thing in the city and another in the country, the left-liberals ended by
being unconvincing everywhere.[35]

Frightened by the results of the 1898 elections, the parliamentary leadership of the Center had ended its long vacillation on the topic and tilted
firmly in the direction of agrarian interests, strongly supporting the new
agricultural protective tariffs. In its campaign, the party aggressively
endorsed these measures in favor of agriculture and boasted that it had
played a key role in bringing them about. Catholic farmers received the
message with approval; the bitter opposition between the Center and the
Bavarian Peasant League, so common in the previous general elections,
was much weaker in 1903, largely because the Peasant League had been
overwhelmed by the Center.

Of course, higher prices for farmers meant higher prices for urban consumers. Catholics had to eat like everyone else, and a group of Christian
trade unionists had even participated in the SPD's public campaign of
1901–2 against the tariffs, some of whom were expelled from the
Christian metalworkers union for their activities. Consequently, the 1903
elections saw the unleashing of the People's Association in defense of the
Center's policy in urban areas. In its training sessions for political agitators, in public meetings it sponsored, and in its extensive pamphlet literature, the People's Association hammered away at a number of themes. It
denounced class egoism and pointed out to the faithful that Catholic
teachings required social classes to cooperate and make concessions to
one another. The group reminded the workers that the Center had
successfully sponsored an amendment to the tariff bill, diverting a
portion of the increased revenues to the social insurance system. At the
urging of the People's Association, the Center nominated loyal Christian
trade unionists in a number of industrial constituencies in western
Germany. The trump card of the People's Association efforts and the
Center campaign more generally was a re-emphasis on the defense of
religion, pointing out that the definite spiritual benefits of a vote for the
Center outweighed the dubious possibility of any possible material gains

---

[35] Besides the sources cited in the previous note, see Elm, *Zwischen Fortschritt und Reaktion*,
pp. 108–12; Blackbourn, *Class, Religion and Local Politics*, pp. 217–19; Liebert, *Wahlen in
Wiesbaden*, pp, 228–29.

to be obtained by voting for the godless Social Democrats or the anti-Catholic liberal parties.[36]

The Center, the left-liberals and the SPD had been the main opposition parties, ever since the Kartell elections of 1887. Often, they had stressed common themes in their campaigns; sometimes, they had cooperated even more closely. By seizing on the issue of food prices, raising it early and often, and making it central to the 1903 election campaign, the SPD had made itself into the sole opposition party, leaving the left-liberals divided on the issue (divided both between the four left-liberal parties, and within at least two of these parties) and the Center as basically a party of the government. Unlike similar political realignments of the Bismarckian era, this one had not been engineered by the government. Quite the opposite, Chancellor Bülow's officials had approached the 1903 elections in the same spirit as those of 1898, not putting themselves forward or pressing political questions on the electorate, but devoting themselves to preventing the election of enemies of the government – usually the SPD and the national minority parties, but, for some, the Center as well.[37]

The Kartell parties also felt the effects of this realignment. They firmly endorsed the new tariff legislation, arguing that it would bring prosperity not just to farmers but to members of all social groups. Downplaying attacks on their traditional rivals – the National Liberals against the Center, the conservative parties against the left-liberals – they concentrated their fire on the SPD, condemning it for its opposition to the "protection of national labor." In other words, they combined the advocacy of protectionism, as well as of other governmental measures in favor of farmers and small business, with anti-socialism. This ideological harmony was reflected in practical cooperation: the twenty-nine constituencies in which two Kartell party candidates stood against each other in 1903 were the fewest since the Kartell elections of 1887 (see also figure 3.7).

As had been the case in 1893 and 1898, the extreme right would not go along with this cooperative effort. However, unlike the 1890s, in 1903 it was less the anti-Semitic parties, deeply divided among themselves and

---

[36] On the Center campaign in 1903 and its background, see, besides the sources cited in the two previous notes, Nolan, *Social Democracy and Society*, pp. 161–62; Sepainter, *Die Reichstagswahlen im Großherzogtum Baden*, pp. 156–57; Bräunche, *Parteien und Reichstagswahlen in der Pfalz*, pp. 151–53; Hattenkofer, *Regierung und Regierte*, pp. 173–74; Hiery, *Reichstagswahlen im Reichsland*, pp. 320–22; Blackbourn, *Class, Religion and Local Politics*, pp. 47–53, 216–17; Loth, *Katholiken im Kaiserreich*, pp. 87, 96–102; Brose, *Christian Labor and the Politics of Frustration*, pp. 160–71.

[37] Fairbairn, "Authority vs. Democracy," pp. 831–37; Liebert, *Wahlen in Wiesbaden*, pp. 225–26.

Table 5.6 *The 1898 voters in the elections of 1903 (percent)*

Vote in 1903	Vote in 1890					
	Right or Extreme Right	Liberal	Minority parties	Social Democrats	Non-voters	Net new voters
Right or Extreme Right	67	13	3	2	6	2
Liberal	13	68	8	11	7	9
Minority parties	2	5	79	0	11	34
Social Democrats	11	9	4	83	10	42
Non-voters	7	6	6	3	67	13
All	100	101	101	99	101	100

ever less capable of engaging in effective political activity, that were the spoilers, as it was the Agrarian League. Opposing the new agricultural tariffs on the grounds that they were not high enough, the League ran fifty-five independent candidates in 1903 – a record number. Independent agrarian or anti-Semitic candidates stood against the conservative parties in just twenty constituencies, but against the National Liberals in seventy-four, and competed bitterly for the Protestant farming vote.[38]

The party that had seized the initiative was the big winner, the SPD share of eligible voters jumping by a third, from 18% in 1898 to 24% in 1903. A spectacular eighty-one Social Democratic deputies took their seats in the newly elected Reichstag. All the other parties registered much more modest changes, the Center and the National Liberals each gaining about two percentage points, the left-liberals and the parties of the right each losing one. Turnout climbed to 76%, rising substantially for both Catholic and Protestant voters. Table 5.6 shows the movements of the voters that lay behind this outcome.

[38] On the 1903 campaigns of the parties of the center–right, right, and extreme right, see Liebert, *Politische Wahlen in Wiesbaden*, pp. 226–28; Sepainter, *Die Reichstagswahlen im Großherzogtum Baden*, pp. 155–57; Bräunche, *Parteien und Reichstagswahlen in der Pfalz*, pp. 273–74, 281–82; Hiery, *Reichstagswahlen im Reichsland*, p. 321; Aschoff, *Welfische Bewegung*, pp. 195–96; Retallack, *Notables of the Right*, pp. 138–41; Puhle, *Agrarische Interessenpolitik*, pp. 222–24; Eley, *Reshaping the German Right*, pp. 239–40.

The 1903 general election was the only one in the *Kaiserreich* characterized both by an increase in turnout and a victory of the left. The 10% of previous non-voters who chose the SPD that year was a new high for the party. The size of the electorate increased substantially in 1903, by almost 9% over 1898, the single largest increase from any one general election to the next in the *Kaiserreich*. The SPD profited heavily from the turnover in the electorate, with almost 4% of the electorate consisting of net new voters who chose the SPD. This is a quite impressive figure, especially considering that the Social Democrats' share of eligible voters grew from 1898 to 1903 by about eight percentage points. The influx from other parties that had been the motor of Social Democrats' growth at the ballot box during the previous decade, however, came to an end. The SPD did enjoy a modest increase in support – net, less than 2% of the electorate – from former voters of the minority parties and parties of the right and the extreme right, but the Social Democrats lost more voters to the liberals than they gained (cf. tables 1.2 and 1.5).

As a comparison with table 5.4 shows, the main difference between the 1898 and the 1903 elections for party groups other than the SPD was that they lost fewer voters to abstention and gained more from previous non-voters. The key question of the 1903 campaign, and the relatively clear fashion in which almost all the parties addressed it, spoke to the voters on all sides of the farm prices/food prices issue – one that had been constantly before their attention for a decade – and brought them to the polls.[39] The 1903 election was also the only election in the *Kaiserreich* turning on economic issues that registered an increase in turnout. In this race among the non-SPD parties to bring supporters to the polls and to mobilize non- or new voters, the minority parties were the clear winners, gaining the largest share of both previous non-voters and net new voters, enabling them to improve their vote totals.

If we look at the results of the 1898 and 1903 general elections by social group and confession, as presented in table 5.7, then we can observe another aspect of the impact of the campaign on the voters.

Turnout among middle-class Protestant voters increased substantially in 1903, reversing a decade-long trend. This was a new development that favored the SPD; the increase in its vote over 1898 was primarily attributable to the growing proportion of middle-class Protestants voting for the party. Avoiding specifically working-class questions, and focusing

---

[39] It is probably no coincidence that the left–liberals and the parties of the right and extreme right, who were divided on the question, were the only ones to suffer even modest losses.

Table 5.7a *The Protestant vote in 1898 and 1903 by social group (percent)*

	Social group							
	1898				1903			
Party group	Farmer	Middle class	Worker	All	Farmer	Middle class	Worker	All
Right	31	7	23	20	37	14	11	19
Liberals	23	29	14	22	22	22	25	23
Minority parties	4	0	4	3	4	0	3	2
Social Democrats	7	29	43	27	3	42	45	34
Non-voters	35	36	16	29	33	22	16	22
All	100	101	100	101	99	100	100	100

Table 5.7b *The Catholic vote in 1898 and 1903 by social group (percent)*

	Social group							
	1898				1903			
Party group	Farmer	Middle class	Worker	All	Farmer	Middle class	Worker	All
Right	6	0	4	4	9	0	2	4
Liberals	7	9	8	8	8	10	11	10
Minority parties	51	39	44	46	54	52	51	52
Social Democrats	1	5	8	4	0	6	13	7
Non-voters	34	48	36	38	30	30	24	28
All	99	101	100	100	101	98	101	101

instead on an issue of concern to a broad range of urban consumers, the Social Democrats garnered the votes of the urban, Protestant middle class, and did so as no other party had been able to do since the elections of 1890. The decline in turnout among the Protestant middle class had been the major reason for the poor showings of the liberal parties in the elections of 1893 and 1898; when many members of this social group came back to the polls in 1903 they did so with a new political prefer-ence.[40]

Protestant farmers, on the other side of the price question, rallied to the parties of the right, which stood for high, or still higher, tariffs. The pro-portion of Protestant agrarian voters choosing the SPD – never large, in any event, but having grown from 2% to 7% in the course of the elections of the 1890s – declined back to about where it had been at the beginning of the Wilhelmine era. Presenting itself as the party of cheap food, the SPD had gained the support of one group of non-working-class Protestant voters, but in doing so it had permanently sacrificed whatever it chance it had to gain the other.

The conservative and extreme right-wing parties also improved their standing among urban middle-class Protestant voters, master craftsmen and small businessmen, benficiaries of policies advocated by the right, such as higher taxes on department stores and consumer cooperatives or the tightening of guild restrictions. This cost the liberal parties additional votes; if the 1903 elections did not end in a fiasco for them as those of ten years previously did, it was primarily because they obtained a substantial proportion of working-class voters. Such voters would have been devout and/or strongly nationalistic: repelled by the agrarian tone of the right-wing parties' campaigns, but unlikely to vote for the godless and republi-can Social Democrats, they moved over to the liberals, setting a trend that would continue in the two following general elections.

The contrast between Protestant and Catholic voters in 1903 was very pronounced and reveals a basic characteristic of Wilhelmine electoral politics. If urban, middle-class Protestants rallied to the SPD on food prices, middle-class Catholics moved to the Center on the religious issue. The 1903 elections are a strong testimony to the remarkable effect of the People's Association on Catholic urban voters: the proportion of both middle- and working-class Catholic voters choosing the minority parties (and most of them, with a few regional exceptions, the Center) increased markedly, even though the party had adopted – and openly defended – a policy that ran counter to their economic interests. Not all Catholics living in urban areas were convinced by the People's Association; a

---

[40] It does not follow that the members of the Protestant middle class who voted for the SPD in 1903 were necessarily the same *individuals*, or even people who worked at the same occupation, as those middle-class Protestants who did not vote in the two previous elec-tions. The strong showing of the Social Democrats among net new voters suggests that younger members of the electorate were voting for the SPD. For the middle class, this would mean primarily salaried employees, a much younger group than independent pro-prietors, so the changing Protestant middle-class vote may also reflect structural changes in the middle class, occurring at the time: the decline in the number of small proprietors and the increase in the number of salaried employees.

growing proportion chose the SPD as well, but since Catholic turnout increased substantially in 1903, this growing strength of the Social Democrats among Catholic voters did not, overall, occur at the expense of the Center.

The increased support for both the Center and the SPD among urban Catholic voters was not distributed equally across Germany, so in a few urban and industrial constituencies, the Social Democrats made substantial gains, bringing them close enough to the Center vote to be a serious challenge to the Catholic party's hold on the seat.[41] The Polish nationalists also improved their vote totals, with the regional and national minority parties in Prussia going from 11% of eligible Catholic voters in 1898 to 13% in 1903 – although the proportion choosing the Center jumped from 35% to 41%.[42] These modest setbacks were more than outweighed by the Center's great victory in southern Germany. The rural insurgencies of 1898 faded quickly, with the founding of Christian Peasant Leagues, their strong clerical endorsement, and the Center's adoption of the program of agricultural protectionism. Once again, the analysis of class and confession in voting does not allow us to detail shifts between the Center and other minority parties among Catholic farmers, but in non-Prussian Germany the Center went from a meager 29% of eligible Catholic voters in 1898 to 40% in 1903, while the other minority parties' share of eligible Catholic voters fell from 14% to 11%. In Bavaria, the Peasant League lost 40,000 votes and five of the eight seats it had won in 1898. Catholic farmers in southern Germany were less disturbed by the Center's support of the government, once the party – and, in effect, the church – endorsed protectionism. The brief moment of the Peasant League as a broad agrarian movement was over; it dwindled to the party of a cranky, anti-clerical and oppositionally minded minority.

In sum, the Center leadership was politically successful by making material concessions to its agrarian supporters and spiritual concessions to its urban ones.[43] The 1903 elections thus demonstrated the continuing

---

[41] In Düsseldorf, for example. Nolan, *Social Democracy and Society*, p. 162.

[42] The gains of the Polish nationalists were somewhat greater than this indicates, since the Hanoverian particularists lost Catholic votes in 1903, the Center putting up candidates against them for the first time. Aschoff, *Welfische Bewegung*, pp. 195–96.

[43] Fairbairn, in "Interpreting Wilhelmine Elections," pp. 40–41, 46–47, argues that the 1898 and 1903 elections turned on what he calls "fairness issues" that is, social and economic questions. In these elections, he asserts, the Center and SPD were successful by opposing the government and stressing fairness issues, while the parties of the right, emphasizing nationalism and loyalty to the government, explicitly disdaining questions of equity, were not. In making such an argument, he slides over the extent to which the Center did noticeably better with Catholic voters in 1903, when it was not in opposition—and promulgated odd notions of equity, to boot—than in 1898, when its campaigns had a noticeably more oppositional political stance.

political efficacy of Catholic confessional loyalties, when they could be mobilized using organizational forms – such as those provided by the People's Association – appropriate to the mass politics of the early twentieth century. The one respect in which the Center was less successful in 1903, namely, in those constituencies where it ran against the Polish nationalists, it was opposing a party that also drew its support from precisely these Catholic confessional loyalties.

The other major political groupings, with their primarily Protestant clientele, were less fortunate. In an election that was very strongly polarized around the issue of food prices, they had to choose one side of the question and lose voters on the other side, or hesitate and lose voters on both sides. This was a strategy that worked for the SPD, because it gained substantially more votes than it lost, but for the liberals and the conservatives the 1903 elections turned into a zero-sum game. Their search – and the search of the national government wishing to improve the parliamentary position of these parties – for a way out of this dilemma would lead directly to the quite different political configuration of the next general election.

The elections of 1907

The more the 1903 campaign progressed, the more the supporters of the liberal and conservative parties became aware of the growing public support for the Social Democrats and of their inability to keep up with the labor party. In the years following the elections, they took steps to reorganize and reorient themselves. We can point to three somewhat different initiatives. One, coming from the ranks of the Kartell parties, involved the founding of the National Association against Social Democracy. Organized by National Liberal and Conservative politicians and well financed by contributions from big business interests hostile to the labor movement, the group soon gained a good 175,000 members. Rather in the manner of the Catholic People's Association, which also had a strongly anti-Social Democratic (although not so openly reactionary) orientation, the group trained speakers and organized speaking tours for them; it printed and distributed a wide array of pamphlets and fliers denouncing the SPD.[44]

The second, specifically centered on the National Liberal Party,

---

[44] Dieter Fricke, "Der Reichsverband gegen die Sozialdemokratie von seiner Gründung bis zu den Reichstagswahlen von 1907," *Zeitschrift für Geschichtswissenschaft* 7 (1959): 237–80; Mattheier, "Drei Führungsorganisationen," pp. 246–48; Retallack, *Notables of the Right*, pp. 155–56; Eley, *Reshaping the German Right*, pp. 228–35.

involved the intensification of an ongoing process of organizational consolidation and expansion. Since the late 1890s, the party had been busy encouraging the founding of local political clubs and creating a central national organization to tie them together. The results of the 1903 elections, slightly encouraging in that the National Liberal vote and the number of deputies the party elected increased for the first time since 1887, but also dismaying, in view of the much greater successes of the SPD, intensified this process. In 1901 a national organization of "young" (under the age of thirty-five) National Liberals was founded, a group on the left-wing of the party (i.e. anti-agrarian), but also one given to a more energetic style of campaigning. The numbers and activities of these groups grew rapidly in the early years of the twentieth century. Efforts were also intensified at the local level, a good example of which might be developments in Essen. Dismayed by the large increase in the SPD's vote there in 1903, and by the poor showing of the National Liberals, two party members founded a "National Workers Association of the Krupp Works in Essen," a company union devoted to opposing the efforts of the labor party in the city's largest employer. In 1905, a broader "National Association" was created in Essen, a mass membership, well-organized constituency association for the National Liberals and Free Conservatives, the two parties which represented the Protestant and nationalist element in the region. By 1908, its 4,500 members were a good 1,200 more than the SPD could manage in the city.[45]

The third initiative came from the ranks of the left-liberal parties that had suffered their third straight defeat at the polls in 1903 and had seen all of their different previous strategies (open and active opposition to the government and guarded support for it, an unqualified defense of laissez-faire and a qualified renunciation of it, a campaign directed against both the parties of the right and against the Social Democrats, and one directed primarily against the right) fail to gain the support of the voters. On the initiative of the smallest of these parties, the German People's Party, the left-liberal politicians began to consider both a merger of their parties and a new political strategy to go along with it. The death of Eugen Richter in 1906, unrivalled leader of the largest party on the bourgeois left, and unreconciled enemy of both a merger and a search for new directions, helped the process along substantially. Although the union of all the left-liberals into a single party only came about in 1910, before this the parties were able to agree on a new public image, central to which was

---

[45] Nipperdey, *Die Organisation der deutschen Parteien*, pp. 94–102, 151–52; Bajohr, *Zwischen Krupp und Kommune*, pp. 79–81, 107–8.

the move toward a more energetic support for the government's imperialist foreign policy.[46]

All these initiatives, explicitly or implicitly took aim at the SPD, but they tended to involve a hostility to the Center as well. The National Association against Social Democracy made no effort to cooperate with the Center, or organize Catholics loyal to it.[47] A revived and more energetic National Liberalism would be, true to the party's tradition, a more anti-clerical one; the Young National Liberals, in particular, were fiercely anti-clerical and vehemently hostile to the Center. Finally, the new orientation among the left-liberals involved abandoning the tacit or sometimes open cooperation with the Center in an anti-governmental coalition that had existed since the days of the Kartell elections of 1887.

In keeping with the greater independence of civil society from the state, typical of Wilhelmine Germany, all these initiatives stemmed from the parties themselves, not from the government. In taking such steps, however, the politicians were quick to keep the government informed of them and they were quite welcome to Chancellor Bülow. Those eighty-one Social Democratic deputies elected in 1903 meant that in working with the Reichstag, particularly in seeking funds for his imperialist foreign policy, he was forced to cooperate with the Center. Although this had proved possible, it was tending to undermine his standing with right-wing elements at the Imperial court, who were not terribly fond of the Catholic party.

Consequently, the chancellor seized the opportunity to break with the Center and start a campaign against it and the Social Democrats, a campaign based on close cooperation between the government and the liberal and conservative parties. Bülow's moment came in December 1906 when the Reichstag was debating a supplemental appropriations bill to pay for more troops to be sent to German Southwest Africa (today's Namibia) to complete the suppression of a native uprising – that is, to conclude the wholesale slaughter of uncooperative indigenous tribespeople. As might be expected, the Social Democrats opposed the appropriations, while the liberal (even the left-liberal) and conservative parties were willing to approve them. When the Center parliamentarians, following the lead of the youthful, active, and oppositionally inclined deputy, Mathias

[46] Dieter Düding, *Der Nationalsoziale Verein 1896–1903: Der gescheiterte Versuch einer parteipolitischen Synthese von Nationalismus, Sozialismus und Liberalismus* (Munich and Vienna: R. Oldenbourg, 1972), pp. 175–93; Joachim Reimann, *Ernst Müller–Meinengen senior und der Linksliberalismus in seiner Zeit: Zur Biographie eines bayerischen und deutschen Politikers (1866–1944)* (Munich: Stadtarchiv München, 1968), pp. 37–47; Wolf, *Liberalismus in Frankfurt am Main*, pp. 68–72; Simon, *Die württembegischen Demokraten*, pp. 78–90, 118–19; Elm, *Zwischen Fortschritt und Reaktion*, pp. 112–23, 144–69.
[47] Suval, *Electoral Politics*, p. 138.

Erzberger, voted against the expenditures and brought the bill down to defeat by a narrow margin, Bülow dissolved the Reichstag before the end of its regular term and called for new elections.[48] These have come to be known, following the derisive sobriquet of the Social Democrats, as the "Hottentot elections." Like their predecessors in 1878, 1887, and 1893, they marked the attempt by the government to determine the outcome of the elections by focusing the campaign on nationalist issues. Unlike the previous, largely unsuccessful Wilhelmine venture in that direction in 1893, the government's efforts paid off handsomely in 1907. All the elements lacking in the earlier campaign, namely close cooperation between the government and the political parties supporting it, as well as a common campaign among the governmental parties, were present fourteen years later. There is another, equally important difference between the failed and the successful nationalist elections. Between 1893 and 1907 there had developed a wide variety of special interest groups and nationalist associations, specializing in mass political action – the Agrarian League, the Navy League, the Kyffhäuserbund (the national federation of veterans' associations), the National Association against Social Democracy, to name just some of the largest and most important. In 1907, these groups, working jointly with the government and the parties endorsing it would be unleashed on the electorate with considerable effect.

Following on the dissolution, Chancellor Bülow called on representatives of the parties of the right and extreme right, the National Liberals, and the left-liberal parties to cooperate at the elections, forming what came to be known as the "Bülow bloc." Although the cooperation between the parties was far from perfect – the right-wing parties and the left-liberals never losing their mutual mistrust – the "patria" committee, a national coordinating group with representatives from all the Bülow bloc parties, did meet regularly in Berlin. It funneled money to the parties and to the nationalist mass associations campaigning for them, both from governmental discretionary funds and from the contributions of big business.[49]

Thus, well prepared and, by the standards of pre-1914 German politics, well coordinated, the election campaign of the governmental parties was characterized by two main themes. One was the combination of

[48] Crothers, *The German Elections 1907*, pp. 29–102; Loth, *Katholiken im Kaiserreich*, pp. 113–120; Winfried Becker, "Kulturkampf als Vorwand: Die Kolonialwahlen von 1907 und das Problem der Parlamentarisierung des Reiches," *Historisches Jahrbuch* 106 (1986): 59–84.

[49] Crothers, *The German Elections of 1907*, pp. 160–63; Dieter Fricke, "Der deutsche Imperialismus und die Reichstagswahlen von 1907," *Zeitschrift für Geschichtswissenschaft* 9 (1961): 538–76.

imperialism and nationalism. The pro-governmental forces insisted that the elections were about Germany's role in the world: its attempts to acquire a great colonial empire, in doing so "developing from a European into a World Power . . ." They were also about "national honor," a referendum on whether or not to support soldiers fighting in the field against the "wild hordes," whether to leave German women and children unprotected against the "wild man's lust for murder."[50]

As in previous state-sponsored nationalist elections, affirmation of the nation implied hostility towards its enemies. Previously, the enemy had been sought within (1878) or seen across the Rhine in France (1887, 1893); now, the enemies were colonial subjects, with Africans portrayed as savage murderers and rapists, although it was German soldiers who were actually doing the murdering and raping in Africa. The year 1907 stands out as one of the relatively few times when this sort of racist politics, so common in the English-speaking world and well represented in France, played a major role in central European politics, in contrast to the anti-Semitic or anti-Slavic racism that had become a fixture of German political life since the 1890s.

The second theme of the governmental campaign flowed logically from the first, an attack on the parties opposing measures necessary for improving Germany's power and prestige and thus giving aid and comfort to the enemies of the nation. Sometimes this appeared as a general attack on parliamentarianism. Conservatives and liberals distributed pamphlets calling on the voters to back the government, the representative of the national will, against the quarreling, particularist, and petty political parties, namely those opposing the government. Along with such a broad attack on the government's enemies went a campaign directed at particular opposing parties. It is hardly surprising that the Social Democrats were a main target, particularly denounced by the parties of the right, but receiving the blows of all the candidates of the Bülow bloc. Armed with the extensive material provided by the National Association against Social Democracy, bloc candidates could denounce the labor party as unpatriotic and cosmopolitan, as an advocate of godlessness and immorality, its leaders a group of swindlers and ne'er-do-wells, engaging in debauchery with money fraudulently collected from the workers.[51]

---

[50] Quotes from Crothers, *The German Elections of 1907*, pp. 105, 109, 112. More generally on this theme, ibid., pp. 105–19; Suval, *Electoral Politics*, p. 138; Fricke, "Der deutsche Imperialismus," pp. 570–71; Sepainter, *Die Reichstagswahlen im Großherzogtum Baden*, pp. 161–62.

[51] Suval, *Electoral Politics*, pp. 137–39; Crothers, *The German Elections of 1907*, pp. 142–48; Reinders, "Sozialdemokratie und Immigration," pp. 87–88; Paetau, *Konfrontation oder Kooperation*, pp. 179, 181.

Yet the most striking and, to contemporaries, unexpected element of the 1907 elections was not the attack on the SPD so much as the campaign launched against the Center. Tapping deep feelings of resentment against a party that had held the dominant position in the Imperial parliament ever since the elections of 1890, the bloc politicians lashed out at the "Centrist yoke," at the "domination of the Center, which finally became unbearable, even to our long-suffering government."[52] It was clear to more sophisticated contemporaries and to later historians as well, that for the liberal politicians differences with the Center on colonial policy were a pretext for the attack on the Catholic party rather than the reason for it. In doing so, the liberals were able to set the tone of the campaign, taking the initiative away from the conservative parties, who wanted to make the SPD the main target of the Bülow bloc. Chancellor Bülow himself took a more ambiguous stance: the government's declaration on the dissolution of the Reichstag named the Center as one of the parties representing the enemies of the nation, along with the national minorities and the SPD, but the authorities also negotiated – ultimately unsuccessfully – with the Center on cooperation in specific constituencies. In the end, Bülow was willing to indulge the anti-Center campaign, and the government encouraged the nomination of "national Catholic" candidates, who presented themselves as loyal to the church but hostile to the "anti-national" political opinions of the Center.[53]

Such candidacies were not particularly successful because the campaign of the liberal parties did not make these fine distinctions between the Center on the one hand, and the Catholic Church on the other, but moved in an increasingly anti-clerical and anti-Catholic direction. Both the National Liberals and the progressives denounced "clericalism" and "obscuranticism," and condemned an "impatient clergy bent on persecution." The former party called for an end to circumstances in which the Pope, with his Center and Polish nationalist deputies, ruled Germany; the latter asserted that "as long as a part of the nation receives its orders for the settlement of political affairs from the Vatican, we will find ourselves in a state of civil war."[54]

[52] Quotes from Crothers, *The German Elections of 1907*, p. 123; on this point. cf. Sepainter, *Die Reichstagswahlen im Großherzogtum Baden*, p. 162.
[53] On Bülow's policies, cf. the different judgements in Loth, *Katholiken im Kaiserreich*, pp. 121–22; Crothers, *The German Elections of 1907*, pp. 120–23, 137–38; Becker, "Kulturkampf als Vorwand," Fricke, "Der deutsche Imperialismus," and Peter–Christian Witt, *Die Finanzpolitik des Deutschen Reiches von 1903 bis 1913* (Lübeck and Hamburg: Matthiesen Verlag, 1970), pp. 158–59. On the national Catholic candidacies, see Horst Grunder, "Rechtskatholizismus im Kaiserreich und in der Weimarer Republic unter besonderer Berücksichtigung der Rheinlande und Westfalen," *Westfälische Zeitschrift* 134 (1984): 107–55, esp. pp. 127–29.   [54] Quotes from ibid., pp. 126–27

Indeed, the 1907 elections became increasingly a war of religion. Just as the National Association against Social Democracy served as a clearing house for the campaign against the SPD, so the Protestant League – a group whose anti-Catholic political propaganda had been firmly rejected by Chancellor Bülow in 1903 – distributed material directed against the Center. The central theme of the liberal campaign could be summed up by the commentary of the *Dortmunder Zeitung*, on the dissolution of the Reichstag and the forthcoming elections. "May a whiff of Luther's anger and Luther's courage run through our nation: away from servitude to Rome, on to truth and freedom!"[55]

Having had the decades old burden of opposition lifted from their shoulders, the left-liberal parties conducted the most aggressive campaign. Emphasizing their nationalist sentiments and even sometimes informing the voters that a vote for them was the express wish of the chancellor, the parties of the bourgeois-left could mix nationalism, imperialism, and racism with the advocacy all sorts of social and political reforms, from woman suffrage, to an end to confessional segregation in public education, to lower grain tariffs.[56] This left-liberal campaign was not unique, but a variation on a theme of aggressive campaigning by the bloc parties, in close conjunction with the government and the nationalist mass associations. Officials of the Colonial Office took to the hustings on behalf of the bloc; civil servants were pressured to campaign or at least to vote for the candidates of the national parties. On election day, the authorities made arrangements to drive patriotic but enfeebled voters to the polls. In some areas, the officials even reverted to the Bismarckian practice of pressuring tavernkeepers to refuse to allow the opposition groups to hold meetings. Veteran Hanoverian particularists insisted that the pressures exerted against them were the worst they could remember, even more severe than in the Kartell elections of 1887.[57]

Much the same can be said of the nationalist associations. Members of the veterans' association went from door to door distributing leaflets, and encouraging or assisting people to go out and vote. Their leadership

---

[55] Quote from Loth, *Katholiken im Kaiserreich*, p. 121. On the Protestant League in 1903 and 1907, see Smith, *German Nationalism and Religious Conflict*, pp. 123–26, 141–42. More generally, on anti–Catholicism in the election campaign, Crothers, *The German Elections of 1907*, pp. 126–29.

[56] On the campaigns of the left–liberals, cf. Moring, *Die Sozialdemokratische Partei in Bremen*, pp. 88–100; Liebert, *Politische Wahlen in Wiesbaden*, pp. 242–43; Frank, *Die Brandenburger als Reichstagswähler*, pp. 92–93, 114–15, 165; Hess, *Geschichte Thüringens*, pp. 394–95.

[57] Crothers, *The German Elections of 1907*, pp. 106–7, 164–65; Aschoff, *Welfische Bewegung*, p. 198; Witt, *Die Finanzpolitik des Deutschen Reiches*, p. 157 n. 29; Frank, *Die Brandenburger als Reichstagswähler*, pp. 73–75.

noted that such groups could only be truly effective in elections conducted with a "national slogan." The Navy League and the National
Association against Social Democracy organized large-scale public-
speaking tours of prominent members and professional agitators. With
the assistance of these groups, the national parties were able to conduct a
mass election campaign, complete with many public rallies, the posting of
placards, the distribution of fliers, leaflets and "get-out-the-vote" drives
on election day, the equal of anything that the Center of the Social
Democrats could do.[58] As I have already shown in this book, it is possible
to see the development of the campaign styles of liberal and conservative
parties from notables to mass politics as a long, slow process, running
through every decade of the empire's electoral history. But if there was a
single turning point, a moment when the liberal and conservative parties
could match the campaigns of their rivals, then it would be the elections
of 1907.

The minority parties and the SPD thus found themselves on the defensive against well-prepared governmental forces in a snap election, with
relatively little time to campaign between the dissolution of the Reichstag
on December 16, 1906 and the first round of the general elections on
January 25, 1907. Caught by surprise, the Center and the Social
Democrats struggled to get their own mass electoral apparatus into
motion. They did, although compared to their well-prepared efforts in
the previous general elections, with less effect.

At first, the Center presented itself to its voters as it had in 1903, as a
cautious supporter of the government. Party speakers insisted that the
Center approved of German colonialism, provided it was carried out in
proper, moral fashion with close cooperation between the authorities and
missionaries and an end to questionable practices of government officials,
referring to party exposés of the travels of the governor of Southwest
Africa with a young woman, not his wife. But as the attacks on the party
and on the Catholic Church increased, the Center politicians and the
Catholic clergy – who were even more active than usual on behalf of the
party in 1907 – shifted gears and turned to claiming that a new
Kulturkampf was in the offing and called on the faithful to support their
party in defense of religion. The Bavarian Center newspaper, *Der*

---

[58] Fricke, "Der Reichsverband gegen die Sozialdemokratie," pp. 273–77; Saul, "Der
'deutsche Kriegerbund,'" pp. 146–51; Crothers, *The German Elections of 1907*, pp.
113–19; Nipperdey, *Die Organisation der deutschen Parteien*, p. 91; von Saldern, *Auf dem
Weg zum Arbeiterreformismus*, p. 81; Hansjoachim Henning, "Kriegervereine in den
preußischen Westprovinzen: Ein Beitrag zur preußischen Innenpolitik zwischen 1860
und 1914," *Rheinische Vierteljahrsblätter* 32 (1968): 430–75, esp. p. 454; Eley, *Reshaping
the German Right*, pp. 256–60.

Bayerische Kurier, called on Catholics to "Unite! unite in the battle for the defense of your most sacred relics, your religion, your faith!" This attitude of fundamental opposition to a hostile national government, typical of Bismarckian electoral politics, began to carry over into the discussion of other issues by the party's politicians. Mathias Erzberger, the Center deputy whose attacks on the government's colonial policy had provided the pretext for the dissolution, campaigned for the party throughout the country, not just in his Württemberg constituency, persistently denouncing the government and the liberals.[59]

The success of the appeal to Catholic confessional solidarity, in the tradition of the *Kulturkampf*, is particularly apparent when one considers what happened in 1907 to the predominantly Protestant minority party, the Hanoverian particularists. The same anti-Catholic propaganda that reinforced the loyalty of the Center's clientele, proved powerfully appealing to the Lutheran supporters of the particularists. The National Liberals and the Protestant League repeatedly informed Hanoverians that the party's deputies were following a course that would leave the Protestant church "defenseless against ultramontane Jesuitism and the whims of the Pope." Many Lutheran clergymen, key supporters of the particularists, "believed the idiotic agitation to the effect that we [the particularists] want to make the people into Catholics," and spoke on behalf of the National Liberals at public meetings. The party was devastated, winning just one seat after its share of votes cast in the province of Hanover dropped by over a third.[60]

Caught by surprise, and lacking its previous edge in mass campaigning, the SPD had difficulty finding an effective theme. The party played up the cost-of-living question, which had worked so successfully for it in 1903, but then the SPD, as a result of its off-year agitation had seized the initiative and set the tone for the campaign. This time it was the government and the national parties that posed the theme of the election and the Social Democrats were forced to campaign on their terrain. The party reiterated its opposition to bearing the costs of the navy and the empire; it stressed, unlike the Center, its principled hostility to militarism and imperialism. It condemned colonialism; one SPD speaker in Westphalia even compared Germany's insurgent African subjects to Hermann, the ancient Germanic opponent of Roman Imperial rule, and a hero of twentieth-century, right-wing German nationalism. The party activists redoubled their efforts in the expectation that a larger, more expensive

---

[59] On the Center campaign, Crothers, *The German Elections of 1907*, pp. 129–36 (quote from p. 135); Loth, *Katholiken im Kaiserreich*, pp. 121–29; Wender, *Wahlen und Sozialstrukturen in Ludwigshafen*, pp. 449–55; Hiery, *Reichstagswahlen im Reichsland*, pp. 338–45.   [60] Aschoff, *Welfische Bewegung*, pp. 198–99.

campaign, reaching more people than ever before, would bring the SPD more votes and more seats in the Reichstag.[61] The campaign produced another upward jog in turnout, rising from the 76% of 1903 to a remarkable 84% of eligible voters, with Protestant and Catholic turnout increasing about equally. The election's big winners were the liberal parties, whose share of the eligible electorate increased by about five percentage points, up by about one-fourth over 1903. The parties of the right enjoyed a two percentage point increase to a little over 15% of eligible voters. If the Bülow bloc parties had done well with the voters, the opposition groups had been less successful: both the minority parties and the SPD could not increase the share of eligible voters over 1903; since the turnout increased, their share of votes cast suffered a modest decline. The mechanics of the single member constituency system produced a very different result in terms of parliamentary mandates: the Center and the Polish nationalists actually gained deputies over 1903, while the SPD lost almost half its parliamentary representation, falling from eighty-one to forty-three seats. The upshot was that the parties of the Bülow bloc gained a majority of the seats, pushing the Center from its previously dominant position in the Reichstag, not because the Center lost any seats but because the Social Democrats did.

Table 5.8 gives the voter movements occurring in the Hottentot elections.

Most of the story this table tells is in the columns giving the 1907 votes of the 1903 non-voters and the SPD voters. Party loyalty of SPD voters, usually considerably above that of the voters of other party groups in Wilhelmine elections, was equal to or lower than them in 1907. About one-fifth of those who voted for the SPD in 1903, when food prices were at the center of public interest, chose one of the parties of the Bülow bloc four years later in a campaign centered on nationalist issues. Relatively few of the liberal and conservative voters of 1903, on the other hand, went over to the SPD – the labor party's net losses to the Bülow bloc parties making up about 3% of the entire electorate, with more than 90% of that loss suffered to the liberal parties. The minority parties, in 1907 clearly in opposition to the government and at least as much under attack from the authorities and the national parties as the Social Democrats, were noticeably more successful in holding on to their voters.

Almost half (46%) of the non-voters of the previous election voted in

---

[61] Crothers, *The German Elections of 1907*, pp. 146–53; Nolan, *Social Democracy and Society*, pp. 177–79; Liebert, *Wahlen in Wiesbaden*, pp. 242–43; von Saldern, *Auf dem Weg zum Arbeiterreformismus*, pp. 81, 85–88; Moring, *Die Sozialdemokratische Partei in Bremen*, pp. 99–100; Paetau, *Konfrontation oder Kooperation*, pp. 181, 447 n. 298; Reinders, "Sozialdemokratie und Immigration," pp. 90–91.

Table 5.8 *The 1903 voters in the elections of 1907 (percent)*

Vote in 1907	Vote in 1903					
	Right or Extreme Right	Liberal	Minority parties	Social Democrats	Non-voters	Net new voters
Right or Extreme Right	77	13	4	3	9	2
Liberal	9	72	6	18	15	11
Minority parties	6	5	83	1	10	29
Social Democrats	4	7	3	74	12	45
Non-voters	4	3	4	4	54	13
All	100	100	100	100	100	100

1907, a figure exceeded only in the Kartell elections of 1887. The opposition minority parties and Social Democrats did not do badly with previous non-voters, the proportion that they gained being pretty typical for post-1890 elections, but the 24% of non-voters who rallied to the liberal and conservative supporters of the government was the best result these parties had obtained since the Kartell elections of 1887. It was ten percentage points above their previous high in Wilhelmine Germany (in 1893), and the only Wilhelmine election at which they captured a larger share of the previous non-voters than the minority parties and the SPD, the original parties of political mass mobilization. The latter's appeal to new entrants to the electorate helped keep their losses within bounds.

Table 5.9, giving the vote by confession and social group, helps identify further which groups of voters were most susceptible to the nationalist campaign.

Although turnout for all Protestant social groups increased from 1903 (see table 5.7), the increase was greatest for farmers and the urban middle class. It was the pro-governmental, Bülow bloc parties who gained by the increase in voting in the Protestant population; the oppositional SPD netted no voters from it. Among Protestant farmers, liberals and the parties of the right benefitted about equally from the growth in electoral participation, but among the urban middle class the liberals were the big winners, their share of this social and confessional group's vote going from 22 to 31%. In the Marxist tradition, a number of Social Democratic commentators on the 1907 elections attributed the party's many close

Table 5.9 *The vote in 1907 by confession and social group (percent)*

Party group	Protestant Farmer	Protestant Middle class	Protestant Worker	Protestant All	Catholic Farmer	Catholic Middle class	Catholic Worker	Catholic All
Right	42	14	13	20	16	5	0	7
Liberals	28	31	27	29	10	12	13	12
Minority parties	4	0	3	2	56	52	59	56
Social Democrats	6	41	45	34	1	8	13	8
Non-voters	20	15	12	15	17	22	15	18
All	100	101	100	100	100	99	100	101

(Confession spans Protestant and Catholic columns)

defeats by the liberals to the votes of a treacherous and vacillating petit bourgeoisie – an explanation that has been seconded by historians of the labor movement, and was in fact what the government was hoping to accomplish.[62] The figures in table 5.9 suggest that such an explanation was probably correct.

Although turnout among Catholic voters increased to about the same extent as among Protestants, the political consequences of the growing participation differed by confession. If Protestant turnout rose most among farmers and the urban middle class, the growth in Catholic turnout was about equal among all social groups. When more Protestants came out to vote, the governmental parties benefitted exclusively; growing Catholic participation helped the governmental, Bülow bloc parties and the oppositional minority parties about equally. The SPD, on the other hand, received no net increase in votes from the rising turnout of either Protestant or Catholic voters.

On closer examination, we can note that much of the increase in the Catholic vote for the governmental parties went to the conservatives; the 7% of eligible Catholic voters they obtained in 1907 was the right-wing parties' best result in Wilhelmine elections. Some of the growth in the Catholic conservative vote was the result of Center candidates stepping

[62] Carl Schorske, *German Social Democracy 1905–1917: The Development of the Great Schism* 2nd edn (New York: John Wiley & Sons, 1965), pp. 63–66; Moring, *Die Sozialdemokratische Partiei in Bremen*, pp. 99–100; Fricke, "Der deutsche Imperialismus," p. 551; Paetau, *Konfrontation oder Kooperation*, p. 181.

down in favor of conservatives, but this cannot have been the whole story, since the percentage of eligible Catholic voters choosing one of the right-wing parties in those constituencies where the Center ran candidates increased from 3% in 1903 to 6% in 1907. It does seem plausible, though, that Catholics who were convinced by the nationalist and racist appeals of the Bülow bloc would have preferred to vote for one of the conservative parties, since they had largely refrained from the anti-clericalism and Protestant bigotry that had so dominated the liberals' campaign and so strongly impressed public opinion.

We can further underscore the extent to which the 1907 liberal campaign against the Center and the Catholic Church backfired among Catholic voters by considering regional differences in the Catholic vote. In non-Prussian Germany, where liberal and anti-clerical sentiments were more prevalent in the Catholic population, the share of eligible Catholic voters choosing one of the liberal or conservative parties just increased from 13% in 1903 to 15% in 1907. In Prussia, on the other hand, Bülow bloc parties went from 13% to 20% of eligible Catholic voters over the same period, with about 70% of that increase due to the rise in Catholic votes for the parties of the right.

We can conclude our analysis of the Catholic vote by noting its differentiation by class. Of eligible Catholic blue-collar workers 51% chose one of the minority parties – above all, the Center – in 1903; 59% did in 1907. Of the growth in the minority party vote over the two elections, 86% is attributable to this increase in blue-collar support. When the clergy and the Center politicians called on the faithful to respond to attacks on their religion, the workers stepped forward. In 1907, at least, they were the truest sons of the church, a fidelity also apparent in the stagnation of their support for the SPD.[63]

The Hottentot elections of 1907 elections seem in many ways a pendant to the Kartell elections of twenty years previously. Common to both were a dissolution of the Reichstag, a campaign planned by the government to focus on national issues, an increase in turnout that benefitted primarily the governmental parties (in 1887 the Kartell, in 1907 the Bülow bloc), a shift of votes from left to right, and a defeat of the main secular left-wing opposition (in 1887 the progressives, in 1907 the SPD), while the minority parties, relying on their ethnic and religious ties to the voters, were able to defy the nationalist campaign. There are, however, three differences between the elections that can be noted, all related to the

---

[63] Of course, some of those Catholic working–class voters who chose the minority parties were voting for the Polish nationalists, who obtained their best results in Upper Silesian constituencies in 1907, but in doing so they were also choosing a party with close ties to the church.

changes in political culture and political practice between Bismarckian and Wilhelmine Germany.

First, the 1887 campaign was very much the government's affair, the Kartell parties doing its bidding. Twenty years later, the government played more the role of a coordinating agent among independently acting political parties and nationalist mass associations. Although these groups generally followed the government's guideline, they could and did take off on their own. We can see this above all in the liberals' introduction of a strong note of anti-Catholicism and anti-clericalism, rather independently of the government's plans, or at least to a greater extent than the authorities might have wished.

Second, the SPD was a mass political party, able to counter, at least in part, nationalist agitation, even when taken by surprise. It was a more effective and worthy opponent of the government than the hapless left-liberals of the Kartell elections, who were tied down by the traditions of notables' politics and unable to respond to officially sponsored nationalist slogans. The estimates of voter movements bear this out. As a percentage of the eligible electorate, the SPD's net losses to the Bülow bloc parties in 1907 were about half the net losses of the progressives to the Kartell parties in 1887. We can also see a difference between the two opposition parties in their differing success in mobilizing the unmobilized, previous non-voters or new entrants into the electorate: non-voters and net new voters choosing the left-liberal parties in 1887 made up about 1% of eligible voters in that year; members of the same two groups voting for the SPD were almost 5.5% of the 1907 electorate. In both 1887 and 1907, the secular left-wing parties suffered greater losses to the governmental parties than did the minority parties, suggesting that appeals to nationalism could be most effectively countered by appeals to ethnic or religious solidarity than by economic or political arguments tailored to rational self-interest. But the greater ability of the SPD to counter these nationalist appeals in 1907 implies both that it was more closely connected to its voters than the left-liberals had been twenty years previously and that the nationalist appeals of 1907 were less effective with the voters than those of 1887. Germans could believe that they were really in danger from the French army, but found it harder to imagine African tribesmen as a threat to the nation.

In some ways, the 1907 elections were a curiously Bismarckian interlude in the midst of Wilhelmine politics. Although certainly Wilhelmine in the unprecedented practice of mass politics by all the parties, the campaign that year did not center on economic questions as elections from 1890 onwards usually did, but on the contrast between a Protestant/national/governmental cause, and a Catholic/particularist/oppositional response, so characteristic of Bismarck's day. Voters responded much as they had under Bismarck too, Protestants turning out to vote against the (confessionally determined) enemies of the nation and to vote for the parties representing the national cause, while Catholics turned out to vote for the parties of their religion, enemies of the national project. Unlike the case in Bismarckian elections, there was a large and powerful Social Democratic Party in 1907, only it could not find any way to intervene in such a campaign to increase the size of its electorate.

A member of the pro patria committee wrote a memo very much impressing Chancellor Bülow, asserting that the Protestant petit bourgeoisie, stirred up by an anti-Catholic election campaign, would turn out to vote for the liberal and conservative parties – and thus against the SPD.[64] This is largely what happened in 1907: both by intent and by chance, the anti-clerical, anti-Catholic campaign of the liberals did not weaken the position of the minority parties against whom the campaign was directed; if anything, it encouraged Catholics to turn out and vote for them. It did, however, succeed in cutting off the Social Democrats from any further increases in support from the Protestant middle class and Catholic workers, the two major sources of the rise in the SPD's vote totals since 1890, and in doing so dealt the Social Democrats the one electoral defeat they would experience in Wilhelmine Germany.

The elections of 1912

The pattern set in 1878 and 1887 (when a Reichstag, elected in a campaign centered on nationalist issues, passed unpopular economic measures and thus set the stage for subsequent general elections on economic questions with a different political outcome) continued after 1907. However, in one respect, the political transition from the general elections of 1907, which were based on nationalist issues, to those of 1912, which were based on economic issues, differed from the predecessor pairs of 1878/1881 and 1887/1890. In the first two instances, the parties that profited from the nationalist agitation were forced to defend their economic decisions to the voters; in 1912, the liberals, the beneficiaries of the vigorous nationalist campaign of 1907, were busy criticizing the economic decisions made by the Reichstag that they had been so instrumental in electing, while the Center, a determined opponent of the nationalist agitation, was hard at work defending these decisions.

The economic question that caused this turnabout was not the agricultural tariffs/food prices issue that had been central to Wilhelmine politics.

[64] Fricke, "Der deutsche Imperialismus," p. 551.

Rather, it was another form of the clash between agricultural producers and urban consumers, this time about taxes. The combination of the government's plans for an expansive foreign policy, calling for large increases in expenditure on the navy, with the growing demands of an increasingly elaborate social insurance system, produced a chronic problem of balancing the Imperial government's budget. In 1909, the government's proposal for a substantial tax increase broke apart the ranks of its parliamentary supporters.

Part of this tax increase was to involve the creation of an inheritance tax. The conservative parties refused to go along with such an idea, which they asserted would pose a danger for landed property. Defying their partners in the Bülow bloc, they joined with the Center in drawing up a new finance bill that raised revenues by a combination of indirect taxes on items of mass consumption such as beer, tobacco, matches, and tea, and by others weighing on urban business interests, such as taxes on stock transfers and payments by check. Since the campaign of 1907 had resulted in fewer SPD but more Center deputies, such an alternative to the post-1907 governmental coalition of the liberal and conservative parties, quickly dubbed by contemporaries the "black-blue bloc" (i.e., clerical-conservative), was able to gain a majority. Repudiated by his parliamentary supporters, and having ever fewer friends in the emperor's entourage, Chancellor Bülow resigned; his successor, Theobald von Bethmann-Hollweg agreed to accept the decision of the new parliamentary majority on taxes.[65]

Once again, the parties, if not instituting parliamentary government (for it was the emperor and his advisers in court who chose Bethmann-Hollweg, not the parliamentary majority) had brought about a political realignment. The liberal parties moved to the left, the National Liberals expelling from their caucus the deputies with close ties to the Agrarian League who had voted for the black-blue bloc's finance reform. They and the left-liberals, the latter united in 1910 into the Progressive People's Party, even moved, cautiously and reluctantly, toward cooperation with the SPD. Such a "Great Bloc," as contemporaries called it, actually came into existence in the elections to the parliaments of Baden and Bavaria, although attempts to put such a union of the left into electoral or parliamentary practice on the national level were never successful.[66]

This realignment of the parties also affected the economic interest

---

[65] Witt, *Die Finanzpolitik des Deutschen Reiches*, pp. 199–304; Loth, *Katholiken im Kaiserreich*, pp. 131–80.
[66] Witt, *Die Finanzpolitik des Deutschen Reiches*, pp. 304–11; Beverly Heckart, *From Bassermann to Bebel: The Grand Bloc's Quest for Reform in the Kaiserreich, 1900–1914* (New Haven and London: Yale University Press, 1974).

groups and nationalist mass associations. The National Association against Social Democracy, a product of cooperation between the National Liberals and the conservative parties, was badly damaged by the growing differences between them. It was additionally weakened by scandals involving some of its leading officials and so had neither the finances nor the public support to work as effectively as it had in 1907. If an influential group on the right of the political spectrum was in decline, the changes in the tax law in 1909, favoring agriculture and hurting business interests, spurred the creation of a new economic interest group, the Hanseatic League. A federation of business associations, with liberal parliamentarians well represented in its leadership, this organization was devoted to achieving a better consideration of urban business interests (as against agrarian ones) in government policy. To accomplish this, the league's leadership was willing to consider the idea of an urban alliance between business interests and the labor movement, the economic pendant to the political parties' great bloc. Taking a leaf from the book of its enemy, the Agrarian League, the business group financed most of the liberals' 1912 election campaign, as well as distributing fliers, putting up posters and holding mass meetings under its own aegis; it also paid the costs for the founding of a liberal farmers' organization, the German Peasants League, that would challenge the hold of the Agrarian League on Protestant small farmers, and thus threaten the basis of the conservative parties' electorate. The outraged agrarians immediately denounced the new farmers' organization as the work of a Semitic conspiracy.[67]

As a result of these realignments of the parties and the organizations that campaigned for them (or at least financed their campaigns), the general elections of 1912 were the first in the history of the empire to be primarily a contest of left against right, pitting the Social Democrats, the Progressives, and most of the National Liberals against the Center and the conservative parties. These distinctions between left and right did not conform to those between the opposition and the government. Bethmann-Hollweg may have come into office as a result of the creation of a Center-conservative alliance, but his position was not dependent on it and he neither endorsed it nor sought to coordinate government policy with it. Turning down demands by right-wing figures in the court, the government, and the political parties, the chancellor refused to engineer a dissolution over the question of further naval expansion and coordinate another nationalist campaign. Whether such a move would have been successful is an open question (the precedent of the 1893 dissolution was

[67] Mattheier, "Drei Führungsorganisationen," pp. 243–56; Mielke, *Der Hansa–Bund*, pp. 29–33, 113–18, 150–52, 159–60 and passim; Puhle, *Agrarische Interessenpolitik*, pp. 144–46.

not encouraging), but in any event Bethmann-Hollweg's government did not support any one party or group of parties in 1912, and, in general, intervened to a modest extent in the elections, especially compared with the efforts of the authorities in 1907. The chief goal of the government in 1912 was to see that as few Social Democrats as possible be elected. Given the deep divisions that ran between the other parties, however, even this relatively modest effort proved difficult to carry out.[68]

The campaigns of 1912 generally conformed to the pre-election alignment of the parties, and so represented a substantial change, when compared to the Hottentot elections of 1907.[69] Nowhere was this change more noticeable than in the position of the National Liberals. Except for its right-wing minority, representing the interests of the agrarians, and, to a certain extent, those of heavy industry, the party had taken a stand against the black-blue bloc. As a result, in 1912, National Liberal and conservative candidates faced each other in seventy-six constituencies, three times as many as they had in 1907. In the elections of that year, candidates of the extreme right, the anti-Semitic parties and the Agrarian League, had stood against the National Liberals in only thirty-three constituencies, the very lowest figure since these parties had come onto the national political scene in 1893. In 1912, the number of constituencies with such opposing candidacies doubled to sixty-six.

In consequence, there were a number of campaign themes that the SPD and both liberal parties had in common, most importantly, the condemnation of the tax bill of 1909 and a call for a more equitable distribution of the burdens of taxation. For all their alignment, the three parties remained quite different, their distinctiveness most apparent in their attitude towards the military. The National Liberals, true to their party tradition, praised the navy and called for higher arms expenditures, seconded in this by the Progressives, following the pattern of support for an aggressive foreign policy that they had adopted in 1907. In contrast, the SPD denounced militarism and its candidates spoke often and loudly about the looming dangers of a great European war. The National Liberals asserted that currently existing tariffs were acceptable, and they should not be raised any higher, while both the Progressives and the Social Democrats demanded lower tariffs, especially on the import of foodstuffs. The SPD hit hardest on this issue, the party's agitation helped along by a sharp increase in retail meat prices occurring shortly before the elections. The background to this inflationary surge – a poor harvest for feed grains

---

[68] Witt, *Die Finanzpolitik des Deutschen Reiches*, pp. 337–45; Bertram, *Die Wahlen zum Deutschen Reichstag*, pp. 119–38; an interesting local study is Kropat, "Der Beamte und Politik in wilhelmischer Zeit."

[69] On these alignments, see Bertram, *Die Wahlen zum deutschen Reichstag*, pp. 13–96.

and the opposition of conservative politicians and agrarian interest groups to increased meat imports in order to lower prices for consumers – fit in perfectly with a perennial Social Democratic campaign theme and made a substantial impression on public opinion.

The Center and the parties of the right, in contrast, endorsed the tax law of 1909, insisting that it was equitable to all concerned and had successfully resolved the government's budget problems. Both defended the existing tariff system, with the conservative parties, as might be expected, calling for still higher tariffs on agricultural imports. Just as the parties of the left differed among themselves, so did the partisans of the black-blue bloc. The right-wing parties vigorously endorsed Germany's military establishment and called for still greater expenditures on the armed forces, a call the Center did not second. While the conservatives vigorously condemned the SPD, Center politicians and the Catholic clergy were more prone to discuss dangers to religion, pointing to the party's past record of defending the faith and calling on the voters to choose it for this purpose once more.[70]

As contemporaries noted and later historians have observed, these views were simply hammered into the voters, the forms of mass campaigning used by all the parties reaching new heights. Turnout remained at the impressive levels of 1907, although there was a modest differentiation by confession, with Catholic participation rates dropping a few percentage points while Protestant rates increased. The SPD was the big winner, its share of eligible voters rising by five percentage points to over 29%. The quirks of the single-member constituency system that had worked against the party in 1907 now came back in its favor, with the number of seats it gained rising from 43 to 110, not just a new high for the SPD but also the most seats any one party in Wilhelmine Germany had ever obtained. The liberal parties' share of eligible voters stayed constant at 23%, very modest gains for the left-liberals counterbalancing the equally modest declines of the National Liberal party.

---

[70] On campaign themes in 1912, see Bertram, *Die Wahlen zum Deutschen Reichstag*, pp. 167–73; Witt, *Die Finanzpolitik des Deutschen Reiches*, pp. 340–41; Mielke, *Der Hansa–Bund*, pp. 157–62; Sepainter, *Die Reichstagswahlen im Großherzogtum Baden*, pp. 167–71; Bräunche, *Parteien und Reichstagswahlen in der Rheinpfalz*, pp. 300–1; Nolan, *Social Democracy and Society*, pp. 214–17; Blackbourn, *Class, Religion and Local Politics*, pp. 227–28; Loose, "Der Wahlkampf des liberalen Reichstagskandidaten Carl Braband," Hiery, *Reichstagswahlen im Reichsland*, pp. 366–402; Aschoff, *Welfische Bewegung*, pp. 202–3; Liebert, *Wahlen in Wiesbaden* pp. 259–62; Moring, *Die Sozialdemokratische Partei in Bremen*, pp. 150–53; Paetau, *Kooperation oder Konfrontation*, pp. 187–89; Wender, *Wahlen und soziale Strukturen*, pp. 486–94; Suval, *Electoral Politics*, pp. 194–97, 226; Klöcker, *Die Sozialdemokratie im Regierungsbezirk Aachen*, pp. 111–19; Reinders, "Sozialdemokratie und Integration," pp. 91–95; Groh, *Negative Integration und revolutionärer Attentismus*, pp. 270–74. All these sources also contain accounts of the unprecedented extent of the campaign.

Table 5.10 *The 1907 voters in the elections of 1912 (percent)*

Vote in 1912	Vote in 1907					
	Right or Extreme Right	Liberal	Minority parties	Social Democrats	Non-voters	Net new voters
Right or Extreme Right	52	23	3	1	1	1
Liberal	30	61	10	8	4	19
Minority parties	3	4	71	1	6	33
Social Democrats	10	8	6	87	19	37
Non-voters	6	4	10	4	70	9
All	101	100	100	101	100	99

The proportion of eligible voters going to the parties of the right and extreme right declined by about two percentage points; that of the minority parties by three percentage points, with both the Center and the regional and national minorities losing voting share. The black-blue blocs' losses in Reichstag seats were greater, but the debacle that party leaders feared was in the making was averted.[71] Table 5.10 gives the voter movements leading to these results.

Three main points about the election emerge from these figures: the reasons for the success of the SPD, the decisions of the voters for the minority parties and the relationship between the liberal and conservative parties.

In complete contrast to 1907, when the SPD had suffered from voter defections, the party's campaign in 1912 inspired a remarkable loyalty among its electorate, far greater than that of any other party group. Indeed, the party loyalty of SPD voters was as great as that of minority party voters in the *Kulturkampf* elections of 1874. Building on this firm base, the Social Democrats gained substantial shares of previous non-voters and net new voters, as well as making a net gain of about 2% of the electorate from the parties of the black-blue bloc. When the liberal parties opposed the SPD, as in 1907, the Social Democrats lost voters to them; now that they were allied, losses and gains balanced each other out.

Of all the party groups, the minority parties lost the most voters to abstention. Now that religion was no longer in danger, and nationalist

---

[71] Loth, *Katholiken im Kaiserreich*, p. 198

issues were more peripheral than they had been in 1907, some of the minority party voters dropped out of politics. This had been the case in the transition from the 1887 to the 1890 elections as well (table 5.1), but then 23% of the 1890 minority party voters had abstained, as against just 10% of the 1907 voters in 1912. The development of a network of affiliated associations among the minority parties, especially the Center and the Polish nationalists, made it possible to rally the troops more effectively, even when religion was not in danger. On the other hand, the loss of 16% of these parties' previous voters to the left was a substantial amount by the standards of the minority parties, reflecting their relative vulnerability in a campaign on economic issues where they were taking an unpopular side.

In some ways the most interesting result of the 1912 elections was the enormous movement of voters between the liberal and the right-wing parties. Of the entire electorate in 1912, 9% consisted of conservative voters who had switched to the liberals, or liberals who had switched to the conservatives. This was the highest figure of this kind in the history of the *Kaiserreich*. Since there were relatively few instances of conservative candidates stepping down in favor of liberals or vice-versa (see figure 3.7), most of this voter movement occurred in competitive situations.

In view of the change in party alignments between 1907 and 1912, such a substantial movement of voters is hardly surprising. The transition from the nationalist solidarity of the Hottentot elections to the dramatic change in political fronts over the tax law of 1909, whose results were brought home to the liberal and conservative electorate by the ceaseless agitation of the Agrarian and Hanseatic Leagues, had undoubtedly left behind voters who could not stomach the changes in allegiance of the party they had previously chosen. These voter movements both confirm and refute Karl Rohe's thesis of a national voting bloc in Imperial Germany.

Over 80% of the 1907 voters of the liberal and right-wing parties chose one of those parties in 1912. Voters who were discontented with the conservatives went over to the liberals, and vice-versa. In other words, at these two elections, there was clearly a pool of voters shared by the liberal and conservative parties. Yet national is precisely what they were not: it was the breakdown of the national orientation that these parties had demonstrated in the Bülow bloc of 1907 that led voters to go from one party group to the other. If the liberals and the parties of the right had a group of voters in common in 1912, they fought over them far more than sharing them amicably.

A look at the voters' choices by confession and social group, given in

Table 5.11 *The vote in 1912 by confession and social group (percent)*

	Confession							
	Protestant				Catholic			
Party group	Farmer	Middle class	Worker	All	Farmer	Middle class	Worker	All
Right	40	15	7	18	12	4	0	5
Liberals	31	29	26	28	13	15	12	13
Minority parties	4	0	3	2	57	45	46	49
Social Democrats	8	45	54	39	0	14	22	12
Non-voters	17	12	10	13	19	23	20	21
All	100	101	100	100	101	101	100	100

table 5.11, will draw out the analysis of the last general elections of the German Empire.

Even though there had been a very substantial movement of voters between the liberal and conservative parties from 1907 to 1912, the overall political preferences of Protestant farmers and the middle class, the main supporters of these parties, changed relatively little as compared to 1907 (see table 5.9). In other words, the changes must have balanced themselves out, with about as many Protestant farmers switching from the liberals to the conservatives as vice-versa. In contrast, the Protestant working-class vote changed a good deal more. The SPD increased its share by 20% (nine percentage points) – the single largest increase between any two elections in the Wilhelmine era – and obtained, for the first time ever, the support of an absolute majority of working-class Protestants eligible to vote. The big losers of working-class support had been the conservatives, perhaps not too surprisingly in an election where food prices had been central and rural–urban distinctions sharp.

Conservatives had suffered equally large losses among Protestant working-class voters in 1903, when food prices and an urban–rural conflict had also dominated the election campaigns: then, the liberal parties had profited, the SPD picking up urban voters primarily among the middle class. By 1912, the SPD seems to have been reaching its limits with Protestant middle-class voters, perhaps because of the increasingly energetic efforts of the liberal parties and organizations affiliated with them, such as the Hanseatic League, directed at this group.

The creation of the black-blue bloc also had its effect on Catholic voters. The minority parties could only hold their 1907 levels of support among farmers; they lost a substantial number of urban voters. The Center Party's tilt toward agarian interests told against it in 1912 as it had not in the 1903 elections; urban Catholic voters were less willing to accept spiritual consolations for higher food prices. The minority parties' losses were particularly pronounced among working-class voters: for the first time, less than half of Catholic workers voted for these parties. A greater proportion of Catholic workers abstained in 1912 than had in 1907, but the big change was the large increase in the percentage of them voting for the SPD.

This switch in Catholic working-class votes certainly corresponds to the results seen in the constituencies. In 1912, the Center lost three predominantly Catholic urban/industrial constituencies to the SPD – Würzburg, Cologne and Düsseldorf – for the first time in general elections. The labor party came close in a number of other such constituencies as well. In Essen, it reached the runoff against the Center. The local party leadership was so sure that the city's Protestant nationalist voters who had chosen the National Liberals in the first round would vote against their long-term ultramontanist enemies in the second round of balloting that it made preparations for a large-scale victory celebration. The festivities fizzled when the National Liberals of Essen, on the party's right wing, so much closer to the blue-black bloc than most National Liberals, and under heavy pressure from the authorities to boot, threw their support to the Center and ensured the election of its candidate in the runoff.[72]

There were Social Democratic festivities in Aachen, even though the Center won an absolute majority of votes cast in the first round of balloting. There, the SPD had come within 900 votes of forcing a runoff, with potentially good results, since the Aachen liberals were more left wing, or at least more anti-clerical, than their counterparts in Essen. This unexpectedly good showing in an industrialized but deeply and devoutly Catholic city, where the Social Democrats had long been godless pariahs, was an enormous encouragement to local party members and they celebrated their results by literally dancing in the streets.[73] This celebration was a sign of the German labor party's successes among the urban laboring population of both confessions in the very last general elections of the German Empire.

---

[72] Rohe, Jäger and Dorow, "Politische Gesellschaft und politische Kultur," p. 472; Loth, *Katholiken im Kaiserreich*, pp. 197–98. This alliance in the runoff elections between Center and National Liberals existed in two other Ruhr Basin constituencies, Duisburg and Bochum, in 1912 as well.

[73] Klöcker, *Die Sozialdemokratie im Regierungsbezirk Aachen*, pp. 373–74.

There are four ways in which we can view the elections of 1912. First, it was the quintessential Wilhelmine election, the one in which mass politics was at its most massive, when all the parties and the interest groups and mass associations affiliated with them engaged in an enormous multimedia campaign for voter support. Also in the Wilhelmine trend, the parties and the affiliated groups did so ever more independently of the national government, that had little success in shaping either the nature of the campaign or its outcome.

The elections of 1912 bear strong similarities to those of of 1881 and 1890, elections fought on economic issues and won by the left, immediately following elections with campaigns on nationalist lines, that were won by the right. In all of these cases, voters mobilized by the governmental and right-of-center parties at the first of a pair of two elections switched their votes to left-of-center parties at the second. The voter movements from the 1907 to the 1912 elections were rather more complex than their predecessors in the 1878/1881 and 1887/1890 pairs, because of the shift in political alignments that occurred midway through the session of the Reichstag elected in 1907. The conservative parties who triumphed in the assassination elections of 1878 and then raised tariffs and indirect taxes in the subsequent Reichstag session had to face the voters in 1881; the Kartell parties, chosen during the war scare of 1887, met their electoral fate three years later. In contrast, the liberal parties, which were the biggest winners of the Hottentot elections, refused to go along with the increase in indirect taxes in 1909, so that it was the conservative parties and the Center who had to face the voters on this question, and concede votes to the SPD and to the liberals as well.

In terms of net voter movements, though, it was only the SPD that profited from this change, since many right-wing voters who had supported the liberals because of their nationalist appeals in 1907 were unwilling to go along with them when they moved to the left. These right-wing voters dropped the liberals for the parties of the right in 1912, so that the liberal losses to the conservatives equalled the conservative losses to the liberals. Having no such nationalist voters in its 1907 electorate, the Social Democrats were in no danger of losing them.

The year 1912 also marked the last of three Wilhelmine general elections in which the agrarian issue, the linked question of farm and consumer food prices, was central to the campaign. In all of these elections – those of 1893, 1903, and 1912 – the SPD gained votes; it was the anti-agrarian party, following a course that guaranteed it urban support but cost it dearly in the countryside. The Center was able to withstand the potentially threatening effects of competing economic interests on its religiously based clientele relatively well in 1893 and 1903, but had to accept losses in 1912, albeit ones that the party was able to keep within bounds. The first of these agrarian-issue elections was a triumph for the parties of the right and a disaster for the liberals, but the two twentieth-century elections on this theme brought a lot of shouting and screaming, and a considerable amount of voter movement, but relatively little change in the vote totals of these two party groups.

Finally, 1912 was the year of the working class at the polls. Although the main issues of the campaign were not class-specific, with the dangers of war, indirect taxes, and rising food prices affecting everybody, working-class voters responded more to them than did others. This proletarian response cut across confessional lines, a rare development in a political system where confession and occupation were far more important in determining voter choices than was class. The SPD had received the support of 27% of eligible working-class voters (of both confessions) in its breakthrough election of 1890, that figure rising slowly to 30 or 31% in 1893 and 1898, and to 33% in 1903 and 1907. In 1912, it jumped to 42% of eligible working-class voters, 49% of votes – just short of a majority – cast by workers. If the era of Wilhelmine elections began with a dramatic victory of the Social Democrats at the polls – one it owed to broad support from Protestant townspeople, making it an urban Protestant people's party – it ended with the SPD appearing as more of an inter-confessional labor party than it had ever been before.

6   A century of democratic elections

This final chapter, both conclusion and epilogue, is divided into four parts. The first is a summary and reformulation of the results of the analysis of elections in Imperial Germany. Then, in each of the three subsequent sections, these results will become the basis for a comparison. I will begin by considering the extent to which the results confirm or refute some of the common explanations of the reasons for voting in Imperial Germany, and offer my own suggestions as to how we might understand the electoral system of the *Kaiserreich*. The second comparison will be between the general elections held under the empire and those of the Weimar and Federal Republics. This will make it possible to develop some notion of long-term voting trends in Germany under a democratic franchise. Finally, I compare these trends in Germany with developments in other countries of Europe and in North America.

Elections, parties, and voters in the *Kaiserreich*

Elections

I will sum up the results of the work under the three rubrics given in the heading above. Starting with elections, it seems to me that two main results emerge from the analysis. The first is the contrast between the Bismarckian and Wilhelmine eras, or, more precisely, between the general elections of 1871–87 and those of 1890–1912. Table 6.1 illustrates one important feature of that contrast by dividing the electorate into one of five groups, defined by behavior in two subsequent elections: (1) party loyalists, those who voted for the same party grouping; (2) switchers, who went from one party grouping to another; (3) the mobilized and demobilized, who moved between not voting and voting, in either direction; (4) the non-voters, eligible voters who did not vote at both of two subsequent elections; (5) the net new voters.

The figures show that elections in Bismarckian Germany occurred in the era of the non-voters. Even though turnout ran between 50% and

265

Table 6.1 *The German electorate, 1871/74–1907/12 (percent)*

Vote at two subsequent elections	Election year pairs				
	1871/1874–1874/1877	1877/1878–1878/1881	1881/1884–1884/1887	1887/1890–1893/1898	1898/1903–1903/1912
Stay with party group	35	39	43	45	52
Switch party group	10	11	6	16	15
Between party and non-voting	19	21	23	15	12
Stay non-voter	31	29	24	19	14
Net new voters	5	—[a]	4	5	7
Total	100	100	100	100	100

Note:
[a] The electorate hardly increased in size at all between 1877 and 1881, so there is no figure for net new voters for the 1878 and 1881 elections.

75% of eligible voters, about one-half of all the voters at each general election were either longer-term non-voters (over two subsequent general elections) or had been mobilized or demobilized especially for that election.

The era of non-voters was also the era of large swings in the vote a party, or group of parties, might receive. The minority parties in 1874, the Conservatives in 1878, the left-liberals in 1881, and the Kartell parties in 1887 all enjoyed very large increases in vote totals, their support among eligible voters increasing from 54% to 160%, either as the direct result of the mobilization of previous non-voters or indirectly so, by gaining the votes of non-voters mobilized by another party at the previous general elections. The Social Democrats' election victory of 1890 was the last in this series of large swings and also marked the transition to a new era in which non-voters played less of a political role.[1]

If the elections of Bismarckian Germany took place in the era of non-voters, those after 1890 occurred in the era of the political parties. The greatly expanded campaigning and organization of the parties and the

---

[1] The 160% increase in the left-liberal vote between 1878 and 1881 (from 5 to 13% of eligible voters) is a bit misleading, since it includes many instances of voters choosing the same deputy, who had gone from the National Liberals to the breakaway Secession. Still, the increases vote totals of 75% for the Center between 1871 and 1874 or the Social Democrats from 1887 to 1890, are impressive enough.

associations connected to them dried up the reservoir of non-voters that had fed the dramatic changes in party strength in the first two decades of the empire. The single largest increase in the percentage of eligible voters casting their ballot for any one party or group of parties was the one-third increase the SPD enjoyed between 1898 and 1903; other large swings included the liberal parties' loss of one-quarter of their previous voting support in 1893, and their gaining a similar amount in 1907. The increase in party loyalty among Wilhelmine voters did not mean a decline in party switching. Quite the opposite, the proportion of the electorate consisting of party switchers reached an all time high after 1890. Party switching was not the opposite of party loyalty, but a complement to it. In other words, the post-1890 increase in party loyalty among voters, the greater proportion of them switching party groups from one election to another and the growing stability of vote totals all had the same cause: the decline in the proportion of the electorate consisting of non-voters, whose mobilization, or lack of it, was the basis of the large swings in vote totals before 1890.

The second main point to make about the elections stems from a different perspective achieved by examining elections one at a time, rather than averaging their results over a decade. Here, I would stress the extent to which developments were not smooth and continuous; rather, individual elections could create a sharp break in the electoral system. There are four such elections that stand out in this respect: those of 1874, 1878, 1887, and 1907. In saying this, let me emphasize what I do not mean. I am not asserting that these elections set the trend for future developments, that they were "realigning" elections, in the sense that such a term is used by political scientists to describe the development of American electoral politics: an election that produces large changes in voter loyalty, changes that continue for a whole further series of elections until the next realignment.[2] With the possible exception of the 1874 elections – and then only for Catholic voters – none of these elections realigned the electorate permanently. The victorious parties did not repeat their successes for years, but, in fact, generally suffered substantial losses the next time that they faced the voters.

Indeed, the pattern of mobilizing elections, with campaigns centered on nationalist issues, the drawing into the electorate of previous non-voters, and victories for parties of the right, followed by elections centered on economic issues, voters switching party groups, and successes of the

---

[2] See Byron E. Shafer (ed.), *The End of Realignment? Interpreting American Electoral Eras* (Madison: University of Wisconsin Press, 1991) for a useful collection of essays on the concept of realignment in American political history, including the question of whether there is such a thing at all.

Table 6.2 *Mobilizing and post-mobilization elections in imperial Germany (percent)*

Vote at two subsequent elections	Type of election					
	Mobilizing			Post-mobilization		
	1877/78	1884/87	1903/1907	1878/81	1887/90	1907/12
Stay with party group	40	47	54	39	47	54
Switch party group	9	6	14	12	18	19
From non-voting to party	14	20	10	5	4	4
From party to non-voting	11	5	3	13	9	5
Stay non-voting	26	18	12	32	19	10
Net new voters	—[a]	4	6	—[a]	4	8
All	100	100	99	101	101	100

Note:
[a] The electorate hardly increased in size at all between 1877 and 1881, so there is no figure for net new voters for the 1878 and 1881 elections.

left, produced much of the electoral dynamics of the *Kaiserreich*. Table 6.2 compares the movements of the voters in the mobilizing elections and right-wing victories of 1878, 1887, and 1907, with those of the subsequent general elections of 1881, 1890, and 1912, which resulted in a victory for the left. It uses the same categories as table 6.2, with one refinement: it gives movement in both directions between non-voting and one of the parties, instead of lumping them both together.

Comparing the voter movements of each of these mobilizing elections (on the left-hand side of the table) with its subsequent post-mobilization election (on the right-hand side), we can note two decisive changes. The mobilizing elections were mobilizing in that substantially more previous non-voters turned out to vote than previous voters abstained.[3] The post-mobilization elections, on the other hand, showed the opposite effect, with a greater number of voters slipping into abstention. The proportion

[3] The elections of 1878 might seem an exception, with 14% of the electorate that year going from non-voting to choosing a party, while 11% went from a party to non-voting. If we just take voters in Prussia, however, where (as noted in chapter 4), the major change in turnout took place, we find that 16% of the Prussian electorate went from non-voting to voting, while just 7% went in the other direction.

of voters who switched parties, however, increased significantly in these post-mobilization elections.

Thus, we need to understand changes in party voting strength as the result of a cycle of elections. Interpretations that contrast elections on nationalist issues with those on economic issues, or that play off voters who were mobilized by the authorities' appeals, and those mobilized against the government, although not incorrect, miss an important point about the interrelationship of these two kinds of elections and two kinds of voter movements. Nationalist elections, by bringing previously passive voters into the electorate, set the stage for economics issues elections; voters who responded to the government's appeals in one election could vote against the government at the next.[4]

We can combine these two main results, the contrast between the Bismarckian politics of the non-voters and the Wilhelmine politics of the parties, and the discontinuities experienced at individual elections, into one perspective. The elections of 1874 and 1878 were partial political mobilizations: of Catholics at the first and Prussian Protestants at the second of these two rounds at the polls. The changes they brought in their wake remained correspondingly partial. At the other end of the history of the *Kaiserreich*, the elections of 1907 occurred in an era of greater voter participation, so there were fewer previous non-voters to mobilize, and their political effect was correspondingly more limited. There remains the Kartell elections of 1887. They occurred in the era of the non-voters, when a very large minority of the German electorate did not turn out regularly to vote. Their mobilizing effect was also enormous – the 28% increase in participation rates over 1884 was the single largest between any two consecutive general elections – and extended to all Germans, Protestants and Catholics, Prussians and non-Prussians. Both the climax of the era of non-voters and its conclusion, they were the central elections in the history of the empire.

Parties

In conjunction with the results on elections, we can discuss the development of the political parties. A plausible way to understand this development would be to consider it in four phases, each more or less corresponding to a decade in the history of the empire. Karl Rohe has suggested that the 1870s were a decade of "primitive political accumulation," when the political parties mobilized voters and developed a loyal

---

[4] These comments are directed against interpretations along those lines by Fairbairn, "Interpreting Wilhelmine Elections," and Anderson, "Voter, Junker, *Landrat*, Priest."

clientele in the first German elections held under a democratic and direct suffrage.[5] This is a suggestive formulation, and one that helps make sense of the politics of the decade. At various points in the 1870s the conservative, liberal, and minority parties all reached levels of support equal to or greater than what they would experience in subsequent elections.

Stated quite so baldly, this thesis does not do justice to the differing developments of the party groups in the initial decade of the empire's history. Both the minority parties and the conservatives enjoyed a sharp, once only increase in votes, the former in 1874 and the latter in 1878, bringing them up to substantially higher levels of voter support that they would, by and large, maintain in future elections. These changes resulted primarily from the mobilization of previous non-voters and, to a lesser extent, from winning over former liberal voters. In contrast, the liberal parties enjoyed a substantial vote at the very beginning of the empire and maintained it with modest ups and downs throughout the decade, compensating for their losses to the minority parties and conservatives by gains from previous non-voters and, secondarily, from the Social Democrats. If there was a single election that shaped the liberal electorate, it was that of 1881, which restructured the voting support of the National Liberals and the left-liberal parties, and kept it that way for the two subsequent decades.

The single biggest problem with the thesis of a "primitive political accumulation" is that it cannot be applied to the Social Democrats. What was to become Germany's largest political party, a whole party grouping unto itself, enjoying more voter support than any two other parties put together, struggled throughout the 1870s with a hostile state and power elite and a largely indifferent popular electorate. The Social Democrats' votes went up and down with changes in the extent of political repression. The crucial electoral indicator for a party that put up as many candidates as possible to gain for the purposes of agitation every last vote, namely the percentage of eligible voters choosing the Social Democrats in the constituencies where they ran candidates, showed no change. At best, one can say that the Social Democrats developed some regional strongholds in the 1870s, including Hamburg, Schleswig-Holstein, greater Berlin, and Saxony, which would also be strongholds of the party, albeit on a much expanded scale, in future elections.

The era of political primitive accumulation gave way to a period of party stasis in the 1880s. It was not that the votes for the parties, or their share of the electorate, remained the same in that decade: these fluctuated

---

[5] Rohe, *Wahlen und Wählertraditionen*, ch. 3. Rohe includes in this era of primitive political accumulation the elections to the North German Reichstag of 1867 and to the all-German tariff parliament of 1868, that have not been considered in this study.

substantially. Rather, the party loyalties established in the 1870s remained firm in the general elections of 1884 and 1887. Most of the movement in that decade, particularly in the Kartell elections of 1887, was the result of the mobilization of previous non-voters; the proportion of the electorate switching party groups, as table 6.1 shows, reached an all-time low.[6]

This party stasis came to an end with a bang in the general elections of 1890: the percentage of the electorate switching party groups reached an unprecedentedly high level, one that would not be matched until the very last prewar elections in 1912. The 1890 elections also marked – and it is no coincidence that these two developments went together – the breakthrough of the Social Democrats, their jump into a new stage of popular support that the other parties had achieved in the 1870s. The elections of 1890 were to the Social Democrats what 1874 had been to the Center or 1878 to the Conservatives, but the victory of the labor party in the 1890 elections also differed fundamentally from those previous breakthroughs. For the other parties, their victories in the 1870s marked high points; rarely, if ever, would they gain a greater share of eligible voters; for the Social Democrats, the 1890 elections were the start of a further advance that would double their share of the electorate by 1912. The mix of previous non-voters and voters switching from other parties also differed: previous non-voters made up 25% of the minority electorate of 1874 and 30% of the conservative electorate of 1878, but just 7% of the Social Democratic voters of 1890; voters switching from other party groups were 21% of 1874 minority voters and 28% of 1878 conservatives, but 38% of the Social Democrat supporters in the party's breakthrough year.

The 1890 elections thus marked the upsetting of the party system that developed in the political primitive accumulation of the 1870s and had been frozen in place during the following decade. For the remainder of the 1890s, the electorate remained in flux as the three basic determinants of political life changed: the relationship of the state to the electoral process, the nature of the issues raised in election campaigns, and the organization of the parties (including the associations related to them and the agitation these groups carried out). The main protagonists of the politics of Bismarckian Germany, the National Liberals, the Center, the progressives, and the Conservatives, struggled to redefine themselves in this new political arena. All lost voter shares in the 1890s to the SPD, to new political groups such as the anti-Semites or the Peasant Leagues, and to

[6] These figures were calculated using the party groups conservatives, liberals, minority parties and Social Democrats. If one replaces conservatives and liberals with Kartell and progressives and recalculates the figures on voter movements during the 1884 and 1887 elections, the results differ by less than one percentage point.

abstention as well. Thus we can summarize the results of this decade in terms of the growth of the SPD, the success of splinter parties, the decline of the previous major parties, and a drop in voter turnout.[7]

Having completed this painful process of redefinition and reorganization, the main Bismarckian parties were able to regain lost terrain in the empire's three twentieth-century general elections and to re-emerge a little below their previous high points. They accomplished this at the expense of the smaller parties and, primarily, by gaining the support of previous non-voters, since the SPD continued to increase its share of the electorate after the turn of the century. In another sense, though, the liberals, the conservatives and the Center were not, by 1907 or 1912, back to where they had been in 1877 or 1884. Although their share of the eligible electorate was comparable, in the earlier period most of the remaining electorate had been non-voters; after 1900, most of the electorate not committed to these parties voted for the SPD. Thus, the Bismarckian parties' share of votes cast and, ultimately, seats in the Reichstag declined, although the connections between a party's votes and its parliamentary seats in a single-member constituency, majority vote system is generally, and was in this specific instance as well, not as direct as it is in one based on proportional representation. The 110 SPD deputies taking their seats in Berlin after the 1912 elections are nonetheless the best measure of the extent that the major political parties of Bismarckian Germany had, after 1900, only been able to check and partially reverse the decline they suffered in the decade of the 1890s.

The voters

The best place to start a consideration of German voters over the years 1871–1912 is with figure 6.1, which gives the turnout rates by confession in the empire's general elections.

Participation rates among Protestant voters increased steadily as time went on, ultimately doubling between 1871 and 1912. Modest falls in their turnout, in 1881 and during the 1890s, did little to work against the upward trend. This is exactly what we might expect, and there is an obvious global explanation of the trend in terms of the expansion and improvement of the quality of public education, the increasing circulation of the press, the growing urbanization of the German population, the rise in membership and organization of voluntary associations, and the increasing extent of organization, agitation, and campaigning on the part

---

[7] Declines in the established parties, development of smaller parties and falling turnout: the 1890s in German electoral politics offers many parallels with the 1990s.

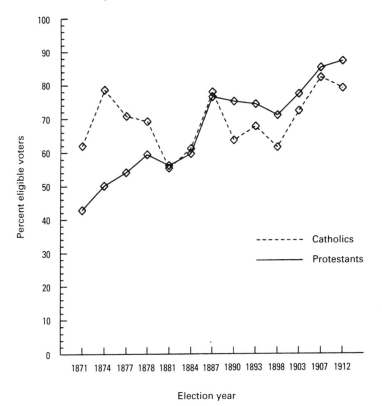

6.1 Turnout by confession, 1871–1912

of political parties and their affiliated organizations. Whether all these developments are summed up teleologically under the heading of "modernization" or not, they are all a part, and an empirically correct one, of the standard picture of the development of German and European society in the half-century preceding the First World War.

This global explanation would be fine if all Germans had been Protestant; or, to put it differently, it only works if one pretends, as many accounts of German history do, that Catholics did not exist. The dashed line in figure 6.1 which represents the Catholic turnout shows no such long-term increase; indeed, the participation rate in the empire's second general election in 1874 was higher than at all but one subsequent election. Since Catholics also went to public schools, read newspapers, moved to cities, joined organizations, and the like, it is hard to understand why these should not have had the same effect on them as they did on Protestants. If a high voter turnout is a result of "modernity," then perhaps Catholics just never became "modern," or maybe they were "modern" long before Protestants, or, alternatively, they were "modern" for a while and became less so.

A preferable way to understand the solid and the dashed lines in figure 6.1 is to realize that confessional differences profoundly divided the German electorate, as they did all of Central European society. The same political events or socioeconomic processes could and did produce different voting behavior in Protestants or Catholics. Voting and, more broadly, political participation had a different meaning to members of the two Christian confessions.

The single most important motivation for Catholic voters, one that overrode all others, was what might be called their primal trauma: the experience of being the losers of the wars of German unification and finding themselves in a nation-state inimical to their religious interests. Elections that rubbed on this raw nerve, as did the *Kulturkampf* elections of 1874, the Kartell elections of 1887, and the Hottentot elections of 1907, brought Catholics to the polls in unprecedented numbers. Protestants had a complementary response, an affirmation of the German nation-state, that also brought them to the polls in greater numbers in those three elections, particularly in 1887. If complementary, the two responses were not symmetrical: affirming the nation-state was just one of many compelling motivations for Protestants to vote, lacking the dominant force that opposing the state, or, at least its policies, had for Catholics.

We can expand this observation to a broader one. The single most important line of division in the electorate of the German Empire was confessional. A large majority of Catholics who voted cast their ballot for the minority parties. Averaging 71% over the thirteen general elections of the empire, the figure fell below 70% at just three elections: the initial ones in 1871 and the two final ones of 1907 and 1912.[8] Over all the general elections, an average of 91% of the minority party voters were Catholics, the figure falling below 90% (to just 85%) only in 1871. In contrast, only 2–3% of Protestants eligible to vote ever supported the minority parties. The electorate of all the other parties was generally 90% or more Protestant, with the one significant exception of the National Liberals.

Both the exceptions, the Catholics who did not vote for the minority parties and the Protestants who did, show the way confessional division

[8] Note that this figure – minority party vote as a percentage of Catholics actually voting (and thus excluding non-voters) – is different from and substantially higher than the figures of support for the minority party among Catholics eligible to vote, including non-voters, given in chapter 2 .

was built into the very foundations of the German nation-state. A large proportion of the Catholics who did not vote for the minority parties – primarily those living in southern Germany, but including others in Prussia as well – were anti-clerical, or at least opposed to the neo-orthodox, "ultramontane" religious tendencies that had gained the upper hand in the Catholic Church, both in Germany and more generally, during the second third of the nineteenth century. They expressed their opposition to this development by voting for the National Liberals, the party of the predominantly Protestant German nation-state, whose creation the Catholic Church and a nascent political Catholicism had bitterly opposed. In contrast, the main group of Protestants to support a minority party, the Hanoverian particularists, did so because they vehemently opposed the Prussian annexation of the once independent Kingdom of Hanover, an annexation that had come about because of the Hanoverian government's military alliance with and military action in support of Austria, Prussia's enemy in the war of 1866, the decisive one for the creation of the German Empire.

When we combine these two confessionally differentiated aspects of voting behavior, that is, the differences between Protestants and Catholics with regard to turnout and party loyalty, we have the two main forms of voter movements from one election to another in the *Kaiserreich*: the movement of Catholic voters between supporting the minority parties and not voting on the one hand, and, on the other, the movement of Protestant voters among the liberal, conservative, and social democratic parties, in the context of a gradually rising turnout. These were the dominant feature of elections in Bismarckian Germany; after 1890, they were supplemented by others, but remained a major aspect of political life. In Bismarck's day, the relationship between the kind of election and the amplitude and direction of these two voter movements is unambiguous. Catholics, starting at a higher level of participation than Protestants in 1871, went from non-voting to supporting the minority parties in those elections loaded with confessional and and national significance, 1874 and 1887 in particular; otherwise, their turnout was likely to decline.[9] Protestant voters moved to the governmental parties of the right in "national issues" elections, those of 1878 and 1887, and to the oppositional parties of the left in 1881, an "economic issues" election. The 1874 elections were something of an exception for Protestant voters because then the liberal parties were the governmental parties.

We can pose another kind of question about the voters in the

---

[9] Anderson, in "Voter, Junker, *Landrat*, Priest," p. 1470, talks about the political mobilization of Germany's Catholics in the 1870s, as a result of the *Kulturkampf*, without noticing their demobilization when other issues came to the fore.

Bismarckian elections, namely to ask about specfic groups within each of the two confessions. For instance, which Protestants were most likely to vote for the conservatives, which for the liberals and which for the Social Democrats? Were the shifts from left to right and vice-versa among Protestant voters the results of the movement of any one group, or common to all of them? Similar questions arise about Catholic voters: which were the occasional supporters of the Center; which were mobilized in the confessionally crucial elections of 1874 and 1887; which were the exceptions, who voted for the liberal parties? These sorts of questions are much more difficult to answer, because the lack of adequate census data makes it impossible to develop something comparable to the rough estimates on social group and voting available for Wilhelmine elections.

One answer to this question is a regional one. Before 1890, Protestants in Prussia, particularly in its East Elbian provinces were more likely to vote for the conservatives; Protestants outside of Prussia for the liberals; Protestants in a few scattered areas, for the Social Democrats. Catholics outside of Prussia, that is, in southern Germany, were far more likely to move between abstention and supporting the minority parties than were their Prussian counterparts, who were steady minority party voters with relatively little fluctuation.

Of course, "region" is in part a shorthand for a mixture of different political traditions and social structures. Jürgen Winkler, for instance, has demonstrated that in the 1870s the liberal parties obtained their best results in those parts of Germany whose inhabitants had sympathized with the left during the revolution of 1848. Conservatives, on the other hand, had the most support in areas that been either on the left or the right during the mid-century revolution, but whose inhabitants had then been pro-Prussian and anti-Austrian. Moving from political tradition to social structure, Winkler has also noted that in the first decade of the empire the liberal parties were strongest in predominantly Protestant and urban constituencies, while the conservatives did best in Protestant and rural ones – although liberals managed reasonably good results in such areas as well.[10]

These investigations suggest the possibility of an analysis of Bismarckian political parties in terms of social structure. In doing so, we could take a conventional tack and assert that among Protestants the conservatives had their strongest support from farmers; liberals from the urban middle class; and Social Democrats from workers. For Catholics, it might be plausible to suggest that the urban middle class included a higher proportion of exceptional Catholic voters, those who did not support the Center, while one might expect to find the erratic voters,

[10] Winkler, *Sozialstruktur*, pp. 152, 183–85, 190–91.

those who moved from not voting to supporting the minority parties, in the rural population. At least with regard to Protestants, I am not so sure that such assertions are entirely correct. If we consider the evidence from local studies, from the estimates of voting by class and confession in 1890 (the first election of the Wilhelmine era, when some traces of Bismarckian voting must have remained), and from the not terribly reliable estimates of voting by class and confession in 1887 (the last of the Bismarckian elections) a somewhat different picture emerges.

I have provided in table 6.3 the vote by confession and social group in these two elections. Before interpreting the figures, I should note two caveats that make this analysis a speculative exercise. First, it is risky to say something about the Bismarckian general elections (seven such elections over a period of sixteen years) on the basis of one at the very end of the series and one at the beginning of the next period of electoral history. Additionally, the estimates for 1887 are suspect, since the figures on social composition of each of the seventy-seven regions used in the ecological regressions are derived from the census of 1895. In the eight years between 1887 and 1895, Germany experienced a spurt of industrialization and urbanization, undoubtedly increasing the proportion of workers and probably of the urban middle class as well, and decreasing the proportion of farmers in the labor force. Consequently, the estimates of how "workers" and the "middle class" voted in 1887 include a number of individuals who were actually farmers. Even with these cautions, however, the figures in table 6.3 do suggest something about social class and voting in Bismarckian Germany.

While the conservative parties did have strong support among Protestant farmers, it seems likely that farmers also voted in substantial numbers for the liberal parties, as Winkler's analysis of rural and urban voting patterns in the 1870s suggests. In elections where the liberals did well, they may have garnered more support from the agrarian population than the right-wing parties did. The conventional wisdom, according to which the liberal parties were the domain of the Protestant middle class, certainly seems to have been the case, although at the end of the Bismarckian era some middle-class Protestant voters were already supporting the Social Democrats.

The latter party was not the choice of the majority of Protestant workers; even if we allow that a number of the "workers" in 1890 (and particularly in 1887) were really farmers, it still seems that most Protestant workers in Bismarckian Germany who went to the polls cast their ballot for a party other than the Social Democrats. This speculative conclusion is confirmed by what we know about the party's election victory of 1890: most of the voters coming to the socialists that year had

Table 6.3a *The Protestant vote in 1887 and 1890 by social group (percent)*

| | Social group | | | | | | | |
| | 1887 | | | | 1890 | | | |
Party group	Farmer	Middle class	Worker	All	Farmer	Middle class	Worker	All
Right	37	2	41	26	27	3	28	19
Liberals	31	62	16	37	34	59	8	34
Minority parties	3	0	4	2	4	0	4	3
Social Democrats	2	13	20	12	2	19	36	20
Non-voters	27	24	19	23	33	18	24	25
All	100	101	100	100	100	99	100	101

Table 6.3b *The Catholic vote in 1887 and 1890 by social group (percent)*

| | Social group | | | | | | | |
| | 1887 | | | | 1890 | | | |
Party group	Farmer	Middle class	Worker	All	Farmer	Middle class	Worker	All
Right	14	1	5	8	12	0	2	6
Liberals	8	25	10	13	6	15	5	9
Minority parties	55	40	71	56	49	33	51	45
Social Democrats	0	2	2	1	0	7	8	4
Non-voters	23	32	12	22	33	46	33	36
All	100	100	100	100	100	101	99	100

voted for the conservative or liberal parties in 1887. If, as seems probable, there were many Protestant workers among these new supporters of the Social Democrats, then the Protestant working-class vote must have been cast primarily for other parties in the Kartell elections, and, perhaps, in the previous general elections of the empire.[11]

[11] In view of the very large mobilization of previous non-voters in 1887, it is also possible that working-class voters who went from the Kartell parties in 1887 to the Social Democrats in 1890, had not previously been regular voters.

Turning to the Catholic vote, we see rather more of the conventional wisdom preserved. While the minority parties were the preferred choice of all Catholic social groups, the urban middle class was the group least likely to vote for them and most likely to support the liberals. The ratio of minority party votes to liberal votes among the Catholic urban middle class in 1887 and 1890 was between 1.5:1 and 2:1, while for the other Catholic social groups it was between 7:1 and 10:1. The figures show the Catholic working class of Bismarckian Germany as both the strongest supporter of the minority parties and also the group that moved in the largest numbers from voting to abstention. I am least sure of this result, once again because some of the "workers" were actually part of the Catholic agrarian population. Still, regions with a large Catholic working class, such as the Ruhr and Upper Silesian industrial areas, were strong-holds of the Center Party before 1890, so there may be something to this speculation.

To sum up the results of this analysis, we might suggest that in Bismarckian Germany the urban middle class was a decided and consis-tent supporter of the liberal parties. Protestant farmers were divided between the liberals and conservatives, perhaps on regional lines (east Elbian Germany primarily conservative, west Elbian, liberal; or areas with a left-wing past, liberal, areas with a pro-Prussian past, conserva-tive), perhaps from election to election as well. The Protestant working class divided its vote – once again, perhaps along regional lines – between the conservatives, liberals, and Social Democrats. Among Catholics, the urban middle class was also the strongest supporter of the liberals, although Catholics from all social classes supported the minor-ity parties more strongly than any other. In other words, if there was a counterweight to the confessional division of the electorate in Bismarck's day it was the extent to which the liberal parties represented the urban middle class of both confessions. About half of eligible middle-class voters in 1887 and 1890 voted for the liberal parties; no other group of parties could get as much as 30% of the eligible voters of any social group.

A good deal of the movement of the electorate in Wilhelmine Germany followed a similar, if somewhat modified path. Overall, Protestant turnout increased between 1890 and 1912, as it had between 1871 and 1887, although less linearly than in Bismarck's day, since all of the increase in the participation of Protestant voters came after 1900, while the decade of the 1890s saw a modest decline in turnout. Protestant voters also continued to move between the non-minority political parties. In Bismarckian Germany, though, a large majority of such voters moved between the liberal and conservative parties; after 1890, an ever larger number of them moved to or from the SPD. Also, as in Bismarck's day, elections on national issues favored the pro-governmental parties; those on economic issues were more likely to benefit the opposition. Of course, the SPD changed things here as well, taking over from the left-liberals the role of the main opposition party among Protestant voters.

Catholic turnout also fluctuated after 1890 if less than before, with a high point in the Hottentot elections, a piece of Bismarckian politics in the middle of the Wilhelmine era. In contrast to the Bismarckian era, the turnout of Catholic and Protestant voters was closer to being synchronized after 1890, suggesting a certain progress toward the creation of a national political life encompassing both confessions, although by no means evening out their very distinct voting preferences. While the movement of Catholic voters between the parties also increased over the pre-1890 period, a good deal of it took place among the minority parties: from the French nationalists to the Center, from the Center to the Polish nationalists, from the Center to the Bavarian Peasant League and back. Nationally, at certain elections, such as those of 1893 and 1898, and in certain regions – much of Bavaria, Upper Silesia, and Alsace-Lorraine – this movement of Catholic voters among the minority parties probably exceeded that of Catholic voters between the minority parties and the other parties. Once again, the rise of the SPD produced a change, with a growing (although even in 1912 still quite modest) number of Catholic voters moving over to it.

Wilhelmine Germany saw more of a realignment among Protestant voters. Although the liberals continued to receive a substantial Protestant farming vote, the parties of the right became the dominant element for Protestant agrarian voters, starting with the general elections of 1893. (In regional terms, this meant a more substantial vote for the right-wing parties in west Elbian Germany.) The extent of the conservative victory would be even greater if one were to count among the right-wing votes those cast for National Liberal candidates endorsed by the Agrarian League. The liberal predominance among the Protestant middle class vanished quickly in the 1890s; many of the members of this social group who abandoned the liberals found their way, after a period of low turnout, to the Social Democrats; others went off to the conservatives. Finally, the SPD quickly obtained a strong position among Protestant workers, although it never had the completely dominant role there that later historians have imputed to it, or that the liberal parties had previously enjoyed with the Protestant middle class.

This realignment among Protestant voters was largely a result of the change in German politics from elections centered on the clash between governmental and oppositional parties to those focused on economic questions, particularly the farm prices/food prices issue. The Social

Democrats, and the conservatives, with their agrarian supporters and anti-Semitic fringes, were best placed to take advantage of the issue, while the liberal parties alienated much of their middle-class base of support by continuing to campaign on Bismarckian themes in the 1890s or by refusing to take a stand on this key economic question. Liberal support among the Protestant middle class improved only in 1907, an election fought on Bismarckian lines, whose nationalist and anti-Catholic themes evidently appealed to these parties' one time core voters. The liberals maintained their position with this group in 1912, largely by coming down openly on the anti-agrarian side of the major socioeconomic debate in Wilhelmine Germany.

A mark of the continuing significance of confessional differences in Wilhelmine politics is the extent to which Protestant voters were much more divided over food and farm prices than their Catholic counterparts. The Center, facing a challenge from farmers' interests within its own ranks in the 1890s, and espcially from the Bavarian Peasant League, moved to an increasingly pro-agrarian political stance. This solidified the party's support among Catholic farmers, yet did not cost it much in the way of votes from urban voters. The contrast between the Protestant and Catholic middle class in Wilhelmine Germany is particularly glaring: the former moved primarily to the SPD, the party of low food prices, and, to a lesser extent, to the right-wing parties, who stood for high farm prices and government intervention on behalf of the middle class. The latter moved in the opposite direction, with the dominant trend being increased support for the Center, a party whose position on economic issues grew ever more similar to that of the conservatives, while many fewer came to support the anti-agrarian Social Democrats. The farm prices/food prices question did tell against the Center among a relatively small group of Catholic workers, who left the party in the 1903 and 1912 elections, ones in which various forms of the agrarian issue were at the heart of the campaign. The upshot was that the working class was the only Catholic social group whose support for the minority parties declined in Wilhelmine Germany.

Confessional differences thus remained the primary factor dividing the German electorate after 1890, as they had been before. The countervailing factor in Bismarckian politics, the middle-class support for the liberals, cutting across class lines, no longer existed on the eve of the First World War: the liberals had become a party enjoying about the same amount of support from all social groups, My estimates are that in 1912 23% of farmers, 25% of the middle class and 21% of workers voted for one of the liberal parties. One could argue that working class support for the SPD had emerged as a countervailing force, and it is certainly true that 42% of eligible working-class voters supported the Social Democrats in the last prewar general elections. However, these general elections were the only ones in which more than one-third of eligible working-class voters cast their ballots for the SPD. I would rather suggest that besides confessional difference the other main factor determining voter behavior in the Wilhelmine era was the agrarian issue, but it was an issue that affected voters from each confession differently, moving all urban Protestants – but only working-class Catholics – to support anti-agrarian political parties at the polls. In that sense, the importance of confessional divisions in German electoral politics increased rather than declined after 1890.

Empirical results and explanatory initiatives

Let us now consider some of the more general explanations of voter behavior in the *Kaiserreich* in the light of the results summarized above. Since most contemporary explanations have taken Rainer Lepsius's milieu thesis as their starting point, it seems reasonable to begin our considerations with a critique of Lepsius's ideas. There are three inter-related problems that emerge from Lepsius's description of the connection between sociomoral milieus and political parties in the German Empire: an exaggeration of the connection between parties and social or confessional groups, an overly static view of the electorate, and a questionable account of the relationship between change and stability in party voting and between change and stability on the part of the voters.

First, while Lepsius is certainly correct in suggesting that certain social and confessional groups favored political parties, he greatly understates the extent to which members of these groups had more varied voting choices and also the extent to which party electorates were coalitions, reaching across class and occupational lines. Protestant farmers may have voted for the conservative parties (including their anti-Semitic and agrarian fringes) in greater numbers than for any other party group, but this does not mean that all Protestant farmers voted for the conservatives – many chose the liberals, in some elections as many as or more than voted for the conservatives – or that farmers made up all, or even the over-whelming majority, of the conservative electorate. Precisely the same point can be made about the Protestant working class and the Social Democrats. While in Bismarckian Germany, the urban Protestant middle class may have been closely connected to political liberalism (although, even then, there were clearly many Protestant farmers and workers who voted for the liberal parties), this connection no longer existed in the Wilhelmine era. Lepsius's categories come closest to the empirical results of the ecological regressions in associating the Catholic vote with the Center. It is there that his description of a sociomoral milieu, a stable and long-lasting formation in which a political party represents the interesection of religious, cultural and regional traditions, with economic, social and organizational structures, fits the electoral politics and the social reality of Imperial Germany most closely. One problem with Lepsius's work is the way he extends the milieu concept from Catholics and the Center to different groups of German Protestants.

The second, and perhaps the chief, difficulty I can see in the milieu thesis is that it presents an overly static picture of the electoral universe. Contrary to the whole idea of a milieu, whose members are firmly, almost indissoluably, tied to a political grouping, voters moved across the lines of party groups in substantial numbers. There were fewer of them, to be sure, than those who remained loyal to their party grouping, but enough to determine the outcome of an election. At certain elections – 1874, 1881, 1890 come to mind – these movements of voters across the lines of party groups shook up the entire system. It was only in the elections of 1884 and 1887 that voters stuck with party groupings in the way that the milieu thesis implies they should have (see table 6.1).

This overly static viewpoint extends to Lepsius's discussion of non-voters in the electoral system of the *Kaiserreich*. The one place that he assigns them a role, namely in accounting for the growth of the Social Democratic vote, is precisely where they were not of major significance. The surges in turnout accompanying certain elections do not appear in his analysis, nor does the process of losing voters to abstention and regaining them later on – of substantial importance for the relationship between the Center or the liberal parties and the electorate in Wilhelmine Germany.

Finally, the milieu thesis suffers from a form of the ecological fallacy. Lepsius uses the fact that the vote for groups of political parties stayed the same or changed relatively slowly as proof that the supporters of these parties must also have stayed the same or changed equally slowly. However, the results of the ecological regression analyses suggest something different. As I put it in the discussion of the minority parties, stability in vote totals was often a dynamic stability, as political parties lost some supporters but gained others. The minority parties, for instance, lost voters to the other parties after 1890, but maintained their strength by recruiting previous non-voters and new entrants into the electorate. While the liberal parties lost much of their Protestant middle-class support in Wilhelmine Germany, they made up for part of it by recruiting a growing number of Protestant working-class and Catholic voters. In 1912, a large number of previous conservative voters chose one of the liberal parties, while many former liberal voters moved over to the parties of the right, but these large voter movements tended to cancel each other out, producing relatively little change in the net vote of these two party groups.

Lepsius in effect anticipates some of these criticisms by asserting that industrialization and urbanization began to dissolve the sociomoral milieus, and that toward the end of the Wilhelmine era one can observe the political consequences of such a dissolution, consequences that would only increase after the First World War.[12] It is probably the case that the predictions of his theory of milieus explain the voting patterns of Bismarckian Germany better than they do those of the Wilhelmine era. However, to describe the Wilhelmine era in terms of an incipient decline of both the sociomoral milieus, and of their political significance, seems to me to miss much of what actually occurred in that period. If the liberal, conservative, and minority parties lost portions of their electorate, they also won over new voters, both developments that can be traced to the growing salience of new political issues, above all the agrarian question, that realigned the electorate. At the same time, previously existing lines of division within the electorate, such as the distinction between Protestants and Catholics remained significant, or even increased in importance.

Consequently, I think that we need to say farewell to the milieu thesis, a remark I make with regret, since I am one of many historians who have been inspired by Lepsius's ideas. While they have served well in promoting investigations of political culture in a system that combined universal manhood suffrage with authoritarian government, in a more advanced stage of research they tend to obscure more than they illuminate. When examined more carefully and using more sophisticated methods, Imperial Germany's voters appear as a more complex, mobile, and diverse group than the static model of sociomoral milieus, based on crude global statistics of party vote, suggest that they were.[13]

Karl Rohe's theory of voters divided into differing political camps, themselves encompassing different milieus, as well as individuals not necessarily affiliated with any given milieu, is a more effective way to understand the electoral dynamics of Imperial Germany. In particular, it helps to explain the combination of party loyalty with occasional drastic shifts in political affiliation among German voters before the First World War. Yet, if more flexible than Lepsius's theories, Rohe's work still contains elements of rigidity within it, which weaken somewhat the validity of some of his interpretations. There are three main aspects of his work that can be

---

[12] Lepsius, "Parteiensystem und Sozialstruktur," pp. 65–67.
[13] A similar conclusion in Winkler, *Sozialstruktur*, p. 434.

taken up here, each showing substantial elements of insight, and each vitiated to a greater or lesser extent by an excessively rigid treatment. First is
the concept of the camp as a group of voters set off from and hostile to
other groups of voters; second, the idea that if electoral politics was organized into camps, voters were not placed on a left–right political spectrum; and third, the notion that there were three main camps in German
politics: the clerical, the Social Democratic and the national, this last
composed of supporters of the liberal and conservative parties.

In Rohe's scheme of things, voters usually stayed within their camps,
only sometimes jumping suddenly from one camp to another and staying
there permanently. We can observe such jumps in 1874, when the minority parties received an influx of voters from the liberals and conservatives,
and 1890, when the Social Democrats suddenly gained supporters from
previous voters in all the other political parties. As Rohe's theory suggests, these changes in support were permanent. I might suggest that such
a theory needs to be modified slightly to consider the importance of previous non-voters, either directly for the minority parties or indirectly for the
Social Democrats, and also to allow for a certain modest peeling away,
either into abstention or back to other parties, of those voters whose loyalties had changed so suddenly, but the basic outlines seem correct.

What does not seem correct, though, is to assert that there was no voter
movement back and forth between the camps. Particularly in Wilhelmine
Germany, there were a considerable number of swing voters who went
back and forth between the liberals and the SPD, and, to some extent,
between the liberals and the minority parties. The camps were rather
more permeable, or perhaps became so over time, than the basic formulation might suggest.

The idea that voters were not aligned on a left–right political spectrum
is also helpful in explaining the general elections of 1874 and 1890, particularly the great breakthrough of the Social Democrats at the latter date.
As we saw in chapter 5, this was primarily a result of voters of the Kartell
parties on the right and center-right, zipping all the way across the political spectrum to the extreme left. Rohe's concept of political camps also
explains the modest if steady movement of voters from the conservative
and minority parties to the SPD during the Wilhelmine era: these voters
were changing camps and once they did, they would not go back. It does
not, however, account for the movement of voters back and forth between
the liberal parties and the Social Democrats in the same period. If some
SPD voters at one election were willing to vote for liberal candidates at
the next, but not for conservative or Center candidates, this is difficult to
explain except in terms of an ideological affinity, ultimately stemming
from some connecting point on a left–right political spectrum.

The weakest aspect of Rohe's work is his notion of a national voting bloc, an electoral camp reaching from the Conservatives to the south German Democrats, taking in National Liberals and anti-Semites on the way. Rohe is certainly right in saying that many voters shifted back and forth between the liberal and the conservative parties, and that such shifts accounted for a large proportion of all voters who shifted between party groups at any two elections. However, it is a long way from this observation to the existence of a national camp in the elections of the *Kaiserreich*. First, there were other substantial voting shifts involving liberal and conservative voters: to the minority parties in the 1870s, and to the SPD in the Wilhelmine era, shifts rivalling in extent those among the liberal and conservative parties. Second, most of the voters going from the liberals to the conservatives, or vice-versa, did so in a competitive situation. The extent to which liberal and conservative candidates stood down for each other in elections where they competed against minority parties or the Social Democrats has been exaggerated by Rohe, who has generalized a bit too hastily from his excellent empirical studies of the politics of the Ruhr industrial area to circumstances in all of Germany.[14] Finally, the national parties did not share a common, Protestant middle-class electorate. A very large majority of Protestant farmers (including farm laborers) did vote for either the liberal or conservative parties; they may have been something akin to a national voting bloc. Their urban, middle-class counterparts, however, gave an increasing proportion of votes for the SPD after 1890 and particularly after the turn of the century.

There certainly were regions, such as the predominantly Catholic parts of western Germany, Alsace-Lorraine, or Prussian Poland, where the liberal and conservative parties did cooperate and their supporters did form a national camp. We can also point to the general elections of 1874 and 1877, during the years of the *Kulturkampf*, in which there was an unusually large amount of cooperative vote-switching between the liberal and conservative parties; and to the general elections of 1887 and 1907, when the conservatives and some or all of the liberals cooperated in a campaign centered around national issues. Yet at those elections, the national voting bloc was not very strongly in existence: voters in 1887 and 1907 were less likely than at other elections to switch between the liberals and the conservatives; when the two cooperated in a nationalist sense, their voters stuck with their party groups. When the liberal and conserva-

---

[14] On this point, I agree with the criticisms of Kühne, "Wahlrecht-Wahlverhalten-Wahlkultur," pp. 520–22.

tive parties openly opposed each other, as happened in 1881, 1893 or 1912, then their voters were more likely to switch among them. In other words, when the liberals and the conservative presented political alternatives, publicly suggesting different policies, or displaying a different attitude toward the government, the voters were more likely to move from one party group to the other, than when the liberal and conservative parties cooperated in a nationalist campaign.

Turning to the third major group of interpretations, what we might call the English school – with its insistence on a greater instability of the voters, its pointing to the significance of the 1890s as the decade when the masses entered political life, and its emphasis on the importance of political protest for voting behavior – we find a similar mixture of interesting suggestions and questionable assertions. The one point on which I am in greatest agreement with these authors is in their emphasis on the instability of the electorate, the extent to which at least Protestant voters were not imprisoned in milieus or camps.

The results of the ecological regressions also substantiate Blackbourn's and Eley's identification of the 1890s as a decade of substantial movements of voters between and within party groups, marking a break from the Bismarckian elections. It was also a period that saw the rise of the SPD and the relative decline of the main actors in Bismarckian party politics – the Conservatives, the Center, the National Liberals, and the Radicals, all of whom experienced losses in voting support to a greater or lesser extent. The last decade of the nineteenth century was also when economic interest groups and nationalist mass associations were formed, and political parties reorganized in ways that would decisively reshape campaigning in the empire's three twentieth-century general elections.

The problem is that these new developments did not go along with an increasing mass political participation. Turnout declined at at every single Reichstag election in the 1890s, and the main political parties of Bismarckian Germany lost substantial numbers of voters to abstention, circumstances that make it difficult to see the decade as one in which the masses entered politics. In 1887, on the other hand, the masses had entered politics: the increase in turnout over the previous election was greater that year than at any other time in the history of the empire, and participation rates broke 70% for the very first time. Yet the 1887 elections involved neither organizational nor substantive novelties; they were conducted along the lines of notables' politics, and on issues that very clearly belonged to the initial period of the history of the empire. It would not be unfair to say that much of the formation of interest groups and mass associations, as well as the reorganization of the liberal parties and the Center in the 1890s occurred precisely because the masses were not in politics, to counteract the effects of declining turnout and political apathy that so contrasted with the remarkable excitement of the 1887 elections.[15]

There is no question that using the ballot as a form of political protest was a major factor in German elections, whether in the 1890s or at any other time. The *Kulturkampf* elections also come to mind, as do the left-liberal victory of 1881 and the SPD's successes in 1903 stemming from a protest vote against the rising cost of living. Yet alongside such use of the ballot for protest against the existing political or socioeconomic state of affairs, we must also set examples of German voters using the ballot to affirm the status quo, especially in the three nationalist elections of 1878, 1887, and 1907. As noted above, in making this observation, I am not doing so to weigh the two forms of voting against one another, to argue that Germans were subservient to state authority, or that they were defiant and resisted it, but to point out the interrelationship between these two attitudes: affirmative voters could become protest voters from one election to the next, and protest voters affirmative ones.

In light of the statistical analysis presented in this book, each of the main approaches to understanding voters and voting in Imperial Germany presents both strengths and weaknesses, explaining well some aspects of the electoral system, but offering inadequate accounts of others. Although attempting to present a more comprehensive explanation may simply be pursuing a will-o'-the-wisp, I will nonetheless suggest one, based, very loosely, on the work of the Norwegian political scientist Stein Rokkan. Analyzing voting patterns across the political spectrum in different European countries from the 1920s to the 1960s, Rokkan argued that they had emerged from two main forms of political conflict on the continent from the late eighteenth through the early twentieth centuries. One form of conflict centered around issues of nation-building, involving clashes between church and state, or between the core regions of a nation-state, and the inhabitants of religious, national or regional minorities incorporated into it. The other kind of conflict, socioeconomic in nature, stemmed from industrialization, and typically involved clashes

---

[15] Anderson, in "Voter, Junker, *Landrat*, Priest," p. 1471 n. 75, has forcefully and, in my opinion, quite aptly, criticized Eley's and Blackbourn's description of the 1890s as a period of the masses exploding into politics by pointing to declining turnout. However, her further assertion that their description of political realignment involves an inappropriate generalization from the liberal parties to the whole political spectrum seems more questionable, given the difficulties the Center experienced with voters in that decade and the political realignment and reorganization its leaders had to carry out.

between farming and business interests, or between workers and capitalists.[16]

Rokkan's theory is quite elaborate, and there is a good deal of it that I find less than useful, indeed something of a classic negative example of trying to crush a scattering of empirical data to fit an elaborate, rigid pattern of abstract social science categories, but the great virtue of his work is in understanding voting behavior as the intersection of two differing dimensions or axes of political conflict. Applying this idea to the electoral politics of the *Kaiserreich*, we might see the elections of the Bismarckian era as ones dominated by the creation of a particular version of the nation-state, the German Empire of 1871. In particular, two aspects of the empire, its emergence from a series of wars, and its combination of democratic suffrage and an authoritarian, non-parliamentary executive provided central electoral themes.

One aspect of Bismarckian elections was voters being asked to endorse or to condemn the very existence of the empire as a nation-state created by warfare in which a number of ethnic and regional minorities, but, more importantly, the Roman Catholic population of central Europe, had been losers. Here, we can see a peculiarity of German political development, the linkage between the creation of a unified nation-state and conflict between the two Christian confessions, a connection that had been apparent ever since national unification had first emerged on the political agenda in the revolution of 1848. That the newly created nation-state quickly adopted a policy of anti-clerical hostility to the Catholic Church, a policy contemporaries understood as a continuation of the wars of German unification by other means, only increased the sharpness of the political conflict. One central axis of voting behavior in Bismarckian Germany thus ran along the overlapping lines of Protestant/Catholic, anti-clerical/clerical, victors of the wars of unification/losers of these wars.

There is another aspect of Bismarckian elections that we can point to, reflecting the other main aspect of constitution of the empire, the anti-parliamentary nature of the executive. Voters were frequently asked to endorse or condemn the specific policies of the government, a government that would stay in office no matter what the voters did. This created a different kind of conflict from the one described above, since policies of

---

[16] See Rokkan and Lipset, "Cleavage Structures, Party Systems, and Voter Alignments: An Introduction," in Lipset and Rokkan (ed.), *Party Systems and Voter Alignments*, pp. 1–64; a useful discussion of the influence of Rokkan's theories (in my opinion, often the least useful aspects of them) on German electoral studies can be found in Kühne, "Wahlrecht-Wahlverhalten-Wahlkultur," pp. 506–8; and a good account of problems emerging when Rokkan's theory is applied to German elections is found in Rohe, *Wahlen und Wählertraditionenen*, pp. 22–25.

the executive changed in ways that the nature of the state could not. Bismarck could go from free trade to protectionism, from having liberal to having conservative bureaucrats advise him and still remain chancellor, but the results of the wars of 1866 and 1870–71 could not be undone and the *Kaiserreich* remain the *Kaiserreich*. Consequently, the voting alignments that ran along the axis of pro-governmental/anti-governmental parties and issues were more varied. Voters rarely crossed the political line separating winners from losers of the wars of unification; if they did so, as in 1874, then it was only once. The mostly Protestant portion of the electorate that moved between pro- and anti-governmental conservatives and liberals – the various parties making up the conservative and liberal groupings could each be pro- or anti-governmental, and at different times were – did so more frequently. Such pro- and anti-governmental alignments often centered, to be sure, around economic issues, but they were issues of the extent of the government's involvement in the economy, and came to the electorate in the form of endorsement or rejection of government policies.[17]

If elections in Bismarckian Germany were about nation-building in the sense of concerning conflicts over the newly created nation-state, they were also about nation building in a quite different sense, namely about the creation of a national electoral system. This is another way of saying that the years before 1890 were the era of the non-voters, when a large portion of the electorate either did not vote at all, or voted sporadically, being mobilized at one particular election – and different groups of voters were mobilized at different elections – to vote for a particular party. In part gradually, in part by spasmodic changes in one direction or another, turnout increased over a decade and a half and was also synchronized, with both Catholic and Protestant, Prussian and non-Prussian turnout coming to move in the same direction and to about the same extent from one election to the next. Ordinary voters were thus incorporated into a nationally encompassing electoral system, a process concluded in the elections of 1887 and 1890.

These patterns of voter alignments created in Bismarckian Germany, particularly the distinction between Catholics and Protestants, did not cease to exist or even to become less significant in the Wilhelmine era. Rather, they were overlapped by and intersected with a new dimension of voter alignment created by conflict over economic questions. The main one was the agrarian issue, a clash over the weight of the economic and

---

[17] The alignments were also a bit different from the ones Rokkan presents as typical economic questions, since they were not between agricultural and industrial interests but between free-traders and protectionists, in both the agricultural and non-agricultural sectors of the economy.

fiscal burdens to be borne by the farm and the non-farm sector of the economy. The primary arena of the agrarian issue was the conflicting demands for higher farm and lower grocery prices, although after 1909 questions of tax burdens played an increasingly significant role, both in parliamentary and electoral politics. Many of the long-term trends in Wilhelmine elections – the rise of the SPD, the reorganization and consolidation of the position of the parties of the right, the initial difficulties of the Center and the liberal parties in the 1890s, and their recovery, albeit with limitations, after the turn of the century – were closely related to the positions taken by voters and by politicians on the agrarian issue.

This version of socioeconomic conflict differs in important details from the one that Rokkan presents in his theory. While Rokkan talks of conflicts between agricultural and business interests (perhaps having the British Corn Laws in mind), the agrarian issue pitted farmers against business, consumer, and labor groups. Rokkan also asserts that conflicts between capitalists and the working class led to the rise of labor or socialist parties in Europe, but electorally the SPD profited most from an emphasis on the agrarian issue. The party's exploitation of this issue enabled it to build a broad coalition of urban consumers that helped make up for the fact that substantial segments of the working class – particularly nationalists and churchgoers – remained outside of its orbit.

It is paradoxical that the SPD, the paradigmatic Marxist party of the Second International, whose leadership and, to a surprising extent, its modestly educated rank-and-file members, debated party policy in terms of class struggle and class consciousness, had its greatest successes with the electorate when campaigning on quite different matters. One might almost say that the Social Democrats, in calling for free trade in foodstuffs, lower taxes, and lesser government expenditures on armaments, gained voters on left-liberal issues, in ways that the left-liberal parties could not. One reason for this was that the SPD did not link these issues, as the left-liberals did, to a rigid and inflexible advocacy of laissez-faire and hostility to any government intervention in the economy, a point of view that was clearly unpopular with German voters, as the persistent long-term failure of progressive political efforts in such a direction demonstrated.

More generally, we can note the lack of class as a primary line of division in the Wilhelmine electorate. Class had its moments, the election victories of the SPD in 1890 (probably) and 1912 were both primarily a result of movements of working-class voters, but when compared to the divisions between Catholics and Protestants or between farmers and non-farmers, those between workers and the (admittedly very broadly defined) middle class were quite modest. Class did gradually develop into a political dividing line among Germany's Catholics; in the Wilhelmine era, Catholic blue-collar workers went from being the strongest support-ers of the minority parties to the weakest. Here, we can see the political effects of class division, or, more broadly, divisions on socioeconomic issues, mediated through confession. This suggests another way that Rokkan's analysis needs modification: the two dimensions of conflict cannot really be understood as dimensions, that is as completely separate and distinct factors influencing voters' choices; rather, they interacted with and modified each other.

If the Bismarckian elections had been the era of the non-voters, characterized by lower and sporadic turnouts, substantial and abrupt changes in party strength at the polls, weak political parties, loosely led and organized in the style of notables' politics, and also by an electoral system managed and dominated by the executive branch of government and centered around support for or opposition to it, then the Wilhelmine era marked a fundamental break with this setup. It was an era of the political parties, where turnouts were higher and voters were conse-quently both more loyal to their party groups and more likely to move between them, where changes in party voting strength were more gradual, and, finally, where elections were increasingly the domain of the parties and the associations affiliated with them. These groups set the themes of the campaigns and carried them out in ever more elaborate and costly fashion, with an ever greater degree of organization and ever greater and more varied mass public appeal. All these developments demonstrated and can be summed up under the heading of the emancipation of civil society from the state; yet, and this seems to me to be characteristic of the state of affairs in Imperial Germany, they neither implied nor led to the creation of a parliamentary form of government. Parties campaigned with the authorities and against them, or went off in altogether different directions, but the state remained an independent, autonomous – if, admittedly, not always terrible effective – element of electoral politics, one separate and distinct from the representatives of the people and the parties and other organizations who brought them into parliament.

This last point about the relationship between the state and civil society can serve as a lead in to some general reflections on the methodology of historical studies of elections. Such studies can be understood as having four separate levels, and it is important to distinguish between them. The first level is that of the voters, their choice of party (or, of course, non-voting) by group characteristics, such as class, occupation, confession, region, nationality, race or gender. One might also wish to know about the movements of voters, the extent to which they stayed with a given party from election to election, moved in and out of non-voting or switched from one party to another. This is the very fundamental level of the electoral process, yet, at least in the era between the end of public oral voting and the beginning of public opinion polling, the most difficult to investigate, requiring the use of regression techniques that yield only a partial, limited, and approximate picture.

A second level is that of party members, people belonging to political clubs, local branches of a national party, or other kinds of political associations. Membership lists, if available, provide handy and methodologically unproblematic access to this level of political life. Sometimes, if several successive lists have been preserved, one can even investigate levels of commitment and fluctuations in membership. The third level, closely related to the second, is that of activists, local leaders or committee members, electors in a system of indirect elections, and the like. Here, we have the leading elements in local or provincial political life; information about them is often more easily obtainable than for those at the first two levels.

The fourth and final level is that of parliamentary representative. At this level, the appropriate form of information is not the one historians most often use – the social or confessional (or gender or racial) composition of a party's representatives, since parliamentary deputies, by the nature of their job, are a special and unique group. More appropriate is a consideration of a party's parliamentary stance, the legal measures it proposes, the issues it raises in parliamentary debate and to the electorate, considered in relation to the first three levels of political life. If a political party, for instance, strongly supports agricultural protective tariffs, it would be logical to see how farm and non-farm voters responded to it at a subsequent election.

It is important to realize that the same groups of people are not necessarily involved in these different levels of political life. For instance, as we have seen in this book, the heavily working-class membership of the Wilhelmine SPD went along with an electorate that was not equally proletarian, but contained a substantial middle-class element. In other words, one cannot and should not draw inferences about one level of the political process from another. It is bad enough that historians describe the social composition of a party's electorate from figures on its membership, but when they do it from similar calculations on the composition of its parliamentary delegation, as is often the case, it is simply a methodological abomination. A truly comprehensive study of political life, particularly one dealing with an era of democratic suffrage, ought to grasp separately and then connect together all four levels. Admittedly, problems of sources will often make this impossible, but historians ought at least to understand the conceptual differences between the different levels of political life.

German elections in the twentieth century

In this section, I will take some of the results of the ecological analysis of the general elections of the German Empire, combine them with the results of similar analyses of other authors on the elections of the Weimar Republic and with polling data from the post-Second World War era, and create a long-term picture of the German electorate. I will not try to develop a party by party, election by election analysis of twentieth-century voting as I have done for the *Kaiserreich*, but will look more briefly at two themes. One is the long-term trend across the shattering political discontinuities and different forms of government in twentieth-century Germany. For this, I will consider the differing support that the party groupings had in these years and the changes in preferences of key groups of voters leading to such results. The other is a comparison of the electorate in different regimes, contrasting movements of voters in the empire, and the Weimar and Federal Republics. For this theme, the focus will be on the spectacular rise of the Nazi Party, seeing the extent to which it had parallels or precursors during the *Kaiserreich*. More generally, I will note the extent to which movements of voters in the Weimar Republic differed from those under the empire or after the Second World War.

A problem arises in analyzing such long-term trends or engaging in broad comparisons over decades, one that is not unique to Germany, but is particularly pronounced there – namely, the issue of compatibility. One obvious form of incompatibility is boundary changes: the German Empire of 1871, the German Republic of 1919, the Federal Republic of Germany in its 1949 boundaries and the Federal Republic of Germany in its 1990 boundaries encompassed different territories and different populations. Although all had a democratic franchise in national or federal elections, the nature of that franchise also changed considerably. Germany's republican governments used some form of proportional representation, as against the single member constituency, majority vote system of the empire. Women received the vote in 1919, and the voting age went from twenty-five to twenty in the Weimar Republic, and then to twenty-one in 1949 and eighteen in 1972. Finally, the contrast between an autonomous executive and a weaker, legislative branch of government, with primarily negative powers disappeared after 1919. Whether the politicians and the voters liked it or not, as long as the republican constitutions functioned, Germany has had a parliamentary regime.

There is an additional problem that must be faced: the changing content of the social or confessional categories used to analyze political life. Do workers at the turn of the twentieth century, who put in a sixty-hour week at a job requiring heavy physical labor, and who lived in two-room apartments without toilets or central heating, belong to the same social group as their proletarian counterparts of the 1980s or 1990s, driving fast cars, working a thirty-five-hour week and vacationing every year in Mallorca? Is the married, middle-aged male bookkeeper of the Wilhelmine era, the paterfamilias with his stiff collar, black coat, careful handwriting and array of tricks for shortening the arithmetic he did by hand, a member of the same lower middle class of salaried employees as the single young woman who runs accounting software on a PC, and goes to a disco on weekends? One might suggest that the content of confession is more stable than that of class, but did the German Catholic family of the turn of the century, with its ten or twelve children, have an even remotely comparable relation to their religion as today's German Catholic family with one or two children? Can we compare the conservative, monarchist Wilhelmine Protestant pastor, who advocated Luther's teachings and German imperialism with equal fervor, to his contemporary, bearded (or female), pacifist, third-world oriented counterpart, who may or may not believe in God?

To these questions I could add further ones about the compatibility of my methods of ecological analysis with those used by Jürgen Falter in studying the elections of the Weimar Republic, and about the compatibility of such analysis with the survey research informing us about voting after the Second World War. There is no real answer to any of these questions, other than to say that in spite of all these differences, I do think there remains something comparable over a long period of time in the political system, the parties that acted in it, and the social and confessional categories used to analyze it. The figures presented in this selction all relate to Germany within its boundaries of the time, and the social categories are defined by the official statistics of each era. Whenever possible, I will note how changes in the group of eligible voters might have affected the election results or where problems in the methods of analysis could render comparisons problematic.

Some long-term trends

As was the case in the *Kaiserreich*, to show and analyze long-term developments in twentieth-century German politics, we need to bring together many different German parties into a few general party groupings. However, the changes in the party structure between 1900 and 1994 were greater than between 1871 and 1912, so that the party groups are rather more ragged. The results in this section refer to six such groups: (1) The parties of the right, encompassing the right-wing and extreme right-wing parties of the *Kaiserreich*, the DNVP and the various fascist parties of the Weimar Republic, including the Nazis. After 1949, much of the previous electorate of the parties of the right was incorporated into the Christian Democrats, so that I have not charted right-wing parties separately in the Federal Republic, but included them under the heading of "other." (2) The liberal parties, including the National Liberals and the left-liberals of the empire, their successors in the Weimar Republic, the DVP and the DDP, and the FDP in post-1945 Germany. (3) The Christian parties, including the Center in the empire, the Center and the BVP in the Weimår Republic, and the CDU/CSU after the Second World War. (4) The labor parties, including the SPD in the empire, the SPD, USPD, and KPD in the Weimar Republic; after 1945, the SPD and the KPD until the latter's prohibition. I have included the various successor parties to the KPD, the DKP, and PDS among them, under the rubric "other." (5) Other parties, a varying category, that includes primarily the national and regional minorities in the empire, the many regional and splinter parties in the Weimar Republic, and a number of different political parties in the Federal Republic: in the years after 1949, mostly regional and refugee parties; in the mid-1960s, primarily the neo-Nazi NDP; in the 1980s, mostly the Greens; in the post-unification elections of 1990 and 1994, the Greens and the PDS. This is a regrettably heterogeneous group, a grab-bag category; unfortunately, I can think of no other consistent way to deal with it. (6) Finally, there are the non-voters.[18]

Figure 6.2 gives us a view of the support enjoyed by the different party groups in the free and open general elections between 1903 and 1990.

The easiest party group to describe is the liberals, whose share of the electorate has shrunk steadily over the long run. While the contemporary joke that the initials of the liberal FDP stand for "fast drei Prozent" (almost three percent) is a bit exaggerated, it is clear that the long-term decline in liberal support, begun in the decade of the 1890s, was only temporarily reversed in the last general elections of the German empire, and has continued ever since. In contrast to the liberals, the vote for the parties of the right stabilized in the Wilhelmine era, and these parties were able to maintain the same position through most of the Weimar Republic.

---

[18] In the following figures, the post-1914 elements come from Jürgen Falter, Thomas Lindenberg, and Siegfried Schumann, *Wahlen und Abstimmungen in der Weimarer Republik: Materialien zum Wahlverhalten 1919–1933* (Munich: Verlag C. H. Beck, 1986), p. 44; Gerhard A. Ritter and Merith Niehuss, *Wahlen in Deutschland 1946–1991: Ein Handbuch* (Munich: Verlag C. H. Beck, 1991), pp. 100–4; and "Germany's New Politics," Special issue of the *German Studies Review* 1995, p. 273. Voting results for the Federal Republic are all *Zweitstimmen*.

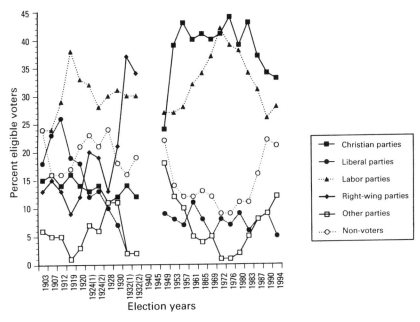

6.2 German parties in the twentieth century

The sharp increase in right-wing votes after 1928 is of course attributable
to the rise of the Nazis; the fact that no right-wing party has received as
much as 5% of the votes in a general election of the Federal Republic can
presumably be attributed to the Nazis, too.

The Christian parties have been the great success story of twentieth-
century German politics. Their success was not obvious at first, since the
Center and its affiliate, the Bavarian People's Party, did slightly worse
with the voters in the Weimar Republic than the Center had before the
First World War. This decline in the Christian party vote in the Weimar
Republic would have been much steeper had women not received the
vote. In those elections in which the ballots were counted separately by
sex (such a separate count was not carried out in the whole country nor at
all elections), women preferred the Center and the BVP over men by a
ratio of 1.5:1.[19] The founding of an interconfessional Christian political

---

[19] Falter et al., *Wahlen und Abstimmungen in der Weimarer Republik*, p. 83. As the figures in
Falter et al. show, the Center was the major party experiencing the largest discrepancy in
the vote by sex. Women preferred the conservative DNVP to men by about 1.2:1; men
preferred the communists to women by about 1.4:1, and the Nazis in 1930 (data on later
elections being too fragmentary to say much) by about 1.1:1. The other major parties
were supported by men and women in almost equal proportions.

party after 1945, the CDU and its Bavarian affiliate the CSU, on the other hand, dramatically reversed the fortunes of the Christian political parties by successfully bringing together the Catholics who had voted for the Center, with a good deal of the largely Protestant former liberal and conservative electorate, producing the dominant party of the Federal Republic. In contrast to the circumstances in the Weimar Republic, the CDU/CSU has been successful among voters of both sexes. In the 1950s and 1960s, women voted for it more frequently than men, by a ratio of about 1.2:1, but since then both men and women have voted for the Christian Democrats in about equal percentages.[20] Although the party's high point came in 1957, when the CDU/CSU became the only party in German history ever to receive an absolute majority of votes cast, and the voters have been somewhat less favorable to it over the past decade, figure 6.2 shows that the Christian Democrats have consistently outpaced all their rivals at the polls.

The history of the relationship between the labor parties and the twentieth-century German electorate has been marked by a series of ups and downs. These parties' vote steadily increased from the turn of the century until the general elections of 1919, held shortly after the overthow of the Kaiser and the proclamation of a German republic. Afterwards, the labor movement, split between Social Democrats and communists, declined at the polls to a point about where it had been in 1912. Following the Second World War, the SPD gradually improved its vote totals (the communists, both before their prohibition in 1956 and after their relegalization in 1968, could find little support among voters in the Federal Republic), although remaining behind the CDU/CSU, only overtaking it once at the ballot box, in 1972, the SPD's best year ever. Since then, SPD support at the polls declined steadily; it is unclear whether the 1994 elections are just a temporary break in that trend or the beginning of a new upswing.

The other parties have had a substantial share of the voting population on three separate occasions: in the middle years of the Weimar Republic, in the early years of the Federal Republic, and since the elections of 1980. All have been periods of political turmoil and economic crisis. In the earlier years, the other parties drew their voters from the center and the right; more recently, voters for other parties have come from the left. Turnout in German general elections has been consistently and impressively high throughout the twentieth century. It was even higher after the

---

[20] Ritter and Niehuss, *Wahlen in Deutschland 1946–1991*, pp. 224–25. Overall, differences in voting preference by gender in twentieth-century Germany have been smaller and less important for election outcomes than differences by confession, occupation, class, and often region.

Table 6.4a *The Protestant electorate, 1903–87 (percent)*

Party group	Election years					
	1903–12	1920–28	1930–32	1953–65	1969–76	1980–87
Right	19	20	37	—[a]	—[a]	—[a]
Liberals	27	17	4	9	6	8
Christian	0	1	0	33	32	30
Labor	36	35	36	40	50	43
Other	2	6	6	5	2	6
Non-voters	17	21	17	13	11	13
All	101	100	100	100	101	100

Note:
[a] Included under "other."

Second World War than before, peaking between 1972 and 1983, when a truly astounding 90% of eligible voters went to the polls, only to decline somewhat since then.

I will now present some figures on voting by confession and social group over the course of the twentieth century, which may help to explain how the trends considered above came to pass. Table 6.4 gives the vote by confession between 1903 and 1987.[21]

Probably the most important trend emerging from the table is the gradual decline in the distinction between Protestant and Catholic voters over the course of the twentieth century. This tendency toward a confessional equalization of the vote appeared in two phases. The first and smaller one occurred during the Weimar Republic; its characteristics

[21] In tables 6.4–6.7, results for the Weimar Republic are taken from Falter and Zintl, "The Economic Crisis of the 1930s and the Nazi Vote," p. 74–77; for the general elections 1953–1983, from Schmitt, *Konfession und Wahlverhalten*, pp. 313–16; for the general elections of 1987, from *Germany at the Polls: The Bundestag Elections of the 1980s* ed. Karl H. Cerny (Durham: Duke University Press, 1990), p. 285. (Breakdowns of the electorate by class and confession are not available for the elections of 1919 and 1949.) I need to make two notes on the use of this material in this and subsequent tables. First, the USPD vote for 1920 and the KPD vote for 1953 are given in the respective sources under "other," so I have assumed that the proportion of voters of different confessions choosing these parties is about the same as that of all voters. Second, the figures for the Federal Republic are based on public opinion polling, which gives no indication of non-voting. For lack of anything better, I have assumed that post-1949 turnout rates were the same for all groups under consideration. Empirical studies of voter participation in the Federal Republic have shown relatively small differences, with most of the differences that do exist being along age or regional lines, that is to say on different criteria than used in this study. See Ralf-Reiner Lapies, *Nichtwählen als Kategorie des Wahlverhaltens* (Düsseldorf: Droste Verlag, 1973) and Peter Schoof, "Wahlbeteiligung und Sozialstruktur in der Bundesrepublik: Eine Aggregardatenanalyse für den Zeitraum von 1972 bis 1980," *Politische Vierteljahresschrift* 22 (1981): 285–304.

Table 6.4b *The Catholic electorate, 1903–87 (percent)*

Party group	Election years					
	1903–12[a]	1920–28	1930–32	1953–65	1969–76	1980–87
Right	5 (4)	4	15	—[b]	—[b]	—[b]
Liberals	12 (11)	4	2	4	3	6
Christian	41 (49)	43	40	56	55	50
Labor	9 (8)	12	16	22	31	25
Other	11 (7)	8	5	5	1	5
Non-voters	22 (22)	29	22	13	11	13
All	100 (101)	100	100	100	101	99

Notes:
[a] Figures in parenthesis give the Catholic vote in those constituencies where the Center Party ran candidates.
[b] Included under "other."

included a decline in the liberal vote of both confessions, and an increase in the proportion of Catholics supporting the labor parties, so that the ratio of Protestant to Catholic support for these parties declined from the 4:1 of the last three general elections of the empire to 2.25:1 in the last three free general elections of the Weimar Republic (that is, excluding the balloting of March 1933, already affected, in at least some areas, by Nazi terror). Although in these last elections of the Weimar Republic, the parties of the right and the extreme right – and from 1930 onwards, this meant primarily the Nazis – clearly enjoyed more support among Protestants than Catholics, the difference was a good deal less than at the end of the empire, with the ratio of Protestant to Catholic support for the parties of the right falling from 4:1 to about 2.5:1.

The second and more dramatic phase of this equalization of confessional voting behavior occurred after the Second World War, with the founding of the CDU/CSU, a party with strong Protestant support, which the pre-1933 Center never had or really ever aspired to have. However, this is not the only feature of confessional equalization of the vote in the Federal Republic. The proportion of Catholics casting their ballot for the labor parties continued to increase after 1949 as it had before 1933, and support for, or, more precisely, lack of support for the liberal parties has been ever more closely equalized among voters of the two Christian confessions. By the 1970s, German liberalism had finally shed the nineteenth-century Protestant and anti-clerical character of its electorate, only not by gaining more Catholic voters but by losing Protestant ones.

This concept of an equalization of voting behavior by confession has the disadvantage of diverting attention away from the relationship between Catholic voters and the Christian political parties in the course of the twentieth century. Particularly relevant in this respect is the change in electoral systems from the empire to the Weimar Republic. In the single-member constituency, majority vote election system of the empire, the Center did not put up candidates in all constituencies, and could not be chosen by all Catholic voters, while in the system of proportional representation in the republican constitutions it and its successor parties could be, so the appropriate basis of comparison between the empire and later developments is the Catholic support for the Center in those constituencies where it did run candidates. From that basis, it is clear that Catholic voters were gradually moving away from the Christian parties after the First World War, particularly when one considers that the Catholic electorate was potentially more favorable to the Christian parties during the Weimar Republic than under the empire: women had the vote and the Catholic French and Polish voters who cast their ballots in favor of the national minority parties were no longer living in Germany. Yet in spite of these favorable factors, the proportion of Catholics supporting the Christian parties had declined by the early 1930s to a level lower than at any time since 1871. If one assumes that the ratio of 1.5:1 for female to male support for the Center and the BVP, found in the scattered instances of counting the votes separately by sex, is more generally valid, then only about 32% of Catholic men were voting for the Christian parties at the end of the Weimar Republic, a very substantial decline from the 50% who did so two decades previously. Such a low level of support had never been seen at any time in the history of the empire.[22]

After the Second World War, though, the proportion of Catholics voting for the Christian parties increased sharply relative to that of the Weimar Republic, and, averaged over several elections, exceeded its previous high water marks in the *Kaiserreich*. The hegemonic position of the Christian political parties in the politics of the Federal Republic is thus a result of their interconfessionality – their ability to attract Protestant voters as well as greater Catholic support. This increased Catholic support has weighed more heavily on the total vote since in pre-unification West Germany, Catholics and Protestants made up about equal proportions of the electorate, against the two-thirds Protestant and one-third Catholic voting population of the empire and the Weimar Republic.

The all-time record of Catholic voting for Christian parties came in the

[22] Jürgen Winkler's contention in *Sozialstruktur*, pp. 331–32, that there was no real decline in Catholic support for the Center between 1900 and 1930 does not take into account these changes in the electoral system and in the voting population.

Christian Democrats' great victory at the general elections of 1957, when 63% of eligible Catholics cast their ballots for the Christian parties, a far higher percentage than at almost any general election of the *Kaiserreich*. If we restrict ourselves to just those constituencies where the Center ran candidates, then we can find comparable figures in only two elections – 58% of eligible Catholics in 1874 and 62% in 1887. These three high points of Catholic support for the Christian political parties are suggestive because they demonstrate a fundamentally different relationship between Catholic voters, Christian parties, and the state. In the *Kaiserreich*, the Center was most successful as a party of existential opposition to the existing regime, as its enormous support in the *Kulturkampf* elections of 1874 and the Kartell elections of 1887 testify. Its close identifiction with the government of the Weimar Republic, on the other hand, was not appreciated by Catholic voters. However, in the Federal Republic, this relationship has been turned around: the CDU/CSU has been the party of government more often than not and, further, has been closely identified with the regime itself, a party of existential endorsement rather than existential opposition, never more convincingly than in 1957 at the high point of the era of Konrad Adenauer. In other words, the Federal Republic has been the Catholic voters' Germany in a way that the nation-state created by Bismarck in 1871 never was.

Looking at the final columns of tables 6.4a and 6.4b, which give the vote by confession in the general elections of 1980, 1983, and 1987 (the last three before reunification), we can see that for all the decline in confessionally distinctive voting, a clear confessional division continued to exist among West German voters. If we take the proportion of voters choosing parties of the left – the labor parties (the SPD) and the Greens (who were the large majority of the voters under the rubric of "other" in those years) – and the proportion choosing the Christian parties (the CDU/CSU), we find that among Protestants the ratio was approximately 5:3 in favor of the left, while for Catholics it was almost precisely the opposite, 5:3 in favor of the Christian Democrats. Even though fewer Germans than ever went to church, they continued to vote along confessional lines.[23]

Turning from confession to the other main factors in voting behavior analyzed in this book – namely, class and occupation – we find greater difficulties in elucidating long-term trends. One problem is the period of the Weimar Republic. The social categories chosen by Jürgen Falter and his

[23] In this respect, things have not changed substantially in the post-unification general elections of 1990 and 1994. See Wolfgang G. Gibowski, "Germany's General Election in 1994: Who Voted for Whom?" in *German Studies Review*, special issue on "Germany's New Politics," 1995: 91–114.

Table 6.5a *The vote of Protestant workers, 1903–87 (percent)*

Party group	Election years					
	1903–12	1920–28	1930–32	1953–65	1969–76	1980–87
Right	10	13	26	—[a]	—[a]	—[a]
Liberals	26	10	2	4	5	5
Christian	0	6	7	23	25	23
Labor	48	52	48	57	59	55
Other	3	5	5	4	1	5
Non-voters	13	13	13	13	11	13
All	100	99	101	101	101	101

Note:
[a] Included under "other."

co-workers for their ecological analysis of the elections then are different from the ones I have used for the elections of the empire, so that our results are not entirely compatible. In addition, Falter's figures are inconsistent and on many points clearly incorrect. Although they will be employed to some extent in the following tables, I will note their problematic features. My categories are comparable with those used by Karl Schmitt in his excellent study of confession and voting in West Germany, so that the results from the empire and the Federal Republic can be more easily compared. Here, however, one does need to note that the social composition of the German electorate has changed much more drastically than its confessional composition. In particular, farm voters, who were a good quarter of the electorate in the first third of the century, have declined rapidly from about 20% of those gainfully employed in 1950 down to just 3% in 1987.[24] Thus in considering differences in election results between the early and the late twentieth century, one needs to take into account not just the changes in voting preferences of individual social and occupational groups, but also the changing importance of such groups in the respective societies.

Table 6.5 gives the vote of German blue-collar workers in the twentieth century.

Turning to the votes of Protestant workers, we might first note that there seems to have been strikingly little change in their voting preferences between the last elections of the empire and those of the Weimar

---

[24] Figures in Ritter and Niehuss, *Wahlen in Deutschland 1946–1994*, p. 53. With the lowered voting age, and the rising age of entry into the workforce, the employed population and the voting population were much closer after the Second World War than in the *Kaiserreich*.

Table 6.5b *The vote of Catholic workers, 1903–87 (percent)*

Party group	Election years					
	1903–12	1920–28	1930–32	1953–65	1969–76	1980–87
Right	1	11	23	—[a]	—[a]	—[a]
Liberals	12	9	3	2	2	4
Christian	52	22	19	43	48	44
Labor	16	24	30	35	38	35
Other	—[b]	5	6	6	1	3
Non-voters	20	28	19	13	11	13
All	101	99	99	99	100	99

Notes:
[a] Included under "other."
[b] Included under "Christian."

Republic. In particular, the proportion supporting the labor parties remained just about the same. However, the figures for the Weimar Republic come from Jürgen Falter's work, and his definition of workers includes agricultural laborers, while mine does not. If we assume (certainly incorrectly, but probably not wildly off the mark) that all the Protestant farmers in the *Kaiserreich* who voted for the SPD were agricultural laborers, we find that an average of some 40% of Protestant workers – as Falter defines them – voted for the German labor party in the three general elections prior to the First World War. In other words, the communists and the Social Democrats together received a modestly higher level of support from the core constituency of the labor movement than did the SPD alone before 1914. Yet the increase was not great, particularly over the 1912 elections, when the SPD received the votes of 47% of Protestant workers (once again using Falter's definition). In fact, we might want to suggest that there was something of a plateau of support for the parties of the labor movement on the part of its Protestant workers between 1912 and 1932, with about half of the labor movement's core constituency supporting it at the polls, a figure exceeded only in the general elections of 1919 and 1920, held under the impact of the German Revolution of 1918 and its overthrow of imperial rule.

Unfortunately, this comparison is in part vitiated by problems with Falter's figures. According to table 6.5a, about 6 or 7% of eligible Protestant working class voters chose the Center or the BVP in the Weimar Republic, an assertion contradicting everything we know about voting patterns in pre-1933 Germany, and incompatible with Falter's own estimates, given in table 6.4a, that virtually no Protestant voted for the Christian parties. There is clearly a problem with the statistical procedures followed by Falter, leading him to attribute a certain percentage of Protestant workers' votes to inappropriate parties. The figures in table 6.5b, giving the vote of Catholic workers, reinforces this suspicion. Even noting that Catholic working-class votes cast for the Polish or French nationalists are included in the rubric Christian parties in the 1903–12 column of table 6.5b, the decline in their support of the Christian parties between the last elections of the empire and the elections of the Weimar Republic is implausibly large. Presumably, the votes for the Center and the BVP that Falter has incorrectly attributed to Protestant workers belong to Catholic members of the working class and other social groups. The idea that Catholic workers in the Weimar Republic were more likely to vote for the parties of the labor movement (and from 1930 onwards for the Nazis) and less likely to vote for the Center than in the last general elections of the empire is certainly reasonable, but the extent of the change, particularly the decline in support for the Christian parties, has been exaggerated by problems in Falter's calculations.[25]

With some relief, we can go on to the figures for voting in the Federal Republic, since the definition of worker used in Karl Schmitt's fine work, from which I take this material is about the same as the one I have used for the empire, and the polling data, for all their problematic features, are at least not subject to the difficulties of ecological regression analysis. They show that the Christian parties have improved their support among Catholic workers in comparison to the Weimar Republic (although, once again, the extent of the improvement is probably exaggerated by weaknesses in Falter's calculations) and have been persistently at a level comparable to what the Center achieved at the beginning of the twentieth century. Most importantly, they demonstrate that working-class support for the labor parties has been at an historic high point in the three decades following the Second World War. This has been primarily the result of the higher proportion of Catholic workers choosing the SPD after 1949, bringing Catholic and Protestant working-class support for the party closer than it was in the past, but the proportion of Protestant workers – the German labor movement's political core constituency – casting its vote for the SPD has increased after the Second World War as well. Indeed, I am tempted to say that the close identification of the Protestant working class with the labor movement, which the conventional wisdom about the Social Democrats assigns to the nineteenth century, actually only came to pass in the second half of the twentieth.

[25] The appendix includes some speculations on how these errors might have arisen and why they are not a problem for my estimates of voting by class and confession.

Table 6.6a *The vote of the Protestant middle class, 1903–87 (percent)*

Party group	Election years					
	1903–12	1920–28	1930–32	1953–65	1969–76	1980–87
Right	14	13	28	—[a]	—[a]	—[a]
Liberals	27	22	6	16	9	11
Christian	0	10	11	41	36	35
Labor	43	27	33	26	44	35
Other	0	4	4	5	1	7
Non-voters	16	24	19	13	11	13
All	100	100	101	101	101	101

Note:
[a] Included under "other."

Between 1953 and 1987, at least 45% of the entire working-class electorate voted for the labor parties (in 1953 the communists and the Social Democrats; afterwards, just the SPD) at every single election, a level of support never reached before the First World War when the Social Democrats only got above a third of the working-class vote in one election. In the SPD's two great election victories of 1969 and 1972, over half of all eligible workers cast their ballot for the party, the only time that the SPD has ever had the support of a majority of the working class at the polls.[26] Another way to put this is to note that in the general elections of 1983, widely and justifiably regarded as a serious defeat for the SPD, 46% of eligible working-class voters chose the party, a higher proportion than the estimated 42% who voted for the SPD in its great Wilhelmine election victory of 1912.

Let us now consider middle-class voters. Here, Falter's figures are not at all congruent to mine, since instead of dividing the non-working-class population into an urban middle class and farmers, he separates them into the civil service and the salaried employees on the one hand, and economically independent farmers and urban proprietors on the other. Consequently, in table 6.6 (showing the middle-class vote in twentieth-century Germany) the figures for the Wilhelmine era and for the Federal Republic are for the vote of the entire urban middle class, while those for the Weimar Republic are for its largest section, the civil servants and salaried employees.[27]

[26] All the labor parties put together – that is, the SPD, the USPD, and the KPD – probably achieved a similar level of working-class support in the revolutionary general elections of 1919 and 1920.

[27] The voting choices of the urban middle class in the Federal Republic have been calcu-

Table 6.6b *The vote of the Catholic middle class, 1903–87 (percent)*

Party group	Election years					
	1903–12	1920–28	1930–32	1953–65	1969–76	1980–87
Right	3	16	32	—[a]	—[a]	—[a]
Liberals	12	14	4	8	3	8
Christian	50	13	13	61	58	55
Labor	9	24	24	14	28	20
Other	—[b]	4	5	5	1	5
Non-voters	25	30	22	13	11	13
All	99	101	100	101	101	101

Notes:
[a] Included under "other."
[b] Included under "Christian."

The deficencies in Falter's estimates for the Weimar Republic are particularly glaring in this table since it is most improbable that 10% of the Protestant salaried middle class voted for the Center or that only 13% of their Catholic counterparts did.[28]

However, if we compare Falter's results with other, more carefully worked studies of voting in the Weimar Republic, and with the figures in table 6.6 giving middle-class voting preferences in the first two decades of West Germany, then some general trends do emerge. The Protestant middle-class vote really did shift away from the SPD in the Weimar Republic as compared to the *Kaiserreich*, perhaps even more than is shown in table 6.6a, since it just gives the vote of the salaried middle class, who may well have been stronger supporters of the labor movement than independent businessmen and craftsmen.[29] Support for the SPD among the Protestant urban middle class was twenty percentage points lower in the early years of the Federal Republic than it had been in the last years of the empire. It only came up to those levels in the heyday of the SPD in the late 1960s and early 1970s, and has declined since then, although this

lated from the figures in Schmitt, *Konfession und Wahlverhalten*, pp. 315–16 by averaging his two categories, *Selbstständige* (outside of agriculture) and *Angestellte + Beamte*; a similar procedure was used for the figures from 1987 in Cerny, *Germany at the Polls*, pp. 286–87.
[28] In addition, the figures on support for the Nazis among the salaried middle class given by Falter in *Hitlers Wähler*, pp. 283–84, differ considerably from those in Falter and Zintl, "The Economic Crisis of the 1930s and the Nazi Vote," p. 75. To the best of my knowledge, Falter has never explained any of these discrepancies.
[29] Winkler, "Die soziale Basis der sozialistischen Parteien in Deutschland," pp. 169–70, has also noted the sharp decline in Protestant white-collar support for the SPD at the polls between 1912 and the elections of the Weimar Republic up through 1924.

decline is largely attributable to a growing vote for the Greens. Middle-class Protestants have continued to vote for liberal political parties to a greater extent than most other Germans, even though the liberal vote of this group, like all others, has declined substantially in the course of the twentieth century. The middle-class Protestant vote in Germany has gone on a long journey since 1871. Beginning with the liberal parties in the early decades of the *Kaiserreich*, it moved to substantial support for the SPD in the years before the First World War, before veering back to the center and the right between 1919 and the early 1960s, only to return to the left since then, at first offering strong support to the SPD, later for the Greens as well.

The course of the middle-class Catholic vote is less clear, though this is largely because the figures for the Weimar Republic seem so unreliable. Although a fairly substantial minority may have chosen the liberal parties in the first decades of the empire, from the early twentieth century onwards, the Catholic middle class has strongly supported the Christian political parties, never more pronouncedly than in the era of Konrad Adenauer during the 1950s. Catholic middle-class support for the SPD has increased in the twentieth century, but has remained at modest levels compared to either the Protestant middle class or to the Catholic working class. The only question remaining is the extent to which this support for the Christian parties weakened in the Weimar Republic. It probably did, and it does seem plausible to assert that more Catholic middle-class voters went off to the parties of both the left and the right; but a valid estimate of the extent of the Center's losses and other parties' gains among this social and confessional group must await more accurate calculations.

If confessional distinctions among German voters have gradually been reduced in the course of the twentieth century, especially after 1949, differences between the working class and the middle class have become more pronounced. In the last three general elections of the *Kaiserreich*, an average of 33% of eligible urban middle-class voters cast their ballots for the SPD, as against 36% of eligible working-class voters. Even if we allow that ambiguities in census definitions mean that some of those middle-class Social Democrats were really workers, the gap between the social groups was not wide. In the Federal Republic, it has been much wider. In the general elections between 1953 and 1965, an average of 47% of blue-collar workers eligible to vote chose the SPD as against just 20% of eligible middle-class voters. The blue-collar:middle-class gap narrowed to 50:37% in the general elections of 1969, 1972, and 1976, only to widen again to 46:28% in the last three general elections of pre-unification West Germany. If one includes the Greens along with the SPD as more generic parties of the left, then in those three last pre-unification elections 50% of eligible working-class voters chose parties of the left as against 35% of the middle class.

A final question we can pose here is whether class distinctions had over-taken confessional ones in West German elections during the 1980s. As noted above, Catholics preferred the Christian parties to those of the left (SPD and Greens) by a ratio of 5:3, or 1.7:1 in that decade, with Protestants' choice being almost the exact opposite. In those same elec-tions, working-class voters preferred parties of the left over the Christian parties in the 1980s by a ratio of 1.5:1, while middle-class voters pre-ferred the CDU/CSU by 1.3:1, so that the voting gap between social classes, although substantially wider in the 1980s than in the early twenti-eth century, was still a little less than the voting gap between the confes-sions, even though that had narrowed considerably over the years. We can calculate this ratio for social and confessional groups, thus giving us an even more precise idea of the influence of class and confession on voting. In the last three elections of the pre-unification Federal Republic, Protestant workers chose the left-wing parties over the Christian ones by a ratio of 2.6:1, the Protestant middle class by a ratio of 1.2:1. Catholic workers voted for the Christian parties over the left by 1.2:1, the Catholic middle class by 2.2:1. In sum, confession and class determined the behav-ior of German voters toward the end of the twentieth century as confes-sion and occupation had done at the beginning.

Occupation and confession have remained an important determinant of voting choices. Of Catholic farmers who voted in the general elections of 1983 91% voted for the CDU/CSU, this preference falling below 90% (between 70 and 80%) in just two elections, those of 1953 and 1980. But by the 1980s, farmers were a very small portion of the population, influ-ential enough to get the German government to endorse the Common Market's bizarre agricultural policies but lacking the numbers to swing elections one way or another. Table 6.7 concludes this long-term survey of voting by class and confession with figures on the farm vote through the mid-1970s, the last time when farmers made up over 5% of gainfully employed West Germans. Once again, the occupational definitions for the elections of the empire and the Federal Republic are the same, but for the elections of the Weimar Republic I have had to use Jürgen Falter's figures for economically independent voters, of whom some 40–50% were actually farmers.

After noting for a third and last time the implausibility of Falter's esti-mates showing large number of Protestants voting for the Christian parties in the Weimar Republic and suspiciously small numbers of Catholics choosing the Center (as well as very implausibly large numbers

Table 6.7a *The vote of Protestant farmers, 1903–76 (percent)*

Party group	Election years				
	1903–12	1920–28	1930–32	1953–65	1969–76
Right	40	26	49	—[a]	—[a]
Liberals	27	16	4	15	12
Christian	0	11	7	56	60
Labor	6	8	8	7	14
Other	4	5	8	9	4
Non-voters	23	35	25	13	11
All	100	101	101	100	101

Note:
[a] Included under "other."

Table 6.7b *The vote of Catholic farmers, 1903–76 (percent)*

Party group	Election years				
	1903–12	1920–28	1930–32	1953–65	1969–76
Right	12	8	18	—[a]	—[a]
Liberals	10	9	4	3	2
Christian	55	44	36	78	83
Labor	0	12	16	2	5
Other	—[b]	7	6	5	0
Non-voters	22	19	19	13	11
All	99	99	99	101	101

Notes:
[a] Included under "other."
[b] Included under "Christian."

voting for the labor parties), I would suggest that the overall effect of this table is to delineate a strong preference among Protestant farmers for parties of the right, although a minority did vote for the liberals and even the Social Democrats. Of Protestant independent businessmen and farmers 49% voted for the parties of the right and the extreme right – that is to say, primarily the Nazis – in the elections of 1930–32. If we note that the Nazis polled their best results in predominantly Protestant and rural areas, and that many of their Protestant working-class voters were proba-bly agricultural laborers, it is very likely that a higher percentage of Protestant farmers supported the Nazis, forming the core of their constituency.[30] In this respect, it would seem appropriate to trace a continuity of right-wing voting among Protestant farmers, beginning with the farm crisis of the 1890s, the successes of the agrarians and anti-Semites in exploiting it, the failure of the SPD's agitation among the rural population and the general helplessness of the liberal parties when faced with the agrarian issue. After the Second World War, Protestant farmers' right-wing preferences took a generally more benign turn, as they became the strongest supporters of the CDU/CSU in the Protestant population. An admittedly small minority, though, apparently pined for the "good old days" of the Third Reich, since the large vote under "other" was especially pronounced in those elections when the neo-Nazi SRP and NPD were at their greatest extent.

As we have seen, support for the Christian parties in the Federal Republic was greater among Catholics than at any other time in the twentieth century, in fact at any other time since Germany held elections based on universal manhood suffrage. Table 6.7b, shows that this move to the Christian parties was most pronounced among Catholic farmers. Both differing categories of analysis and the problematic features of Jürgen Falter's calculations leave unclear the extent to which Catholic farmers deserted the Center and its affiliates in the Weimar Republic (the impact of woman suffrage may have been significant here as well), but if there was a decline in Catholic agrarians' support for the Christian parties during the Weimar years, they more than made up for it in the Federal Republic.

Looking back over the entire period from the beginning of the century to the end of the pre-unification Federal Republic, we can see the long-term increase in the vote totals of the labor and Christian parties as the most significant developments. These were the result of three main factors. First, there was the extent to which these parties improved their support in their core constituencies, the working class for the labor parties and Catholic voters for their Christian counterparts. From 1912 through 1932, the labor parties enjoyed stronger support from the working class than ever before. This development was hidden from view by the bitter split in the labor movement between communists and Social Democrats, meaning that a growing proletarian loyalty to the labor movement was divided among two political parties. The increase in support was also not consistent, workers' votes for the labor parties rising from 1912 through the elections of 1919–20, then declining to a level of about the last prewar

---

[30] Cf. Falter, "War die NSDAP die erste deutsche Volkspartei?" p. 39; similarly, Winkler, *Sozialstruktur*, pp. 376–77.

elections. The largest increase in working-class voting for the labor movement – particularly pronounced among Catholic workers, but occurring among their Protestant counterparts as well – came after the Second World War.

The story for the Christian parties is a bit different, these parties suffering a decline in Catholic voting support between 1912 and 1932. It was relatively modest to be sure, but only because women received the vote in 1919 and Catholic womens' adherence to the Center Party and the BVP helped to compensate for male Catholics' declining willingness to vote for it. The resurgence of Catholic support for the Christian parties in the 1950s and 1960s was pronounced, most so among Catholic farmers.

The second main factor in the rise of the labor and Christian parties was changes in the composition of the electorate. The Social Democrats' long inability to connect with Germany's farmers was finally rendered politically innocuous in the 1970s, when the agrarian population dwindled to near insignificance. Granting woman suffrage in 1919 was a boon to the Christian parties, and the larger proportion of Catholics in pre-unification West Germany (as compared with both its predecessor states and reunified successor) gave more weight to the stronger Catholic support for the Christian parties after 1949.

The third factor, the one most emphasized (probably overemphasized) in standard accounts, was the ability of the two parties to gain support outside of their core constituency. Such support has generally not accumulated in gradual or linear fashion, but has come in sudden jumps or shown substantial ups and downs. A sudden change was the way that large numbers of Protestants – particularly farmers and the middle class, but some workers as well – started voting for the CDU/CSU in 1953 and have done so ever since.[31] A development with little pre-1933 precedent (in spite of endless labors on the part of historians to find one), it permanently and totally changed the nature of German electoral politics and was the single most significant factor in creating a hegemonic role for the Christian Democrats in the politics of the Federal Republic.

The relationship between middle-class voters and the parties of the labor movement shows the other side of the coin. Strong support by the Protestant middle class for the SPD in the decade before the First World War was followed by a period of sharp decline, from 1919 until the early

---

[31] Although polling data is lacking, ecological analyses have shown that with a few regional exceptions, such as Schleswig-Holstein, quite a modest proportion of Protestants chose the CDU or CSU in the very first general elections of the Federal Republic in 1949. Jürgen Falter, "Kontinuität und Neubeginn. Die Bundestagswahl 1949 zwischen Weimar und Bonn," *Politische Vierteljahresschrift* 22 (1981): 236–63.

1960s, modest increases in middle-class Catholic support for the labor movement only partially counteracting this trend. German middle-class voters of both confessions have moved to the left since then, first to the SPD, later to the Greens. Still, the only general election in the Federal Republic in which support for the parties of the left by middle-class voters in general, and by Protestant middle-class voters in particular, has surpassed the levels of the years 1903–1912 was the SPD's great triumph of 1972.

These three factors, or more precisely, their mirror image, also throw some light on the other main development of German politics, the gradual decline of the liberal and conservative parties, the sudden breakthrough of the Nazis in 1930 and after, and the weakness of the extreme right after 1949. It is certainly one of the best-known facts about the politics of the Weimar Republic, ascertained long before the development of complex statistical methods, that there was a large group of voters who, by the late 1920s, had become increasingly disenchanted with the liberal and conservative parties, moving off to abstention or to one of the many splinter parties. Such voters included the old core of the "national" electorate, Protestant farmers and part of the Protestant middle class, but also Protestant middle-class voters who had supported the SPD before the First World War, as well as those working-class and Catholic voters who were not regular supporters of the labor or Christian parties. The difficult economic and political circumstances of the Weimar Republic made it impossible for the divided labor movement or the exclusively Catholic and clerical Center party to reach out to them. Instead, it was the Nazis who did. Jürgen Falter's estimates of the voter movements leading to the rise of the NSDAP (which I think are more reliable than his figures on voting by class and confession) show that about three-quarters of the Nazi electorate came from outside the regular clientele of the Christian and labor parties. In other words, they were those voters who in the empire and early Weimar Republic had chosen the liberal and conservative parties and – after experiencing just what their choice of Nazism had meant – in the Bonn regime swelled the ranks of the Christian and Social Democrats.

Different voting regimes

The considerations mentioned in the previous paragraph lead into the main question of this section: can the elections of the Weimar Republic be considered unique in comparison with those of the preceding and successive regimes – especially in view of the rise of the Nazi Party? A good place to start is with the fluctuation of the electorate. Following along the lines

Table 6.8 *Stability and change in the twentieth-century German electorate (percent)*

	Election year pairs				
Vote at two subsequent elections	1898/1903–1907/12	1920/24(1)-1924(2)/28	1928/30–1932(1)/32(2)	1957/61–1969/72	1972/76–1983/87
Stay with party group	52	42	48	62	69
Switch party group	15	26	25	11	20
Between party and non-voting	12	17	14	15	—[a]
Stay non-voter	14	15	14	13	12
Net new voters	7	—[a]	—[a]	—[b]	—[c]
Total	100	100	100	101	101

Notes:
[a] Not calculated.
[b] Included with "between party and non-voting."
[c] Included with "stay non-voter."

of tables 6.1 and 6.2, table 6.8 offers some figures on stability and change in the German electorate at different points in the twentieth century.[32] These results are not entirely compatible since they are based on somewhat different methods of calculation and since the party groups are different for each period. The figures from the *Kaiserreich* are based on the four party groups used in the previous chapters (conservatives, liberals, minority parties, SPD); for the Weimar Republic, there are six party groups, (1) labor parties (SPD, KPD, USPD); (2) Catholic parties (Center and BVP); (3) liberal parties (DDP and DVP); (4) the conservative DNVP; (5) the Nazis; and (6) the other parties. In the elections of the Federal Republic, the groups are simply the individual political parties, the SPD, FDP, CDU/CSU, and whatever smaller parties were at the polls in any given year.

[32] For the Weimar Republic, figures are calculated from Falter and Zintl, "The Economic Crisis of the 1930s," pp. 78–79. (I have assumed that all the votes given as "other" in 1920 were actually cast for the USPD and have calculated them as part of the labor party vote.) For the years 1957–72, the figures are taken from Hans D. Klingemann and Franz Urban Pappi, "Die Wählerbewegungen bei der Bundestagswahl am 28. September 1969," *Politische Vierteljahresschrift* 11 (1970): 11–83, esp. p. 122, and Peter Hoschka and Hermann Schunck, "Schätzung von Wählerwanderungen: Puzzlespiel oder gesicherte Ergebnisse?" in ibid. 16 (1975): 491–539, esp. p. 537; for the years 1972–87, from David P. Conradt, *The German Polity* 5th edn (New York and London: Longman Publishing, 1993), p. 124.

In spite of these differences, the elections of the Weimar Republic stand out as ones where the percentage of voters staying with the same party group was low and the percentage switching from one party to another unusually high. This was a persistent feature of elections in the Weimar years; the Nazi triumphs of 1930 and 1932 were in this respect little different from preceding elections. In contrast, the elections of the Federal Republic have been characterized by noticeably greater party loyalty and rather smaller amounts of party switching.[33] The available figures for the West German elections only begin in 1961, thus leaving out earlier ballots when the votes for the parties changed considerably and there must have been a much greater proportion of the electorate switching parties, particularly between the elections of 1949 and 1953. If this was the case, then we could divide twentieth-century German elections into two main periods: the pre-1914 and (probably) post-1953 eras, when party loyalties were strong and switching between party groups relatively modest; and an intermediate period of instability, when parties were newly formed or vanished from the political scene and when voters shifted their choices around more than they had in the past. It is difficult not to identify these two eras in political and socioeconomic terms: the eras of voter stability were also periods of prosperity and constitutional continuity; the intermediary era encompassed four decades of warfare, revolution, dictatorship, drastic political and constitutional change, and almost uninterrupted economic crisis. Under these circumstances, it is remarkable that the voters did not switch parties even more than they actually did.

It is certainly no coincidence that the rapid and massive rise in the fortunes of the Nazi party occurred in this period of electoral lability. The sevenfold increase in the Nazi share of eligible voters between 1928 and 1930, from 2% to 15%, had no precedent in the era of a democratic franchise in Germany. But it was followed by a doubling of the proportion of eligible voters choosing the Nazis to 31% in the general elections of July 1932. This was comparable to the greatest increases in vote totals during the *Kaiserreich*: the minority parties between 1871 and 1874, the left-liberals between 1878 and 1881, and the Social Democrats between 1887 and 1890. All of those, though, had been achieved in the era of non-voters, when a good deal of the electorate did not vote on a regular basis and was not firmly tied to any party. From the 1890s onward, when 70% or more of eligible German voters went to the polls, even the sort of increase in support the Nazis enjoyed between 1930 and 1932 – itself, a

---

[33] The greater extent of switching party groups in the last column of table 6.8 may represent a growing number of swing voters, or it may just be an artifact of the method of calculation that ignores those individuals who move between voting and not voting.

considerably more modest rise than between 1928 and 1930 – had been unknown.

If the speed and enormity with which the Nazi Party attracted its voters was unprecedented, was their social composition and previous political allegiances equally so? In other words, did the Nazi electorate represent a fundamentally new political coalition, drawing voters across social and confessional boundaries in a way that had never been done before? Jürgen Falter has argued strongly for an affirmative answer to this question. Suggesting that the NSDAP was Germany's first "people's party," Falter has noted that "the NSDAP was the first larger party in the history of German elections that was able to overcome the milieus defined by traditional sociopolitical conflicts." The crux of such an assertion is Falter's estimate that in the three general elections of 1930 and 1932, about 39% of the Nazi voters were workers, 19% salaried employees and civil servants, and 42% independent businesmen and farmers.[34]

Even accepting the validity of Falter's estimates (and, as we have noted above, there are clearly problems with them), the question arises of whether the results they represented were unprecedented.[35] The SPD of 1912, whose 29% of eligible voters, was just two percentage points below the Nazi peak in the general elections of 1932, was also a political party with a socially varied electorate: 54% workers, 41% from the urban middle class (including independent businessmen, professionals, salaried employees and civil servants), and 4% farmers. If we note, following Falter's definition of social categories, that many of the workers who voted for the Nazis were farm laborers, and that farmers were probably disproportionately over-represented in his category of "independent businessmen and farmers," we could suggest that the SPD of 1912 and the NSDAP of 1932 were both people's parties, drawing support from a wide range of social groups, but that the two parties' respective strengths and weaknesses were complementary. The Nazis were a good deal more successful among farm voters than the SPD ever had been, and the Wilhelmine SPD had more support in large cities, from both the working-class and middle-class electorate, than the Nazis could obtain.[36]

Another example of a political grouping with a wide range of support would be the liberal political parties, which together averaged a respectable 21% of eligible voters in the three last elections of Imperial Germany.

[34] Falter, "War die NSDAP die erste deutsche Volkspartei?" pp. 42, 45.
[35] While the problems noted above occur in Falter's estimates of the votes of each social group by confession, he obtains his estimate for each social group as a whole by combining his confessionally specific estimates, so that if there are problems with these, then there will be problems with their combination.
[36] On the Nazis as a party whose core voting support was in the Protestant farming population, cf. Winkler, *Sozialstruktur*, pp. 376–79.

This liberal electorate was composed of some 34% workers, 42% urban middle class, and 23% farmers (see table 3.7), a social composition probably very similar to the electorate of the NSDAP. Indeed, Falter's own figures suggest that in the early years of the Weimar Republic, the liberal parties and especially the conservative DNVP had a broad basis of support in different social groups.[37]

Another important element of representativeness of any political party – especially a German one – and of its ability to attract voters across the boundaries of milieus is the confessional composition of its electorate. In 1932, according to Falter's figures, some 83% of the Nazi voters were Protestants and 17% Catholics. This figure, little different from the 85% of SPD voters in 1912 who were Protestant and 15% Catholic, marks the NSDAP as a political party of the era of strong confessional differences in the German electorate. It did not have the interconfessional appeal of the National Liberals, in this respect the champion party of the *Kaiserreich*, with an electorate some 75% Protestant and 25% Catholic. Among its contemporaries, the NSDAP could not match the inter-confessionality of the communists, whose calls for atheistic revolution resonated among both nominally (very nominally, one assumes) Protestant and Catholic voters, bringing them an electorate with a confessional composition about the same as that of the National Liberals in the *Kaiserreich*.[38] None of these results can compare with the way the confessions have mixed at the ballot box in the Federal Republic. There, between 60% and 65% of the CDU/CSU's voters have been Catholic, while Protestants have made up between 60% and 70% of the electorate of the other major parties.

To reinforce his description of the Nazis as a people's party – one that could draw voters across the lines of milieus – Falter has noted that about a quarter of the Nazi voters in the general elections of 1930, the year of the party's great breakthrough, had voted for either one of the labor parties (mostly the SPD) or the Center and the BVP in the previous elections of 1928. This too, was not unprecedented: my estimates are that

[37] Falter and Zintl, "The Economic Crisis of the 1930s and the Nazi Vote," p. 74. In "War die NSDAP die erste deutsche Volkspartei?" Falter presents a "people's party index" that purports to show that the Nazis had the most representative electorate of any German party for the general elections from 1928 to 1933 (p.36). However, from 1930 to 1932 the Nazi index of representativeness is either equalled or surpassed by the DNVP and the left-liberal DDP, a party on the verge of dissolution, something that should cause one to wonder about the index's validity.

[38] Calculated from figures on the communist vote by confession in Falter and Zintl," The Economic Crisis of the 1930s," p. 77, and on the confessional composition of the German population in Falter et al., *Wahlen und Abstimmungen in der Weimarer Republik*, p. 88. Falter's figures show that a slightly greater percentage of Catholics voted for the labor parties – SPD and KPD – than for the Nazis in the general elections of 1930 and 1932.

22% of the liberal voters in the Hottentot elections of 1907 had voted in 1903 either for the SPD or one of the minority parties. In fact, if we compare the Nazi victories with the classic right-wing general elections in the *Kaiserreich*, those of 1887 and 1907, we see no evidence of an increasing movement of voters across the boundaries of political groups. Of the SPD voters of 1884, 13% chose the Kartell parties in 1887; 21% of the SPD voters of 1903 voted for one of the parties of the Bülow bloc in 1907. By contrast, just 8% of the labor party voters of 1928 chose the Nazis in 1930, and 11% of these parties' voters in 1930 did so in the elections of July 1932. Movement away from the Catholic political parties in these victories of the right in the *Kaiserreich* and the Weimar Republic was more modest, and steadier: 8% of the 1884 minority party voters chose one of the Kartell parties in 1887; 11% went from one of those parties to the Bülow bloc in 1907; 9% went from the Center and the BVP to the Nazis in 1930 and 11% in 1932.

In other words, Falter's assertion that the Nazi Party had created an unprecedented electoral coalition, is based on a comparison of his rigorous analytical studies with the vague suppositions about previous elections inherent in Rainer Lepsius's milieu thesis – suppositions, as we have seen, that were largely unproven and almost certainly empirically incorrect. In light of the results on voting in the *Kaiserreich* presented in this book, I find the idea of an unprecedented composition of the Nazi electorate – as against the rapidity with and extent to which it increased – unconvincing. In this respect, more helpful than Lepsius's contention (taken up by Falter) that the Nazis represented an end to the politics of milieus, is Karl Rohe's assertion that the Nazis were the latest manifestation of the "national" camp in German politics.

Most Nazi voters had previously chosen either the liberals or the conservatives, or had been non-voters or supporters of one of the splinter parties, these last two groups themselves made up in large part of former liberal or conservative voters. The social and confessional composition of the Nazi voters – a large proportion of Protestant farmers and of the urban middle class, a somewhat smaller proportion of Protestant workers, and a still smaller group of Catholics – looks less novel when one remembers that both the liberal and the conservative parties had, even in the *Kaiserreich*, attracted an equivalent measure of both Protestant working-class and Catholic support. Finally, the sudden breakthrough of the NSDAP at the polls appears less mysterious if we realize that it did not involve crossing previous lines of allegiance so much as rallying one constituency that had previously been shared, sometimes amicably, sometimes competitively, by two different party groups, both of which, as a consequence of the social, economic, and political crises of the Weimar Republic, had lost the confidence of their voters.[39]

This line of argument is particularly appropriate to understanding the connection of the Nazi Party to the politics of the German Empire. While the pre-1914 anti-Semitic parties certainly anticipated the Nazis in many of their campaign themes, and also, to a certain extent, in their political style, they were most unlike the NSDAP in remaining splinter groups, with a very limited national appeal and, at best, a certain regional basis of support. To be sure, the strongholds of the anti-Semitic movement in the *Kaiserreich*, parts of Hessen and Saxony, were later centers of support for the Nazis, but the latter attracted large numbers of voters across a much greater range of the country. These covered most of the bastions of the liberal (including the left-liberal) and the conservative parties of the empire; in 1932 the Nazis had obtained a share of eligible voters of the order of what all the liberal and conservative parties together reached between 1903 and 1912.[40]

Thus, if we take as characteristic of the rise of Nazism a dynamic, aggressively nationalist and strongly anti-socialist and anti-Catholic mass politics, uniting liberal and conservative voters, and winning over a minority of the labor and Christian party electorate, and ask what in the electoral politics of the *Kaiserreich* showed similar traits, the answer would have to be the campaign of the Bülow bloc parties in the Hottentot elections of 1907. In a sense, Nazism would be the perfection of what these parties were groping towards but unable to reach. Perhaps more cautiously, we could say that if the Bülow bloc was the liberal-conservative, anti-socialist and anti-Catholic mass politics of the Wilhelmine era, while the NSDAP represented the same sort of politics in much sharper, more extreme, more racist and anti-Semitic, and more militarized form, a result of the intervening quarter century of total war, defeat, revolution, and social and economic crisis.

Only after these experiences were the former liberal and conservative voters really fused together into a national voting bloc. It would be an exaggeration to describe Rohe's concept of a national camp in German politics as a projection of the Nazi electorate back onto the politics of the

[39] For a similar interpretation of the rise of Nazism, in the sphere of street demonstrations and political self-representation, see the excellent work of Peter Fritzsche. *Rehearsals for Fascism: Populism and Political Mobilization in Weimar Germany* (Oxford and New York : Oxford University Press, 1990).

[40] At their high point, in the general elections of July 1932, 31% of all eligible voters, 38% of Protestant eligible voters, 16% of Catholic eligible voters and 21% of working-class eligible voters chose the Nazis. Comparable figures for all the liberal and conservative parties together, averaged over the general elections of 1903, 1907, and 1912, are 35% of all eligible voters, 46% of Protestants, 17% of Catholics, and 28% of workers.

Kaiserreich. But it was the Nazis who overcame all the internal differences within such a national voting bloc, as had never really been possible before 1914, and brought such a bloc into existence all across Germany, and not just in certain regions of the country, as had been the case under the empire.

In this respect, we could argue that the rise of the Nazis was a part of the third of three long-term voting trends in Germany, during the era of a democratic franchise. The first was the development of a Catholic bloc, placing a substantial portion of the Catholic electorate behind church-related political parties. Emerging in the 1870s, this bloc has remained in existence ever since in a process of dynamic stability, compensating for losses among some Catholic voters with gains among others, and for modest defeats in some elections with convincing victories at others, and maintaining itself through changes in society, religious practice, the circle of those eligible to vote, and the changing relation of Catholics to the German state or states.

The second trend was the emergence of a labor electorate, about twenty years after the formation of the Catholic bloc. Grouped around a Protestant, working-class core constituency – and one that has remained a core constituency for a good century since 1890 – this labor electorate has had periods of growth (roughly 1887–1919 and 1957–72) and decline (1920–32 and 1972–1990/94), largely a result of its changing fortunes with Catholic working-class and Protestant middle-class voters. These swings have been accompanied by three long-term developments, two favorable and one unfavorable. Gradually increasing levels of support in the core constituency and a declining proportion of the population working in agriculture, an area closed to the labor electorate, have helped the SPD, while the decline of the blue-collar labor force in the past quarter century (more modest in Germany than in other economically advanced countries) has hurt the party's chances at the polls.

The third trend concerns the voters not belonging to either of these two blocs – Protestant farmers, certainly, but members of the Protestant urban working and middle classes, and some Catholics as well. Divided among and fluctuating between the various liberal and conservative parties in the *Kaiserreich*, they were never united behind any one of them. Of all the parties in the *Kaiserreich*, the National Liberals of the 1870s probably came closest to achieving such a unity. The Nazis brought this group together as no party ever had previously. Following the end of the Nazi regime, this group has dissolved as a political bloc, most of its members voting for the CDU/CSU but some for the Social Democrats, with a smaller group – albeit one fluctuating in size (larger in the 1950s and since 1980 than in the intervening decades) – choosing one of the various smaller political parties active in the Federal Republic (one of the neo-Nazi groups, the [liberal] Free Democrats, or the Greens).

Democratic electorates in Germany and elsewhere

Comparing voting trends in Germany and other countries of Europe and North America in the age of the democratic franchise would be an enormous task, a whole book in itself – and one that probably could not be written, given the relative scarcity of ecological analysis of elections in the era before public opinion polling, and the inconsistencies and limitations of survey data. Consequently, the comparisons I can make will be limited and the conclusions to be drawn from them extremely tentative. I have found it possible to make even such limited and tentative comparisons for two main themes: trends in turnout and volatility (percentage of voters switching parties, movements of previous non-voters and the like) on the one hand, and, on the other, the social and confessional bases of voting, particularly for the labor parties.

I have only been able to find long-term estimates of trends in voter movement, comparable to those presented in the previous sections of this chapter, for three countries, the United States, Sweden, and Denmark. Figures from the United States cover the most ground, from the 1850s through the 1960s, but they are generally partial, covering just some states, and sporadic. The results from the two Scandinavian countries, on the other hand, are a good deal more comprehensive, including the entire national territory, and all or most pairs of general elections, but they begin later, since universal manhood suffrage was only introduced in the first decades of the twentieth century. Table 6.9 offers the material from the United States. All the columns give voter transitions between one presidential election and the subsequent one, leaving aside (because not comparable with voting systems in European countries) the movements from presidential to off-year elections.[41]

[41] First two columns calculated from Gienapp, *The Origins of the Republican Party 1852–1856*, pp. 482–85, 527–31 (unweighted averages of the eight states); third column from Allan Lichtman, "Political Realignment and Ethnocultural Voting in Late Nineteenth Century America," *Journal of Social History* 16/3 (Spring 1983): 54–82, esp. p. 63; fourth from Allan Lichtman, *Prejudice and the Old Politics: The Presidential Election of 1928* (Chapel Hill: University of North Carolina Press, 1979), p. 213; final two columns from V. O. Key, *The Responsible Electorate: Rationality in Presidential Voting 1936–1960* ed. Milton C. Cummings, Jr. (Cambridge, MA: Havard University Press, 1966), p. 20 (using figures on pre-election preferences). Paul Kleppner, in his *Continuity and Change in Electoral Politics 1893–1928* (New York: Greenwood Press, 1987), p. 82 n. 23, has criticized Lichtman's estimates for 1896, only his own figures on transitions from 1892 to 1894 and 1894 to 1896 (pp. 79–80) are fairly similar, the main difference being that Kleppner takes into account new voters entering the electorate while Lichtman does not.

Table 6.9 *Voter transitions in the American electorate (percent)*

Vote at two subsequent elections	Presidential election year pairs					
	1848/52 Eight northern states	1852/56 Eight northern states	1892/96 All non-southern states	1924/28 All non-southern states	1936/40–1944/48 All voters	1948/52–1956/60 All voters
Same party	58	28 (56)	77	43	68	60
Switch parties	5	39 (11)	2	13	14	12
Between parties and non-voters	12	8	8	13	18[a]	28[a]
Stay non-voters	11	12	13	31	—[b]	—[b]
New voters	15	14	—[b]	—[b]	—[b]	—[b]
All	101	101	100	100	100	100

Notes:
Figures in parentheses in second column count Free Soil and Whig voters of 1852 as members of same party group as Republican voters in 1856; figures out of parentheses count them as members of different party groups.
[a] Previous non-voters and newly eligible voters choosing a party.
[b] Not calculated.

The figures for the nineteenth century show quite high levels of political participation among American voters. Outside the South, turnouts ranged from 60% to 80% of those eligible; even in the post-Civil War (but pre-Jim Crow) South of the 1870s and 1880s, in spite of unsystematic if often violent efforts to prevent African-Americans from voting, some 60% of adult men went to the polls.[42] Thus American voters, throughout this period, were at least as likely (and generally rather more likely) than their German counterparts to go to the polls. When they did go, their party loyalty was a good deal stronger: the proportion of the electorate staying with the same party over two elections was some twenty to thirty percentage points higher in the North American republic than in the German Empire (see table 6.1). Even the U.S. presidental elections of 1856, generally regarded as a quasi-revolutionary transformation of the party system, setting the stage for the outbreak of the Civil War, seem less of a drastic change, if one counts the Whig and Free Soil voters of 1852 as part of the same political grouping as the Republicans, the party that replaced them at the polls in 1856. It might be objected that the gap of a

[42] An overview of political participation in the post-bellum south in Paul Kleppner, *Who Voted? The Dynamics of Electoral Turnout, 1870–1980* (New York: Praeger Publishers, 1982), pp. 18–19; a detailed analysis in Kousser, *The Shaping of Southern Politics:*.

half-century between the 1852/56 and 1892/96 pairs could conceal all kinds of political gyrations. Dale Baum has developed voter transition estimates for every pair of presidential elections in Massachusetts between 1856/60 and 1904/1908: his figures show that an average of just 5% of the electorate switched parties between any two subsequent elections.[43] Massachusetts is, of course, not the whole United States, and there were undoubtedly greater voter movements in other states or regions, particularly in connection with the rise and decline of third parties, but these figures do suggest something of the extraordinary stability of the American electoral system in the late nineteenth century.[44] Such strong party loyalties among American voters do cast doubt on the idea, implicit in Rainer Lepsius's theory of sociomoral milieus, that German voters in the *Kaiserreich* were unusually and undemocratically rigid in their voting choices.

The last three columns, showing American voting in the twentieth century, show the gradual development of a somewhat greater movement among voters between political parties; although I have not been able to find any figures directly bearing on it, this has certainly increased since the 1960s. The elections of 1928, which almost certainly had an unusually high proportion of voters shifting parties – in view of the campaign of a major third-party candidate in 1924, but not in 1928, and the unprecedented circumstance of the Democrats nominating a Catholic presidential candidate – brought party loyalty and vote-switching among American voters to about the point where they had been for German voters in the Wilhelmine era. The Weimar electorate, in contrast, was a good deal more unstable (see table 6.8). After the Second World War, the ratio of voters staying with the same party to those switching parties was about the same in the United States as in the Federal Republic.

If voting patterns in the United States and Germany have, in this respect, converged, they have diverged in another. Turnout in twentieth-century German general elections has been consistently high, ranging from 75% to 90% of eligible voters. In American presidential elections, on the other hand, it has declined almost continuously, from some

[43] Dale Baum, *The Civil War Party System: The Case of Massachusetts, 1848–1876* (Chapel Hill and London: University of North Carolina Press, 1984), p. 21. The maximum proportions switching were 15% in 1860 and 10% in 1864; after the Civil War, the proportion switching never rose above 8%, reaching low points (0% and 1% respectively) in 1868 and 1904.
[44] In table 6.9, the Populist voters of 1892, who voted for the Democratic–Populist fusion candidate of 1896 are counted as having stayed with the same party group; if they were counted as shifting parties, the percentage of voters staying with the same party would just decline to 73% and the percentage switching parties would increase to 6%.

Table 6.10a *Voter transitions in twentieth-century Scandinavian elections: Sweden (percent)*

	General election pairs				
Vote at two subsequent elections	1911/1914(1)-1914(2)/1917	1917/20–1921/24	1924/28–1936/40	1944/48	1964/68
Same party group	46	35	50	60	72
Switch party groups	7	9	7	9	9
Between parties and non-voters	26	26	22	17	11
Stay non-voters	21	30	21	14	8
All	100	100	100	100	100

75–80% at the beginning of the century to around 50% at the end, with just a modest increase over the years 1932–60.[45]

Table 6.10 provides estimates of voter movements in twentieth-century Danish and Swedish elections.[46]

Voters in Scandinavian countries have shown very high levels of party loyalty throughout most of the era of democratic suffrage, with the number of voters staying with their parties outnumbering those switching by margins of between 4 and 15:1. This is a particularly remarkable result considering that the system of proportional representation used in both Sweden and Denmark, with many parties on the ballot across the entire country, makes it particularly easy for voters to cross party lines. The contrast between the steady Scandinavian electorates and their more volatile German counterpart is particularly pronounced in the decades of the 1920s and 1930s. After the Second World War, on the other hand, party loyalty in German increased, while, in Denmark at least, it declined, leading to a gradual convergence in the pattern of voter transitions.[47]

I am rather reluctant to draw drastic conclusions from such frag-

[45] Kleppner, *Who Voted?*, p. 112 and passim.
[46] Figures for Sweden are from Sten Berglund, Søren Risbjerg Thomsen, and Ingemar Wörlund, "The Mobilization of the Swedish Vote. An Ecological Analysis of the General Elections of 1928, 1948 and 1968," in Berglund and Thomsen (eds.) *Modern Political Ecological Analysis*, pp. 63–77, esp. pp. 73–75, and, by the same authors, "The Mobilization of the Swedish Electorate (1911–1940)," in ibid., pp. 78–90, esp. pp. 80–85; for Denmark, calculated from Thomsen, *Danish Elections*, pp. 143–86 (eliminating voters who died between elections). I have identified party groups as the individual political parties, except that I have grouped the Social Democrats together with the smaller left-socialist and communist parties as labor parties.
[47] On the (relatively) drastic change in political scenery introduced by the Danish elections of 1973, see Thomsen, *Danish Elections*, p. 90.

Table 6.10b *Voter transitions in twentieth-century Scandinavian elections: Denmark (percent)*

Vote at two subseqent elections	General election pairs					
	1920/24–1926–29	1929/32–1935/39	1939/43–1947/50	1950/53(1)–1957/60	1960/64–1968/71	1971/73–1977/79
Same party group	63	62	63	68	69	60
Switch party groups	4	5	9	5	8	18
Between parties and non-voters	11	9	11	9	8	11
Stay non-voters	14	12	8	11	7	6
New voters	9	12	8	6	8	6
All	101	100	99	99	100	101

mentary material. In particular, it would be helpful to have comparable figures from elections in France, the country with the longest history of universal manhood suffrage. Still, these figures do suggest that in the late nineteenth and first half of the twentieth centuries German voters were not unusually static or limited in their choices of party. Quite the opposite, they appear to have been more unstable than their counterparts in other countries under democratic suffrage regimes, more willing to cross party boundaries. By the 1960s and 1970s, German voters' propensity to cross party lines seems to have been about at the level of their Scandinavian and American counterparts. It is hard to say if these cases represent a broader trend toward a levelling out of voter movements among the parties in North America and Western Europe. Some scattered survey data, unfortunately analyzed incompatibly with the figures cited above, suggest that they do.[48]

Other countries, however, seem to show different patterns. In Great Britain, for instance, in the seven general elections held between 1964 and 1983, an average of just 46% of the voters chose the same party at two consecutive elections, 13% switched parties, 31% voted in one but not the other of the two consecutive elections, and 11% were persistent non-voters. Party loyalties were thus weaker in the UK and non-voting more common than in most of continental Europe. (It is not impossible that

[48] Ian Budge and Dennis Farlie, *Voting and Party Competition: A Theoretical Critique and Synthesis Applied to Surveys from Ten Democracies* (London and New York: John Wiley & Sons, 1977), p. 282.

voter movements in the United States at this time would have been similar.) Italian voters, at least until quite recently, seem to have stuck with their parties, or if they moved, they did so only between politically related groups, such as the communists and the socialists. In the Netherlands, a considerable stability of voting patterns in the 1950s gave way to much heavier switching among the voters in the 1970s, reaching the very high figure of 35% of the entire electorate in the general elections of 1972. In any event, German voters do not seem to have occupied an extreme position, either with regard to mobility or stability, since the Second World War.[49]

One of the reasons that material on this topic is so scattered and hard to find is that post-1945 studies of the electorate are generally based on public opinion polling, and, to put it bluntly, a lot of people lie to the pollsters about not having voted, thus rendering polling-based estimates of turnout very unreliable. Survey data on voting by social or confessional characteristics, on the other hand, are less subject to such difficulties. Table 6.11, bringing together ecological analysis and survey results, offers some figures on the proportion of workers who voted for labor parties in Western Europe and for the Democrats in the United States, in the twentieth century. The entry in each cell is the percentage of votes cast by blue-collar workers for such parties. It would have been nice to have been able to give the more relevant percentage of eligible voters, but, as just noted, such information is often not available from the polls. The figures in parentheses under the entries give the years of the elections, when they do not span the entire period under consideration.[50]

There are two observations that can be made about this table, one general point and one concerning Germany in particular. First, the numbers in table 6.11 are a critical commentary on an idea common

[49] Richard Rose, *Voters Begin to Choose: From Closed-Class to Open Elections in Britain* (London and Beverly Hills: SAGE Publications, 1986), p. 152; Samuel H. Barnes, "Secular Trends and Partisan Realingnment in Italy," in Russell J. Dalton, Scott C. Flanagan, and Paul Allen Beck (eds.) *Electoral Change in Advanced Industrial Democracies: Realignment or Dealignment?* (Princeton: Princeton University Press, 1984), pp. 205–30, esp. pp. 218–21, and Galen Irwin and Karl Dittrich, "And the Walls Came Tumbling Down: Party Dealignment in the Netherlands," in ibid., pp. 267–97, esp. p. 288.

[50] Sources for table 6.11: sources cited in nn. 21, 41, and 46; and Herbert Döring, "Wählen Industriearbeiter zunehmend konservativ? Die Bundesrepublik Deutschland im westeuropäischen Vergleich," *Archiv für Sozialgeschichte* 29 (1989): 225–71, esp. p. 235; Adam Przeworski and John Sprague, *Paper Stones: A History of Electoral Socialism* (Chicago and London: University of Chicago Press, 1986), pp. 150–53; Herbert Kitschelt, *The Transformation of European Social Democracy* (Cambridge and New York: Cambridge University Press, 1994), p. 44; Paul Abramson, John H. Aldrich, and David W. Rohde, *Change and Continuity in the 1980 Elections* (Washington, DC: Congressional Quarterly Press, 1982), pp. 98, 105, 110; Gerald Pomper et al., *The Election of 1988: Reports and Interpretations* (Chatham, NJ: Chatham House Publishers, 1989), pp. 133–34.

Table 6.11 *Working-class voters and labor parties in twentieth-century Europe and North America (percent)*

	General election years				
Country	1900–19	1920–49	1950–69	1970–79	Since 1980
Germany	43 (1903–12)	53 (1920–32)	54	53	53 (1980–87)
Sweden	65 (1911–17)	71	78	68	—
Denmark	—	84	79	77	—
France	—	—	47 (1956–68) 67 (1950s)	67 (1976–79)	51 (1984–87)
Italy	—	—	71 (1950s)	66 (1976–79)	64 (1984–87)
UK	—	—	65 (1950s)	54 (1976–79)	42 (1984–87)
USA	—	c.70[a] (1944–48)	c.55[a]	c. 43[a] (1972–80)	47[b] (1984–88)

Notes:
[a] White workers, only.
[b] All workers.
A dash indicates that no information is available.

among historians and social scientists, the notion of a golden age of class consciousness: a time, sometime before the First World War, or perhaps the Second, when workers were workers, the bourgeoisie were the bourgeoisie, and classes knew where they stood – and acted politically in appropriate fashion. Since then, the argument continues (sometimes made with nostalgia for the "good old days", sometimes with manifest pleasure at their disappearance), class distinctions have blurred, with the workers owning cars and the bourgeoisie wearing jeans; and other contrasts – say of race and gender, or between different value systems – have come to dominate citizens' consciousness and political life.[51]

Yet, if we take as one modest measure of the political expression of class consciousness the proportion of workers voting for a labor party, the figures in table 6.11 provide no support for such an idea. In the three

[51] A particularly elegant formulation of this view can be found in Eric Hobsbawm, *The Age of Extremes: A History of the World, 1914–1991* (New York: Pantheon Books, 1994), pp. 305–10.

countries for which estimates reach back to the beginning of the century, the proportion of workers casting their ballot for a labor party has shown no long term decrease. If we remember that turnouts were noticeably lower at the beginning of the century (one estimate, for instance, is that it was not until 1928 that over half of Swedish workers voted in a general election), then the proportion of eligible working-class voters choosing a labor party has actually substantially increased over the course of the century. Although no one has done regression estimates of class-based voting in France or Great Britain before the beginning of the public opinion polling era around 1950, it seems likely from the relatively modest vote totals that the Labour Party and the French socialists and communists received before the Second World War, that the percentage of working-class voters choosing such parties must have generally been lower than after 1945.[52]

In this general context, what stands out for Germany is the relative stability of the working-class vote, with slightly over half of it cast for labor parties since the First World War, and slightly less than half for other parties. (Remember that we are talking here about the percentage of votes cast for a labor party, not, as in table 6.5, about the percentage of eligible voters: with rising turnout, this measure of working-class support for the labor parties has increased.) German workers have never shown Scandinavian levels of support for the labor parties, but their loyalty to them has also never consistently sagged below 50%, as has been the case with French workers in the glory days of Charles De Gaulle, with workers in the period of Republican domination of American politics since 1968, or with British workers in the age of Margaret Thatcher. This has been primarily the result of confessional divisions within German society, with Protestant workers' support for the labor parties consistently a bit less than that of their Scandinavian counterparts, while only a minority, if at times a substantial one, of Catholic workers ever choosing such parties.

The German labor parties were thus limited in their working-class support. But unlike their counterparts in Sweden, who did very well among agricultural and forest laborers, or in France and Italy, whose support from small peasants, tenant farmers and agricultural laborers was regionally very substantial, the countryside remained almost off limits to the SPD and its successor or rival parties – a politically decisive

---

[52] The one country for which such an argument might hold is the United States, although, of course, the Democrats were not (and are not) a political party comparable to European social democratic, communist or labor parties. Even in the US, in view of the substantial working-class vote for the Republicans before the New Deal era, one would have to wonder how a comparison between the first and the last decades of the century would turn out.

fact in the first half of the twentieth century, when farmers were still a substantial proportion of the labor force in most advanced, industrial economies. There were other countries, such as Denmark, where the farming population resolutely rejected the labor movement, but there the Social Democrats did unusually well among craftsmen and small businessmen, and salaried employees.[53] The SPD enjoyed comparable levels of support from these social groups before the First World War – but only among Protestants; in the Weimar Republic, the labor parties' attraction for the entire middle-class sector of both confessions seems to have declined.

It is the combination of these two elements, an electorate powerfully divided along confessional lines, with a labor party that could only obtain a modest foothold outside the working class, that were unique to Germany before 1933.[54] They stem from the two major facts of popular politics in the *Kaiserreich*: first, the dominant reality of the Bismarckian era, the creation of an authoritarian German national-state as a result of warfare that Catholics lost and Protestants won, leading to the division of the electorate into confessional blocs, with fundamentally different attitudes toward the nation-state. This division limited the possibilities for the SPD, not just among Catholic voters, but among Protestants (including working-class Protestant nationalists) as well. The second was the centrality of the agrarian issue to the electoral politics of Wilhelmine Germany, that would shut the SPD out of the farmers' vote and bring it Protestant, urban middle-class support – a support, however, that was tied primarily to this issue and so declined substantially with the coming to the fore of other social and economic questions in German politics after the First World War.

It is precisely this group of voters, nominally Protestant and nationalist, opposed on confessional grounds to the Catholics and their Center Party,

[53] On these points, see Lewin, Jansson, and Sörbom, *The Swedish Electorate*, pp. 142–45; Laird Boswell, "The French Rural Communist Electorate," *Journal of Interdisciplinary History* 23 (1992/93): 719–49; Dogan, "Political Cleavage and Social Stratification in France and Italy," in Lipset and Rokkan (eds.) *Party Systems and Voter Alignments*, pp. 129–95, esp. pp. 141–50; Thomsen, *Danish Elections*, p. 97.
[54] Smaller countries with a confessionally mixed population, such as Switzerland or the Netherlands, have experienced similar forms of confessional division at the electorate. Among the countries listed in table 6.11, only the United States has had similar confessional divisions to that of Germany, and while Catholics in the US have generally preferred the Democratic Party and white Protestants have preferred the Republicans, the confessional division of the electorate has been less sharp than in Germany, with the possible exceptions of the presidential elections of 1928 and 1960, when the Democratic Party nominated Catholic candidates. On this point, cf. Gienapp, *Origins of the Republican Party*. p. 540; Baum, *The Civil War Party System*, p. 91; Kleppner, *Continuity and Change in Electoral Politics*, pp. 189–90; Lichtman, *Prejudice and the Old Politics*, passim; and Abramson, Aldrich, and Rohde, *The Elections of 1980*, p. 105.

distant for both economic and ideological reasons from the labor movement, that was both unique to Germany and formed the core of the Nazi constituency. In making this observation, I do not mean to assert that Nazism was an inevitable result of either Bismarck's policies of blood and iron or of the agitation of the Agrarian League. It would take the First World War, with its militarization of everyday life, the German Revolution of 1918/19, and its disruption of the accustomed political life of the empire, the virtually permanent economic crisis of the years 1919–32, and the inability of the politicians of the Weimar Republic to do anything about it, to unite a group of voters that had previously voted for often mutually hostile liberal and conservative or splinter parties behind a fascist political movement. Nonetheless, the group of voters so united was a product of the political and constitutional regime of the German Empire.

In this respect, the second half of the twentieth century has decisively changed German electoral politics. The decline of the agricultural population, the creation of an interconfessional CDU/CSU, and the resulting dissolution of the Protestant-nationalist bloc of German voters has created a new political situation, one rather more like that of other European countries, where a majority of blue-collar voters and a minority of middle-class ones vote for a labor party (or, more recently, a left-wing environmentalist party), and the other portions of the electorate choose, in varying proportions, right-of-center liberal, conservative or Christian Democratic ones.[55] Other elements of older voting patterns, particularly the confessional division of the electorate, remain, albeit in weakened form, but in a number of crucial respects the era of the Kaiser's voters has come to a close.

[55] For figures of the non-proletarian vote for labor parties since the Second World War, showing a gradual convergence between different European countries, see Przeworski and Sprague, *Paper Stones*, pp. 150–53.

Technical appendix

In this appendix, I first discuss the nature of the sources used to develop the estimates of voting given in the body of this book. Then I outline the different mathematical methods that can be used in ecological regression and explain the specific choices I made in order to derive the estimates. Finally, I present tables giving the basic results of the different regression equations and fitting procedures, so that readers can check my interpretations of them and develop their own.

Sources

The election returns

Constituency-level election returns for each general election in Imperial Germany were published in one of the official state statistical publications, either the *Statistik des Deutschen Reiches* or the *Vierteljahrsschrift zur Statistik des Deutschen Reiches*.[1] I consulted these materials directly, and developed my electronic database by entering them into the computer. Of course, the validity of calculations on the returns and inferences about the voters drawn from them depends on the honesty and reliability of the election returns.

The count in the Reichstag elections appears generally to have been an honest one, formal and informal institutional arrangements allowing for a good deal of oversight. If German elections were probably less marked by fraud than, say, ones in America at the same time, intimidation was another matter. In many constituencies and at many elections, secrecy of the ballot was more nominal than real; government officials, clergy, employers, and other influential parties found ways to know who voted for whom and the voters knew that they knew it. Protests about intimidation of voters constantly came before the Reichstag committees charged

---

[1] A complete list of the specific volumes in which the returns have been published is conveniently available in Ritter and Niehuss (eds.) *Wahlgeschichtliches Arbeitsbuch*, pp. 183–84.

with validating members' credentials and these committees frequently annulled results because of the intimidation of voters. Thus, all I can say is that the vote may have been counted honestly, but it may not always have reflected the voters' convictions.[2]

Going from honesty to adequacy, the tabulation of the published election returns demonstrate the precision, comprehensiveness, and reliability classically associated with German bureaucracy. The returns are complete and internally consistent. If one sums up the votes cast for the individual parties, plus the number of scattered and invalid votes, one obtains exactly the figure for the total number of votes cast, in each constituency and at every election – an impressive result when all the arithmetic had to be done by hand. Of course, a problem arises here as well: the *Statistisches Reichsamt* that performed the tabulations had to use the figures sent in by local officials.

These officials did not just have to send in the returns, but were responsible for two other key pieces of information: the number of eligible voters and their confessional composition. Hermann Hiery, whose book on the Reichstag elections in Alsace-Lorraine includes an excellent account of the mechanics of voting and vote counting, has noted that the municipal government of Strasbourg was not up to the task of keeping the electoral register. Failing to purge the deceased and departed voters from the rolls, it grossly exaggerated the number of eligible voters and hence depressed the turnout rate.[3] However, in the regressions used to calculate, for instance, the percentage of Catholics and Protestants who were non-voters, the constituency of Strasbourg-city persistently appears as an outlier, an observation where the proportion of non-voters is much higher than would be expected according to the overall relationship, and is generally the only (or one of the few) observation to appear as such. This suggests that the incompetence of the municipal officials of Strasbourg was an exception rather than the rule.

The other point that needs to be cleared up concerns the question of the confessional composition of the electorate. The figures given in the official statistics are the proportion of the entire population in each constituency who are Catholic or Protestant, rather than the proportion of eligible voters. In his pioneering study of Catholic voters and the Center Party from the 1920s, Johannes Schauff suggested that because Catholics had a higher birth rate than Protestants, and hence a larger proportion of the population under voting age, these figures tend to underestimate the pro-

---

[2] On these points, see Suval, *Electoral Politics*, ch. 3; Anderson, "Voter, Junker, *Landrat*, Priest"; and Hiery, *Reichstagswahlen im Reichsland*, pp. 401–25.

[3] Hiery, *Reichstagswahlen im Reichsland*, pp. 116–18.

portion of Catholics in the actual electorate.[4] Most subsequent historians, if they have considered this issue at all, have accepted Schaff's assertions. The Catholic birth-rate may have been somewhat higher than the Protestant one, especially in Wilhelmine Germany, but one could imagine countervailing factors, such as higher infant mortality rates, different rates of emigration, differing proportions of non-citizens, or even differing proportions of women. We cannot tell directly because censuses in the *Kaiserreich* never cross-tabulated the population by confession and age. The statistical material on the elections, however, allows an indirect investigation. For most elections, the proportion of Catholics and Protestants (including Jews and others) in each constituency is given, along with the proportion of the population that was eligible to vote. By using the methods of ecological inference (see the next section), it is possible to develop estimates of the proportion of each confession eligible to vote.

For all the data prior to 1905 (the last year for which there are published figures), the estimates show that the proportion of Catholics eligible to vote was as high, or sometimes even slightly higher than the proportion of Protestants. The figures for 1905 – 21.1% Catholics eligible to vote as against 22.3% of Protestants – are fairly close to Schauff's estimates. However, the regression did not produce a very good fit, the coefficient of determination (R^2) just 0.069. I tried something different, dividing the constituencies into two groups: those in eastern Germany with a large ethnic Polish population, and the rest of the empire. The regression for the heavily Polish areas had a much higher R^2 of 0.303. Estimates derived from it showed that in these areas only 18.6% of Catholics were eligible to vote, but 21.2% of non-Catholics. For the rest of Germany, the R^2 was very low, only 0.012, and the estimates were that 21.8% of Catholics and 22.3% of non-Catholics were eligible to vote.

In short, there was no difference in the proportion of the different confessions eligible to vote, except perhaps in the last peacetime decade of the empire, and then almost all the difference in the percentage of eligible voters among the confessions was attributable to the ethnically Polish population. Schauff's procedure of attributing this difference to all Catholics and to the whole history of the empire is incorrect. The simplest thing to do, and what I have done, is just to use the figures on the confessional composition of each constituency as they are without any adjustment.

This investigation of the published election returns suggests that they

---

[4] Schauff, *Das Wahlverhalten der deutschen Katholiken*, pp. 71–74.

are fairly reliable and can be taken at face value. The only remaining issue is the attribution of the votes in each constituency to different political parties. There is evidence that in scattered cases these were not always correct; especially in the 1871 elections, the Social Democrats seem to have been undercounted. I have not attempted to make any corrections to the returns, since nothing suggests that errors were widespread. In entering the returns into the computer, I have used the following combinations of parties.

(1) The party group "conservatives" or "right" includes the Conservatives, Free Conservatives, Christian-Social Welfare Party, the various anti-Semitic parties, the Agrarian League, the *Wirtschaftliche Vereinigung*, and the various *Mittelstand* candidates.

(2) Besides the National Liberals themselves, I have included under the National Liberals, smaller moderate liberal groupings, such as the *Liberale Reichspartei* or the Löwe-Kalbe caucus, all "National Catholic," "National Labor Party" and generically "National" candidates, as well as otherwise undesignated "Liberal" candidates.

(3) The left-liberals include votes cast for the Progressives, the German People's Party, the National Liberal Secession of 1881, the Radical Party (*Deutsch-Freisinnige Partei*) and its offshoots, the Radical People's Party (*Freisinnige Volkspartei*) and the Radical Alliance (*Freisinnige Vereinigung*), the National-Social Welfare Party (*National-Sozialer Verein*), the Progressive People's Party and the Democratic Alliance, as well as any generically progressive or radical candidates.

(4) The minority parties include the Center; the Hanoverian particularists, or Guelphs, as they were commonly known, as well as other, smaller, particularist groups; the French, Danish, Polish, Lithuanian, and Masurian nationalists; and the Bavarian Peasant League.[5] A fair case could actually be made for including the last named party with the liberals, but when all is said and done, placing it with the parties of the religious, national, and regional minorities seems more appropriate.

(5) The Social Democrats include the General German Workers' Association (Lassalleans), the Social Democratic Labor Party (Eisenachers), the Socialist Labor Party of Germany, the party that emerged from their unity congress in 1875, and the Social Democratic Party of German (SPD), as the party called itself from 1891 onwards. Also included here is the labor party of the Saar Basin miners that ran its own candidates in 1890.

---

[5] I have counted votes for the Center Party of Alsace-Lorraine as cast for the national Center Party, rather than for one of the French nationalist or autonomist groups.

(6) As noted in the introduction, non-voters also include those who cast scattered or invalid ballots, these last two a very small proportion of the electorate.

One final problem remains, namely what to do about candidates who stood for office as independents, representing no party. Sometimes, one sees a pattern in which one party, the National Liberals say, have a large majority in a constituency at one election, an independent has an equally large majority at the next, and the National Liberals do again at the third. In such cases, I have counted the independent candidate as really belonging to the surrounding party. Otherwise, I have entered the votes for such independents under the rubric of the Free Conservatives.

The census data

If using the election returns was relatively straightforward, the same cannot be said for the census data, which required a good deal of manipulation before it was in a form appropriate for the regression analysis. There were three main problems that had to be solved: (1) arranging the census and election returns into geographically identical units; (2) extracting from the occupational and industrial censuses of 1895 and 1907 that portion of the population eligible to vote; (3) dividing the eligible voters by class and confession.

The first problem was the most straightforward. I compared the boundaries of the Reichstag constituencies with those of the units used in the census returns.[6] Since the latter were larger or the same size as the former, to obtain comparable units I had to combine Reichstag constituencies. For Prussia and Bavaria, this involved grouping together all the constituencies in a *Regierungsbezirk*, for the medium-size states of Baden, Württemberg, Saxony, and Hessen-Darmstadt, as well as Alsace-Lorraine, it involved a grouping by similar units (which went by different names in the different states), although additionally, several of these units had to be combined together; for the smaller states and the Hanseatic cities, the entire state was the unit needed for comparison. After all the combining was done, I had seventy-seven such units for the 1895 census and seventy-eight for the 1907 census. (The difference arose from the creation of an additional Prussian *Regierungsbezirk* – Allenstein – in the province of East Prussia in the intervening years.)

Once this was done, I turned to the task of extracting the eligible voters from the census returns. The first step, eliminating women (who were

---

[6] Boundaries of the constituencies are given in *Vierteljahrshefte zur Statistik des Deutschen Reiches* 16, 3 (1907): 84–118. The figures on the confessional composition of the constituencies according to the 1905 census can also be found there.

ineligible to vote), was simple since both the 1895 and 1907 commercial and industrial censuses consistently offered figures differentiated by sex. The next step, eliminating men under the age of twenty-five, active duty soldiers, and those receiving poor relief, living in asylums or in prison, was not too much more difficult. For the population engaged in agriculture, forestry, and fishery; manufacturing, mining and crafts; commerce, transportation and finance; and domestic service and miscellaneous day labor (the "A," "B," "C," and "D" categories of the German census), the census offered figures categorized by age and sex. These occupations were also broken down by social standing, distinguishing independent owners of a business or farm, salaried employees, and wage earners (the "a," "b," and "c" categories of the German census). For Prussia and Bavaria, the figures on the population by age were only available at the level of the province or larger unit, each containing several *Regierungsbezirke*, but it seemed reasonable enough to assume that the age distribution of the population of each province would not differ very much in each *Regierungsbezirk*.[7]

For the "E" group of the census, those in the professions, the army, and state service, this same procedure would have been inappropriate, since it would have included a number of active duty soldiers over the age of twenty-five who were not eligible to vote. In this case, what I did was to subtract from the male members of the "E" group all the active duty soldiers, and assume that everyone remaining was eligible to vote. This procedure has two small problems: the census category of active duty soldiers included the paramilitary police, the gendarmerie, who were eligible to vote (although this eligibility had long been legally in doubt and definitive court rulings were only issued after 1900); the remaining civilian members of this group might have included some men under twenty-five who would not have been eligible to vote. Both groups, however, would not have been very large, so the distortions introduced here are slight.[8]

The last category, those not gainfully employed (the "F" group in the German census), presented another problem. The returns did distinguish members of this group by sex, but not by age. What I did in this case was to divide the group by the census's sub-categories. I assumed that all the men in the sub-category of "rentier," that is, persons living off their capital or receiving a government pension, were eligible to vote, while the men in the other categories – secondary school and university students

---

[7] Figures for 1895 in *Statistik des Deutschen Reiches* n.s. vol. 106; for 1907 in ibid., n.s. vol. 206. The age breakdown in 1895 includes the category 20–30 years, so I have assumed that one-half of those in this category were eligible.

[8] On the question of whether gendarmes counted as active duty soldiers or not, see Hiery, *Reichstagswahlen im Reichsland*, p. 118.

not living with their families, and inmates of jails, poor houses, and asylums for the insane and retarded – were ineligible. This procedure might incorrectly include a few wealthy young men under the age of twenty-five as eligible, and exclude some older students, but once again the inaccuracies introduced would be extremely slight.[9]

Putting all these results together, I was able to obtain for each of the seventy-seven or seventy-eight units the number of men eligible to vote for each of the occupational and social categories, that is, the number of agricultural proprietors eligible to vote, the number of industrial workers, of commercial and financial salaried employees, and so on. What remained was to divide each of these categories by confession, and this presented some difficulties. For the smaller states, where the unit of observation was the entire state, there was no problem; the figures on occupations and the social groups within them were also divided by confession.[10] For the larger states of the empire, on the other hand, the figures on the population by confession were only given by province (as in Prussia) or by still larger units (Bavaria), or for the entire state, while the figures on the population by *Regierungsbezirk* did not include any material on confession.[11] This had also been the case with the division of the population by age, and I found it unproblematic to assume that the age-distribution of the population across an entire province or smaller state was constant; such an assumption, however, would have been impossible for confession. To take one example, the Prussian province of Westphalia was divided into the heavily Roman Catholic (about 90%) *Regierungsbezirk* of Münster, the predominantly Protestant (about 66%) *Regierungsbezirk* of Minden, and the *Regierungsbezirk* of Arnsberg, where the population was fairly evenly divided between Catholics and Protestants. A similar point could be made about the subdivisions in the Province of Silesia, with Oppeln, heavily Catholic, Liegnitz mostly Protestant, and Breslau about equally divided by confession.

Consequently, I had to devise a way to estimate the proportion of the population of each occupational and social group in each *Regierungsbezirk* belonging to each confession. I knew the proportion of the entire popula-

---

[9] The 1895 census figures for the city of Berlin, in *Statistik des Deutschen Reiches* n.s. 108 (1897): 15–16, do not give a breakdown of the "F" group by sub-categories. I have assumed that the proportion of members of this group eligible to vote in 1895 was the same as it was in 1907, the census of that year providing a breakdown of the sub-categories.

[10] For the figures on the population by confession, see the source given in note 6 above.

[11] These detailed breakdowns of the population are in *Statistik des Deutschen Reiches* n.s. 104 (Prussia, except for the city of Berlin, 1895); n.s. 105 (other larger states, 1895); n.s. 108 (city of Berlin, 1895); n.s. 204 (all of Prussia, including the city of Berlin, 1907); and n.s. 205 (other larger states, 1907).

tion in each *Regierungsbezirk* belonging to each confession, and, since provinces were made up of these *Regierungsbezirke*, I also knew the proportion of the population in each province made up of each confession.[12] In addition, the census figures told the proportion of the population in each occupational and social group in any province that belonged to each confession. Assuming that the ratio between the confessional proportions of the entire population of the *Regierungsbezirk* and the province was the same as was that of the specific occupational and social groups, I was able to calculate the latter.

Expressed mathematically, this procedure is very simple. Let "A_r" be the proportion of members of a given social and occupational group in a *Regierungsbezirk* belonging to a given confession (say the percentage of agricultural laborers who are Catholic) and "A_p" be that same proportion in the entire province. Let "W_r" be the proportion of the entire population in the *Regierungsbezirk* belonging to the same confession, and "W_p" be the proportion of the entire population in the province belonging to this confession. Then the assumption being made is that: $\dfrac{Ar}{Ap} = \dfrac{Wr}{Wp}$. As pointed out in the previous paragraph, we know A_p, W_r, and W_p, so that the proportion of agricultural laborers who are Catholic in an individual *Regierungsbezirk* is given by $A_r = \dfrac{Ap \cdot Wr}{Wp}$.

This procedure thus gave me estimates of the number of members of each class and occupational group belonging to each confession in each *Regierungsbezirk*. I then checked by adding them up and comparing the results with the census figures for each province. The total numbers of members of each occupational and social group always came out right, and the numbers of each confession usually did, but in a few cases, the proportions of the confessions obtained by adding the estimates from the *Regierungsbezirke*, differed by 10% (or somewhat more) from the proportions given in the census figures. I therefore adjusted these results, using the proportional iterative fitting procedure described in the section below.

After all this, I had obtained figures on the number of Catholic agricultural laborers, Protestant agricultural laborers, Catholic salaried employees in industry, mining and crafts, Protestant salaried employees in this sector, and so on, for each of the seventy-seven or seventy-eight units. Combining these class and occupational groups together into the six

---

[12] The proportion of the population in each *Regierungsbezirk* and province belonging to each confession is according to the source cited in note 5, above.

larger units that I discussed in the introduction (farmers, workers, and middle class, each divided by confession) I was then able to obtain the proportion of the electorate in each unit belonging to each of these groups. Two questions arise from this procedure. How well do these figures approximate the electorate? In view of the relatively small number of units obtained after this elaborate processing of the census data, were there any better alternatives?

To answer the first question, there are some checks that we can perform by comparing the results of my manipulations of the 1907 census with the figures on eligible voters for the elections held that year. After processing the census material, I came up with a figure of some 13.84 million eligible voters; the official returns give 13.35 million, so there is an overestimate of some 3.6%, not too bad, especially considering that the elections were held at the beginning of the year and the census at the end, and the eligible electorate was increasing at the rate of about 0.5% per year. The confessional proportions are closer: the 1905 census figures that form the basis for the confessional breakdown of the individual constituencies give the entire population as 36.4% Catholic; my calculations of the eligible electorate from the 1907 census are that it was 35.8%.

The confessional composition of each of the seventy-eight units of observation, drawn from the official material in the 1905 census and from my calculations on the 1907 commerical and industrial census is also extremely close, differing by more than three percentage points in only one instance. The estimates of the total population in each unit are generally this close as well, but sometimes show greater differences. Sometimes my estimates of the neighboring *Regierungsbezirke* deviate in opposite directions: say, 5–8% higher in one and 5–8% lower in the next, a result occurring because the boundaries of the constituencies, usually contained within a *Regierungsbezirk* flowed over into another. I decided that these deviations were not a serious problem, since there was no reason to think that they introduced inaccuracies into the social and confessional composition of the electorate, as against its size.

In some cases, though, the estimates from the commercial and industrial census for all the observations in a given region were higher than the official figures on eligible voters. I would attribute this surplus to the presence of non-citizen workers, as these discrepancies were found in border districts – southern Bavaria, Saxony, parts of Prussian Poland – and in the Ruhr Basin and Lorraine, both industrial regions with many migrant laborers. These worried me more, and I tried adjusting for the surplus by assuming that it occurred in the working-class population and subtracting these "excess" workers, on the assumption that they were foreigners and ineligible to vote. However, when I ran regressions with these adjusted figures, they differed from the original ones only at the fourth decimal place, so I decided that these differences simply did not matter.

All these adjustments, just to create a data set with a relatively small number of observations, might give the reader pause. It was possible to have more observations but I would say that the cost of these was losing far too much information. The censuses of 1895 and 1907 did include returns at the *Kreis* level (a much smaller unit than the the *Regierungsbezirk*) from which one could have calculated figures on most of the 397 constituencies, rather than the larger 78 units of combined constituencies. However, these census returns just give the proportion of the population in each occupation: they are not broken down by age, sex, social class, or by confession. Thus, much of the meaningful information one might want is missing. One can, for instance, calculate the relationship between a party's vote and the proportion of the entire population employed in industry, but not the proportion of industrial workers, or Protestant industrial workers. Furthermore, since these figures are not modified by either sex or age, calculations on them relate the party vote not to the eligible voters but to the general employed population, a quite different group.

In spite of these difficulties, both Jürgen Winkler and Jürgen Schmädeke have used the lower administrative level census returns in their work. Some questionable decisions they made compound the unreliability of results calculated from these figures. Schmädeke, for instance, simply disregards the entire "F" group of the census, rentiers, and pension recipients. He also increases the number of people employed in agriculture in 1895 by 17.86% to allow for an ostensible undercount of family members employed on family farms – ignoring the obvious fact that such people employed on their family's farm were likely to have been women, under age, or both, and hence not part of the electorate. While not taking such evidently dubious steps, Winkler does use figures from the 1907 census to analyze the elections of the 1870s, although in the intervening three decades industrialization had progressed rapidly, with considerable declines in the proportion of the population engaged in agriculture and corresponding increases in the proportion in industry and services.[13]

More detailed information for smaller administrative units is available for censuses taken after the First World War. Jürgen Winkler, in an interesting and convincing study of the labor electorate between 1912 and

[13] Schmädeke, *Wählerbewegunbg*, 1: 51 n. 113; Winkler, *Sozialstruktur*, pp. 246–47, 251, 254, 261, 270.

1924, written before his book and somewhat separate from it, has proceeded this way, analyzing the 1912 elections with material from the occupational and industrial census of 1925.[14] The thirteen-year gap, however, seems like an awfully long time, especially since it includes the First World War and the subsequent economic chaos, to say nothing of the fact that portions of prewar Germany were no longer in postwar Germany and so would have to have been excluded from the caluclations. Needless to say, extrapolating backwards to elections before 1912, would make things even worse.

Additionally, and in some ways more importantly, census returns in the Weimar Republic did not cross-tabluate the population by confession and social group. They give, for instance, the proportion of workers in each *Kreis* and the proportion of Catholics, but not the proportion of workers who were Catholic. Jürgen Falter dealt with this situation by multiplying the proportion of each confession by the proportion of each occupation. That is, if the eligible population of a given *Kreis* was 40% working class and 30% Catholic, he calculated that 12% $(0.4 \times 0.3 = 0.12)$ were Catholic workers.[15] Such a procedure, however, assumes that the social composition of the Catholic and Protestant populations were the same. In the *Kaiserreich*, where the census did cross-tabulate occupation or class and confession, this was not the case: Catholics were over-represented in agriculture, crafts, and among the working class, and under-represented in the ranks of salaried employees, professionals, and owners of businesses.[16] For both these reasons, it seemed best to me to stick with the 1895 and 1907 census returns from larger administrative units, in spite of the fact that the number of observations that I could derive from them was less than I would have liked. I used the 1895 census to develop estimates of class and confessional voting for the 1887, 1890, 1893, and 1898 elections; I used the 1907 census to calculate estimates for the empire's three twentieth-century general elections.

Ecological inference in theory and practice

Having developed figures on voting and on the composition of the electorate from the election and census returns, the next step was to analyze them using the methods of ecological regression. This section begins with

---

[14] Winkler, "Die soziale Basis."

[15] Lohmoeller et al., "Unemployment and the Rise of National Socialism," p. 366.

[16] The most recent discussion of this fact, one that was well known to contemporaries, is Antonius Liedhegener, "Marktgesellschaft und Milieu. Katholiken und katholische Regionen in der wirtschaftlichen Entwicklung des Deutschen Reiches 1895–1914," *Historisches Jahrbuch* 113 (1993): 203–354.

an explanation of the basic method of ecological inference, using linear regressions. From there it goes on to discuss a modification of this method, the use of non-linear, logistic regressions. Finally, there is an explanation of the problems of impossible results that arise using both methods, the proportional iterative fitting procedure that can be used to deal with these problems, the reasons that the combination of these procedures can produce different results, and the choices that I made between these methods.

Linear regression

Let us begin by imagining an electorate made up exclusively of two groups, g and h (for some of the work done in this book, Catholics and Protestants plus the smaller confessions come to mind). In each constituency, precinct, or other unit of observation, if we understand g and h as referring to the percentage of the electorate belonging to each group, then $g+h=1$. We would like to find out what percentage of each of these groups vote for a given political party. If we say that the percentage of eligible voters choosing that party is y, and g_y is the percentage of members of group g who vote for the party, and h_y is the percentage of group h voting for that party, then we have:

(1) $$y = g \cdot g_y + h \cdot h_y$$

Since $g+h=1$, then $h=1-g$, and we can substitute $1-g$ for h in (1) above, giving us:

(2) $$y = g \cdot g_y + (1-g) \cdot h_y$$

Multiplying out and rearranging terms, we have:

(3) $$y = h_y + g \cdot (g_y - h_y)$$

Equation (3) is a linear equation where the dependent variable is the percentage of eligible voters choosing party y and the independent variable is the percentage of voters belonging to group g. We know these figures for each of our observations (constituency in this case, but could be precinct or other unit). Using the mathematical procedure of ordinary least squares, handily available in a wide variety of statistical programs for personal computers, we can calculate the linear equation of the form $y=a+bx$, that best fits our observations. The constant, that is the "a" of this equation, is h_y, the percentage of members of group h who cast their ballot for party y. The slope, the b of the equation, is $g_y - h_y$. If we add b to a, we have $h_y + (g_y - h_y) = g_y$, the percentage of members of group g voting for party y.

This is the basic, very simple procedure. Many refinements are possible, such as weighting the variables, adding dummy variables, running different regressions for different sub-groups of the observation, and so on. The one refinement I will mention, since it is important for the regressions used in ths book, is that the procedure can be easily expanded to more than two groups. Imagine that the electorate is completely divided not into two groups g and h, but into k groups, $g_1, g_2 \ldots g_{k-1}, g_k$. If g_{ky} is the percentage of group g_k voting for party y, then the corresponding regression equation, used to estimate the percentage of members of each of these k groups voting for party y is:

$$y = g_{ky} + g_1(g_{1y} - g_{ky}) + g_2(g_{2y} - g_{ky}) \ldots + g_{k-1}(g_{[k-1]y} - g_{ky})$$

Obviously, one also does not have to restrict oneself to just one party. Similar regressions can be done for the percentage of groups voting for all parties, including the "party" of the non-voters.

These equations used to produce estimates for ecological inference are ordinary linear equations, so conditions for their validity, such as the normal distribution of the error term, are the same as those of other linear equations. In estimating them, the same care must be taken as with any use of linear regression. The number of independent variables should not be too large for the number of observations; collinearity of the independent variables needs to be avoided; residuals should be checked for normality, the coefficient of variation (adjusted R^2) can be calculated to see the general strength of the prediction, and so on.

Logistic regression

There is an alternative approach to ecological inference, relatively little used, perhaps because it involves mathematically more complex, non-linear equations. However, once again any number of standard statistical programs for personal computers allow one to carry out the calculations with no difficulty. This alternative approach is based on logistic regression, a procedure used in regressions where the dependent variable is dichotomous.[17] One example of the use of logistic regression would be relating home ownership to family income. The dependent variable, home ownership, is dichotomous, one either owns a home or does not, while the independent variable, family income, can take an unlimited range of values. What the logit regression does is to express this dichoto-

---

[17] On logistic regressions, see John H. Aldrich and Forrest D. Nelson, *Linear Probability, Logit, and Probit Models* (Beverly Hills and London: SAGE Publications, 1984),or John Neter, William Wasserman, and Michael H. Kutner, *Applied Linear Regression Models*, 2nd edn (Homewood and Boston: Irwin, 1989), ch. 16.

mous variable as a probability, the odds or the likelihood that a family would own a home, depending on its income.

One can think of voting choice in logistic terms. An individual voter either votes for party y or does not. To come back to the problem of ecological inference, the likelihood that a voter might choose party y could be dependent on whether the voter belongs to either group g or group h, who together make up the entire electorate. If we define y as the likelihood that any individual voter will vote for party y; g as the likelihood that any individual voter will belong to group g; g_y the likelihood that any member of group g will vote for party y; h as the likelihood that a voter will belong to group h; and h_y as the likelihood that any member of group h will vote for party y, then we can write the logistic equation as follows:

$$(4) \qquad \ln\left(\frac{y}{1-y}\right) = g \cdot g_y + h \cdot h_y$$

where ln refers to the natural logarithm.

The probability that any individual voter will belong to group g is just the percentage of eligible voters actually belonging to group g, the same with h. Consequently, just as with linear regressions, $h = 1 - g$, and substituting and rearranging, we can write:

$$(5) \qquad \ln\left(\frac{y}{1-y}\right) = h_y + g \cdot (g_y - h_y)$$

Taking exponentials of both sides, gives us:

$$(6) \qquad \frac{y}{1-y} = e^{h_y + g \cdot (g_y - h_y)}$$

Solving for y, we have:

$$(7) \qquad y = \frac{e^{h_y + g \cdot (g_y - h_y)}}{1 + e^{h_y + g \cdot (g_y - h_y)}}$$

This equation gives us the likelihood that any individual voter will vote for party y; our observations, however, are not based on individual voters but on a constituency full of them. If a constituency has, say, 20,000 eligible voters, we are estimating the likelihood that any one of them would vote for party y 20,000 times.[18] What this means, is that the dependent variable y is not, as with linear regression, the percentage of eligible voters in each constituency voting for party y, but the actual number of voters doing so, and the independent variable is the percentage of voters belonging to group g multiplied by the actual number of voters in the con-

---

[18] This is based on using the method of iteratively reweighted least squares (as I did) to estimate the coefficients of the logistic regression.

stituency. Using these numbers, which are known for each constituency, then it is possible to calculate the regression coefficients, h_y and $g_y - h_y$ of the logistic equation (7) best fitting these observations.

Once we have this equation, we can calculate the likelihood that an individual voter of group g or of group h would vote for party y, or, what is the same thing, the percentage of voters in group g or group h choosing party y. If a voter belongs to group h, then the likelihood of belonging to group g is zero, and substituting zero for g in equation (7) gives:

(8)
$$\frac{e^{h_y}}{1+e^{h_y}}$$

If a voter belongs to group g, then the likelihood of belonging to group g is 1, and substituting 1 for g in equation (7) gives:

(9)
$$\frac{e^{g_y}}{1+e^{g_y}}$$

Just as with linear regression, this method can be extended to include more than two groups and more than one political party.

Impossible results and fitting procedures

We now have two possible methods for estimating the percentage of different groups in the population voting for different political parties, or not voting, methods that produce two different estimates, sometimes fairly close to each other, sometimes rather more distant. The question that arises is which is right, although the more appropriate way to frame it would be which is least wrong. Both methods of ecological regression have the annoying feature of producing mathematically correct but logically impossible results.

A problem frequently occurring with linear regression is that the estimate of the percentage of members of a particular group voting for a particular party is often greater than 100 or less than 0. If one adds together the percentages of members of that group voting for each of the parties and not voting, the sum total of these percentages will usually equal 100 (more or less, allowing for rounding errors and inexactitudes) as it should, since that means that all the members of the group are accounted for, but that sum frequently includes, as I have said, choices of individual parties that are impossible. Sometimes in ecological regression such impossible results suggest that the equation itself represents a poor fit, with a low R^2, which can be improved by introducing new variables or running the equation for different groups of observations separately. At other times – and this was the case with my work – the R^2 was high, in the order of 0.7 or more, indicating a very good fit, yet impossible results turned up.

It is from these circumstances – impossible results in spite of a good linear fit – that the idea of using logistic regressions arises, since the logit curve, estimated in logistic regression, $y = \dfrac{e^{a+bx}}{1+e^{a+bx}}$, looks like a straight line in the middle with a kinking and flattened curve (the technical term is "asymptotic") at either end. Points lying on such a curve, if fitted to a linear equation of the form $y = a + bx$, might have coefficients giving impossible results. Such impossible results cannot emerge in logistic regression, since the estimates for the percentages of group members choosing an individual party (equations [8] and [9]) are always between zero and one.

Unfortunately, avoiding one form of impossibility, logistic regressions fall into another. While the percentage of members of a given group voting for a given party is always logically possible, when one sums up the percentages of members of these groups voting for each party or not voting, the sum is always greater than 100%.[19] In other words, with linear regressions, individual estimates of a group's voting may be impossible, but the sum of all the estimates of one group's voting will be correct, while with logistic regressions, all the individual estimates of a group's voting will be logically possible, but their sum will be greater than 100% and thus logically impossible.

To see how this works in practice, let me give the results of the equations for the voter transition probabilities between the elections of 1907 and 1912. Table A.1a gives the results of the estimates via linear regression; table A.1b, the results via logistic regression.

Although in very general terms, both forms of estimation point in the same direction, there are a number of differences between them and, of course, neither presents results that are all logically possible in the ways explained above: the linear equations lead to individual estimates greater than 100% and less than 0%, while the logistic equations create a situation in which the vote for all parties of individual groups is well over 100%. To get to all logically possible results, Jürgen Falter has developed a proportional iterative fitting procedure for linear regressions, which I have employed, and adapted to the logistic regressions as well.[20]

[19] On this characteristic of logistic estimates, see Thomsen, *Danish Elections*, pp. 66–70. Although the specific method of logistic estimation he develops is idiosyncratic and not universally applicable, the discussion of linear and logistic estimation procedures in Thomsen's book is the best available.

[20] On this procedure, see the brief description in Lohmoeller et al., "Unemployment and the Rise of National Socialism," pp. 366–68, and the more detailed discussion in the article to which they refer, W. Edwards Deming and Frederick F. Stephan, "On a Least Squares Adjustment of a Sampled Frequency Table when the Expected Marginal Totals are Known," *Annals of Mathematical Statistics* 11 (1940): 427–44.

Table A.1a *Voter transitions between 1907 and 1912 calculated using linear regressions (percent)*

Vote in 1912	Vote in 1907						
	Right or Extreme Right	Liberal	Minority parties	Social Democrat	Non-voter	Net new voter	Adjusted R^2
Right or Extreme Right	72.4	28.9	−5.2	−18.3	13.0	1.9	0.75
Liberal	24.6	71.7	2.9	7.1	2.7	20.6	0.60
Minority parties	−1.9	−5.3	92.2	−4.1	6.5	25.8	0.92
Social Democrats	1.3	2.0	0	111.9	5.8	34.8	0.97
Non-voters	3.6	2.7	10.1	3.3	72.0	16.9	0.63
All	100.0	100.0	100.0	99.9	100.0	100.0	

Table A.1b *Voter transitions between 1907 and 1912 calculated using logistic regressions (percent)*

Vote in 1912	Vote in 1907					
	Right or Extreme Right	Liberal	Minority parties	Social Democrats	Non-voters	Net new voters
Right or Extreme Right	88.9	50.9	5.4	2.3	1.8	3.6
Liberal	30.6	82.3	10.3	10.7	4.6	28.3
Minority parties	3.7	6.1	90.9	1.2	8.4	63.2
Social Democrats	7.9	8.7	4.9	95.0	15.9	43.6
Non-voters	7.7	7.0	11.5	7.0	89.7	16.4
All	138.8	155.0	123.0	116.2	120.4	155.1

Basically, what this procedure does is to assume that the impossible results represent either small violations of the assumptions underlying the regression equations and/or are the result of the way the voters were grouped together into constituencies, either of which could produce the impossible results. Falter's procedure involves first re-expressing all the figures as overall percentages and then setting the largest negative figure to zero. In the case of table A.1a, this would be the proportion of 1907 Social Democrats voting for parties of the right in 1912. The 1907 SPD voters made up 22.6% of the 1912 electorate; the regression results are that −18.3% of them chose the parties of the right in 1912, so that −4.1% (0.226×−0.183=−0.041) of the 1912 electorate consists of 1907 SPD voters choosing the right-wing parties in 1912.

One then sets this to zero by adding 0.041 to all the estimates. Once this is done, the figures no longer sum up to 100%, so they are proportionately reduced, the estimates in each row decreased so that they remain in the same proportion to each other but add up to the row marginal. The figures will still not add up correctly by columns, so that a similar proportionate reduction is carried out by columns. The figures will then no longer add up correctly by rows, so the proportional reduction is carried out on the rows; then on the columns again. After this has been done several times – hence the "iterative" in the procedure's name – the figures will add up to exactly the row and column marginals and will total, overall, 100%. At this point, further iterations will not change them.[21]

The same procedure can be used in reducing the estimates obtained from logistic regression, the assumption here being that the inherent over-estimation built into logistic regression gives results that are proportionately correct but too high. The procedure is even simpler in this case since logistic regressions produce no negative results, making the initial step in Falter's procedure – setting the most negative result equal to zero – unnecessary. The calculations can be carried out with a pocket calculator and a very large amount of patience, but with a modest amount of programming knowledge, one can write a program that will perform the iterations automatically, which is what I did.

I calculated the voter transition probabilities using both logistic and linear regressions, applied the fitting procedure to the results, and then considered what criteria I could use to decide which results I would accept. Unfortunately, there is no generally accepted measure of fit for logistic regressions as R^2 is for linear ones, so I could not ascertain which form of regression fitted the observations better and thus could not use that to decide. Another possibility would be to calculate the probability plots of the residuals, thus showing the normality of the error term and use the equations whose error terms were closer to normal, in other words, those whose probability plots were closest to a straight line. When

---

[21] For a mathematical proof that the iterations converge to a final result and that such a result is unique for each initial configuration, see the article by Deming and Stephan, cited in the previous note.

Table A.2a *Voter transitions between 1907 and 1912 calculated with linear regressions, after fitting (percent)*

Vote in 1912	Vote in 1907					
	Right or Extreme Right	Liberal	Minority parties	Social Democrats	Non-voters	Net new voters
Right or Extreme Right	35	19	6	0	14	12
Liberal	25	49	13	12	14	21
Minority parties	11	7	55	6	14	20
Social Democrats	17	14	13	73	19	30
Non-voters	13	10	14	9	39	17
All	101	99	101	100	100	100

I did this, though, the probability plots of the residuals for both kinds of regressions showed little difference between them. Rather than the form of the regression being the deciding factor, in both linear and logistic regression the more constituencies in which a party group put up candidates, the closer to a straight line the probability plot was. Thus, considering the residuals offered no clue as to which form of regression was a better estimate of voter behavior. Along the same lines, reducing the number of observations by dividing Germany into regional groups generally worsened somewhat the linearity of the probability plots. This is why I decided that estimates obtained from regressions on all the constituencies were more reliable than those involving averaging results from separate regressions on constituencies in Prussia and non-Prussian Germany.

Although the final, adjusted results of the two kinds of regression were always in the same direction and of about the same general magnitude, they showed systematic differences, which, I came to realize, related to the fitting procedure. The problem lay in the initial step in Falter's procedure, setting the most negative coefficient equal to zero. This involved adding a figure to all the other estimates, which affected such estimates disproportionately depending on the size of the group being estimated. The smallest group would be the most affected and if the group were small enough, then the figure being added to it would completely overpower, as it were, the results calculated from the regressions. To show what this means, table A.2 gives the results of the fitting procedures on the 1907–12 voter transition probabilities for linear and logistic equations.

Table A.2b *Voter transitions between 1907 and 1912 calculated with logistic regressions, after fitting (percent)*

Vote in 1912	Vote in 1907					
	Right or Extreme Right	Liberal	Minority parties	Social Democrats	Non-voters	Net new voters
Right or Extreme Right	52	23	3	1	1	1
Liberal	30	61	10	8	4	19
Minority parties	3	4	71	1	6	33
Social Democrats	10	8	6	87	19	37
Non-voters	6	4	10	4	70	9
All	101	100	100	101	100	99

The column in table A.2a for net new voters should awaken our suspicions since the adjusted results are furthest away from the initial regression estimates given in table A.1a and are, in fact, very close to the choices for the entire electorate. This should not be too surprising, since net new voters made up just 7.5% of the electorate, meaning that the initial estimates from the regressions of the number of net new voters choosing any one of the individual party groups was between 0.1% (0.001) and 2.6% (0.026) of the entire electorate.[22] But the fitting procedure involves adding a figure (0.041) to each of these entries that is greater or a good deal greater than each of these entries. Consequently, what ends up being adjusted in the fitting procedure is not the regression results for net new voters but the number needed to bring the largest negative entry to zero. A look at table A.2a shows that the distortion generated by setting the most negative estimate equal to zero is greatest for the smallest groups in the electorate, the net new voters, the non-voters of 1907 and the conservative voters of 1907. The smaller the size of the group, the greater the distortion; although I cannot prove it mathematically, my experience suggests that with the smallest groups, like the net new voters in this example, the fitting procedure ends up by reducing them to the average for all voters.[23]

---

[22] Table A.1a shows that 1.9% of net new voters chose the conservatives, or 0.1% of the entire electorate (0.019×0.075=0.001) and 34.8 % of net new voters chose the SPD, 2.6% (0.075×0.348=0.026) of the electorate.

[23] I first noticed this when I tried to calculate voter transition probabilities for all the parties,

The linear and logistic regressions produced the most similar estimates for the elections of the 1890s, when all the party groups and the non-voters were closest in size. In other years, the estimates for the smaller party groups would diverge, so I decided that in this case the linear estimates were unreliable.[24] Consequently, the figures presented in this book for voter transition probabilities are based on logistic regressions, whose resulting estimates have been proportionately reduced. To get some idea of the differences between logistic and linear estimates, the reader might compare my figures on voter transition probabilities in the 1870s with those given by Jürgen Winkler, who calculated these transition probabilities using linear regression and Falter's fitting procedure.[25]

In calculating estimates of voting by confession, the situation was much better: both linear and logistic estimates were very close to each other, and the impossible results were much smaller – the most impossible result being of the order of −2–3% for linear estimates, and the totals for a group summing up to 105% for the logistic estimates. (A few linear regressions even gave estimates without any impossible results.) The sort of problems in the fitting procedure for voter transition probabilities generally did not arise here because the individual estimates were much larger than the figure involved in raising the negative estimates to zero. The estimates obtained from the two kinds of regression were also much closer, the main difference between them being that the linear regressions consistently showed that no Protestant voters chose the Center Party, while the logistic regressions showed that about 2–3% of them did. The development of support for different parties by the different confessions, and the peaks and troughs of such support, were the same in both kinds of regression. The figures given in this book are based on weighted linear regressions, but they could just as easily have been based on logistic regression, with the main difference being that a very small proportion of

not just party groups, and the fitted results for the smaller parties, such as the Free Conservatives and the Anti-Semites, tended strongly and most implausibly toward the mean for all voters. I would have liked to have calculated voter transition probabilities for all parties using logistic regression, but the software package I was using did not allow me to run logistic regressions with so many independent variables, so I was forced to settle for estimates of party groups rather than individual parties. Regressions with so many zeros in them (since individual parties, as opposed to party groups did not put up candidates in many constituencies) might have produced dubious results, in any event, since there would be a large number of observations with an unacceptably high leverage.

[24] This seems to me to be a general problem of the combination of linear regressions and this fitting procedure. When the most negative estimate is large, relative to the estimates for a smaller group, then the results for this group will not be reliable. It is possible that some of Falter's results, especially those giving voting by confession and class, suffer from this problem. Using logistic regressions, which have no negative results, and the fitting procedure, is one possible way to deal with this difficulty.

[25] Winkler, *Sozialstruktur*, pp. 123–28.

Protestants would have been shown as voting for the Center as would a slightly smaller proportion of Catholics.[26]

In contrast to the previous group of regressions, these were only calculated for those constituencies in which the party group put up candidates, and the results reduced by the proportion of voters involved. In 1893, for instance, the right-wing parties ran candidates in constituencies in which 83% of eligible Protestant voters and 58% of eligible Catholic voters lived. In those constituencies, the regressions showed that 28% of eligible Protestants and 8% of eligible Catholics chose one of these parties. Thus, the estimates were that $0.83 \times 0.28 = 23\%$ of Protestant voters and $0.58 \times 0.08 = 5\%$ of Catholic voters in all of Germany voted for one of the parties of the right. This was apparently the procedure used by Winkler in his estimation of voting by confession for the 1870s and the 1900s, since his estimates and mine are almost identical. The occasional one percentage point discrepancy can be explained by the fact that Winkler did not include the fifteen constituencies of Alsace-Lorraine in his analysis.[27]

The most difficult problems lay in developing estimates of voting by class and confession. In the previous groups of regressions, the independent variables were not especially highly correlated and measures of collinearity showed that interaction between the independent variables was not affecting the results. For this case, though, the independent variables were highly collinear – r between a number of them being in the order of ± 0.9 – so that the results of regressions run with any combination of them were extremely unreliable. Attempting to recombine the census categories did not lead to any reduction in collinearity.

Consequently, I was forced to strike out in a new direction and apply, for the first time in ecological regression, a special procedure to deal with collinear independent variables. This procedure, known as ridge regression, involves adding a constant, the ridge constant, at one point in the calculation of the regression results (for those interested, the constant is added to the inversion matrix), to reduce the unreliability caused by collinearity. Statistical theory tells us that there exists a ridge constant whose addition produces better estimates of the regression coefficients than could be obtained from an ordinary linear regression, only this theory provides no way of knowing what that coefficient is.[28]

Since there is an infinite number of potential ridge constants, there is

---

[26] Regressions were weighted by the square root of the number of eligible voters, as suggested by J. Morgan Kousser, "Making Separate Equal: Integration of Black and White School Funds in Kentucky," *Journal of Interdisciplinary History* 10 (1980): 399–428, esp. pp. 425–26. Weighted regressions produced results that seemed slightly more accurate (the differences were usually just a percentage point or two) than unweighted ones.

[27] Winkler, *Sozialstruktur*, pp. 169, 330–31.

[28] On ridge regression, see Neter, Wassermann, and Kutner, *Applied Linear Regression Models*, pp. 411–18.

therefore an infinite number of possible regression coefficients and an infinite number of potential estimates that could be obtained from them. My choice of the ridge constant, and, ultimately, regression result, was not arbitrary (or worse, rigged, designed to produce results I wanted to obtain in advance) but was based on the three following criteria: (1) The variance inflation factor, the measure of collinearity, had to be at appropriate levels – below ten, the rule of thumb minimum for eliminating effects of collinearity, and, preferably, beneath five. (2) The regression coefficients had to be relatively stable, that is an increase in the ridge constant had to produce little change in them. (3) The smallest ridge constant that allowed conditions (1) and (2) to hold was then chosen. In a number of regressions, for instance the ones predicting how Protestant social groups voted for the SPD, the results were the same, regardless of the ridge constant. In others, the initial increases in the ridge constant from zero (when the constant is zero, then there is an ordinary linear equation) changed both the regression coefficients and the variance inflation factor drastically, but after a few increases, in units of 0.01 each, the coefficients did not change much at all, and the results, even with different constants, were very similar.

The procedure for estimating the proportion of members of different social and confessional groups voting for the different party groups was as follows. I ran two linear regressions, one for each confession.[29] One equation would have as independent variables the percentage of Catholic farmers, workers, and middle class, and one would have as independent variables the percentage of Protestant farmers, workers, and middle class. From the first equation one obtained estimates of the percentage of each Catholic social group voting for each party group and from the second an estimate of the percentage of each Protestant social group doing so. These estimates had the usual problems of impossible results, in particular, the proportion of the Protestant, urban middle class choosing the minority parties always being noticeably negative.

Eliminating the impossible results by fitting these estimates directly to the election returns with Falter's fitting procedure produced ridiculous conclusions, such as large percentages of Catholic farmers voting for the SPD, a result of the weakness in the method I mentioned above.[30] Consequently, I fitted the estimates for each confession separately, and fitted them to the results of the previous regressions, on voting by confession. That is, my estimates gave proportions of Protestant farmers, workers, and middle class choosing the different party groups or not

---

[29] I had to use linear regressions, since there is, as far as I know, no comparable procedure for eliminating the effects of collinearity of the independent variables from logistic regressions.

[30] The reader will recall that Falter's estimates of voting by class and confession produced similarly implausible conclusions, and probably for the same reason. Had he and his team applied the procedure suggested below, they might have obtained better results.

voting; the previous set of regressions gave the proportion of all Protestants choosing these groups and not voting. I used those figures as the marginals in the fitting procedure and did the same with the Catholics. The results were much better and, overall, pretty convincing.

The reader may wonder how reliable such results really are, given the many sources of error – from the manipulations required of the census data to the use of an unusual and indeterminate statistical procedure. There are two, very partial replies that I can make. First, ridge regression has the additional virtue of not being sensitive in its results to small changes in the independent variables. Hence, if the manipulation of the census returns produced results that were slightly out – say, there really should have been 45% Protestant workers in an observation instead of 42%, these small changes would not produce much in the way of changes in the estimates. Secondly, I could cross-check my procedures by taking the figures for the seventy-seven or seventy-eight observations, adding together the proportion of the different social groups by confession and using those results to estimate the proportion of all Catholics or Protestants voting for the different party groups. These resulting estimates were within two or three percentage points of those obtained from regressions on all 397 constituencies, an encouraging convergence that increased my confidence in the reliability of the procedure.

Estimates

The estimates are given in three groups: the voter transition probabilities, tables A.3–A.14; the vote by confession, tables A.15–A.27; and vote by confession and social group for the years 1887–1912, tables A.28–A.34. In all three cases, the figures are given as fractions of the entire electorate, summing up to 1. As an example, in table A.3, giving the voter transition probabilities from 1871 to 1874, the 0.051 in the upper left-hand corner says that 5.1% of the 1874 electorate consisted of 1871 voters of the conservative parties choosing the conservatives again in 1874. The 0.019 to the right of it says that 1.9% of the 1874 electorate consisted of 1871 voters for the conservative parties who voted for one of the liberal parties in 1874. The number in the upper right-hand corner, under "All 1871," 0.110, states that 11.0% of the 1874 electorate consisted of voters who had chosen the conservatives in 1871.[31] The 0.090 in the lower left, next to "All 1874," states that 9% of the 1874 electorate consisted of conservative voters. If one wishes to ascertain how many conservatives in 1871 voted for the conservative parties in 1874, one divides 0.051 by 0.110

---

[31] Note that such a figure is not the same as the proportion of the 1871 electorate voting for the conservative parties in 1871, because the 1874 electorate was larger than the 1871 electorate by 6% (the 0.059 in the right-hand column, the total net new voters in 1874).

which gives 0.464, or 46.4%. To find out the proportion of the 1874 conservative electorate consisting of 1871 conservative voters, then dividing 0.051 by 0.090 gives 0.567, or 56.7%.

The reader will note that the marginals, the figures in the extreme right-hand columns and the very bottom rows of the tables, are the actual election returns (or in tables A.28–A.34 the census figures), while all the other entries are estimates of voting behavior calculated from these returns by means of ecological regression. The small differences between the sum of the rows or columns and their respective marginals are the result of rounding-off error.

Table A.3 *Voter transition probabilities, 1871–74*

	Conservative 1874	Liberal 1874	Minority 1874	Social- Democrat 1874	Non-voter 1874	All 1871
Conservative 1871	0.051	0.019	0.017	0.000	0.024	0.110
Liberal 1871	0.008	0.156	0.028	0.002	0.026	0.221
Minority 1871	0.003	0.007	0.105	0.000	0.006	0.120
Social-Democrat 1871	0.001	0.001	0.000	0.008	0.005	0.015
Non-voter 1871	0.024	0.061	0.053	0.026	0.312	0.478
Net new voter 1874	0.004	0.009	0.012	0.006	0.027	0.059
All 1874	0.090	0.253	0.214	0.043	0.400	1

Table A.4 *Voter transition probabilities, 1874–77*

	Conservative 1877	Liberal 1877	Minority 1877	Social- Democrat 1877	Non-voter 1877	All 1874
Conservative 1874	0.047	0.011	0.011	0.000	0.013	0.083
Liberal 1874	0.038	0.147	0.017	0.002	0.029	0.233
Minority 1874	0.004	0.015	0.164	0.000	0.040	0.223
Social-Democrat 1874	0.000	0.012	0.000	0.024	0.003	0.039
Non-voter 1874	0.018	0.033	0.011	0.016	0.299	0.376
Net new voter 1877	0.000	0.015	0.006	0.013	0.013	0.047
All 1877	0.107	0.231	0.209	0.055	0.398	1

Table A.5 *Voter transition probabilities, 1877–78*

	Conservative 1878	Liberal 1878	Minority 1878	Social-Democrat 1878	Non-voter 1878	All 1877
Conservative 1877	0.071	0.005	0.006	0.000	0.025	0.107
Liberal 1877	0.033	0.137	0.017	0.001	0.043	0.231
Minority 1877	0.010	0.005	0.160	0.000	0.035	0.209
Social-Democrat 1877	0.005	0.013	0.001	0.029	0.007	0.055
Non-voters 1877	0.050	0.052	0.018	0.018	0.260	0.398
All 1878	0.169	0.212	0.201	0.048	0.370	1

Table A.6 *Voter transition probabilities, 1878–81*

	Conservative 1881	Liberal 1881	Minority 1881	Social-Democrat 1881	Non-voter 1881	All 1878
Conservative 1878	0.086	0.046	0.012	0.001	0.023	0.169
Liberal 1878	0.022	0.132	0.016	0.004	0.038	0.212
Minority 1878	0.003	0.006	0.142	0.001	0.050	0.201
Social-Democrat 1878	0.003	0.004	0.000	0.025	0.015	0.048
Non-voters 1878	0.019	0.024	0.009	0.003	0.315	0.370
All 1881	0.133	0.212	0.180	0.034	0.441	1

Table A.7 *Voter transition probabilities, 1881–84*

	Conservative 1881	Liberal 1884	Minority 1884	Social-Democrat 1884	Non-voter 1884	All 1884
Conservative 1881	0.087	0.011	0.002	0.001	0.028	0.129
Liberal 1881	0.022	0.152	0.004	0.004	0.024	0.206
Minority 1881	0.011	0.006	0.132	0.000	0.025	0.174
Social-Democrat 1881	0.003	0.002	0.000	0.024	0.005	0.033
Non-voters 1881	0.010	0.050	0.044	0.020	0.304	0.427
Net new voters 1884	0.001	0.002	0.006	0.010	0.012	0.031
All 1884	0.133	0.223	0.188	0.059	0.398	1

Table A.8 *Voter transition probabilities, 1884–87*

	Conservative 1887	Liberal 1887	Minority 1887	Social-Democrat 1887	Non-voter 1887	All 1884
Conservative 1884	0.102	0.001	0.003	0.002	0.016	0.128
Liberal 1884	0.011	0.180	0.005	0.005	0.014	0.214
Minority 1884	0.009	0.009	0.152	0.001	0.010	0.180
Social-Democrat 1884	0.001	0.011	0.000	0.040	0.004	0.056
Non-voters 1884	0.067	0.069	0.046	0.022	0.178	0.382
Net new voters 1887	0.004	0.010	0.008	0.009	0.007	0.039
All 1887	0.193	0.285	0.215	0.078	0.229	1

Table A.9 *Voter transition probabilities, 1887–90*

	Conservative 1890	Liberal 1890	Minority 1890	Social-Democrat 1890	Non-voter 1890	All 1887
Conservative 1887	0.101	0.040	0.009	0.017	0.019	0.186
Liberal 1887	0.018	0.176	0.024	0.030	0.028	0.275
Minority 1887	0.011	0.013	0.131	0.010	0.042	0.207
Social-Democrat 1887	0.003	0.006	0.000	0.063	0.003	0.075
Non-voters 1887	0.008	0.010	0.008	0.010	0.185	0.220
Net new voters 1890	0.001	0.005	0.007	0.012	0.012	0.037
All 1890	0.141	0.250	0.179	0.141	0.289	1

Table A.10 *Voter transition probabilities, 1890–93*

	Conservative 1893	Liberal 1893	Minority 1893	Social-Democrat 1893	Non-voter 1893	All 1890
Conservative 1890	0.067	0.007	0.002	0.005	0.011	0.092
Liberal 1890	0.044	0.157	0.016	0.019	0.049	0.285
Minority 1890	0.008	0.004	0.114	0.003	0.017	0.146
Social-Democrat 1890	0.018	0.010	0.001	0.112	0.018	0.159
Non-voters 1890	0.027	0.015	0.040	0.016	0.176	0.273
Net new voters 1893	0.002	0.005	0.016	0.014	0.009	0.045
All 1893	0.166	0.198	0.189	0.168	0.280	1

Table A.11 *Voter transition probabilities, 1893–98*

	Conservative 1898	Liberal 1898	Minority 1898	Social-Democrat 1898	Non-voter 1898	All 1893
Conservative 1893	0.095	0.022	0.006	0.014	0.018	0.154
Liberal 1893	0.022	0.102	0.011	0.026	0.022	0.184
Minority 1893	0.007	0.020	0.110	0.008	0.031	0.175
Social-Democrat 1893	0.004	0.018	0.001	0.120	0.014	0.156
Non-voters 1893	0.008	0.002	0.024	0.008	0.218	0.260
Net new voters 1898	0.004	0.007	0.032	0.009	0.020	0.071
All 1898	0.141	0.169	0.182	0.184	0.324	1

Table A.12 *Voter transition probabilities, 1898–1903*

	Conservative 1903	Liberal 1903	Minority 1903	Social-Democrat 1903	Non-voter 1903	All 1898
Conservative 1898	0.086	0.016	0.003	0.015	0.008	0.128
Liberal 1898	0.020	0.105	0.008	0.014	0.009	0.155
Minority 1898	0.005	0.014	0.132	0.006	0.010	0.166
Social-Democrat 1898	0.003	0.019	0.001	0.140	0.006	0.168
Non-voters 1898	0.017	0.019	0.031	0.029	0.199	0.295
Net new voters 1903	0.002	0.007	0.030	0.036	0.012	0.087
All 1903	0.132	0.180	0.204	0.240	0.243	1

Table A.13 *Voter transition probabilities, 1903–07*

	Conservative 1907	Liberal 1907	Minority 1907	Social-Democrat 1907	Non-voter 1907	All 1903
Conservative 1903	0.095	0.012	0.007	0.005	0.005	0.124
Liberal 1903	0.022	0.122	0.009	0.012	0.005	0.169
Minority 1903	0.008	0.012	0.158	0.005	0.008	0.191
Social-Democrat 1903	0.007	0.040	0.003	0.167	0.009	0.226
Non-voters 1903	0.020	0.034	0.024	0.027	0.124	0.228
Net new voters 1907	0.001	0.007	0.018	0.028	0.008	0.062
All 1907	0.154	0.227	0.218	0.244	0.157	1

Table A.14 *Voter transition probabilities, 1907–12*

	Conservative 1912	Liberal 1912	Minority 1912	Social-Democrat 1912	Non-voter 1912	All 1907
Conservative 1907	0.074	0.042	0.004	0.014	0.009	0.142
Liberal 1907	0.047	0.128	0.008	0.017	0.009	0.209
Minority 1907	0.006	0.020	0.143	0.013	0.019	0.202
Social-Democrat 1907	0.002	0.017	0.002	0.195	0.010	0.226
Non-voters 1907	0.002	0.006	0.009	0.027	0.102	0.146
Net new voters 1912	0.001	0.014	0.025	0.028	0.007	0.075
All 1912	0.132	0.228	0.190	0.294	0.156	1

Table A.15 *The vote by confession, 1871*

	Party						
Confession	Conservative	Liberal	Center	Other minority	Social-Democrat	Non-voters	All
Protestant	0.084	0.163	0.008	0.011	0.015	0.373	0.653
Catholic	0.033	0.072	0.086	0.023	0.002	0.132	0.348
All	0.117	0.234	0.094	0.033	0.016	0.505	1

Table A.16 *The vote by confession, 1874*

	Party						
Confession	Conservative	Liberal	Center	Other Minority	Social-Democrat	Non-voters	All
Protestant	0.065	0.192	0.000	0.019	0.039	0.314	0.629
Catholic	0.021	0.052	0.169	0.047	0.003	0.079	0.371
All	0.086	0.244	0.169	0.066	0.041	0.393	1

Table A.17 *The vote by confession, 1877*

	Party						
Confession	Conservative	Liberal	Center	Other Minority	Social-Democrat	Non-voters	All
Protestant	0.092	0.181	0.000	0.018	0.053	0.291	0.634
Catholic	0.015	0.050	0.150	0.042	0.003	0.107	0.366
All	0.107	0.231	0.150	0.059	0.055	0.398	1

Table A.18 *The vote by confession, 1878*

	Party						
Confession	Conservative	Liberal	Center	Other Minority	Social-Democrat	Non-voters	All
Protestant	0.142	0.172	0.000	0.020	0.044	0.259	0.637
Catholic	0.027	0.040	0.146	0.036	0.004	0.112	0.364
All	0.169	0.212	0.146	0.056	0.048	0.370	1

Table A.19 *The vote by confession, 1881*

				Party			
Confession	Conservative	Liberal	Center	Other Minority	Social-Democrat	Non-voters	All
Protestant	0.124	0.190	0.000	0.015	0.031	0.281	0.641
Catholic	0.009	0.022	0.130	0.034	0.003	0.160	0.359
All	0.133	0.212	0.130	0.049	0.034	0.441	1

Table A.20 *The vote by confession, 1884*

				Party			
Confession	Conservative	Liberal	Center	Other Minority	Social-Democrat	Non-voters	All
Protestant	0.121	0.194	0.000	0.017	0.052	0.259	0.642
Catholic	0.012	0.029	0.137	0.035	0.007	0.139	0.358
All	0.133	0.223	0.137	0.051	0.059	0.398	1

Table A.21 *The vote by confession, 1887*

				Party			
Confession	Conservative	Liberal	Center	Other Minority	Social-Democrat	Non-voters	All
Protestant	0.166	0.239	0.000	0.015	0.074	0.151	0.644
Catholic	0.027	0.047	0.155	0.044	0.004	0.078	0.356
All	0.193	0.285	0.155	0.059	0.078	0.229	1

Table A.22 *The vote by confession, 1890*

				Party			
Confession	Conservative	Liberal	Center	Other Minority	Social-Democrat	Non-voters	All
Protestant	0.121	0.219	0.000	0.017	0.125	0.159	0.640
Catholic	0.021	0.031	0.132	0.030	0.016	0.131	0.360
All	0.141	0.250	0.132	0.047	0.141	0.289	1

Table A.23 *The vote by confession, 1893*

	Party						
Confession	Conservative	Liberal	Center	Other Minority	Social-Democrat	Non-voters	All
Protestant	0.144	0.165	0.000	0.018	0.150	0.163	0.640
Catholic	0.022	0.033	0.138	0.032	0.019	0.116	0.360
All	0.166	0.198	0.138	0.051	0.168	0.280	1

Table A.24 *The vote by confession, 1898*

	Party						
Confession	Conservative	Liberal	Center	Other Minority	Social-Democrat	Non-voters	All
Protestant	0.126	0.142	0.000	0.017	0.169	0.184	0.638
Catholic	0.014	0.028	0.127	0.038	0.015	0.140	0.363
All	0.141	0.169	0.127	0.055	0.184	0.324	1

Table A.25 *The vote by confession, 1903*

	Party						
Confession	Conservative	Liberal	Center	Other Minority	Social-Democrat	Non-voters	All
Protestant	0.118	0.145	0.000	0.014	0.215	0.143	0.636
Catholic	0.014	0.035	0.147	0.043	0.025	0.101	0.364
All	0.132	0.180	0.147	0.057	0.240	0.243	1

Table A.26 *The vote by confession, 1907*

	Party						
Confession	Conservative	Liberal	Center	Other Minority	Social-Democrat	Non-voters	All
Protestant	0.130	0.183	0.000	0.014	0.215	0.094	0.636
Catholic	0.024	0.044	0.163	0.041	0.029	0.064	0.364
All	0.154	0.227	0.163	0.055	0.244	0.157	1

Table A.27 *The vote by confession, 1912*

	Party						
Confession	Conservative	Liberal	Center	Other Minority	Social-Democrat	Non-voters	All
Protestant	0.114	0.180	0.000	0.012	0.250	0.080	0.636
Catholic	0.017	0.048	0.143	0.036	0.045	0.075	0.364
All	0.132	0.228	0.143	0.048	0.294	0.156	1

Table A.28 *The vote by confession and social group, 1887*

	Party					
Confession and social group	Conservative	Liberal	Minority	Social-Democrat	Non-voters	All
Protestant farmers	0.076	0.063	0.007	0.004	0.057	0.207
Protestant middle class	0.004	0.141	0.000	0.029	0.054	0.227
Protestant workers	0.086	0.034	0.008	0.042	0.040	0.210
Catholic farmers	0.021	0.012	0.081	0.000	0.033	0.147
Catholic middle class	0.001	0.025	0.040	0.002	0.032	0.100
Catholic workers	0.006	0.011	0.078	0.002	0.013	0.109
All	0.193	0.285	0.214	0.078	0.229	1

Table A.29 *The vote by confession and social group, 1890*

Confession and social group	Party					
	Conservative	Liberal	Minority	Social-Democrat	Non-voters	All
Protestant farmers	0.055	0.069	0.008	0.004	0.069	0.206
Protestant middle class	0.007	0.133	0.000	0.045	0.041	0.226
Protestant workers	0.058	0.017	0.009	0.076	0.049	0.208
Catholic farmers	0.018	0.009	0.072	0.001	0.048	0.148
Catholic middle class	0.000	0.015	0.033	0.007	0.046	0.101
Catholic workers	0.003	0.006	0.057	0.008	0.036	0.111
All	0.141	0.250	0.179	0.141	0.289	1

Table A.30 *The vote by confession and social group, 1893*

Confession and social group	Party					
	Conservative	Liberal	Minority	Social-Democrat	Non-voters	All
Protestant farmers	0.069	0.055	0.009	0.011	0.063	0.206
Protestant middle class	0.020	0.088	0.000	0.053	0.065	0.226
Protestant workers	0.056	0.023	0.009	0.086	0.035	0.208
Catholic farmers	0.019	0.009	0.072	0.002	0.046	0.149
Catholic middle class	0.000	0.014	0.040	0.007	0.040	0.101
Catholic workers	0.004	0.009	0.058	0.010	0.030	0.111
All	0.166	0.198	0.189	0.168	0.280	1

Table A.31 *The vote by confession and social group, 1898*

Confession and social group	Party					
	Conservative	Liberal	Minority	Social-Democrat	Non-voters	All
Protestant farmers	0.064	0.048	0.009	0.014	0.071	0.205
Protestant middle class	0.015	0.065	0.000	0.065	0.080	0.225
Protestant workers	0.047	0.030	0.008	0.090	0.033	0.207
Catholic farmers	0.010	0.010	0.077	0.002	0.051	0.149
Catholic middle class	0.000	0.009	0.039	0.005	0.048	0.102
Catholic workers	0.005	0.009	0.049	0.009	0.040	0.111
All	0.141	0.169	0.182	0.184	0.324	1

Table A.32 *The vote by confession and social group, 1903*

Confession and social group	Party					
	Conservative	Liberal	Minority	Social-Democrat	Non-voters	All
Protestant farmers	0.058	0.034	0.007	0.005	0.052	0.156
Protestant middle class	0.034	0.053	0.000	0.103	0.052	0.242
Protestant workers	0.026	0.059	0.008	0.109	0.039	0.242
Catholic farmers	0.010	0.009	0.062	0.000	0.034	0.114
Catholic middle class	0.001	0.011	0.055	0.007	0.032	0.106
Catholic workers	0.003	0.015	0.071	0.018	0.033	0.140
All	0.132	0.180	0.204	0.240	0.243	1

Table A.33 *The vote by confession and social group, 1907*

Confession and social group	Party					
	Conservative	Liberal	Minority	Social-Democrat	Non-voters	All
Protestant farmers	0.066	0.044	0.006	0.009	0.031	0.156
Protestant middle class	0.033	0.074	0.000	0.100	0.036	0.242
Protestant workers	0.033	0.065	0.008	0.108	0.028	0.242
Catholic farmers	0.018	0.012	0.064	0.001	0.019	0.114
Catholic middle class	0.005	0.013	0.055	0.009	0.023	0.106
Catholic workers	0.000	0.018	0.083	0.019	0.020	0.140
All	0.154	0.227	0.218	0.244	0.157	1

Table A.34 *The vote by confession and social group, 1912*

Confession and social group	Party					
	Conservative	Liberal	Minority	Social-Democrat	Non-voters	All
Protestant farmers	0.063	0.048	0.006	0.012	0.027	0.155
Protestant middle class	0.035	0.070	0.000	0.107	0.028	0.241
Protestant workers	0.017	0.062	0.007	0.130	0.025	0.240
Catholic farmers	0.014	0.015	0.066	0.000	0.022	0.116
Catholic middle class	0.004	0.017	0.048	0.014	0.025	0.107
Catholic workers	0.001	0.017	0.065	0.031	0.029	0.142
All	0.132	0.228	0.191	0.294	0.156	1

Bibliography

Abramson, Paul, Aldrich, John H., and Rohde, David W. *Change and Continuity in the 1980 Elections*. Washington, DC: Congressional Quarterly Press, 1982.

Adams, Carole Elizabeth. *Women Clerks in Wilhelmine Germany: Issues of Class and Gender*. Cambridge and New York: Cambridge University Press, 1988.

Aldrich, John H. and Nelson, Forrest D. *Linear Probability, Logit, and Probit Models*. Beverly Hills and London: SAGE Publications, 1984.

Anderson, Margaret Lavinia. "The Kulturkamff and the Course of German History," *Central European History* 19 (1986): 82–115.

"Voter Junker, *Landrat* Priest: The Old Authorities and the New Franchise in Imperial Germany," *American Historical Review* 98 (1993): 1448–74.

Windthorst: A Political Biography. Oxford: Clarendon Press, 1981.

Aschoff, Hans-Georg. *Welfische Bewegung und politischer Katholizismus 1866–1918. Die Deutsch–hannoversche Partei und das Zentrum in der Provinz Hannover während des Kaiserreiches*. Düsseldorf: Droste, 1987.

Bajohr, Frank. *Zwischen Krupp und Kommune: Sozialdemokratie, Arbeiterschaft und Stadtverwaltng in Essen vor dem 1. Weltkrieg*. Essen: Klartext, 1988.

Barkin, Kenneth. *The Controversy over German Industrialization, 1890–1902*. Chicago and London: University of Chicago Press, 1970.

Barnes, Samuel H. "Secular Trends and Partisan Realingnment in Italy," in Russell J. Dalton, Scott C. Flanagan and Paul Allen Beck (eds.) *Electoral Change in Advanced Industrial Democracies: Realignment or Dealignment?* Princeton: Princeton University Press, 1984, pp. 205–30.

Baum, Dale. *The Civil War Party System: The Case of Massachusetts, 1848–1876*. Chapel Hill and London: University of North Carolina Press, 1984.

Becker, Winfried. "Kulturkampf als Vorwand: Die Kolonialwahlen von 1907 und das Problem der Parlamentarisierung des Reiches," *Historisches Jahrbuch* 106 (1986): 59–84.

Die Minderheit als Mitte. Die Deutsche Zentrumspartei in der Innenpolitik des Reiches 1871–1933. Paderborn: Schöningh, 1986.

Becker, Winfried and Morsey, Rudolf (eds.). *Christliche Demokratie in Europa: Grundlagen und Entwicklung seit dem 19. Jahrhundert*. Cologne and Vienna: Böhlau, 1988.

Bendikat, Elfi. *Wahlkämpfe in Europa 1884 bis 1889. Parteiensystem und Politikstile in Deutschland, Frankreich und Großbritannien*. Wiesbaden: Deutscher Universitäts-Verlag, 1988.

Berghahn, Volker A. *Imperial Germany 1871–1914: Economy, Society, Culture and Politics*. Providence and Oxford: Berghahn Books, 1994.

Bergmann, Günter. *Das Sozialistengesetz im rechtsrheinischen Industriegebiet. Ein Beitrag zur Auseinandersetzung zwischen Staat und Sozialdemokratie im Wuppertal und im Bergischen Land 1878–1890*. Hanover: Verlag für Literatur und Zeitgeschehen, 1970.

Bertram, Jürgen. *Die Wahlen zum Deutschen Reichstage vom Jahre 1912*. Düsseldorf: Droste, 1964.

Blackbourn, David. *Class, Religion and Local Politics in Wilhelmine Germany: The Centre Party in Württtemberg before 1914*. New Haven and London: Yale University Press, 1980.

Blackbourn, David and Eley, Geoff. *The Peculiarities of German History: Bourgeois Society and Politics in Nineteenth-Century Germany*. Oxford and New York: Oxford University Press, 1984.

Blank, Robert. "Die soziale Zusammensetzung der sozialdemokratischen Wählerschaft Deutschlands," *Archiv für Sozialwissenschaft und Sozialpolitik* 20 (1905): 507–53.

Blanke, Richard. *Prussian Poland in the German Empire (1871–1900)*. New York: Columbia University Press, 1981.

Bleek, Stephan. *Quartierbildung in der Urbanisierung: Das Münchener Westend 1890–1933*. Munich: R. Oldenbourg Verlag, 1991.

Blessing, Werner. *Staat und Kirche in der Gesellschaft: Institutionelle Autorität und mentaler Wandel in Bayern im 19. Jahrhundert*. Göttingen: Vandenhoeck & Ruprecht, 1982.

Boswell, Laird. "The French Rural Communist Electorate," *Journal of Interdisciplinary History* 23 (1992/93): 719–49.

Bourke, Paul F. and DeBats, Donald A. "Individuals and Aggregates: A Note on Historical Data and Assumptions," *Social Science History* 4 (1980): 229–49.

Breunig, Willi. *Soziale Verhältnisse der Arbeiterschaft und sozialistische Arbeiterbewegung in Ludwigshafen am Rhein 1869–1919*. Ludwigshafen a. Rh.: Stadtarchiv, 1976.

Bräunche, Ernst Otto. *Parteien und Reichstagswahlen in der Rheinpfalz von der Reichsgründung 1871 bis zum Ausbruch des Ersten Weltkrieges 1914*. Speyer: Verlag der Pfälzischen Gesellschft zur Förderung der Wissenschaften, 1982.

Brose, Eric. *Christian Labor and the Politics of Frustration in Imperial Germany*. Washington: Catholic University of America Press, 1985.

Brosius, D. *Rudolf von Bennigsen als Oberpräsident der Provinz Hannover 1888–1897*. Hildesheim: Lax, 1964.

Budge, Ian and Farlie, Dennis. *Voting and Party Competition: A Theoretical Critique and Synthesis Applied to Surveys from Ten Democracies*. London and New York: John Wiley & Sons, 1977.

Burbank, Garin. *When Farmers Voted Red: The Gospel of Socialism in the Oklahoma Countryside, 1910–1924*. Westport: Greenwood Press, 1976.

Busch, Helmut. *Die Stoeckerbewegung im Siegerland. Ein Beitrag zur Siegerländer Geschichte in der 2. Häflte des 19. Jahrhunderts*. Siegen: Forschungsstelle Siegerland, 1968.

Cerny, Karl H. (ed.). *Germany at the Polls: The Bundestag Elections of the 1980s*. Durham: Duke University Press, 1990.

Chrobach, Werner. "Politische Parteien, Verbände und Vereine in Regensburg 1869–1914," *Verhandlungen des Historischen Vereins für Oberpfalz und Regensburg*: 119 (1979): 137–223; 120 (1980): 211–384; 121 (1981): 183–284.

Claggett, William, Loesch, Jeffrey, Shively, W. Phillips, and Snell, Ronald. "Political Leadership and the Development of Political Cleavages: Imperial Germany, 1871–1912," *American Journal of Political Science* 26 (1982): 644–63.

Conradt, David P. *The German Polity*. 5th edn. New York and London: Longman Publishing, 1993.

Conze, Werner. "Politische Willensbildung im deutschen Kaiserreich als Forschungsaufgabe historischer Wahlsoziologie," in Helmut Berding (ed.) *Vom Staat des Ancien Regimes zum modernen Partiestaat*. Munich and Vienna: R. Oldenbourg Verlag, 1978, pp. 331–47.

Crothers, George Dunlop. *The German Elections of 1907*. New York: Columbia University Press, 1941.

Dann, Otto. *Nation und Nationalismus in Deutschland 1770–1990*. Munich: Verlag C.H. Beck, 1993.

Deming, W. Edwards and Stephan, Frederick. "On a Least Squares Adjustment of a Sampled Frequency Table when the Expected Marginal Totals are Known," *Annals of Mathematical Statistics* 11 (1940): 427–44.

Döring, Herbert. "Wählen Industriearbeiter zunehmend konservativ? Die Bundesrepublik Deutschland im westeuropäischenVergleich," *Archiv für Sozialgeschichte* 29 (1989): 225–71.

Dogan, Mattei. "Political Cleavage and Social Stratification in France and Italy," in Seymour Martin Lipset and Stein Rokkan (eds.) *Party Systems and Voter Alignments: Cross-National Perspectives*. New York: The Free Press, 1967, pp. 129–95.

Downs, Anthony. *An Economic Theory of Democracy*. New York: Harpers, 1957.

Düding, Dieter. *Der Nationalsoziale Verein 1896–1903. Der gescheiterte Versuch einer parteipolitischen Synthese von Nationalismus Sozialismus und Liberalismus*. Munich, 1972.

Eichler, Volker. *Sozialistische Arbeiterbewegung in Frankfurt am Main 1878–1895*. Frankfurt: Kramer, 1983.

Eley, Geoff. "The German Right, 1860–1945: How It Changed," in Geoff Eley (ed.) *From Unification to Nazism: Reinterpreting the German Past*. Boston, London and Sydney: Allen & Unwin, 1986, pp. 231–53.

"Notable Politics, the Crisis of German Liberalism, and the Electoral Transition of the 1890s," in Konrad Jarausch and Larry Jones (eds.) *In Search of a Liberal Germany: Studies in the History of German Liberalism from 1789 to the Present*. New York, Oxford and Munich: Berg Publishers, 1990, pp. 187–216.

Reshaping the German Right : Radical Nationalism and Political Change after Bismarck. Yale and New Haven: Yale University Press, 1980.

Elm, Ludwig. *Zwischen Fortschritt und Reaktion. Geschichte der Parteien der liberalen Bourgeoisie in Deutschland 1893–1918*. East Berlin: Akademie-Verlag, 1968.

Elsässer, Konrad. *Die badische Sozialdemokratie 1890 bis 1914. Zum*

Zusammenhang von Bildung und Organisation. Marburg: Verlag Arbeiterbewegung und Gesellschaftswisenschaft, 1978.

Ersson, Svante. "Model Specification and Ecological Inference," in Sten Berglund and Søren Risbjerg Thomsen (eds.) *Modern Political Ecological Analysis.* Åbo: Åbo Akademis Förlag, 1990, pp. 111–30

Ersson, Svante and Wörlund, Ingemar. "Level of Aggregation and Ecological Inference: A Study of the Swedish Elections in 1944 and 1979," in Sten Berglund and Søren Risbjerg Thomsen (eds.) *Modern Political Ecological Analysis.* Åbo: Åbo Akademis Förlag, 1990, pp. 131–47.

Fairbairn, Brett. "Authority vs. Democracy: Prussian Officials and the German Elections of 1898–1903," *Historical Journal* 33 (1990): 811–38.

"Interpreting Wilhelmine Elections: National Issues, Fairness Issues and Electoral Mobilization," in Larry Eugene Jones and James Retallack (eds.) *Elections, Mass Politics and Social Change in Modern Germany: New Perspectives.* Cambridge and New York: Cambridge University Press, 1992, pp. 17–48.

Falter, Jürgen. *Hitlers Wähler.* Munich: Beck, 1990.

"Kontinuität und Neubeginn. Die Bundestagswahl 1949 zwischen Weimar und Bonn," *Politische Vierteljahresschrift* 22 (1981): 236–63.

"The Two Hindenburg Elections of 1925 and 1932: A Total Reversal of Voter Coalitions," *Central European History* 23 (1990): 225–41.

"Die Wählerpotentiale politischer Teilkulturen, 1920–1933," in Detlef Lehnert and Klaus Mengerle (eds.) *Politische Indentität und nationale Gedenktage: Zur politischen Kultur in der Weimarer Republik.* Opladen: Westdeutscher Verlag, 1989, pp. 281–305.

"War die NSDAP die erste deutsche Volkspartei?" in Michael Prinz and Rainer Zitelmann (eds.) *Nationalsozialismus und Modernisierung.* Darmstadt: Wissenschaftliche Buchgesellschaft, 1991.

Falter, Jürgen and Hänisch, Dirk. "Die Anfälligkeit von Arbeitern gegenüber der NSDAP bei den Reichstagswahlen," *Archiv für Sozialgeschichte* 26 (1986): 179–216.

Falter, Jürgen, Lindenberg, Thomas, and Schumann, Siegfried. *Wahlen und Abstimmungen in der Weimarer Republik: Materialien zum Wahlverhalten 1919–1933.* Munich: Verlag C.H. Beck, 1986.

Falter, Jürgen and Zintl, Reinhard. "The Economic Crisis of the 1930s and the Nazi Vote," *Journal of Interdisciplinary History* 19 (1988/89): 55–85.

Farr, Ian. "From Anti-Catholicism to Anti-Clericalism: Catholic Politics and the Peasantry in Bavaria, 1860–1900," *European Studies Review* 13 (1983): 246–69.

Fischer, Ilse. *Industrialisierung, sozialer Konflikt und politische Willensbildung in der Stadtgemeinde. Ein Beitrag zur Sozialgeschichte Augsburgs 1840–1914.* Augsburg: H. Mühlberger, 1977.

Frank, Robert. *Dei Brandenburger als Reichstagswähler.* Vol. 1 1867/71 bis 1912/14. Berlin, Carl Heymanns Verlag, 1934.

Fricke, Dieter. *Handbuch zur Geschichte der deutschen Arbeiterbewegung 1869 bis 1917.* 2 vols. East Berlin: Dietz Verlag, 1987.

"Der Reichsverband gegen die Sozialdemokratie von seiner Gründung bis zu den Reichstagwahlen von 1907," *Zeitschrift für Geschichtswissenschaft* 7 (1959): 237–80.

Friedrich, Manfred. "Die Parteitage des Zentrums in Bayern," *Zeitschrift für Bayerische Landesgeschichte* 36 (1973): 834–76.

Fritzsche, Peter. *Rehearsals for Fascism: Populism and Political Mobilization in Weimar Germany.* Oxford and New York: Oxford University Press, 1990.

Gerhardt, Dittmar. "Zur praktischen Landagitation der deutschen Sozialdemokratie unter den deutschen Kleinbauern in den 90er Jahren des 19. Jahrhunderts," *Beiträge zur Geschichte der deutschen Arbeiterbewegung* 10 (1968): 1091–1100.

"Germany's New Politics," Special issue of the *German Studies Review* 1995.

Gesters, K. *Leopold Sonnemann: Ein Beitrag zur Geschichte des demokratischen Nationalstaatsgedankens in Deutschland.* Frankfurt: Waldemar Kramer, 1976.

Gibowski, Wolfgang G. "Germany's General Election in 1994: Who Voted for Whom?" in *German Studies Review*, special issue on "Germany's New Politics," 1995: 91–114.

Gienapp, William. *The Origins of the Republican Party 1852–1856.* Oxford and New York: Oxford University Press, 1987.

Goch, Stephan. *Sozialdemokratische Arbeiterbewegung und Arbeiterverhalten im Ruhrgebiet. Eine Untersuchung am Beispiel Gelsenkirchens 1848–1975.* Düsseldorf: Droste 1990.

Groh, Dieter. *Negative Integration und revolutionärer Attentismus: Die deutsche Sozialdemokratie am Vorabend des Ersten Weltkrieges.* Frankfurt: Ullstein, 1973.

Grohs, Winfried. *Die Liberale Reichspartei 1871–1874. Liberale Katholiken und föderalistische Protestanten im ersten Deutschen Reichstag.* Frankfurt: Peter Lang, 1990.

Gründer, Horst. "Rechtskatholizismus im Kaiserreich und in der Weimarer Republik unter besonderer Berücksichtigung der Rheinlande und Westfalen," *Westfälische Zeitschrift* 134 (1984): 107–55.

Günther, Wolgang. *Parteien und Wahlen in Oldenburg: Beiträge zur Landesgeschichte im 19. und 20. Jahrhundert.* Oldenburg: Holzberg, 1983.

Guttsman, Wilhelm. *The German Social Democratic Party 1875–1933: From Ghetto to Government.* London: Allen & Unwin, 1981.

Hagen, William. *Germans, Poles and Jews: The Nationality Conflict in the Prussian East, 1772–1914.* Chicago and London: The University of Chicago Press, 1980.

Hanushek, E. A., Jackson, J. E., and Kain, J. F. "Model Specification, Use of Aggregate Data, and the Ecological Correlation Fallacy," *Political Methodology* 1 (1974): 87–106.

Hattenhofer, Peter. *Regierende und Regierte Wähler und Gewählte in der Oberpfalz 1870–1914.* Munich: Stadtarchiv, 1979.

Heckart, Beverly. *From Bassermann to Bebel: The Grand Bloc's Quest for Reform in the Kaiserreich, 1900–1914.* New Haven and London: Yale University Press, 1974.

Heitzer, Horstwalter. *Der Volksverein für das katholische Deutschland im Kaiserreich 1890–1918.* Mainz: Matthias Grünwald, 1979.

Hellfaier, Karl Alexander. "Die sozialdemokratische Bewegung in Halle/S (1865–90)," *Archiv für Sozialgeschichte* 1 (1961): 69–108.

Henning, Hansjoachim, "Kriegervereine in den preußischen Westprovinzen. (Ein Beitrag zur preußischen Innenpolitik zwischen 1860 und 1914)," *Rheinische Vierteljahrsblätter* 32 (1968): 430–75.

Hentschel, Volker. *Geschichte der deutschen Sozialpolitik 1880–1980.* Frankfurt: Suhrkamp, 1980.

Henze, Wilfried. "Die politische Masssenarbeit der Sozialistischen Arbeiterpartei Deutschland in Vorbereitung der Reichstagswahl 1890," *Beiträge zur Geschichte der Arbeiterbewegung* 27 (1985): 29–39.

Herzig, Arno. *Der Allgemeine Deutsche Arbeiter-Verein in der deutschen Sozialdemokratie. Dargestellt an der Biographie des Funktionärs Carl Wilhelm Tölcke (1817–1893),* W. Berlin: Colloquium Verlag, 1979.

Hess, Ulrich. *Geschichte Thüringens 1866 bis 1914.* Edited Volker Wahl. Weimar: Böhlau, 1991.

Hesselbarth, Hellmut. *Revolutionäre Sozialdemokraten, Opportunisten und die Bauern am Vorabend des Imperialismus.* Berlin: Dietz, 1968.

Hiery, Hermann. *Reichstagswahlen im Reichsland. Ein Beitrag zur Landesgeschichte von Elsaß–Lothringen und zur Wahlgeschichte des Deutschen Reiches 1871–1918.* Düsseldorf: Droste, 1986.

Hinscke, Andrea. *"Über die Parteien" und "neben den Gewerkschaften": Der württembergische Landesverband evangelischer Arbeitervereine (1891–1918),* Frankfurt: Peter Lang Verlag, 1989.

Hirschfelder, Heinrich. *Die bayerische Sozialdemokratie 1864–1914.* Erlangen: Palm u. Enke, 1979. 2 vols. vol. 1, 1864–78; vol. 2, 1878–1914.

Hobsbawm, Eric. *The Age of Extremes: A History of the World, 1914–1991.* New York: Pantheon Books, 1994.

Hoch, Gerhard. *Das Scheitern der Demokratie im ländlichen Raum: Das Beispiel der Region Kaltenkirchen/Henstedt-Ulzburg 1870–1933.* Kiel: Neuer Malik-Verlag, 1988.

Hofmann, Klaus Martin. *Die evangelische Arbeitervereinsbewegung 1882–1914.* Bielefeld: Luther-Verlag, 1982.

Hoschka, Peter and Schunck, Herman. "Schätzung von Wählerwanderungen: Puzzlespiel oder gesicherte Ergebnisse?" *Politische Vierteljahrsschrift* 16 (1975): 491–539.

Hunt, James Clark. *The People's Party in Württemberg and Southern Germany, 1890–1914.* Stuttgart: Ernst Klett Verlag, 1975.

Irwin, Galen and Dittrich, Karl. "And the Walls Came Tumbling Down: Party Dealignment in the Netherlands," in Russell J. Dalton, Scott C. Flanagan, and Paul Allen Beck (eds.) *Electoral Change in Advanced Industrial Democracies: Realignment or Dealignment?* Princeton: Princeton University Press, 1984, pp. 267–97.

Jarausch, Konrad H. and Jones, Larry (eds.). *In Search of a Liberal Germany: Studies in the History of German Liberalism from 1789 to the Present.* New York, Oxford and Munich: Berg Publishers, 1990.

Jensen, Jürgen. *Presse und politische Polizei. Hamburgs Zeitungen unter dem Sozialistengesetz 1878–1890.* Hanover: Dietz, 1966.

Jensen, J. F. "Die Ausweisungspraxis der Hamburger politischen Polizei während des Sozialistengesetzes, (1878–90)," *Hamburgische Geschichts- u. Heimatblätter* 21 (1965): 245–52.

Judt, Tony. *Socialism in Provence, 1871–1914 : a Study in the Origins of the Modern French Left*. Cambridge and New York: Cambridge University Press, 1979.

Kamenski, Ted. *Polish Publicists and Prussian Politics: The Polish Press in Poznan during the Neue Kurs of chancellor Leo von Caprivi 1890–1894*. Stuttgart: Steiner-Verlag, 1988.

Kelly, Alfred. *The Descent of Darwin: The Popularization of Darwinism in Germany 1860–1914*. Chapel Hill: University of North Carolina Press, 1981.

Kermann, Rose. "Das pfälzische Kriegervereinswesen nach der Reichsgründung. Aspekte seiner Entwicklung und seiner politischen und gesellschaftlichen Bedeutung," *Mitteilungen des Historischen Vereins der Pfalz* 85 (1987): 279–346.

Key, V. O. *The Responsible Electorate: Rationality in Presidential Voting 1936–1960*. ed. Milton C. Cummings, Jr. Cambridge, MA: Havard University Press, 1966.

Kitschelt, Herbert. *The Transformation of European Social Democracy*. Cambridge and New York: Cambridge University Press, 1994.

Klatt, Ingo. "Sozialdemokratie und Obrigkeit vor dem Ersten Weltkrieg in Schleswig-Holstein. Aktion und Reaktion," *Demokratische Geschichte* 3 (1988): 97–116.

Kleppner, Paul. *Continuity and Change in Electoral Politics 1893–1928*. New York: Greenwood Press, 1987.

Who Voted? The Dynamics of Electoral Turnout, 1870–1980. New York: Praeger Publishers, 1982.

Kleßmann, Christoph. *Polnische Bergarbeiter im Ruhrgebiet*. Göttingen: Vandenhoeck & Ruprecht, 1978.

Klingemann, Hans D. and Pappi, Franz Urban. "Die Wählerbewegungen bei der Bundestagswahl am 28. September 1969," *Politische Vierteljahresschrift* 11 (1970): 11–83.

Klöcker, Michael. *Die Sozialdemokratie im Regierungsbezirk Aachen vor dem 1. Weltkrieg*. Wentorf b. Hamburg: Einhorn-Presse Verlag, 1977.

Knobel, E. *Die Hessische Rechtspartei: Konservative Opposition gegen das Bismarckreich*. Marburg: N.G. Elwert, 1977.

Kousser, J. Morgan. "Ecological Regression and the Analysis of Past Politics," *Journal of Interdisciplinary History* 4 (1973): 237–62.

"Making Separate Equal: Integration of Black and White School Funds in Kentucky," *Journal of Interdisciplinary History* 10 (1980): 399–428.

The Shaping of Southern Politics: Suffrage Restriction and the Establishment of the One Party South, 1880–1910. New Haven and London: Yale University Press, 1974.

"Speculation or Specification: A Note on Flannigan and Zinagle," *Social Science History*. 10 (1986): 72–84.

Kremer, H. J. "Die Krieger- und Militärvereine in der Innenpolitik des Großherzogtums Baden (1870–1914)," *Zeitschrift für die Geschichte des Oberrheins* 133 (1985): 301–36.

Kremer, Hans-Jürgen (ed.). *Mit Gott für Wahrheit, Freiheit und Recht. Quellen zur Organisation und Politik der Zentrumspartei und des politischen Katholizismus in Baden 1888–1914*. Stuttgart: Kohlhammer, 1983.

"Der Volksverein für das katholische Deutschland in Baden 1890–1933. Ein Beitrag zur Organisations- und Wirkungsgeschichte des politischen und sozialen Verbandskatholizismus," *Freiburger Diözesan-Archiv* 104 (1984): 208–80.

Kropat, W. A. "Der Beamte und die Politik in wilhelmischer Zeit. Zur gescheiterten Reichstagskandidatur des Wiesbadener Regierungspräsidenten von Meister im Jahre 1912," *Nassauische Annalen* 83 (1972): 192–201.

Kühne, Thomas. *Dreiklassenwahlrecht und Wahlkultur in Preußen 1867–1914: Landtagswahlen zwischen korporativer Tradition und politischem Massenmarkt.* Düsseldorf: Droste, 1993.

. "Wahlrecht–Wahlverhalten–Wahlkultur: Tradition und Innovation in der historischen Wahlforschung," *Archiv für Sozialgeschichte* 33 (1993): 481–547.

Kutz-Bauer, Helga. *Arbeiterschaft, Arbeiterbewegung und bürgerlicher Staat in der Zeit der großen Depression. Eine regional- und sozialgeschichtliche Studie zur Geschichte der Arbeiterbewegung in Hamburg 1873 bis 1890.* Bonn: Verlag Neue Gesellschaft, 1988.

Lademacher, Horst. "Wirtschaft, Arbeiterschaft und Arbeiterorganisation in der Rheinprovinz am Vorabend des Sozialistengesetzes 1878," *Archiv für Sozialgeschichte* 15 (1975): 111–44.

Langbein, Laura Irwin and Lichtman, Allan. *Ecological Inference.* Beverly Hills and London: Sage Publications, 1978.

Langewiesche, Dieter. *Liberalismus in Deutschland.* Frankfurt: Suhrkamp Verlag, 1988.

Lapies, Ralf-Reiner. *Nichtwählen als Kategorie des Wahlverhaltens.* Düsseldorf: Droste Verlag, 1973.

Lehmann, Hans Georg. *Die Agrarfrage in der Theorie und Praxis der deutschen und internationalen Sozialdemokratie.* Tübingen: J. C. B. Mohr, 1970.

Lepper, Herbert. "Vom Honoratiorenverein zur Parteiorganisation. Ein Beitrag zur 'Demokratisierung' des Zentrums im Rheinland 1898–1906," *Rheinische Vierteljahrsblätter* 47 (1983); 238–74.

"Die 'Septennatswahlen' 1887 im Raume Aachen," *Zeitschrift des Aachener Geschichtsvereins* 82 (1972): 77–110.

Lepsius, M. Rainer. "Parteisystem und Sozialstruktur: zum Problem der Demokratisierung der deutschen Gesellschaft," in Gerhard Albert Ritter (ed.) *Die deutschen Parteien vor 1918.* Cologne: Kiepenheuer & Witsch, 1973, pp. 56–80.

Levy, Richard S. *The Downfall of the Anti–Semitic Political Parties in Imperial Germany.* New Haven and London: Yale University Press, 1975.

Lewin, Leif, Jansson, Bo, and Sörbom, Dag. *The Swedish Electorate 1887–1968.* Stockholm: Almqvist & Wiksell, 1972.

Lichtman, Allan. "Political Realignment and Ethnocultural Voting in Late Nineteenth Century America," *Journal of Social History* 16/3 (Spring 1983): 54–82,

Prejudice and the Old Politics: The Presidential Election of 1928. Chapel Hill: University of North Carolina Press, 1979.

Lidtke, Vernon. *The Outlawed Party: Social Democracy in Germany 1878–1890.* Princeton: Princeton University Press, 1966.

"Social Class and Secularisation in Imperial Germany: The Working Classes," *LBI Yearbook* 25 (1980): 21–40.

Liebert, Bernd. *Politische Wahlen im Wiesbaden im Kaiserreich 1867–1918.* Wiesbaden: Historische Kommission für Nassau, 1988

Liedhegener, Antonius. "Marktgesellschft und Milieu. Katholiken und katholische Regionen in der wirtschaftlichen Entwicklung des Deutschen Reiches 1895–1914," *Historisches Jahrbuch* 113 (1993): 203–354.

Lohmoeller, Jan-Bernd and Falter, Jürgen. "Some Further Aspects of Ecological Regression Analysis," *Quality & Quantity* 20 (1986): 109–25.

Lohmoeller, Jan-Bernd, Falter, Jürgen, Link, Andreas, and de Rijke, Johann. "Unemployment and the Rise of National Socialism: Contradicting Results from Different Regional Aggregations," in Peter Nijkamp, Helga Leitner, and Neil Wrigley (eds.) *Measuring the Unmeasurable*. Dodrecht Boston and Lancaster: Martinus Nijhoff Publishers, 1985, pp. 357–70.

Loose, Hans-Dieter. "Der Wahlkampf des liberalen Reichstagskandidaten Carl Braband 1911/12," in *Aus der Arbeit der Archive: Beiträge zum Archivwesen zur Quellenkunde und zur Geschichte. Festschrift für Hans Booms*. ed. Friedrich P. Kahlenberg. Boppard: Boldt, 1989.

Lorek, Jochen. *Wie man früher Sozialdemokrat wurde. Das Kommunikationsverhalten in der deutschen Arbeiterbewegung und die Konzeption der sozialistischen Parteipublizistik durch August Bebel*. Bonn–Bad Godesberg: Verlag Neue Gesellschaft, 1977.

Lorenz, Eckehart. "Protestantische Reaktion auf die Entwicklung der sozialistischen Arbeiterbewegung. Mannheim 1890–1933," *Archiv für Sozialgeschichte* 16 (1976): 371–416.

Lorenz, Ina Susanne. *Eugen Richter. Der entschiedene Liberalismus in wilhelmischer Zeit*. Husum: Matthiesen Verlag, 1986. Historische Studien Nr. 433.

Lösche, Peter and Walter, Franz. "Auf dem Weg zur Volkspartei? Die Weimarer Sozialdemokratie," *Archiv für Sozialgeschichte* 19 (1989): 75–136.

Loth, Wilfried. *Katholiken im Kaiserreich: Der politische Katholizismus in der Krise des wilhelmischen Deutschlands*. Düsseldorf: Droste, 1984.

Lützenkirchen, Ralf. *Der sozialdemokratische Verein für den Reichstagwahlkreis Dormund–Hörde. Ein Beitrag zur Parteiengeschichte*. Dortmund: Historischer Verein, 1970.

Mallmann, Klaus-Micheal and Steffens, Horst. *Lohn der Mühen. Geschichte der Bergarbeiter an der Saar*. Munich: Beck, 1987.

Mattheier, K. J. "Dreie Führungsorganisationen der wirtschaftsfriedlichen Arbeiterbewegung: Reichsverband gegen die Sozialdemokratie, Förderungsausschuß und Deutsche Vereinigung in der Auseinandersetzung um die 'Gelben Gewerkschaften,'" *Rheinische Vierteljahrsblätter* 37 (1973): 244–75.

Mergel, Thomas. "Christlicher Konservatismus in der Provinz: Politischer Katholizismus in Ostwestfalen 1887–1912," in Joachim Meynert, Josef Mooser, and Volker Rodekamp (eds.) *Unter Pickelhaube und Zylinder: Das östliche Westfalen im Zeitalter des Wilhelmismus 1881 bis 1914*. Bielefeld: Verlag für Regionalgeschichte, 1991, pp. 283–301
Zwischen Klasse und Konfession: Katholisches Bürgertum im Rheinland 1794–1914. Göttingen: Vandenhoeck & Ruprecht, 1994.

Mielke, Siegfried. *Der Hansa-Bund für Gewerbe, Handel und Industrie 1909– 1914: Der gescheiterte Versuch einer antifeudalen Sammlungspolitik* Göttingen: Vandenhoeck & Ruprecht, 1976.

Mittmann, Ursula. *Fraktion und Partei: Ein Vergleich von Zentrum und Sozialdemokratie im Kaiserreich*. Düsseldorf: Droste, 1976.

Mooser, Josef, Meynert, Jochen, and Rodekamp, Volker (eds.). *Unter Pickelhaube und Zylinder: Das östliche Westfalen im Zeitalter des Wilhelminismus 1888 bis 1914*. Beielefeld: Verlag für Regionalgeschichte, 1991.

Moring, Karl-Ernst. *Die sozialdemokratische Partei in Bremen 1890–1914. Reformismus und Radikalismus in der Sozialdemokratischen Partei Bremens*. Hanover, 1968.

Müller, Klaus. "Zentrumspartei und agararische Bewegung im Rheinland 1882–1903," in Konrad Repgen and Stepan Skalweit (eds.) *Spiegel der Geschichte: Festgabe für Max Braubach zum 10. April 1964*. Münster: Aschendorff, 1964, pp. 828–57.

Neter, John, Wasserman, William, and Kutner, Michael H. *Applied Linear Regression Models*. 2nd edn, Homewood and Boston: Irwin, 1989.

Neubach, Helmut. "Parteien und Politiker in Oberschlesien zur Bismarckzeit," *Jahrbuch der Schlesischen Friedrich–Wilhelms Universität Breslau* 13 (1968): 193–231.

Nipkau, Frank. "Tradition der Erweckungsbewegung in der Partiepolitik: Die Christlich-Konservativen und die Christlich-Soziale Partei in Minden-Ravensberg 1878–1914," in Josef Mooser (ed.)*Frommes Volk und Patrioten. Erweckungsbewegung und soziale Frage im östlichen Westfalen 1800 bis 1900*. Bielefeld: Verlag für Regionalgeschichte, 1989, pp. 386–90.

Nipperdey, Thomas. *Die Organisation der deutschen Parteien vor 1918*. Düsseldorf: Droste, 1961.

Religion im Umbruch: Deutschland 1870–1918 . Munich: Beck, 1988.

Nolan, Mary. *Social Democracy and Society: Working-Class Radicalism in Düsseldorf, 1890–1920*. Cambridge and New York: Cambridge University Press, 1981.

Paetau, Rainer. *Konfrontation oder Kooperation. Arbeiterbewegung und bürgerliche Gesellschaft im ländlichen Schleswig–Holstein und in der Industriestadt Kiel zwischen 1900 und 1925*. Neumünster: Wachholtz, 1988.

Parisius, Bernhard. *Vom Groll der "kleinen Leute" zum Programm der kleinen Schritte. Arbeiterbewegung im Herzogtum Oldenburg 1840–1890*. Oldenburg: Holzberg, 1985.

Peschle, K. "Die Bedeutung der liberalen Parteien und der Sozialdemokratie für das politische Leben im Wahlkreis Altena-Iserlohn von der Reichsgründung 1871 bis zum Jahre 1890," *Altenaer Beiträge* NS (1973): 1–150.

Pflanze, Otto. *Bismarck and the Development of Germany*. 2nd edn, 3 vols. Princeton: Princeton University Press, 1990.

Pies, Norbert. *"Hetzer wohnen hier verhaltnismäßig wenige." Geschichte der Arbeiterbewegung am linken Niederrhein*. ed. Günter Pätzold and Karl-Heinz Schlingmann. Marburg: SP-Verlag, 1989.

Pohl, Karl Heinrich. *Die Münchener Arbeiterbewegung: Sozialdemokratische Partei, Freie Gewerkschaften, Staat und Gesellschaft in München 1890–1914*. Munich: K. G. Saur, 1992.

"Ein zweiter Emanzipationsprozeß des liberalen Unternehmertums? Zur Sozialstruktur und Politik der Liberalen in Sachsen zu Beginn des 20. Jahrhunderts," in Klaus Tenfelde and Hans-Ulrich Wehler (eds.) *Wege zur Geschichte des Bürgertums*. Göttingen: Vandenhoeck & Ruprecht, 1994, pp. 231–48.

Pollmann, Klaus Erich. "Von der Bürgerlichen Repräsentation zu Minderheitsparteien: Liberalismus und Parteienentwicklung in Braunschweig 1880–1914," in Bern Rebe, Klaus Lompe, and Rudolf von Thadden (eds.) *Idee und Pragmatik in der politischen Entscheidung: Alfred Kubel zum 75. Geburtstag*. Bonn: Verlag Neue Geselleschaft, 1984, pp. 289–300.

Pomper, Gerald et al. *The Election of 1988: Reports and Interpretations*. Chatham, NJ: Chatham House Publishers, 1989.

Pracht, Elfi. *Parlamentarismus und deutsche Sozialdemokratie 1867–1914*. Pfaffenweiler: Centaurus-Verlags-Gesellschaft, 1990.

Przeworski, Adam and Sprague, John. *Paper Stones: A History of Electoral Socialism*. Chicago and London: University of Chicago Press, 1986.

Puhle, Hans-Jürgen. *Agrarische Interessenpolitik und preußischer Konservativsmus im wilhelmischen Reich 1893–1914*. Hanover: Verlag für Literatur und Zeitgeschehen, 1966.

Pulzer, Peter. *The Rise of Political Anti–Semitism in Germany and Austria*. New York: John Wiley & Sons, 1964.

Reimann, Joachim. *Ernst Müller-Meiningen senior und der Linksliberalismus in seiner Zeit. Zur Biographie eines bayerischen und deutschen Politikers (1866–1949)*, Munich: Stadtarchiv, 1968.

Reinders, Christoph. "Sozialdemokratie und Immigration. Eine Untersuchung der Entwicklungsmöglickeiten der SPD in einem überwiegend ländlich geprägten Reichtagswahlkreis auf der Grundlage der Wahlbewegung von 1893 bis 1912," in Wolfgang Günther (ed.) *Parteien und Wahlen in Oldenburg: Beiträge zur Landesgeschichte im 19. und 20. Jahrhundert*. Oldenburg: Heinz Holzberg Verlag, 1983, pp. 65–116.

Retallack, James. *Notables of the Right: The Conservative Party and Political Mobilization in Germany, 1876–1918*. London: Unwin Hyman, 1988.

Rieber, Christof. *Das Sozialistengesetz und die Sozialdemokratie in Württemberg 1878–1890*. 2 vols. Stuttgart: Müller & Gräff, 1984.

Ritter, Gerhard Albert. *Die Arbeiterbewegung im Wilhelmischen Reich. Die Sozialdemokratische Partie und die Freien Gewerkschaften 1890–1900*. West Berlin: Colloquium Verlag, 1959.

"Die Sozialdemokratie im Deutschen Kaiserreich in sozialgeschichtlicher Perspektive," *Historische Zeitschrift* 249 (1989): 295–362.

Staat Arbeiterschaft und Arbeiterbewegung in Deutschland. Vom Vormärz bis zum Ende der Weimarer Republik. Berlin–Bonn, Dietz, 1980.

(ed.). *Der Aufsteig der deutschen Arbeiterbewegung: Sozialdemokratie und Freie Gewerkschaften im Parteiensystem ind Sozialmilieu des Kaiserreichs*. Munich: R. Oldenburg, 1990.

Ritter, Gerhard Albert and Niehuss, Merith. *Wahlgeschichtliches Arbeitsbuch: Materialien zur Statistik des Kaiserreichs 1871–1918*. Munich: Beck, 1980.

Wahlen in Deutschland 1946–1991: Ein Handbuch. Munich: Verlag C. H. Beck, 1991.

Röhl, John C. G. "The Disintegration of the *Kartell* and the Politics of Bismarck's Fall from Power," *Historical Journal* 9 (1966): 60–89.

Germany without Bismarck: The Crisis of Government in the Second Reich, 1890–1900. Berkeley and Los Angeles: University of California Press, 1967.

The Kaiser and his Court: Wilhelm II and the Government of Germany. trans.

Terence F. Cole. Cambridge and New York: Cambridge University Press, 1994.

Rohe, Karl. "Die Ruhrgebietssozialdemokratie im Wilhelmischen Kaiserreich und ihr politischer und kultureller Kontext," in Gerhard Albert Ritter (ed.) *Der Aufsteig der deutschen Arbeiterbewegung: Sozialdemokratie und Freie Gewerkschaften im Parteiensystem und Sozialmilieu des Kaiserreichs*. Munich: R. Oldenburg, 1990, pp. 317–44, *Wahlen und Wählertraditionen in Deutschland*. Frankfurt: Suhrkamp, 1992.

Rohe, Karl, Jäger, Wolfgang and Dorow, Uwe. "Politische Gesellschft und politische Kultur," in Wolfgang Köllmann, Hermann Korte, Dietmar Petzina, and Wolfhard Weber (eds.) *Das Ruhrgebiet im Industriezeitalter: Geschichte und Entwicklung*. 2 vols. Düsseldorf: Schwann, 1990. 1: 419–507.

Rohrkrämer, Thomas. *Der Militarismus der "kleinen Leute." Die Kriegervereine im Deutschen Kaiserreich 1871–1914*. Munich: R. Oldenbourg Verlag, 1990.

Rokkan, Stein and Lipset, Seymour Martin. "Cleavage Structures, Party Systems, and Voter Alignments: An Introduction," in Seymour Martin Lipset and Stein Rokkan (eds.), *Party Systems and Voter Alignments: Cross-National Perspectives*. New York: The Free Press, 1967, pp. 1–64.

Rose, Richard. *Voters Begin to Choose: From Closed-Class to Open Elections in Britain*. London and Beverly Hills: SAGE Publications, 1986.

Ross, Ronald R. *Beleaguered Tower: The Dilemma of Political Catholicism in Wilhelmine Germany*. Notre Dame and London: University of Notre Dame Press, 1976.

Roth, Ralf. *Gewerkschaftskartell und Sozialpolitik in Frankfurt am Main: Arbeiterbewegung vor dem Ersten Weltkrieg zwischen Restauration und liberaler Erneuerung* . Frankfurt: Waldemar Verlag, 1991.

Rüdel, Holger. *Landarbeiter und Sozialdemokratie in Olstholstein 1872 bis 1878. Erfolg und Niederlage der sozialistischen Arbeiterbewegung in einem großagrarischen Wahlkreis zwischen Reichsgründung und Sozialistengesetz*. Neumünster: Wachholtz, 1986.

Saldern, Adelheid von. *Auf dem Weg zum Arbeiter–Reformismus. Parteialltag in sozialdemokratischer Provinz, Göttingen (1870–1920)*, Frankfurt: Materiales Verlag, 1984.

"Wer ging in die SPD? Zur Analyse der Parteimitgliedschaft in wilhelmischer Zeit," in G. A Ritter (ed.) *Der Aufsteig der deutschen Arbeiterbewegung: Sozialdemokratie und Freie Gewerkschaften im Parteiensystem und Sozialmilieu des Kaiserreichs*. Munich: R. Oldenburg, 1990, pp. 161–83.

Saul, Klaus. "Der 'Deutsche Kriegerbund.' Zur innenpolitischen Funktion eines 'nationalen' Verbandes im kaiserlichen Deutschland. Dokumentation," *Militärgeschichtliche Mitteilungen* 2 (1969): 95–159.

"Der Kampf um das Landproletariat. Sozialistische Landagitation, Großgrundbesitz und preußische Staatsverwaltung, 1890 bis 1903," *Archiv für Sozialgeschichte* 15 (1975): 163–208.

Schadt, Jörg. *Die Sozialdemokratische Partei in Baden von den Anfängen bis zur Jahrhundertwende (1868–1900)*, Hanover: Verlag für Literatur und Zeitgeschehen, 1971.

Schauff, Johannes. *Das Wahlverhalten der deutschen Katholiken im Kaiserreich und in der Weimarer Republik*. ed. Rudolf Morsey. Mainz: Matthias-Grünewald-Verlag, 1975.

Schilling, Donald G. "Politics in a New Key: The Late Nineteenth Century Transformation of Politics in Northern Bavaria," *German Studies Review* 17 (1994): 33–57.

Schloßmacher, Norbert. *Düsseldorf im Bismarckreich: Politik und Wahlen Parteien und Vereine*. Düsseldorf: Schwann, 1985.

"Erzbischof Philippus Krementz und die Septennatswahlen," *Annalen des Historischen Vereins für den Niederrhein* 189 (1986): 127–54.

Schmädeke, Jürgen. *Wahlerbewegung im Wilhelmischen Deutschland*. 2 vols. Berlin: Akademie Verlag, 1995.

Schmidt, Gustav. "Die Nationalliberalen – eine regierungsfähige Partei? Zur Problematik der inneren Reichsgründung 1870–1878," in Gerhard Albert Ritter (ed.) *Die deutschen Parteien vor 1918*. Cologne: Kiepenheuer & Witsch, pp. 208–23

Schmidt, Marianne. "Die Arbeiterorganisationen in Dresden 1871 bis 1890: Zur Organisationsstrukturen der Arbeiterbewegung im Kampf gegen das Sozialistengesetz," *Jahrbuch für Geschichte* 22 (1981): 171–226.

Schmiesser, Wolfgang. *Von der Arbeiterbewegung zur Arbeiterpolitik: Die Anfänge der Arbeiterbewegung in Württemberg 1862/1863–1878*. Hanover: Verlag für Literatur und Zeitgeschehen, 1970.

Schmitt, Karl. *Konfession und Wahlverhalten in der Bundesrepublik Deutschland*. West Berlin: Duncker & Humblot, 1989.

Schoof, Peter. "Wahlbeteiligung und Sozialstruktur in der Bundesrepublik: Eine Aggregardatenanalyse für den Zeitraum von 1972 bis 1980," *Politische Vierteljahresschrift* 22(1981): 285–304.

Schorske, Carl. *German Social Democracy 1905–1917: The Development of the Great Schism*. 2nd edn. New York: John Wiley & Sons, 1965.

Seeber, Gustav. *Zwischen Bebel und Bismarck. Zur Geschichte des Linksliberalismus in Deutschland 1871–1893*. East Berlin, 1965.

Sepainter, Fred Ludwig. *Die Reichstagswahlen im Großherzogtum Baden. Ein Beitrag zur Wahlgeschichte im Kaiserreich*. Frankfurt: Peter Lang, 1983.

Shafer, Byron E. (ed.). *The End of Realignment? Interpreting American Electoral Eras*. Madison: University of Wisconsin Press, 1991.

Sheehan, James J. *German Liberalism in the Nineteenth Century*. Chicago and London: University of Chicago Press, 1978.

Simon, Klaus. *Das württembergische Demokraten. Ihre Stellung und Arbeit im Parteien- und Verfassungssystem in Württemberg und im Deutschen Reich 1890–1920*. Stuttgart, 1969.

Smith, Helmut Walser. *German Nationalism and Religious Conflict: Culture, Ideology, Politics, 1870–1914*. Princeton: Princeton University Press, 1995.

Sperber, Jonathan. *Popular Catholicism in Nineteenth Century Germany*. Princeton: Princeton University Press, 1984.

Stegmann, Dirk. *Die Erben Bismarcks: Parteien und Verbände in der Spätphase des Wilhelmischen Deutschlands*. Cologne: Kiepenheuer & Witsch, 1970.

Steinbach, Peter. "Reichstag Elections in the Kaiserreich: The Prospects for Electoral Research in the Interdisciplinary Context," in Larry Eugene Jones and James Retallack (eds.)*Elections, Mass Politics and Social Change in Modern*

Germany: New Perspectives. Cambridge and New York: Cambridge University Press, 1992, pp. 119–46.

Die Zähmung des politischen Massenmarktes. Wahlen und Wahlkämpfe im Bismarckreich im Sp;iegel der Hauptstadt– und Gesinnungspresse. 3 vols. Passau: Wissenschaftsverlag Richard Rothe, 1990.

Stelzle, Walter. "Die wirtschafltichen und sozialen Verhältnisse der byaerischen Oberpfalz um die Wende vom 19. zum 20. Jahrhundert. Der Streit um Fuchsmühle," *Zeitschrift für Bayerische Landesgeschichte* 39 (1976): 487–540.

Stürmer, Michael. *Regierung und Reichstag im Bismarckstaat 1871–1880. Cäsarismus oder Parlamentarismus.* Düsseldorf: Droste, 1974.

Suvall, Stanley. *Electoral Politics in Wilhelmine Germany.* Chapel Hill: University of North Carolina Press, 1985.

Thomsen, Søren Risbjerg. *Danish Elections, 1920–1979. A Logit Approach to Ecological Analysis and Inference.* Århus: Politicia, 1987.

Thomsen, Søren Risbjerg, Berglund, Sten, and Wörlund, Ingemar. "Assessing the Validity of the Logit Method for Ecological Inference," in Sten Berglund and Søren Risbjerg Thomsen (eds.) *Modern Political Ecological Analysis.* Åbo: Åbo Akademis Förlag, 1990, pp. 12–62.

Thränhardt, Dietrich. *Wahlen und politische Strukturen in Bayern 1848–1953.* Düsseldorf: Droste Verlag, 1973.

Trzeciakowski Lech, *The Kulturkampf in Prussian Poland.* trans. K. Kretkowska. New York: Columbia University Press, 1990.

Weber, Christoph. *"Eine starke enggeschlossene Phalanx." Der politische Katholizismus und die erste Reichstagswahl 1871.* Essen: Klarxtext Verlag, 1992.

Weber, Marie-Lise. *Ludwig Bamberger: Ideologie statt Realpolitik.* Stuttgart: Steiner Verlag, 1987.

Wender, Rolf. *Wahlen und soziale Strukturen in Ludwigshafen am Rhein 1871–1914. Unter besonderer Berücksichtigung der Reichstagswahlen.* Ludwigshafen a. Rh.: Stadtarchiv, 1984.

Wetzel, H.-W. *Presseinnenpolitik im Bismarkschen Reiche 1874–1890.* Bern: Peter Lang, 1975.

White, Dan S. *The Splintered Party: National Liberalism in Hessen and the Reich 1867–1918.* Cambridge, MA: Harvard University Press, 1976.

Wilhelm Liebknecht Briefwechsel mit deutschen Sozialdemokraten Vol. 1 ed. Georg Eckert, Assen: Verlag Van Vorcum, 1973. Vol. 2 (1878–1884) ed. Götz Langkau, Frankfurt: Campus Verlag 1987.

Winkler, Heinrich August. "Vom linken zum rechten Nationalismus: Der deutsche Liberalismus in der Krise von 1878/79," *Geschichte und Gesellschaft* 4 (1978): 5–28.

Winkler, Jürgen. "Die soziale Basis der sozialistischen Parteien in Deutschland vom Ende des Kaiserreichs bis zur Mitte der Weimarer Republik 1912–1924," *Archiv für Sozialgeschichte* 19 (1989): 137–71.

Sozialstruktur politische Tradition und Liberalismus: Eine empirische Längsschnittstudie zur Wahlentwicklung in Deutschland 1871–1933. Opladen: Westdeutscher Verlag, 1995.

Witt, Peter-Christian. *Die Finanzpolitik des Deutschen Reiches von 1903 bis 1913.* Lübeck and Hamburg: Matthiesen Verlag, 1970.

Wolf, Siegbert. *Liberalismus in Frankfurt am Main vom Ende der Freien Stadt bis zum Ersten Weltkrieg (1866–1914)*, Frankfurt: Kramer, 1987.

Wörlund, Ingemar and Berglund, Sten. "The Mobilization of the Swedish Vote. An Ecological Analysis of the General Elections of 1928, 1948 and 1968," in Sten Berglund and Søren Risbjerg Thomsen (eds.) *Modern Political Ecological Analysis*, Åbo: Åbo Akademis Förlag, pp. 63–77.

Wörlund, Ingemar, Berglund, Sten, and Thomsen, Søren Risbjerg. "The Mobilization of the Swedish Electorate (1911–1940)," in Sten Berglund and Søren Risbjerg Thomsen (eds.) *Modern Political Ecological Analysis*, Åbo: Åbo Akademis Förlag, pp. 78–90.

Zangerl, Carl. "Courting the Catholikc Vote: The Center Party in Baden 1903–1913," *Central European History* 10 (1977): 220–40.

Index

Aachen, 62, 262
Adenauer, Konrad, 302, 308
Agrarian League
  founding, 138, 214
  organization and campaigning of, 138,
    148–49, 214, 222, 260, 330
  and the political system, 19, 138–40,
    148, 152, 222, 229, 235, 255, 257
Alsace-Lorraine, 335, 352
  political, religious, and social conditions
    in, 62, 75, 88, 97, 99, 101, 127,
    164–65, 286, 332
  pro-French sentiment in, 66, 77, 99,
    102, 158–59, 166, 197
  voting in, 62, 80, 91, 99, 103–4, 128,
    169, 280
Anderson, Margaret, 7 n.8, 288 n.15
anti-clericalism, 58, 166, 289
  the labor movement and, 58–61, 146
  liberalism and, 146, 162, 254, 262, 300
  in southern Germany, 62, 71, 145–46,
    162, 170, 215, 239, 275
anti-Semitism, 181–82, 191, 213–14,
    217–18, 222, 224, 228, 256, 319
Arnsberg (*Regierungsbezirk*) 337
Association of German Catholics, 76
Augsburg, 100
Austro-Prussian War, 75, 77, 94, 158, 196,
    274, 275, 289–90

Baden, 61, 131, 145, 162, 168–69, 175,
    195, 221, 255, 335
Baum, Dale, 323
Bavaria, 61, 335, 337, 339
  political, social, and religions conditions
    in, 47–48, 71, 76 n.2, 96–97, 99,
    145–46, 162, 168–69, 215–16, 224,
    229, 255
  separatist sentiment in, 164–65, 215
  voting in, 91, 99, 104, 221, 239, 280
Bavarian Peasant League
  ideologies of, 71, 215

organization and campaigning of, 215,
    229
and other political parties, 215, 229,
    279–80
and the state, 96
support for, 71, 221–22, 228, 239, 271
Bayerischer Kurier, 248
Bebel, August, 52, 219
Bennigsen, Rudolf von, 183
Berlin, 86, 130–31, 174–75, 182, 206–7,
    270, 337 nn.9–10
Bethmann-Hollweg, Theobald von,
    255–57
Bismarck, Otto von, 134–35, 182, 259
  and German government, 21, 109, 121,
    132, 160, 190, 203, 212, 302
  political policies of, 51, 165, 174–75,
    179–80, 190, 193–96, 204, 213,
    330
  social and economic policies of, 132,
    180–81
Blackbourn, David, 7, 287, 288 n.15
Blank, Robert, 68
Böckel, Otto, 213
Braunschweig, 61
Breslau (city), 60
Breslau (*Regierungsbezirk*), 337
Bülow, Bernhard von, 231, 234, 242–43,
    245–46, 254–55
BVP (Bavarian People's Party) 298, 301,
    304

Caprivi, Leo von, 212–13, 223
Catholics
  clergy, 59, 80–81, 196
  religious and political opinions of,
    59–63, 101, 162, 165, 170, 193,
    196, 214–16, 233, 252, 295
  and the state, 75, 158–59, 162, 166,
    169–70, 248, 274, 289
  voting behavior of,
    in Bismarckian Germany, 90, 92–93,

Catholics (*cont.*)
    105, 141–42, 162–64, 187–89,
       192–93, 200–1, 267, 269, 275–79,
       289–92
    in Imperial Germany, 3–5, 8, 23, 38,
       61–63, 81–84, 90–92, 94, 143–46,
       152, 273–75, 282
    in modern Germany, 22, 320, 329–30
    in the twentieth century, 299–313,
       317–18
    in Wilhelmine Germany, 10–12,
       67–69, 72–73, 91–93, 99, 103–4,
       105–6, 142, 146–48, 150, 210–11,
       219–21, 227–28, 235–39, 251–52,
       254, 262–63, 279–82, 283
Center Party
    ideologies and policies of, 162, 190,
       196, 233–34, 248
    organization and campaigning of,
       75–76, 80–81, 95, 97–100, 137,
       164, 196, 205, 216–17, 224, 227,
       233–34, 247–48
    and other political parties, 92–93,
       96–97, 161, 191, 205–6, 229, 240,
       255–56, 279–80
    and the state, 96, 158–59, 161–62, 180,
       182, 212, 242–43, 245, 271
    support for
       in Bismarckian Germany, 5, 105, 160,
       163–64, 166, 168–69, 173, 179,
       184, 188, 201, 271, 279, 302
       in Imperial Germany, 4–5, 80–84, 86,
       88, 90–94
       in the twentieth century, 78, 297, 301,
       304–5, 307, 309, 311–12
       in Wilhelmine Germany, 66, 77–78,
       104, 106–7, 219, 221, 225, 228–29,
       235, 238–39, 249, 252, 257, 262,
       263–64, 271–72, 283, 287
Christian Peasant Leagues, 97, 99, 239
classes, social
    definitions of, 31, 65, 67–68, 302–5,
       306, 336–37
    in the electorate, 63–64, 303 n.24
Cologne, 262
Conservative Party
    ideologies and policies of, 138, 167,
       171–72, 181–82, 214
    organization and campaigning of, 138,
       140, 166–67, 171, 216
    and other political parties, 126, 161,
       180, 194, 214, 216, 224, 286
    and the state, 161, 165–66, 171–72
    support for, 109, 173, 178, 217, 266,
       271, 287
CDU/CSU (Christian Democratic
    Union/Christian Social-Welfare

Union) 65, 78, 298, 300, 302, 309,
    311–12, 314, 317, 320, 330

Denmark, 321, 324–25, 327, 329
Dortmunder Zeitung, 246
Downs, Anthony, 3
Düsseldorf, 62, 239 n.41, 267

East Prussia, 126, 335
Elberfeld, 52
elections
    of 1871, 36, 80–81, 129–30, 160–66,
       167–71, 174, 180, 200, 274–75,
       301, 315
    of 1874, 39, 46–47, 80, 82, 85, 111,
       115, 158, 165–71, 172–73, 179,
       197, 266–67, 269, 270, 271,
       273–76, 283, 285, 286, 290, 302,
       315
    of 1877, 39, 171–73, 174, 176–78, 188,
       272, 287
    of 1878, 39, 49, 112, 115, 173–79,
       184–89, 190, 192, 197, 202, 211,
       243, 266, 267–69, 270, 271, 275,
       305
    of 1881, 39, 115, 117, 132, 180–93,
       202, 211, 270, 275, 283, 288, 315
    of 1884, 39, 49, 115, 134, 189–94, 197,
       198–99, 200, 210–11, 269, 272,
       283, 318
    of 1887, 39, 82, 85, 111, 112, 113, 115,
       117–18, 134, 135, 178, 180, 189,
       193–202, 203–5, 207–11, 212, 213,
       216, 219, 234, 243–44, 246,
       252–53, 266, 267–69, 274–76,
       277–79, 283, 287–88, 290, 302,
       315, 318
    of 1890, 39–40, 41–42, 45–46, 49–50,
       56, 85, 101, 117, 134, 189, 204–11,
       213, 217–22, 232, 271, 277–79,
       283, 285, 290, 291, 315
    of 1893, 71, 112, 178, 212–13, 224–28,
       232, 234, 237, 243–44, 250, 255,
       263, 280
    of 1898, 40, 45, 91, 96, 101, 111, 113,
       117, 118, 129, 135, 201, 223–30,
       232, 233, 234, 235–37, 239, 267
    of 1903, 41–42, 45–46, 93, 106, 134,
       211, 230–41, 246, 249–52, 263,
       264, 267, 280, 281, 288, 318–19
    of 1907, 82, 85, 91, 93, 106, 112, 115,
       117, 119, 178, 189, 211, 240–55,
       257–63, 264, 267–69, 274, 281,
       287, 318
    of 1912, 36, 40, 41–42, 45–46, 57, 59,
       64, 66–67, 68, 93, 101, 106, 114,
       115, 117, 119, 129, 135, 189, 211,

DATE DUE
